ONE SQUARE MILE OF HELL

ONE SQUARE MILE OF HELL

THE BATTLE FOR TARAWA

JOHN WUKOVITS

NAL
CALIBER

NAL Caliber
Published by New American Library, a division of
Penguin Group (USA) Inc., 375 Hudson Street,
New York, New York 10014, USA
Penguin Group (Canada), 90 Eglinton Avenue East, Suite 700, Toronto,
Ontario M4P 2Y3, Canada (a division of Pearson Penguin Canada Inc.)
Penguin Books Ltd., 80 Strand, London WC2R 0RL, England
Penguin Ireland, 25 St. Stephen's Green, Dublin 2,
Ireland (a division of Penguin Books Ltd.)
Penguin Group (Australia), 250 Camberwell Road, Camberwell, Victoria 3124,
Australia (a division of Pearson Australia Group Pty. Ltd.)
Penguin Books India Pvt. Ltd., 11 Community Centre, Panchsheel Park,
New Delhi - 110 017, India
Penguin Group (NZ), cnr Airborne and Rosedale Roads, Albany,
Auckland 1310, New Zealand (a division of Pearson New Zealand Ltd.)
Penguin Books (South Africa) (Pty.) Ltd., 24 Sturdee Avenue,
Rosebank, Johannesburg 2196, South Africa

Penguin Books Ltd., Registered Offices:
80 Strand, London WC2R 0RL, England

First published by NAL Caliber, an imprint of New American Library
a division of Penguin Group (USA) Inc.

Copyright © John Wukovits, 2006
Maps copyright © Jeffrey L. Ward, 2006

NAL CALIBER and the "C" logo are trademarks of Penguin Group (USA) Inc.

ISBN-10: 0-451-21847-7
ISBN-13: 978-0-451-21847-6

Set in Fairfield Lt.
Designed by Ginger Legato

Printed in the United States of America

PUBLISHER'S NOTE
Publisher does not have any control over and does not assume any responsibility for author or third-party Web sites or their content.

To my brother, Tom,

whose encouragement and

praise make me smile

with the realization that

my big brother is proud

CONTENTS

I have long been familiar with the story of Tarawa. One of the first pieces I wrote, a magazine article more than twenty years ago, dealt with the subject, and the battle has remained with me ever since. The frightening walk toward shore, so reminiscent of what Steven Spielberg later handed theater audiences in the opening moments of *Saving Private Ryan*, captivated me, and the appalling slaughter that unfolded over the three days of fighting made me appreciate what those young Marines endured to wrest a piece of sand from the enemy.

In the early 1990s I had the pleasure of interviewing one of the main participants, *Time* magazine correspondent Robert Sherrod. His brilliant reportage of the battle printed in the pages of the newsweekly, followed by his moving 1944 book, *Tarawa,* first conveyed the Pacific War's terrible reality to the American people. Over three interviews, he regaled me with tales of his wartime experiences, in which Tarawa played such a prominent part. His insight and comments helped me better understand what unfolded that November in 1943.

Research took me to Quantico, Virginia, and Washington, D.C., where I scoured the official Marine records and the personal papers of participants. I traveled to Laguna Beach, California; Alexandria, Virginia; and San Antonio, Texas, to interview survivors and family members. At each location I gathered material that clarified different features of the fighting and met individuals whose courage of more than sixty years ago was matched by the quiet emotions they retain today. This story exists because of them.

Rather than simply fashion a minute-by-minute account of the fighting that raged at Tarawa, I chose to tell the story through the experiences of a handful of participants. Collectively, these individuals typify what the Marine at Tarawa faced as well as what families and loved ones back home endured. By implication, they also represent the experiences and sacrifices made by the military throughout the Pacific and by their families and friends in the United States.

I included a variety of ranks as well as men with differing responsibilities so that I could better convey the drama of Tarawa, including two corporals who had been boyhood friends, three brothers, a colonel, a corpsman, a combat photographer, and a Medal of Honor winner. These men and their families allowed me to present each aspect of the fighting—the Marine riflemen who carried the brunt of the fighting, the correspondents who covered the fighting, the corpsmen who patched the wounded, the families who anxiously awaited word of their loved ones—and to do so in a more personal fashion than can be done strictly by focusing on official reports.

I would like to thank many people. My agent, Jim Hornfischer, who knows what it takes to write a book, nurtured the project from start to finish. The valuable comments made by my editor at New American Library, Mark Chait, improved the manuscript, while Jeffrey Ward again added his marvelous artistic touch to the maps that adorn the book. Barry Zirby at the National Archives; Fred Allison, Charles Melson, and Gordon H. Heim at the Marine Corps Historical Center; Gale Munro at the Navy Art Collection; and Dr. James Ginther and the staff at the marvelous Marine Corps Research Center in Quantico, Virginia, lent valuable assistance whenever needed. Col. C. W. Van Horne, USMC (Ret.), the executive secretary of the Second Marine Division Association, sent me a list of Tarawa veterans and put me in touch with men who contributed fascinating material to the book. Agent Irene Webb's continued belief in my stories makes me work more assiduously to bring the contributions of World War II veterans to current generations.

This book would not be whatever it is without the assistance of the many men and women I interviewed. Veterans imparted their reminiscences, families opened homes, and loved ones shared letters from long ago. A complete list of the people I talked with is found in the bibliography, but I must thank a few for the enormous contributions they made. The Montague family in Bandera, Texas, and the Seng family in San Antonio spent hours with me around the kitchen table or on the telephone, confiding stories and handing over photographs or priceless letters written in 1942 and 1943. Stanley Bowen and his wife, Marge, welcomed me to Laguna Beach, where they provided a fascinating account of their time in World War II. I never truly grasped how a Marine operated in battle until Robert Muhlbach explained his method of attacking Japanese pillboxes at Tarawa. James Wendell Crain clarified the hectic conditions at Red Beach 1, and James and Dick Meadows added powerful material about their time in the battle. Norman Hatch and William Kelliher proved that battlefield heroes often accomplish their tasks without weapons, while Robert Sherrod movingly explained the wade ashore and the aftermath during his extensive interviews.

I want to mention two men whose valued advice helped me become a writer. Both are now deceased, but their memories and words will influence me until I am gone. My college professor and adviser at the University of Notre Dame, Dr. Bernard Norling, and historian Thomas Buell, who wrote powerful biographies of Adms. Ernest J. King and Raymond A. Spruance, commented on earlier manuscripts and lent encouragement at every step along the way. I cannot thank them enough, and my only hope is that I contribute to history even a portion of what these two gentlemen gave.

My family, as always, made the writing process easier. My brother Tom, a naval aviator during the Vietnam War, encouraged me with his comments on my writing. My daughters, Amy, Julie, and Karen, are spread to the far corners of the nation, but their supportive remarks and their love constantly return home to Trenton. My three grandchildren, Matthew, Megan Grace, and Emma, remind me of my duty to convey to one generation the heroics and nobility of a prior generation. Terri Faitel, my fiancée, supported me not only with her love, but also by carefully reading the manuscript and offering helpful suggestions.

Three people who are no longer with me continue to help through the memories that linger and with the words that remain—my dad, Tom, my mom, Grace, and my younger brother, Fred.

John F. Wukovits
Trenton, Michigan
December 1, 2005

"WHERE'S PEARL HARBOR?"

"The Most Haunting Memory"

Fear, the numbing, paralyzing kind, demolished all thoughts of home for Pfc. Eugene Seng and Pfc. Charles Montague, two San Antonio, Texas, school buddies. As they waded directly into the slaughter inflicted by Japanese mortar shells and bullets in those early morning hours of November 20, 1943, six thousand miles separated them from their homes in the Lone Star State, but it might as well have been sixty thousand, for the two boys, barely out of high school, found themselves trapped in an alien, violent world they could never have imagined.

The staccato crack from machine guns and small arms fire added a menacing beat to the ear-shattering explosions produced by mortar and larger-caliber shells. Shrapnel and bullets screeched by, blocking out the boisterous commands from officers. The normally placid lagoon waters, which should have adorned a travel poster as the image of a luxuriant tropical paradise, instead swirled and churned from the hundreds of eruptions, large and small, kicked up by enemy projectiles. Seng and Montague, like most of the young Marines in the waters off the Pacific atoll of Tarawa, swore that their racing heartbeats drowned out other noises, and they had to strain to hear each other shout, even though they stood mere yards apart as they inched toward shore.

On all sides, shells detonated in bloody geysers, bullets churned the water, which looked as if it were agitated by a storm, and wounded Marines, some hideously disfigured and dying, shouted, even begged, for help.

Montague and Seng had enlisted shortly after Pearl Harbor, swept along by the patriotic fervor that engrossed the nation in the aftermath of that tragedy, but this was way beyond their imaginations. No one in boot camp had warned the pair, who should have instead been sitting through college lectures or courting women, that it would be like this. No battle-hardened Marine veteran cautioned them. No one explained what a hellhole this tiny island would be.

A few hundred yards away, Pharmacist's Mate First Class Stanley Bowen stood in his amtrac (amphibious tractor), waiting to land at the same beach. Only hours ago he and his buddies had joked that the operation would be a minor affair against little or no opposition, one that would certainly be over within one hour. After all, how could anyone on the island live through such a deadly preinvasion bombardment as the one the Navy battlewagons had just delivered? Some Marines, naïve to the point of arrogance, even worried that there would be no Japanese remaining alive for them to kill.

The twenty-year-old Bowen had joined the military seeking vengeance for Pearl Harbor. "We thought we would take care of the Japanese with no problem. It got to the point when we were actually going into battle, I couldn't wait to get in, because we were going to kill Japs right and left. We were just going to go in and shoot those damn Japs."

When Bowen's amtrac climbed over the reef that surrounded Tarawa seven hundred yards from shore, the bullets ringing off the protective armor plating sent a chill through his heart. "I couldn't believe it when we were landing, that they were firing back at us."[1] The situation quickly deteriorated. For the first time, he grasped that an enemy waited on Tarawa's beaches, one who considered Bowen nothing more than another target to obliterate.

The corpsman, whose task on shore was not to fight but to patch up the wounded, prepared for a long day. On Tarawa, his services were apparently going to be in great demand.

Approaching the same beach as Bowen, Pfc. Robert Muhlbach sensed that something was seriously wrong. By now, at least according to his officers, he should have been ashore, combing the shattered remnants of what had once been the Japanese garrison on Tarawa and enjoying a speedy victory, but instead he stood in the neck-deep lagoon water, praying that he would survive the Japanese machine gun bullets that kicked up splashes all about him.

He was not alone, but that concerned him even more. Those Marines wading in the waters nearby him should have been ashore, too. Wherever he turned, Muhlbach watched fellow Marines struggling to reach the beaches. Many, he noticed, disappeared beneath the surface, replaced by a crimson ribbon that dyed the waters red. Was this how he was to die? Drowned before he reached shore and could utilize his expert marksmanship talents against the enemy?

S. Sgt. Norman T. Hatch, a combat cameraman assigned to record the battle on film, sat atop the engine cover and tried to ignore the dangers around him. He had to concentrate, just like the other Marines, but while they clutched their rifles and maybe uttered a silent prayer, Hatch checked his film equipment. He did not intend to miss any of the action because his motion picture camera was not on.

Seng, Montague, Muhlbach, and the others had just taken their first wet steps toward Tarawa, an island in the Pacific that has become synonymous with death and gallantry. In a matter of hours on that humid morning, the Marines had gone from optimism that the operation would be over in a few short hours, to doubting that they would even be alive in five minutes. And as bad as the approach to Tarawa was, worse horrors waited once Seng and Bowen and the other young Americans stepped ashore.

Veteran correspondent Robert Sherrod, who covered the landings for *Time* magazine and who would subsequently report on some of the Pacific War's most brutal clashes, including Iwo Jima and Saipan, concluded forty years later, "I regard Tarawa as the most haunting memory of World War II."[2]

Texas Buddies

In 1938, all that was in the future. Five years before the battle, few things, certainly nothing as life-threatening, disturbed Charlie Montague and Gene Seng's serene high school world of cars, horseback riding, and girls. If you wanted Montague or Seng, everyone knew where to find them—outside Montague's home working on that old jalopy they nicknamed the Hoopie or, in Seng's case, wherever girls congregated. The more diplomatic friends called the Hoopie a car, but the term had to be loosely applied, for in truth it was a work in progress, as if pieced together in the workshop of Dr. Frankenstein—a part patched on here and some fabric sewn on there. The bright red oilcloth used for seat covers especially handed the vehicle its "class." Whenever Montague and Seng had a spare moment from homework or chores, they headed to the garage, picked up their tools, and idled glorious hours transforming the 1932 Chevrolet coupe into a work of art.

As important as the work were the relationships the pair formed. Though popular at San Antonio's Central Catholic High School, Montague, born on December 7, 1922, and Seng, born August 20, 1922, preferred quiet to noise, smaller groups to assemblies, a handful of friends to a host of acquaintances. That was why they liked each other—their similarities created a bond that surpassed casual high school ties. They understood each other.

They also understood risk. Montague encountered that every time he hopped on a horse and galloped about the sprawling family ranch in Bandera, Texas, ninety miles west of San Antonio. He and Seng faced it every time they turned the ignition of their unfinished jalopy and hazarded one of the local roads. Usually one of two things happened—either the contraption broke down somewhere along the way, or an astonished police officer, dubious that such a vehicle, still lacking a roof and fenders, could be safely taken out in public, halted them.

Montague understood risk every time he pulled one of his sporadic pranks, such as shoving a worm into his grandfather's pipe or stuffing a bagged skunk into his teacher's desk. At least Montague came by his traits honestly. His great-grandfather emigrated from Ireland to the United States in 1820, eventually settling in Bandera, then little more than a crude frontier community in the midst of hostile Indians. According to one relative, the great-grandfather, who rose to county clerk, "had a fiery temper and a willingness to fight,"[3] characteristics subsequent Montagues possessed in abundance.

Montague's father was what some would call a man's man. In addition to the immense demands exacted by the eight-thousand-acre Montague Ranch, he simultaneously juggled the duties of two other businesses, the town bank and a firm trading wool and mohair. He loved Charlie and his other three sons but, like many men from that day, kept his feelings bottled inside. He believed he could better express his affection by establishing rigorous standards and by demanding that his sons strive for them. He expected his boys to work as hard as he did, including contributing to exhaustive stints rounding up the sheep and goats and harvesting the seven hundred acres of farmland. "We'd be up long before sunrise and be out in the field until dark,"[4] explained Charlie's younger brother, George, of their summers. Charlie, George, Frank, and Bruce all learned to drive an automobile and tractors before their tenth birthdays.

Though the stolid father considered emotional displays a sign of weakness, he beamed with pride whenever one of his boys concluded what he called their "rite of passage" into manhood. By that he did not mean graduation or marriage, but the day when his sons bagged their first deer. That illustrious moment came for Charlie when he was eleven years old. Charlie returned home to the accolades of a proud father and the knowledge that his trophy would soon adorn the family wall.

The father took quiet pride in his sons' other talents. Charlie played the guitar in a trio with his brothers, Bruce and Frank. Wearing fancy satin shirts festooned with the Montague Ranch crest, the three became so popular that the state government asked them to perform in Dallas during Texas's centennial celebrations in 1936.

Above all, Charlie could shoot. Living on a ranch, with a myriad of wild animals, the boys knew how to handle a rifle, but Charlie outclassed them all. He beamed when a local judge declared him the best shooter in the county, a description he one day validated with a William Tell–like display.

"We were sitting down eating watermelon on my grandma's porch, and about two hundred yards away the cows gathered at the gate," said his brother Bruce. "Grandpa said, 'Charlie, go down and open that gate and let those cows in to water.' One of the guys there, Speedy Hicks, heard Charlie and me arguing about who should open the gate and said, 'You two quit arguing. Neither of you have to walk down there. Just shoot the chain.' Charlie said, 'I don't want to hit the chain and tear it up, but I'll tell you what I'll do. I'll hit that bolt.'"[5] Charlie took dead aim, squeezed the trigger, and smashed open the bolt with a single shot.

Living on a ranch as he did, Charlie Montague felt most comfortable in dusty cowboy boots and clothes, working with the animals or riding his horse. When he jumped into the Hoopie and headed to town for the latest movie, he preferred the adventures of Hollywood cowboys like Tom Mix and Gene Autry. He and Gene Seng spent many weekends roping cattle at the ranch. His fame as a calf roper quickly spread throughout the county, where he so frequently brought home first prize at fairs that rivals avoided entering contests in which they knew Montague would be competing.

Like his father, Charlie maintained a calm, quiet demeanor. "He was more of an introvert, not a talker," said George. "He did a lot of dreaming, reflecting. You never knew quite what was on his mind. He kept his emotions pretty much inside." The introspective youth often played his guitar by himself, deep in thought over some thorny issue.

Those thoughts usually centered about Lucille Miller, one of the prettiest females in the county, whom Montague described as the love of his life. The two made a great couple. Both flashed piercing deep-set eyes beneath gorgeous black hair, and everybody assumed that one day Charlie and Lucille, whom everybody called Billie, would be husband and wife. "I loved his beautiful blue eyes and his coal black hair. He was very handsome."

They first met when a friend fixed them up on a blind date for Billie's junior prom at St. Mary's School. For some reason, they did not see each other for another year, but then as suddenly as he left, Charlie reappeared at her door. "I just wanted to see if you still lived here,"[6] he told a surprised Billie.

From then on the two were inseparable. Billie warmed to Charlie's soft-spoken nature and his love for ranch life. On weekends, she joined the Montague clan for horseback riding and other activities, including being taught how to dance by Mrs. Montague. When Billie had to be treated at the hospital for minor injuries suffered when Charlie struck a parked car, he sent her flowers as a way of apologizing. Plans for the future surfaced. Charlie would prosper in ranch and calf roping, and they would be married.

Gene Seng, too, thought of girls, more often than did most anyone at Central Catholic. "I'm a rose between thorns,"[7] Seng lightheartedly explained whenever one of his three sisters asked him why he had so many girlfriends. The smooth dancer who moved with grace on the dance floor—the romantic waltz was his favorite—navigated with equal ease around females. Montague was a one-woman man, but Seng hoped to be the one man all women wanted. A few bubbled to the top—Una Maloney for one—but Seng made sure he kept the others always in sight. He walked a dangerous tightrope, for he could at any moment incur a girl's wrath should she learn of his escapades.

If one of the many buddies who always seemed to gather at the Seng home in San Antonio lacked a date, Gene would tell him, "My sister will go with you."[8] Lorraine, two years his junior, loved the attention and knew that in turn, if one of her girlfriends needed a date, she could readily offer Gene as an escort.

Seng placed a value on friendship. He and Eugene Aschbacher Jr. camped, hunted, fished, and boy-scouted together, times they remembered the rest of their lives. But as loyal as Seng was to friends, his family occupied the most prominent position in his life. Raised in the Roman Catholic faith, Seng developed close bonds with both parents, who he explained "made me feel like I was something." He fondly recalled hunting and fishing jaunts with his father, experiences Seng called "some of my keenest times" with the man of whom he stated, "I hope I can live to be half the man"[9] he was.

Everyone in San Antonio sports knew Seng's father, who officiated football and basketball games in addition to owning a sporting goods store, so when Gene displayed a similar love, a deeper bond developed with the man he called Daddy, old buddy, and old boy. The affection grew when Gene joined both the football and boxing teams at Central Catholic. In the "Last Will and Testament" section of his senior yearbook, Seng facetiously bequeathed to the junior class one of his sporting accomplishments. "Seng leaves a record for lettering on the Varsity football team, for anyone to shoot at,"[10] stated his final high school bequest.

Father and son could brush aside the concerns of the day on the rugged gridiron, that most male of domains, but Gene also exhibited a tender side, especially toward his mother and sisters. Unlike many teenage boys, Gene openly displayed his affection for his mother. Every Mother's Day he sent a dozen carnations to "my mamasita," or "my sweetheart," and Seng explained that it was from her that he learned most of his values.

Gene's fondness extended to his three younger sisters. He loved to tease them, as do most big brothers, but he also made sure to purchase souvenirs for them whenever he traveled. If one of the girls was in trouble at home, Gene sat down with soothing advice and a sympathetic ear. Lorraine had a habit of running away and hiding whenever she incurred her parents' wrath. She knew that Gene would sooner or later materialize, put his arm around her, quietly mutter, "Come on, Sis,"[11] and lead her back home.

People in Bandera or at Central Catholic High School remarked that if you spotted Gene or Charlie, you would invariably see the other shortly afterward. The relationship extended to their families, who gathered on weekends for fun-filled parties on the Montague Ranch. "Our parents liked Gene," stated Bruce Montague of Charlie's close friend. "He'd come out and have lunch, then go horseback riding and hunt."[12]

While Charlie looked ahead to calf roping or owning a ranch, Gene intended to become an engineer like his grandfather. Gene offered help when friends struggled with their math assignments, and in the summer of 1940 he worked with a survey crew to gain experience in engineering. He attended St. Mary's University in San Antonio with the intention of transferring to Texas A & M as soon as he had enough money.

The future seemed bright for the two Texas friends, but in the distance, storm clouds threatened their idyllic life. Like millions of other people around the world, they had no idea that events in faraway lands would dramatically alter their futures.

Pacific Foes

Neither Montague nor Seng closely followed world events but then, neither did most people in the country. Their lives started and ended within the confines of Bandera County, and other than knowing who Adolf Hitler was and that the

Japanese seemed to be stirring trouble in China, the teenage boys were oblivious to the events that would, one day, place them side by side on an obscure Pacific isle.

By the time Montague and Seng entered high school in the mid-1930s, President Franklin D. Roosevelt had already cast a wary eye to the Pacific. Sources of friction between Japan and the United States existed long before war actually touched their borders in 1941. As early as the late 1800s, American politicians proclaimed that it was the nation's "manifest destiny" to expand beyond its continental borders into the Pacific. They lustfully viewed the lucrative natural resources in the Orient, and intended to develop and maintain an economic presence in the region. American manufacturers also wanted to have a ready market for the vast amount of goods their factories churned out.

Following the successful conclusion of the war with Spain in 1898, the United States received possession of the Philippine Islands. Standing about 1,400 miles southwest of Japan, the Philippines offered numerous rich products, such as oil and rubber, as well as superb sites for military bases. The United States dispatched a garrison army to occupy the subjected nation, and without openly declaring so, conveyed the message to Japan through her actions that the United States, and not Japan, would be master in the Pacific.

Japan occupied a more complex role in the Pacific and Far East than that of the United States. Most Japanese contended that a dominant position in the region guaranteed the nation's survival, while to accept an inferior status would relegate her to the backwaters of world rankings.

As an island nation, Japan had to import much of her raw materials and food products. Since her people could cultivate only a certain percentage of the national need, the nation's leaders had to look elsewhere to fill the rest. Almost 70 percent of the country's supply of zinc and tin came from outside, 90 percent of its lead, and all of its cotton, wool, aluminum, and rubber.

When they sought raw materials from Asia, Japanese leaders collided with European interests. Japan needed rubber, tin, and bauxite from Burma and Malaya, but Great Britain controlled those nations. Indochina's vast rubber plantations contained valuable material, but France held sway in that region. The most coveted product, oil, stood in bountiful amounts in the East Indies, but the Dutch maintained a stranglehold on the region. Everywhere Japan turned, a European nation blocked the path to her future.

Japan yearned to be the preeminent nation in the Pacific and Far East. She, not Great Britain or any other European country, deserved to control the area because she was an Asian land. Besides, she had already built a potent military and with it intended to assert her interests in the region.

The rest of the world took notice in May 1905 when the upstart Japanese Navy soundly defeated the heralded Russian Navy at the battle of Tsushima. For the first time an Asian nation had bested a European power, and both Great Britain and the United States realized that Japan could pose a threat to their own interests. The triumph emboldened Japanese leaders in believing that Japan's destiny lay in the Pacific and the Asian mainland. This aggressive attitude placed Japan and the United States on the path toward war.

"I Can Take It"

William Deane Hawkins had more important things to worry about than what happened in the Pacific. He may have been unusually close to his mother, but no one dared call him a momma's boy, for few individuals exhibited as much grit as this young Kansan. Born April 19, 1914, at Fort Scott, Kansas, to William F. Hawkins and Clara Jane Moon, Hawkins experienced hardship at an early age. While living in Los Angeles, the three-year-old Hawkins suffered agonizing burns to much of his body. A neighbor walked into the Hawkins kitchen carrying a pan of scalding water, and when the toddler, running about as do most three-year-olds, accidentally bumped into her, he was doused with water that inflicted ghastly burns to his upper arms, back, one shoulder, and one leg.

Scarring from the burns was so severe that Hawkins could not straighten out his leg and one arm. Physicians asked his mother for permission to cut the muscles to correct it, but fearing this would cause permanent damage Mrs. Hawkins, a nurse, refused. She spent the next year lovingly massaging the arm and leg for up to three hours each day in an effort to revitalize the muscles. Amazingly, after one year, Hawkins regained the use of his muscles and again started walking. For the first of many times, Hawkins saw how strong the influence of a mother can be.

The hideous scars helped define the man Hawkins, called Deane by family and friends, became. While they prevented him from obtaining some of the things he wanted in life, the scars made Hawkins more determined to prove he had what it took.

His first test occurred when the ten-year-old came home from the El Paso,

Texas, YMCA in tears. When his mother asked why he was crying, Hawkins explained, "When I take off my clothes the kids all look and say, 'Oh, look at Deane!' "[13] Clara calmly told him he had nothing to be ashamed of, that he should never allow teasing about his scars to bother him, and that if he returned the other boys would eventually stop their taunting. Hawkins followed his mother's advice, and the situation improved.

Despite the injuries, Hawkins enjoyed the life of a robust teenager. His father died when Hawkins was eight, but his mother, used to the role of family savior, deftly filled the void. Hawkins supplemented his mother's nursing income by selling newspapers and magazines, by helping at the local pharmacy, and by working as a bellhop in a hotel and as a bank messenger. One summer he even worked as a cowboy, an experience that planted the dream of one day owning a Texas ranch.

Everyone in his high school class knew Hawkins to be a gifted athlete and fun-loving teen. He played in a church basketball league and excelled at swimming, but most evenings he could be found at the YMCA with his close friends, Wallace Love and Ballard McCleskey, trying to decide what to do. The basketball court usually won out, but as the trio grew older and learned to drive, they more frequently hopped into Hawkins's Ford roadster and crossed the border into Mexico to prowl about Juarez's bars, where they could legally drink beer and whiskey.

The good-looking Hawkins felt at ease in the company of his buddies, but in the presence of girls, he retreated into a shell. McCleskey and Love teased Hawkins about his shyness, but they also wished they received as much adulation from the girls. One of his female classmates told Hawkins's mother, "The girls were crazy about him—we all thought he was so handsome—but he never paid much attention to any of the girls except to be polite and friendly to them."[14]

That was because he had the attention of the one female who mattered—his mother. The two chatted about everything, and the dutiful son made the beds and swept the floors at home to help his hardworking parent. He thought nothing of joining her for a ride, whether to the store or for a leisurely country drive. They enjoyed one another's company and were so often seen together that some assumed he was with a sister. "He and I were great pals," recalled his mother, "and used to go to a great many places together—he thought it great fun when someone would say to him, 'Deane, I saw you and your big sister out together last night.' That always pleased him for them to think I was his sister."[15]

Hawkins excelled in the classroom as well, skipping fifth grade in elementary school. At age sixteen, he won a state chemistry essay contest and graduated from high school, then in 1931–1932 attended on a scholarship the Texas College of Mines and Metallurgy, now the University of Texas at El Paso. Hawkins had to leave school and put his graduation plans on hold when the scholarship money ran out.

The seventeen-year-old Hawkins set aside his disappointment and accepted a job with a gas company laying a pipeline through the New Mexico desert. In sweltering conditions the arduous work, which demanded that Hawkins grab one end of a heavy pipe and hoist it onto a pile, exacted a toll on every man. The foreman laughed when he first saw the scrawny Hawkins and cautioned him that stronger, bigger men than he had cracked under the strains of the task. "Sonny, two-hundred-pound men are collapsing on the job," he warned the five-foot-ten-inch, 147-pound laborer, but Hawkins refused to yield. He later wrote his mother of those twelve-hour workdays in the blinding desert sun. "I'm all right now, Mom. The first day or two though, I thought I was going to die. It was pretty tough the next two or three days, too, but now I can take it almost as well as some of these two-hundred pounders."[16]

Adolf Hitler's antics in Europe, which eventually plunged an entire continent into war, bothered Hawkins, but at this stage he believed the affair was none of his country's concern. He told his mother, "I hate war. I don't see why the United States ought to get into it."[17] Like many of his countrymen, Hawkins saw Europe's turmoil as a foreign concern.

Rise of the Japanese Militarists

The Japanese military commanded enormous respect from its population in the 1920s and 1930s. Kiyoshi Ota knew this when he was a young boy in Naokata-shi, Fukuoka Prefecture, in the northern portion of the Japanese home island of Kyushu. Some towns hosted parties when one of their residents entered the military. Schoolchildren collected coins in a drive to finance the construction of a battleship, and it was deemed an honor to serve the emperor.

After his birth in September 1915, Ota enlisted in the Imperial Japanese Navy at Sasebo Naval Barracks on June 30, 1936, as Montague and Seng enjoyed their early years at Central Catholic High School. Rigorous training instilled discipline and an aversion to surrendering. Instructors taught Ota that loyalty to one's unit, faith in commanding officers, and spirit would defeat any foe, no matter how well-armed it might be. Attacking, even in circumstances that produced ghastly casualties, was preferred to surrendering or retreating.

Men trained fourteen hours a day, six days a week, under the watch of dictatorial officers who answered complaints with punishment. Soldiers embarked on marches of twenty-five miles wearing gear that weighed two-thirds of their own body weights, then ran the final mile to prove they still had reserves of strength.

A soldier's life belonged to the emperor, and to suffer defeat was considered an insult to the emperor that brought shame to the soldier's family. The ancient samurai tradition known as Bushido, which meant "way of the warrior," governed his behavior. The samurai were honored fighters in Japan's history, and soldiers of the Imperial Army were to emulate them. "Be it resolved that honor is heavier than the mountains, and death lighter than a feather,"[18] reminded one dictate. A soldier could attain no higher glory than to die in battle.

The military clamored for a new policy that emphasized conquest and expansion. The Army wanted to drive on Russia and northern China—land targets—while the Navy claimed a water advance into Indochina, the Dutch East Indies, and Pacific islands would be better because of the rich natural resources available. Faced with two radically different plans, in 1936 Japan's cabinet compromised and assented to both plans. This decision set in motion a chain of events that could only result in conflict with either Great Britain or the United States—or with both.

The initial aggression that culminated in World War II in the Pacific occurred on September 18, 1931, when a bomb exploded along the Japanese-controlled South Manchuria Railway near Mukden, Manchuria. Units of the Japanese Army had been stationed in Korea since the Russo-Japanese War to protect Japanese interests. Officers of the Kwantung Army, as it was called, immediately launched an invasion to overrun all of Manchuria, which they quickly renamed Manchukuo.

A more serious incident occurred on the Asian mainland on July 7, 1937, when Japanese soldiers opened fire on Chinese troops at the Marco Polo Bridge near Peking, China. Who fired first is unclear, but the Japanese Army used the event as justification to unleash a huge offensive against Generalissimo Chiang Kai-shek's Chinese Army. Within weeks the Japanese Army had pushed Chiang's poorly trained and underequipped forces toward the interior of China, leaving many key Chinese coastal cities open to the Japanese.

The Japanese reacted swiftly and brutally. The worst carnage unfolded in December 1937 at Nanking, where Japanese troops embarked on an orgy of killing and rape. Soldiers used thousands of civilians as live bayonet targets, set afire whole groups of men, women, and children, and raped old and young alike. A war tribunal after the war determined that twenty thousand women between the ages of eleven and seventy-six had been raped, and more than two hundred thousand Chinese murdered.

One American who was present wrote on Christmas Eve that Nanking "is a city laid waste, ravaged, completely looted, much of it burned. The victorious army must have its rewards—and those rewards are to plunder, murder, rape, at will, to commit acts of unbelievable brutality and savagery. In all modern history surely there is no page that will stand so black as that of the rape of Nanking. It has been hell on earth."[19]

The United States protested these criminal acts against a nation with whom they shared sentimental bonds, developed by American missionaries who had long worked in China. Since no nation was willing or able to mount military action to deter the Japanese, the critical words achieved nothing.

American ambassador to Japan Joseph Grew advised President Franklin D. Roosevelt that the nation rode a risky path by attacking Japan verbally without appropriate military force to back up the words. Like Winston Churchill warning the democracies in Europe about the rise of Hitler, Grew urged his nation to build a military machine capable of maintaining order in the Pacific. Roosevelt agreed with his ambassador, but embroiled in rescuing the devastated American economy from the Depression, he unfortunately could do little to stop the Japanese.

The events in China pushed the United States and Japan further apart. More and more, the two viewed each other as bitter foes.

"A Super Place to Grow Up"

Two thousand miles to Texas's west, Stanley Bowen inhabited a vastly different world from the one shared by Montague and Seng, one where glimmer and glamour made headlines—Beverly Hills, California. Born in Los Angeles on January 30, 1923, he attended the famous Beverly Hills High School, the one later featured in a television series, and sat in the same classrooms with future stars. Betty White of *The Golden Girls*, actress Rhonda Fleming, actors Jackie Cooper and Bobby Breen, musician André Previn, and producer Blake Edwards attended school with Bowen. Though Bowen was neither famous nor wealthy like some of his classmates, he found few differences separated them.

"Beverly Hills was a super place to grow up," explained Bowen. "It was a real nice town with one high school, and all the kids from wealthy families and the normal, moderate-income families got along fine. Some kids were driven to school in limousines with chauffeurs, while some of us rode our bikes up to school."[20]

He recalls the time a girl named Joey Paige asked him to her mansion, built by her stepfather, the powerful filmmaker Jack Warner of Warner Brothers. "She would invite us occasionally to her house because she was lonely. They had a theater, a bowling alley, a pool room, and when you wanted to eat, guys would come out with towels over their arms. You could have steak or turkey or chicken, whatever you wanted."[21]

Bowen envied the adulation and fame some students enjoyed, but he learned that one other possession surpassed those advantages—family. His father's job with the Bank of America provided sufficient income for a modest home in Beverly Hills. The close-knit clan attended services every Sunday at the nearby Lutheran church, and the parents emphasized the value of a college education. In many ways, while the children of movie stars inhabited a realm that glittered on the surface yet smoldered underneath, Bowen resided in the more substantial Norman Rockwell–type world where family came before possessions.

Bowen's track coach reminded him of that one day when he claimed that Bowen and the other kids from moderate-income families were the lucky group. "When you finished working out at the gym," the coach explained, "you went on home to family and had dinner. The rich kids would drive us nuts because they'd be hanging around the gym until all hours. We'd have to kick them out. They didn't have a family to go home to."

Bowen benefited from having parents who cared enough to teach him lessons in life. When Bowen, a gifted track star, received a complete scholarship to attend the University of Texas, he rushed to tell his father the good news. All he had to do was pay a standard two-hundred-dollar out-of-state fee, and Texas beckoned.

Bowen approached his father and said, "Dad, I've got this great offer to go to Texas."

"Wonderful," replied his father.

"But I've got to pay a two-hundred-dollar fee to get in."

"Wonderful. Where are you going to get the money?" A confused Bowen saw his chances to attend the University of Texas dwindle, but he later understood what his father tried to do.

"He never gave us a nickel once we turned nine or ten years old. I'm glad now because it taught us a good lesson. We always had small jobs so we could earn what we got."[22]

Like Montague and Seng, Bowen paid scant attention to things happening on the other side of the world. War flared in Europe during the sixteen-year-old Bowen's sophomore year at Beverly Hills High, but Bowen cared more about his next athletic competition and next date. The Japanese and places in the Pacific, with their strange-sounding names, meant even less.

"We Were Very Close"

The three Meadows brothers of Watertown, South Dakota, Jim, Bill, and Dick, knew hardship for most of their early lives. Maybe that is why they grew so close. In the absence of other stabilizing factors, they turned to each other for comfort, companionship, and guidance.

Not that they lacked love and direction from adults. Their mother was a rock of stability, but three teenage boys growing up without a father could be a difficult situation for a working mother.

The hard times began, as it did for millions of Americans, with the stock market crash of 1929. Midwestern farmers, like their father, especially suffered, and that same year the Meadows family lost the farm to the local bank. "We had some difficult times," remembered Dick Meadows, five years old at the time. "I remember him taking furniture out of the house. Mother sold cookies door-to-door. Mom was a fighter."

Their father worked for International Harvester Company, but in 1933 a series of strokes paralyzed him. From then on, the crushing family duties fell to the mother and her father, an attorney in Watertown. Mrs. Meadows entered politics, while the oldest of the three Meadows boys, Jim, helped fill the void left by the incapacitated father. When their father died in 1939, Mrs. Meadows and the boys' grandfather assumed an even greater role in the lives of eighteen-year-old Jim, seventeen-year-old Bill, and fifteen-year-old Dick.

Mrs. Meadows and her father emphasized the importance of an honest day's work and of fulfilling one's responsibilities. All three boys worked odd jobs around town. They mowed lawns for twenty-five cents. Jim delivered milk and cleaned barbershops. Dick emptied shop spittoons, delivered groceries, and worked in a dry cleaner's and a department store. The three had the same values instilled at school, where "we were taught honesty and responsibility, the three r's and the Palmer writing method."

Above all, the Meadows brothers found their most important stabilizing element in each other's company and advice. "We were very close,"[23] stated Dick, especially throughout high school, where the trio joined many of the varsity teams. All three played football, but their biggest success came in track, where as a star sophomore runner, Dick raced in the famed Drake Relays. When school and job duties ended, the trio often headed to the open fields, where they loved to hunt pheasant.

The fields and activities of South Dakota overshadowed world events for the Meadows boys. The brothers from Watertown could not have felt more insulated than in the rolling land of South Dakota, smack in the middle of the American prairie.

Deteriorating Relations

Events would soon drag Seng, Montague, Hawkins, Bowen, and the Meadows boys from their carefree lives. Relations between the United States and Japan worsened in December 1937 when Japanese aircraft attacked the U.S. gunboat *Panay*. The gunboat was removing the last of the American embassy staff from the besieged town of Nanking when a squadron of Japanese aircraft shelled the small boat. Though the sinking *Panay* was clearly marked by American flags as belonging to the United States, the Japanese pilots continued their assault. Two American sailors and one Italian journalist were killed in the attack, which was filmed by a news reporter.

Politicians and citizens in the United States reacted angrily to the news, and for a moment the two nations appeared on the verge of warfare. Hampered by an ill-prepared military, Franklin Roosevelt could do little to assert American power in China, and thus did not want to start a war. Roosevelt demanded that Japan offer a public apology and pay more than two million dollars in damages. Tokyo agreed, and Roosevelt accepted the explanation that the Japanese pilots had incorrectly identified the *Panay* as a Chinese boat. Though both sides avoided war at this time, the affair soured relations between Japan and the United States.

The *Panay* incident handed Roosevelt justification for strengthening his military, though. One month after the gunboat sank, Roosevelt asked for and received from Congress a 20-percent increase in funds for the Navy so it could build enough ships to station a fleet in both the Atlantic and Pacific Oceans.

In September 1940, one year after war broke out in Europe, the Japanese signed the Tripartite Pact with Germany and Italy. The agreement bound each party to declare war on any nation that aligned against one of the three—an obvious attempt to prevent the United States from entering the conflict.

In 1941 Japanese messages, deciphered by American codebreakers, informed the United States of Japan's advance into French Indochina, south of China. Since Hitler had defeated France and the Netherlands, and appeared ready to knock Great Britain out of the war, Japan saw an opportunity to seize European possessions in the Pacific and gain control of their valuable resources.

When Japanese troops moved into Indochina in July 1941, President Roosevelt cut off all trade with Japan, including the flow of oil. He vowed to maintain the embargo until Japan withdrew from both China and Indochina and renounced the Tripartite Pact. Roosevelt's actions ignited additional war preparations in Japan.

In November 1941 a war warning went out to every American military post in the Pacific. The message bluntly stated: NEGOTIATIONS WITH JAPAN LOOKING TOWARD STABILIZATION OF CONDITIONS IN THE PACIFIC HAVE CEASED. AN AGGRESSIVE MOVE BY JAPAN IS EXPECTED WITHIN THE NEXT FEW DAYS. Since the Japanese military had sent large forces to Indochina, United States military commanders dismissed the idea that Pearl Harbor was endangered. Most predicted that war would start in the Philippines or the Far East.

During November 1941 six Japanese aircraft carriers, protected by two battleships, three cruisers, and nine destroyers, moved toward a remote harbor in the Kurile Islands, the northernmost regions of the Japanese home islands, to prepare for the secret voyage across the Pacific. Under strict radio silence, the fleet weighed anchor on November 26 and steamed toward Hawaii. The armada, under the command of Vice Adm. Chuichi Nagumo, steamed along a rarely traveled northern route across the Pacific to avoid being detected by foreign steamers. Three fleet submarines patrolled the waters in advance of Nagumo's ships, and twenty-seven other submarines arrived at positions ringing Oahu, the island locale of Pearl Harbor.

Shortly before dawn on December 7, the fleet arrived at its launch point 230 miles due north of Oahu and prepared its aircraft for attack. At the same time, other Japanese forces approached their launch points in the Far East. Adm. Isoroku Yamamoto sent his attacking fleet one final message, the same one used in battle thirty-six years earlier by Adm. Heihachiro Togo when Japan annihilated the Russian fleet at Tsushima: THE RISE OR FALL OF THE EMPIRE DEPENDS UPON THIS BATTLE. EVERYONE WILL DO HIS DUTY WITH UTMOST EFFORTS.[24]

"We'll Stamp Their Front Teeth In"

Each generation experiences an epochal moment so powerful, so emotional, so painful, it is as if society had been suddenly rent into two distinct sections—the time before the event and the time after. Baby boomers witnessed the Kennedy assassination; Americans in the early years of the new century suffered through September 11. Anyone above the age of six on December 7, 1941, can recall with distinct clarity what they were doing the moment they first heard the news that the Japanese had attacked the American naval base at Pearl Harbor in Hawaii.

As Dick Meadows leisurely cleaned the local barbershop in Watertown, South Dakota, a job he inherited when brother Jim left for college, he turned on the portable radio and listened to music. So far, that Sunday had been like all the others, unspectacular in its boredom, but the job of sweeping floors and cleaning sinks provided him with a little spending money and helped his mother with expenses at home. Somehow, the music made the chores less burdensome. How could you not move more sprightly when you listened to such great 1941 hits as "Dancing in the Dark" by Artie Shaw, Glenn Miller's "Chattanooga Choo Choo," and "Blues in the Night" by the lovely Dinah Shore? Benny Goodman, Frank Sinatra, Stan Kenton, Peggy Lee—all could transform a dreary day of labor into an exciting, toe-tapping afternoon.

Suddenly, at 12:26 P.M. (2:26 eastern standard time) a terse voice cut into the program and curtailed Meadows's reverie. Simultaneously, Meadows and millions of Americans across the country listened to the somber statement. LADIES AND GENTLEMEN, WE INTERRUPT THIS BROADCAST TO BRING YOU AN IMPORTANT BULLETIN FROM THE UNITED PRESS. FLASH! WASHINGTON—THE WHITE HOUSE ANNOUNCES A JAPANESE ATTACK ON PEARL HARBOR. STAY TUNED FOR FURTHER DEVELOPMENTS TO BE BROADCAST AS THEY ARE RECEIVED.[25]

Shaking off his momentary disbelief, Meadows telephoned his mother with news of the attack.

In Beverly Hills, Stan Bowen rustled out of bed after his usual late Saturday night. Like Meadows, he turned on the radio to news that Pearl Harbor had been bombed. "Honest to God, we didn't know where Pearl Harbor was," said Bowen, a sentiment matched by many of his countrymen that fateful Sunday. Wherever it was, he knew an Oriental country on the far side of the Pacific had the audacity to assault his nation. Vengeance quickly replaced anger. "We thought we would take care of the Japanese with no problem."[26] Bowen assumed he would soon be in the military, but that caused little concern. He felt he needed a little adventure in his life.

Charles Wysocki Jr. had just returned to his Milwaukee home with his family after attending church services. His father, as always, sat in his favorite chair reading the paper, while his mother and sisters headed to the kitchen to prepare lunch.

About noon Wysocki's father turned on the radio to listen to his favorite program, but instead of the expected entertainment, they tuned in to an announcement that the Japanese had attacked Pearl Harbor.

"We looked at each other and wondered—'Where's Pearl Harbor?'"[27]

When the radio announcer mentioned Hawaii, Wysocki and his father pulled out a few maps and some old geography books to find out where Hawaii was.

In two waves, the Japanese destroyed 188 aircraft and damaged another 159, sank or damaged 18 ships (including 7 battleships), killed 2,403 American sailors and soldiers, and wounded another 1,178. This was accomplished at the cost of 29 Japanese aircraft and pilots lost, and 1 large and 5 midget submarines destroyed.

A stunned nation was slow to react, but once it did, emotions served both to vent anger as well as to unify a country. "Over the U.S. and its history there was a great unanswered question," stated *Time* magazine. "What would the people, the 132,000,000, say in the face of the mightiest event of their time?

"What they said—tens of thousands of them—was: 'Why, the yellow bastards!'"

The first man to arrive at the Norfolk, Virginia, recruiting station bluntly expressed his reason for being there. "I want to beat them Japs with my own bare hands." More than two thousand people in Dallas were watching the movie *Sergeant York* at the Majestic Theater when news of the war was announced. A long silence ended in boisterous applause and a spectator promising, "We'll stamp their front teeth in."[28]

On December 8 in Washington, D.C., in words that have resonated through the years, President Roosevelt asked Congress to declare war on Japan. He began in a deliberately slow cadence to ensure his nation grasped the significance. "Yesterday, December 7, 1941—a date which will live in infamy—the United States of America was suddenly and deliberately attacked by naval and air forces of the Empire of Japan."

It was as if, with his words, he had drawn a line of demarcation that separated the lives of the Meadows brothers, Bowen, Hawkins, Montague, and Seng into two segments. With that famous speech, they were about to leave behind one world—the civilian—and enter another—the military. A world of familiarity and comfort would be replaced by an unknown future against a known enemy.

A nation listened as the man who had steered the country through the depths of the Great Depression admitted that the nation had suffered grievous harm. "The attack yesterday on the Hawaiian Islands has caused severe damage to American naval and military forces. I regret to tell you that very many American lives have been lost."

Roosevelt then methodically listed the places that Japan had attacked—Malaya, Hong Kong, Guam, the Philippine Islands, Wake Island, Midway Island. As he spoke each name, he symbolically yanked Bowen farther from his life in Beverly Hills. Each utterance placed Seng's and Montague's dreams on hold. Each phrase added miles between Hawkins and his mother.

The president exuded an optimism that Bowen and the rest felt from the first moment when he promised a satisfactory end to the war. "With confidence in our armed forces—with the unbounding determination of our people—we will gain the inevitable triumph—so help us God."[29]

The Japanese had underestimated the impact of the surprise attack on the American people. Debate between isolationists and interventionists vanished, and men and women rallied to the cry "Remember Pearl Harbor." The smoldering wreckage at Pearl Harbor united the nation in a way that could not have been achieved in any other manner.

One crucial difference separated the president's public optimism from the optimism that fueled the nation. Roosevelt's was finely crafted in an effort to rally his people. Theirs, including Montague's, Seng's, and Bowen's, was based upon naïveté. They had no idea how horrid the war would be.

Winston Churchill, who governed a nation in retreat in both the European and Pacific theaters, did. As he later wrote of the early weeks of conflict, "In all the war I never received a more direct shock. . . . As I turned over and twisted in bed the full horror of the news sank in upon me. . . . Over all this vast expanse of waters Japan was supreme, and we everywhere [were] weak and naked."[30]

"TOKYO, WE ARE COMING"

"A Slow, Mounting Anger"

For the thousands of men already in the military on December 7, war meant continuing their careers on a different scale. Most men who fought in World War II, however, did not intend to make the armed forces their permanent occupation. They willingly signed up for one of the branches with the thought that once the war terminated, they would return to their civilian lives. In the interim, they put their careers, hopes, and expectations on hold while they temporarily inhabited a strange new world, one filled with violence and bloodshed.

The sentiment, according to the racial attitudes of the times, was clear. They would exterminate the Japanese as if they crushed irritating insects. One noted newspaper correspondent, Ira Wolfert, wrote of the Japanese, "The kind of human being that he himself has become is wrong and has no place any more on earth." A June 1942 patriotic parade coursed through the streets of New York City featuring a popular float titled *Tokyo: We Are Coming*. A newspaper account described it as "a big American eagle leading a flight of bombers down on a herd of yellow rats which were trying to escape in all directions."[1] This would be a struggle pitting good versus evil, freedom versus dictatorship, civility versus barbarity.

Marine Corps recruiting posters reflected those emotions. "If you got an itch to grab a Nip by the stacking swivel you're hitching with the right outfit," stated one poster, while another promised, "You'll get action and a chance to slap the Jap."[2]

The day after Pearl Harbor, young men flooded recruiting stations around the country, forcing many to remain open twenty-four hours a day, seven days a week. According to *Time* magazine, the nation met the war's first days "with a deepening sense of gravity and a slow, mounting anger."[3]

William J. Bordelon, like Seng and Montague a graduate of Central Catholic High School, enlisted on December 8 despite his father's advice to think of his mother and at least wait until after Christmas. "Dad, I have a job to do," replied the son. "If I wait until after Christmas, I will lose two weeks doing that job." Classmates were hardly surprised, as Bordelon's dedication in ROTC vaulted him to the battalion major by his senior year, the top-ranking cadet, and his class prophecy stated, "Military first, last and always."[4]

Thus the young men pulled out of train stations with Marine recruits waving to families and singing patriotic songs. The young men did not expect a summer camp. After all, the military built a reputation on harshness, but how long could it possibly take the mighty United States to defeat such a backward nation as Japan, one that resorted to trickery to attack Pearl Harbor?

Along with his brother Jack and friend Larry Kavich, Stan Bowen enlisted in the Navy a few days after Pearl Harbor, mainly because his father had been a Navy quartermaster during World War I. When the recruiting officer learned that Bowen and Kavich had taken first-aid classes in college, he offered them what he called a can't-miss opportunity. "I can make you hospital apprentices first class," the recruiter promised. "You'll wear three stripes on your sleeves instead of one, a red cross on your left arm, get paid more and if you don't like the Medical Corps you can transfer to any other branch of the Navy *and* you won't lose your rating."[5] Bowen especially liked the extra five dollars per month he would earn, so he and Kavich quickly agreed.

Though he had signed with the Navy, he was not due to be inducted until after receiving a telegram indicating when he should appear at the Los Angeles induction center. When Jack received his notice to report on December 29, Stan accompanied him to the ceremony. Stan thought he heard his name called when a chief boatswain's mate started roll call, but assumed it had to be some mistake. His concern deepened when his brother frantically waved to get his attention. Jack told him that when he heard Stan's name, he had answered the roll call for him, fearing that his brother might be in trouble if they thought he failed to show up.

Stan walked over to the chief boatswain's mate, confident he could quickly straighten out the confusion. He explained that he had not yet received his telegram and was thus not packed and ready to depart.

"Are you Stanley Bowen?" the chief asked, his tone more of irritation than solicitousness.

"Yes."

"Then fall in!"

Bowen started to object, adding that he had a grand New Year's Eve bash planned, but another curt "Fall in!" quieted him. The dejected Stan joined his brother and headed off to camp without any personal items or the opportunity to say good-bye to friends.[6]

Bill Meadows joined the Marine Corps in May 1941, before the war, while Jim entered in May 1942, six months following the attack. Hoping to be stationed with his older brother, Jim asked to be placed in the same outfit when he completed boot camp, a request the Marines readily granted.

Dick chafed back in Watertown, but the high school junior faced an uphill struggle. The 1942 movie *Wake Island*, which depicted the heroic Marine stand against overwhelming enemy forces on a tiny Pacific atoll, increased his desire to be with his brothers. "Isn't it something how a movie like that can inspire you when it's all killing and misery? But it did inspire me," explained Dick Meadows. "William Bendix, the fortitude, how they kept repelling the Japanese, ten-to-one odds didn't bother them. I think they kind of used that as a recruiting movie."

The five-foot-eight-inch, 142-pound Dick Meadows put on hold his dreams of playing football or becoming a track coach and decided to drop out of high school in his junior year to enter the Marines. When he mentioned the idea to his principal, the administrator replied, "You might as well, Dick. You're a lousy student."

Dick had his heart set on the Marines, but an avid Army recruiter hotly pursued the youth. Every time the recruiter spotted Meadows, he asked when he was joining the Army. Meadows's answer never varied—he was joining the Marines.

And so it seemed, until one day the recruiter called Meadows and said, "Well, Dick, I got you." Meadows asked him what he meant, and the Army recruiter explained that the Marines had closed their enlistments.

A shaken Meadows saw his dreams crumbling. He told his mother, who happened to have been a high school classmate of the area's Marine recruiting officer. After she telephoned her former associate, Meadows traveled to the post office and talked with the officer. He explained that the Marines had indeed cut off their enlistments but added, "I know about your brothers, and I know your mother, and I'll date your papers back and put you in ahead of the closing date."

By the slimmest margin, Dick Meadows avoided the Army, but worried his mother in the process. She repeated many times that if anything happened to him because of his being in the Marines, she would never be able to forgive herself.[7]

"A Tearful Good-bye"

Charlie Montague struggled with a problem many men faced. He loved Billie and wanted to marry her, but he also knew his country needed him and every other healthy young man. The training in his high school ROTC classes inculcated a sense of duty, and he could no more ignore it than he could go against the wishes of his mother. Should he first flee with Billie, marry her, then join the Marines, or should he simply leave and wait to marry her until after the war?

Charlie talked about the matter with Gene Seng, who urged him to delay marrying until after the war. Seng believed that Charlie would be foolish to set plans in the uncertain times they faced. When Charlie received similar advice from the parents of the seventeen-year-old Billie, he began to waver. They had forbidden her older sister from marrying at an early age, and wanted Charlie and Billie to wait as well. After much debate, the four compromised. Charlie would enlist in the Marines with his good buddy, Gene Seng, as previously planned, then return after boot camp near San Diego and marry Billie.

After making his decision to enlist, Gene visited every relative in the area, including his grandparents and five sets of aunts and uncles, to say good-bye. He then threw a huge going-away party with friends. The group talked and laughed into the night, sharing jokes and memories of high school.

Following the party, on February 3, 1942, Gene and Charlie hopped on a train for Houston to enlist. When they were accepted, Gene's pride gushed out. "We are now U.S. Marines," he told his family. "We passed the most grueling physical I ever hope to go through."[8] He and Charlie were fortunate, as the Marines rejected twelve of the thirty young men who appeared that day.

That the pair would enlist together surprised no one in the San Antonio–Bandera area. Having experienced many great times in high school and after, and now inspired by the patriotic fervor of the times, Seng and Montague did what came naturally—they joined as a pair.

They also typified America's younger generation, the men who would be expected to carry the brunt of the fighting. Rather than shirk the responsibility, they eagerly embraced it, partly out of a sense of impatience—the sooner you start, the sooner you return—but mostly from ignorance as to what war would actually be like. In late 1941–early 1942, patriotism dwarfed reality.

In early February 1942, the Montague and Seng families, along with Billie, drove to the train station to greet Charlie and Gene. The two were on their way to boot camp near San Diego, and the train from Houston had a scheduled stop in San Antonio.

Around 2:00 A.M., Gene said good-bye to his parents, three sisters, and brother Ralph, while Charlie and Billie managed to sneak off for an all-too-brief moment alone together, during which time they kissed and promised to write each other. With time dwindling, Charlie and Gene boarded the Southern Pacific train.

"We were so proud that he was going," said Patsy of brother Gene. "We were so glad that our big brother was in the service."[9]

"It was a tearful good-bye," said Gene's brother, Ralph. "They were in a hurry to join the service. Everybody wanted to go into service. Everybody wanted to go over and kill 'em a Jap."[10]

As the train slowly chugged out of the San Antonio station, George Montague shouted his good lucks as his brother and Gene stood on the train's steps and waved good-bye, then raced to the back of the train for a final glimpse of family. Billie could hardly contain her emotions, but she at least drew comfort from the fact that her loved one would soon return and they would be married.

Gene and Charlie settled in for the lengthy ride aboard the Santa Fe Streamliner to San Diego. More accustomed to the dry, flat lands of Texas, the pair marveled at the variety of scenery as the train wound west. "This was the land they loved," George Montague wrote of the Texas countryside through which the pair traveled. "But that was why they were leaving. Leaving their fathers and mothers and aunts, and sweethearts, because they loved them."[11]

Gene sent a quick letter home when he and Charlie arrived in San Diego. Despite the prospects of physicals, inoculations, and drills, Gene's spirits remained high. "Tell the rest of the folks we got out here O.K. and are ready for plenty of hard work quick—Then plenty of hard action—quick."[12]

A Marine "Scars and All"

Pearl Harbor energized William Hawkins as if he had been struck by lightning. Despite his boyhood accident and his hatred of war, duty called the young man. He quickly told his mother, "I've got to go. I'm going to see if the Marines will have me."[13]

He did not consider the Army or Navy because those branches had earlier rejected him. When he was seventeen years old, Hawkins tried to enter the Naval Academy at Annapolis, but he lacked the necessary political connections to obtain a congressional appointment. Rather than give up, Hawkins convinced two of his friends, James Colley and William Abbott, to enlist in the Navy with him. Once accepted, Hawkins figured he could enter the Academy by working hard, gaining the confidence of superior officers, and taking the sailors' merit examination.

When the recruiting officer examined the trio, he readily accepted Colley and Abbott, but rejected Hawkins because of his scars. "I never hated to turn down anyone so much in all my life," the recruiter told Hawkins. "You're the kind of boy the Navy wants."[14]

Devastated, Hawkins hurried home and cried. His mother attempted to console him, but Hawkins could only mutter, "Just think, Mom, it was my idea and then they take Bill and Junior and turn me down."[15] Hawkins next tried the Army Air Corps at Randolph Field in San Antonio, but again the scars ruled him out.

In a December 1941 visit to his mother, Hawkins told her that, as a last resort, he would try the Marines. When they accepted him on January 5, 1942, an ecstatic Hawkins told his mother he was a Marine, "scars and all."

Before leaving for boot camp, the five-foot-ten-inch, 147-pound Hawkins made an unusual prediction that he shared with his close friend, Ballard McCleskey. He stated that he doubted he would make it back from the Pacific.

A stunned McCleskey hardly knew what to say. "Aw, come on, Deane, I'll see you after the war, whether you think so or not," countered McCleskey.

"Nope," replied Hawkins. "You won't! Well, we've had fun though."[16] Hawkins never explained what compelled him to make the depressing prediction, but he wisely kept it from his parent.

The hardest part for Hawkins would be leaving his mother. She had nursed him through his horrible burns, provided comfort and understanding, given words of advice when others spurned him, and been a continuous source of love for him. Now he had to say good-bye for the duration of the war. Hawkins knew she could take care of herself—she always had been a survivor—but he worried about her if something bad happened to him.

Duty and Artistry

Some of the men who would fight on Tarawa had already joined the Marines before December 7. Unlike the civilians, they had chosen the military as a career. War meant new posts and orders, but it was just another stop in their routine. Strife or not, they would have been in the military.

One was Norm Hatch. Acquaintances always seemed to use the words *active* and *independent* to describe him. Born March 2, 1921, in Boston, Massachusetts, Hatch had a knack for escaping even life-threatening situations. While still in grade school, one winter night Hatch and two classmates jumped onto a slow-moving freight train, intending to ride it until it halted a few miles down the track. Rather than slowing, the train gained speed and sped out of Boston.

"This train is going to Maine!" Hatch shouted to his friends. "I'm going to jump. If my old man ever catches the fact that I've been jumping these trains, he's going to kill me." Hatch leaned out the side of the racing boxcar to peer down the track, waited until he spotted a large snowbank, jumped into it, then hit the ground and rolled around.

Shaken but unhurt, Hatch returned home, riding part of the way by jumping onto the back of a streetcar and hanging on as the vehicle took him closer to home. Hatch climbed into bed before his parents realized anything was awry. His two companions, too frightened to jump from the speeding train, rode all the way to Portland, Maine, before being rescued. Hatch, fearing his stern father's reaction, refrained from telling him of the incident until many months later.

As if a racing train were not enough, the youthful Hatch survived multiple encounters with the most feared mobster of the day. A drawback to his father's job of selling luxury cars was that the company often transferred him. One of those moves took the Hatch family to Chicago, where they lived in the exclusive Lexington Hotel, infamous as being the headquarters for Al Capone and his gang. Hatch's father, whose clientele included many of the top mobsters and bootleggers of the day, warned his son to be careful of what he said or did whenever he rode the elevators or walked through the lobby, but Hatch found little to fear. "They were all big Italians and they liked kids and they always gave me quarters to buy ice cream, and a quarter was a lot of money. Italians are very family-oriented, so a young kid was pleasurable to have around."[17]

Not surprisingly, Hatch found the classroom to be somewhat restrictive. He maintained decent grades, but a world existed outside the windows that begged discovery. In high school, once again living in Boston, Hatch fell in love with the ocean. He spent every spare moment either along the harbor, working on the yachts of wealthy Bostonians, or in a fishing boat earning fifty cents an hour. He so reeked of fish that when he returned home, no matter how cold the weather, Hatch's mother made him clean up outside.

At the same time, Hatch inherited a sense of duty. No matter how inconsequential the task, Hatch's father expected it done correctly, without shortcuts or expedients.

"He had no shades of gray," said Hatch of his father. "It was either right or it was wrong." He "believed in getting a job done and in getting it right, and he didn't have much favor for anyone that didn't. I knew him to be a man of strength and character. He didn't back down on anything, and that's what made it so hard to deal with him as a kid."[18]

Besides the importance of duty, Hatch inherited an artistic bent from his mother. Many summers the family moved to an art community in New England where his mother, a high-spirited intellectual woman, mingled with artists and studied their work. Through her, Hatch developed an appreciation for images captured on canvas, an interest he quickly turned into a love for images caught on film.

Hatch joined the Marines in June 1939, intending to use his love of photography in that branch of the service. After completing basic training, Hatch joined the staff of the Marine magazine, *Leatherneck*. His photographic talent so impressed fellow workers that the Marines recommended him for a spot in the prestigious newsreel course conducted by the March of Time, a national newsreel service.

The Japanese attacked Pearl Harbor before Hatch completed his training in the newsreel class. Once he finished, he helped instruct future groups, then in September 1942 joined the 2d Marine Division's Photo Section. What he experienced and where he went the next few years would now be determined by where superior officers, in most cases far from the scene, sent the division.

"We Were All Gung Ho"

Robert Muhlbach always knew what he wanted—combat. Ever since his uncle, a Marine in World War I, had regaled him with tales of battlefield splendor, Robert intended to be a soldier. He loved it all—the sleek uniforms, the precise drills, the shiny medals, and the weapons. New York's Bronx High School of Science offered nothing he wanted.

A detachment of Marines in full blues at the 1939 New York World's Fair convinced Muhlbach to join that branch, but one obstacle stood in his way. At fifteen years of age, he was three years below the minimum age to legally join. Unfazed, Muhlbach forged a birth certificate and entered the Marines in early 1941.

Muhlbach thrived in boot camp. He earned expert rifleman status, then headed to sea aboard the battleship *Wyoming* for duty in the Atlantic Ocean as part of an admiral's detachment.

Muhlbach and the other Marines heard the rumblings emanating from the Pacific and guessed that they would soon have to slug it out with the Japanese. Most had friends in the Pacific, or they talked with men aboard ship who had recently been stationed there, so they knew more about the brewing troubles than did most of their countrymen.

On December 7 the *Wyoming* was steaming five hundred miles off the Iceland coast when news of the Pearl Harbor attack electrified the detachment. Every Marine aboard requested a transfer to the Pacific, where most of the fighting involving Marines was sure to take place. "We were all gung ho about getting in the Fleet Marine Force and going over there and getting revenge on the Japs,"[19] said Muhlbach.

Unfortunately, the admiral denied every request. He would have difficulty in wartime finding adequate replacements for his detachment, so he took the easiest step—he froze Muhlbach and the others in their current assignment. Unless the admiral's ship steamed to the Pacific, Muhlbach would be on the sidelines while his Marine brethren fought the war. Caught in the excitement of Pearl Harbor, the seventeen-year-old Muhlbach decided to take drastic measures once the ship reached Norfolk, Virginia.

"The only way to get off the ship was to go over the hill. At that time, if you went over the hill and you got caught or were turned in to the same naval district, you went back to your ship and were tried and court-martialed there. If you got turned in at a different naval district, you got tried and court-martialed there, so I hitchhiked to New York and turned myself in at the Brooklyn Navy Yard."

A summary court-martial handed Muhlbach thirty days in the brig and a $150 fine, a heady amount considering he earned only $30 a month from the Marine Corps, but he willingly suffered the inconveniences in order to obtain a chance to fight the Japanese. "More than half the detachment [from his ship] went over the hill,"[20] stated Muhlbach.

Rather than sending him back to his ship, the Marine Corps included Muhlbach on a troop train formed out of men in the brig. The train transported

Muhlbach to Camp Elliott near San Diego, the final stop before heading to the Pacific. Though the ride proved far from comfortable—the Marines sat on hard seats, waited in line to use the facilities, and carried combat packs, tin helmets, and Springfield rifles—few complained. They were about to deliver payback for the insults suffered at Pearl Harbor and Wake Island.

"A Complete Scary Time"

When most newly inducted Marines, like Montague and Seng, walked through the portals into boot camp, they left the civilian world and entered the military. The train bearing Dick Meadows provided an example. When the group of twenty-five fresh recruits arrived in San Diego, the neophyte Marines hopped off the train singing the Marine Hymn. They thought they made an impressive sight, but crusty Marine sergeants quickly dispelled that notion. "A whole bunch of Marine sergeants were standing there with their hands on their hips, and boy, did we catch hell! It was a shock. We thought we were Marines, but they were going to let us know we weren't."[21]

For Meadows and the other enthusiastic recruits, now much subdued, it was only the first of many challenges shattering their preconceptions of the military and the war. Milwaukee resident Charles Wysocki realized civilian life, as well as the comforts of home, had disappeared until war's end almost as soon as he arrived in San Diego. He had barely walked into camp when a sergeant told him to pack up his civilian clothes and mail them home, since he would no longer need them. Most of the items meant little, but Wysocki stared at a beautiful pullover sweater he had long cherished. Though he hated to part with that vestige of civilian life, "I had to let it go."[22]

Seng and Montague could part with their civilian clothes. They just hoped to retain each other's company. Together they could better face what lay ahead. Together they could bring a touch of home to what was fast becoming a rigid, physical world.

But would the Marines accommodate them? Fortunately, fate smiled on the pair. Seng stated that he and Charlie were "just flat lucky." He explained, "We were organized this morning into platoons and squads and were put in the same squad and bunk. We are just about the only buddies that got to stay so close." Seng added, "I imagine we will stay this way for quite a while now—I hope for good."[23]

Montague, Seng, and the others received their uniforms and a bucket of toiletries, the cost of which would be deducted from the first monthly paycheck of twenty-one dollars. A sergeant then marched them to their barracks, where they packed their civilian clothes and donned the uniforms that marked them—if they satisfactorily passed boot camp—as Marines instead of civilians. Recruit Melvin Traylor later wrote, "They now owned you body and soul."[24]

The two most important items in their immediate careers as Marines now entered their lives—their rifles, and their drill instructor (DI). Seng and Montague had to call their rifles—whose serial numbers they committed to memory—their best friend. "My rifle is my girlfriend,"[25] Gene Seng wrote to his sister, quite an admission for a healthy young man with an avid interest in females.

Routine became the word of the day for the recruits. Profane drill sergeants interspersed an amazingly rich vocabulary of swear words with marching, hiking, shooting, and drilling, most of it done in double time.

"We got up at 5:00 this morning and have been on the go ever since," wrote Gene Seng to his family. He explained that his left side felt numb from all the shots he had been given. "From what I have seen of this place already it is going to be plenty rough. My sergeant told us that it wouldn't be just damned rough he said in the Marines it was ____ rough—and I think he meant it."[26]

Afterward their DI barked that "we were all nice boys, but they didn't need boys in the corps, they needed men."[27] The DI added that his job was to break them down and rebuild them as Marines, and to that end he would keep them busy sixteen hours a day, between 0500 (5:00 A.M.) and 2200 (10:00 P.M.), with one hour for lunch.

The horrible food matched the miserable training conditions, which seemed designed to break any but the sturdiest. Seng and Montague, now shorn of their hair and looking like every other young Marine, engaged in a litany of drills, marches, and classes.

Gene Seng stated that after the first day he was "as sore as a football player the second day of the season." He added his fear that this "was just the beginning."[28]

For the first three weeks of boot camp, Montague and Seng drilled endlessly, sat through lectures on basic tactics and weapons, and learned the proper use of bayonets, explosives, and hand grenades. Seng explained that he learned how to handle himself in battle, "for the most part musketry, close order drill, combat principals [sic] and signals, and bayonet drill,"[29] which he executed until he nearly collapsed from exhaustion. They spent the next three weeks at the rifle range, where they learned how to fire the Springfield '03 rifle and the .45 pistol.

Through it all, the two remained friendly with everyone. Cpl. Henry Duke, who shared the same tent with Montague, whom they called Monty, and Seng, said, "They were real nice. They were honest country boys. Good guys."[30]

Their dream of sticking together almost ended when both came down with sore throats and headed to sick bay. Seng was treated and released, but Montague had to remain in sick bay. "It scares me because if he stays there three days we will be separated for good—he will be put in another outfit for missing out," wrote Seng.

Happily for the two, Charlie, whom Seng called his sidekick, suddenly reappeared and all was well. Seng mentioned that "the damned fool sneaked out because he was scared he would not get back to our outfit. I was so glad to see him I could have kissed him. Hope he don't die—I think I would die too."[31]

Degradation was the recruits' constant companion, as their sergeants attempted to strip away their individualities and mold them into a unit. From their shaved heads to the derogatory names, everything was designed to fashion a fighter. Should any Marine violate the rules, a drill sergeant dealt with it immediately and harshly. Most carried a stick, ostensibly for measuring, but typically used to smack butts, ribs, or fingers. Occasionally, irate drill sergeants resorted to swift kicks in the rear with their heavy boots if necessary.

When one man from Tennessee refused to shower, much to the chagrin of his bunkmates, the drill sergeant gathered the men and said he was going to illustrate how the Marine Corps handled such a situation. The young man had to run around the parade ground, holding his rifle high, yelling, "I am a dirty Marine."[32] After that the other men in his unit gave him a "bath," using sand instead of soap. The recruit from Tennessee, and every other man watching, never forgot to bathe after that spectacle.

Albert Gilman said that training was "a complete scary time. You became nothing when you went there. It was culture shock. Total discipline. When I came home, though, I hurdled a five-foot hedge. They taught you to do things I never felt I could do."[33]

Corpsmen like Stanley Bowen, for instance, learned how to use plasma and sulfa powder and how to set splints, and Hawkins headed to scout-sniper school started by the famed Marine Jim Crowe, a man Hawkins would again meet on Tarawa. No matter where they ended, each man learned hand-to-hand combat techniques. If a Marine doubted he had entered a world alien from the civilian realm, this exercise removed them, for he came face-to-face with the notion that one day he would have to fight an enemy he could see, whose face and eyes glared back at him with the intent to kill, who stood feet away and would give no quarter in a struggle that would result in someone's death.

Hawkins shone above most of the other recruits and easily gained the respect, not only of every superior officer, but also of the men he eventually commanded. Upon completion of boot camp, Hawkins was named the outstanding member of his platoon, then on March 14, 1942, was promoted to private first class.

Hawkins wrote his mother that he was "trying to be an example to a bunch of 190-pounders when I am so pooped that I hardly know how I am standing up on my own feet, but I'll do it if it kills me." Hawkins gained such respect from his superiors after working as a clerk in intelligence that one officer wrote, "I relied very heavily on Hawkins as my senior NCO because he was quite knowledgeable. . . . I looked to him to provide the leadership in the section required of a second in command. It was apparent that he was a person of superior intellect and educational background as compared to the other enlisted persons in the section."[34]

"We Are Now Full-Fledged Marines"

Seng and Montague kept close touch with family members back home. On one of his first days in boot camp, Seng asked his mother to write often, as "your letters seem to put something in my backbone with your sweet encouragement." He requested that they send photos of the family, since "you would be surprised how much those pictures keep you closer to me," and mentioned that he and Charlie were sending a photograph home of the two. "They are going to be my Mother's Day present to you, sweetheart."[35]

He enjoyed drawing pictures for his youngest sister, seven-year-old Peggy. In one letter he drew himself lying prone at the rifle range, and later sketched a boat bearing Charlie and him overseas. On both letters, Gene included hugs and kisses from both Charlie and himself.

As they had been brought up to do, Seng and Montague turned to their faith in awkward times. "Charlie and I went to Confession and Communion last Sunday and to Communion today," Seng wrote his parents in March. "It makes me feel better about the whole deal." Sister Gabriella, a nun who taught both boys, sent them scapular medals to wear about their necks, and in June Gene "went to Communion for you, Daddy, Sunday for Father's Day."[36]

Whenever they could, Gene and Charlie headed to San Diego to catch a movie or a dance, or even traveled to Los Angeles to tour Hollywood. While Charlie remained faithful to Billie, Gene always seemed to have a new female in his life, always on a short-term basis. He referred to Mary, Mary Jean, Patty, and Grace in letters home, and mentioned that he met a nice girl at a USO dance "and through some tall talking finally managed to get her phone number." The girl invited Gene to her home, where he had a great time, and added, "I only hope that I can keep up my good luck."[37]

On another occasion, Gene took a date into San Diego to hear the Bob Crosby orchestra, but mishap more than mischief marked a night that used up his available money supply. "I got my date home late," explained Seng, "because we had to wait so long for the bus and caught hell from her ma. I had to get a taxi back to the base because the buses had quit running which cost a small fortune in itself." Reflecting on it later, Seng concluded, "But I guess it was worth it all—I think."[38]

Seng's jovial ways eventually caught up to him when he erroneously mailed a letter meant for one girl in an envelope addressed to a second. The blunder caused some embarrassment, but did not deter him from continuing his pursuit of the opposite sex.

"I guess I committed the greatest mistake I could have," he wrote to his sister Lorraine. "Billie wrote me and told me that she found out from some place that I had gotten part of a letter I wrote to Mary Jean McBride mixed with one I wrote to Una. I haven't heard from Una for quite a while and I was wondering why—now I know—Ouch! It is one hell of an embarrassing situation to put it mild. Let me know what you can and after this I am going to be very careful about not getting my letters mixed. . . . I guess I tore my pants with Una now. I always do something to ruin my deals with the girls—Oh well." Seng could not have been too worried, however, for in the next paragraph he thanks Lorraine for sending Patty Pin's address and asks for Grace Swimmer's.[39]

Hints appeared in Seng's letters that the time for departure drew closer. On Easter Sunday, Gene talked more about the world situation than normal. "It sure was funny celebrating Easter without the swellest most dear family in the world. It especially seemed like there was something not there at church this morning. But I guess that it is high time everyone is forgetting our own personal wants and think about what the people of this country will lose if they don't. The Bishop of San Diego gave the sermon at Mass this morning and he brought out in fine manner how our fight today parallel [sic] the fight of the Crusaders."[40] Seng mentioned in early June that some Marines left six weeks after arriving in boot camp, so he and Charlie would likely soon be on their way to the Pacific.

Before heading overseas, Montague hoped to return to Texas, where he and Billie would marry, but the Marines had other plans. Developments in the South Pacific required a rapid buildup in strength to halt the Japanese at a place called Guadalcanal. Similar to what befell many other couples around the country over the next four years, Charlie and Billie placed their wedding plans on hold until the war ended. Gene, who had helped persuade Charlie to wait, promised Billie he would look after his friend now that they were ready to embark for the war zone.

"Well at last I am free," Seng wrote home. "We are now out of boot camp and full-fledged U.S. Marines. It is sure one *hell* of a good feeling to be free again. Charlie and I were both put in the same line outfit and at long last are bunking in the same tent." Seng explained that at first the Marines were going to put him into a different company, "but I put up such a kick that they left me as is." He added that he received his monthly pay—$5.41 after deductions—but that "I bet money we can get the job we are in here for done better than any other branch."[41]

"I Never Got to Say Good-bye to the United States"

Leaving for boot camp was an emotional experience for the young Marines, but at least they remained inside the United States, where family and loved ones stood relatively close by. A war that unfolded on the far side of a vast ocean had not yet wrenched them from familiar surroundings.

That changed with the troop transports bound for Pacific destinations. Pfc. Charles Wysocki boarded the same ship with Gene Seng, the USS *President Hayes*. When reveille awoke him the next morning, Wysocki headed topside to scan the California coastline, but "there was none—only water and more water—we had put out to sea—I and the others knew—we were on our way— where, we did not know."[42] Rather than the comfortable California landscape, Wysocki stared at an unknown future.

Once the country's borders disappeared over the horizon, the Pacific took on two identities—it became an immense barrier of water separating them from everything familiar and friendly, and it acted as a speedy path ending inevitably in combat. Each day the men steamed farther from their families and closer to danger. The war that had appeared so distant in 1939 now loomed real and ominous. The sole advantage was that many headed toward the South Pacific oblivious to what waited.

To their surprise, Montague and Seng were placed into different platoons and boarded separate ships. After not seeing Charlie in over a week, Gene wrote home, "I sure miss that guy."[43]

Instead of immediately leaving San Diego, Seng and Montague waited aboard their transports for three weeks. As the days wound on, morale plummeted. "I am ready to go and am getting tired of waiting around,"[44] Seng wrote home. He added that some men had gone over the hill because the ceaseless waiting got to them.

Stanley Bowen, now a naval corpsman assigned to the Marines, had already said his good-byes to his parents when he boarded in San Diego what he called "this God-awful boat,"[45] a dilapidated vessel that rumor stated Adm. Richard Byrd had used to go to the South Pole. For the next three weeks they remained in port, existing on a steady diet of cramped quarters and horrible food.

When the ship finally left, one sight affected him—for an hour a dirigible floated above, looking for enemy submarines. For the first time since he left Beverly Hills, Bowen came face-to-face with the thought that he could be harmed or killed. For Stanley Bowen, the war had drawn much closer, even though he could still see the California coast.

Unlike Bowen, Dick Meadows traveled to the Pacific in style. He and five thousand other Marines climbed aboard the luxury liner *Lurline*, and although the ship bulged with troops, she bore herself with the dignity attached to such a vessel. Gorgeous murals adorned the ceilings, and other trappings reminded the men that another world existed outside their own, yet they still realized they were headed to war. Scuttlebutt stated that they would retake Wake Island, a small atoll that had been seized in December 1941 after mounting an heroic defense, but no one knew for sure.

Meadows could not erase two events from his mind, despite the abundance of shipboard attractions. The first occurred on land. "It was tough and we were homesick and all, and I remember it was Christmas Eve," Meadows later said. "We marched to see a movie. Would you believe the movie was *Holiday Inn*, and I tell you, that was the saddest-looking bunch of guys you ever saw. There were plenty of tears in the theater. We filed out of there, and somebody talked. The sergeant made us do a couple of laps around the parade ground, which must be six blocks long by one block wide, and we had to double-time around it on Christmas Eve. It was pretty rough."[46] Meadows could rarely recall feeling any lower than that Christmas of 1942. Being an optimist, he looked ahead to Christmas of 1943, which he believed had to be better.

The second event happened shortly afterward as the *Lurline* pulled out of San Diego. Instead of standing at the rails with the rest of the Marines as the ship left, Meadows stood guard duty outside the purser's office belowdecks and missed the exit. "When I got off duty, I went up on deck and all I saw was ocean. I never got to say good-bye to the United States, and it kind of hit me between the eyes. I had hoped to be on deck and watch the country fade away, like in the movies. That bothered me."[47] The war had taken Meadows away before he had been ready.

The *President Hayes* and Gene Seng finally left San Diego on July 1, 1942. Steaming in the same escort were an aircraft carrier, a heavy cruiser, a light cruiser, several destroyers, and three other troop transports, including the USS *President Adams* with Charlie Montague aboard. Nine days later the convoy crossed the equator, where Gene, Charlie, and the other first-time crossers of the equator experienced the initiation known as the King Neptune ceremony.

"It was fun," explained Seng, "but plenty rugged to say the least. When we got through we were covered from head to foot with grease, paint, red lead and welts." He added his hair was "clipped to the bone in nice wide patches and it was a couple of days before I could sit down comfortably."[48]

One day after the joviality, aircraft from the carrier spotted an enemy aircraft. Fun and lightheartedness quickly dissipated.

"Hell Bent for Somewhere"

The Marines approached a difficult situation. At no time during World War II was the outlook any bleaker than in the first days of May 1942. The American Navy had been manhandled at Pearl Harbor, the American Army had been forced off the Philippines, and the American Marines had surrendered at Wake Island and Guam. The British lost much of its fleet as well as its two major possessions in the Far East, Singapore and Hong Kong. After three hundred years, the Dutch lost the Indies. The only news that energized the American public—the electrifying defenses at Wake Island and Bataan—resulted in additional defeats.

The Japanese attack at Pearl Harbor had forced the American military to quickly remedy the twenty-year miasma that had crept into the Armed Forces since the end of World War I. The devastating effects of the Great Depression left the nation with limited resources for its military. Combined with the prevailing mood of isolationism that gripped the country, the United States stood ill-prepared to fight either Germany in Europe or the Japanese in the Pacific. The nation now had to play a dangerous game of catch-up and count that the forces on hand could hold off the enemy until additional men streamed out of training camps and supplies gushed out of American factories.

Japan's stunning race through much of the Far East and western Pacific knocked the United States on its heels. After a six-month period of inaction, the U.S. Navy scored triumphs at the battle of the Coral Sea and at Midway. Those encounters were, however, defensive in nature. To win the war, the United States had to mount its own offensive drives and recapture land seized by Japan.

Men like Charlie Montague and the Meadows brothers formed the underpinning of a giant military juggernaut that coalesced from training camps around the nation and gathered at debarkation ports on the West Coast, eager to head overseas and put the Japanese in their place. San Diego and other West Coast locations bulged with the Marines and Navy personnel who would provide America's initial military response to December 7.

The bloody march to Tokyo introduced to American citizens names and places that normally appeared in *National Geographic*. Largely unknown in 1943, within a few months the Gilbert Islands, Tarawa, and Betio would become all too familiar to newspaper readers in the United States. For some families, the names became synonymous with death.

Some of the men who fought at Tarawa gained combat experience in America's first Pacific offensive. When the Japanese constructed an airfield in the Solomon Islands, northeast of Australia, in August 1942, the United States rushed a contingent of Marines to prevent its completion. The men who fought there received their first taste of South Pacific jungles, heat, humidity, insects, and crocodiles. They battled an experienced Japanese Army that had honed its skills in China. They eventually left victorious, but weakened from wounds and malaria. In the process they gained priceless battlefield experience that they could later impart to the many fresh recruits who would join them for Tarawa.

Gene Seng concluded in late July, while still aboard the *President Hayes,* that his introduction to combat could not be far off. On July 26 the ship headed southwest, "hell bent for somewhere."[49] More telltale signs appeared in the next few days—additional ships joined the convoy, and Seng received orders to change from khaki uniforms to dungarees and steel helmet. When, on August 2, the Catholic chaplain gave everyone conditional Last Blessing—a rite used in the event of imminent danger and death—Seng knew he would soon meet the Japanese. His suspicions were confirmed the next day when officers informed Seng's unit it would land on August 7 at Tulagi in the Solomon Islands.

Seng enjoyed a spectacular view of the August 7 landings from his spot aboard the transport. Before the first wave headed in, battleships and cruisers commenced a bombardment of the islands that Seng called "quite a show." Japanese aircraft attacked the transports and bracketed Seng's ship with bombs, an experience the young man never forgot. "Believe me I was truly s-c-a-r-e-d!"[50] he wrote in his diary.

Because they were in different units, Montague and Seng landed on separate islands in the Solomons—Montague with the force assigned to remove the Japanese from Gavutu, while Gene Seng joined those headed to the nearby island of Tulagi. Both manned a .30-caliber machine gun, but carried little beyond what was absolutely essential. Lt. Col. Merritt A. Edson, who gained fame and a Medal of Honor for his actions at Guadalcanal with the Marine Raiders, told his men to travel lightly. "Don't worry about the food. There's plenty there. Japs eat, too. All you have to do is get it."[51]

Two and a half miles long and half a mile wide, Tulagi was the seat of the British government's presence in the Solomons, with the governor's residence standing at the island's southeast end. The island was defended by three hundred Japanese of the 3d Kure Special Naval Landing Force, nicknamed Japan's Marines, some of the finest troops Tokyo had.

The Marines on Tulagi were the first American forces to encounter Japanese land tactics. Japanese in heavily fortified trenches, dugouts, caves, and tunnels provided stiff opposition to the novice Marines. Sniper fire reduced their ranks, and nighttime counterattacks pushed the young Americans to their limits.

Three thousand yards to the east, Charlie Montague participated in the Marine assault on the island of Gavutu. The outnumbered Japanese mounted a stiff resistance, but five days of hard fighting eliminated the small garrison. In the absence of flamethrowers or bangalore torpedoes, Marines had to use hand grenades to clear out caves, a costly tactic.

Montague, Seng, and their cohorts had just witnessed a preview of what lay ahead for American forces as they advanced through the Pacific toward Japan. The Americans might have the numerical advantage, but a determined foe was going to exact a heavy price. The boys from Texas mirrored the thoughts of every Marine when they hoped this would be as rough as the war got.

Back in Texas, both families tried to ascertain clues as to where their sons were. Gene's little brother, Ralph, constantly updated a large Pacific map upon which he recorded news of the war, and whenever any of the Montagues and Sengs attended a movie, they avidly scoured the Movietone News features in hopes of glimpsing either Charlie or Gene. Patsy Seng one time swore she saw her brother in a panoramic view of a transport, but no one could be sure.

Both families hoped to hear from their sons, but days and weeks passed without any word. "There has been no news from our precious Charlie since July 4," wrote one of his aunts to Billie. "So we take for granted he is some-where in the Pacific." The aunt added, "We try to believe in the old adage that 'no news is good news'—but under the circumstances it is just a little difficult to be satisfied with it. I know you feel the same way."[52]

When the Seng family had learned nothing of their son by early September, despite news accounts detailing the Solomons campaign, Gene's father sent a letter asking for help from the American Red Cross. He received a reply on September 18 which stated, "We are glad to inform you that as far as we are able to learn he [Gene] has not been reported as a casualty by Marine Head-quarters on any of its official lists received through September 8, 1942."[53] The letter added that they could not divulge Gene's whereabouts because of mili-tary restrictions.

"I Looked Death in the Face"

Everyone in the Solomons sensed that Hawkins was a senior officer in the making. He fought and patrolled with his men, even taking his turn at the vul-nerable point position along with privates and corporals. He made them feel they were as important as he was, that teamwork counted more than individu-ality, and that he would risk anything to help bring them back alive. Chaplain Wyeth Willard, who shared a tent in the Solomons with Hawkins, stated that the indomitable officer "seemed not to fear enemy bullets or death itself."[54]

Herbert Estes, a pharmacist's mate who knew Hawkins on Guadalcanal, said that even though Hawkins had been promoted from the ranks, he retained the same common touch he exhibited as a corporal. Always sporting a mustache and a smile, Hawkins led through example, not intimidation. Estes claimed his men would "go to Hell and back for him."[55]

Hawkins wrote his mother in late 1942 of the pride he felt for his men. "The Marines have never resigned themselves to fate. Each time we go into battle we go with the idea of running roughshod over the Nip (which we usually do) hoping that by doing so we will hasten the end. We give vent to all our pent-up emotions by attempting to annihilate our opposition—the cause of our being here."

He added a chilling thought later in the letter when talking about the nature of fighting on Guadalcanal. "No quarter was given or asked by either side" in the bitter combat. Yet, at the same time, his experiences made him more optimistic about his future. Instead of assuming he would die in the Pacific, he now stated, "I looked death in the face and found it was pretty liberal. I am confident nothing will ever get me now. I'll live a long life and die of old age."[56]

By the time he landed in the Solomons, Hawkins had been promoted to sergeant. Within one month, after ably leading his men on numerous patrols behind enemy lines to gather intelligence, Hawkins was commissioned a second lieutenant.

The Sengs and Montagues finally received news from their sons. In a letter written on August 25 but not received until late September, Gene wrote, "I am 'live and kicking' and doing fine as far as health." He mentioned that the Marines had "quite a scrap but the Japs just didn't have it," and asked his parents to "tell Roy and Pete and the rest of the gang we are giving these yellow devils hell and some day not very far off they are going to learn not to mess with the U.S." He concluded by telling his parents not to worry. "With God's grace I'll be back and this war will be over soon."[57]

In subsequent letters Seng informed his family that he and Charlie were back together. He wrote he was doing "better than before. The main reason is that Charlie & I are back together again. I was transferred into his outfit the other day. We are even on the same machine gun—I was made assistant gunner to him."[58] Montague's platoon sergeant, at Charlie's urging, arranged for the friends to be back together.

It did not take long for Gene to mention females. In one letter he referred to two more girls—Connie and Mary Jean—and in another stated, "Since I haven't seen a woman in six months it will be quite a novelty to even see one again."[59]

As was true with every soldier in the Pacific, the holidays made Gene Seng thankful for what he had and eager to see what the future brought. In his Thanksgiving letter, Seng mentioned he and Charlie were still on Tulagi, that they went to Mass and Communion, and "one of the biggest things I have to be thankful for today is that I have the swellest family back there waiting and praying for my coming back."[60]

Christmas seemed more somber. Gene read and reread letters from home "until they are just about worn out." He added, "With God's indulgence maybe next Christmas will be back to normal—here's hoping and praying."[61]

"HAVE YOU MADE OUT YOUR WILL?"

"You Gave Us Life"

A welcome respite from the fighting followed the Solomons. Battered and bruised from their first encounter with the enemy, Montague, Seng, and the other survivors from the 2d Division steamed out of the humid islands and headed two thousand miles southeast to New Zealand, where they would rest and recuperate before training for their subsequent mission. Paradise, in the guise of friendly New Zealanders and idyllic countryside, awaited them.

The lengthy sea voyage ended in a sight that rejuvenated the weary boys. As the transports headed into Wellington Harbor, Marines lined the decks to gawk at New Zealand's capital, resting lovingly on hills and slopes that reminded many of San Francisco's beautiful terrain. The city beckoned to the Marines with its promise of rest, liberty, and most importantly, women. New Zealand offered a sanctuary from the rigors of combat and provided a welcome substitute for the safe, secure life they had left behind in the United States.

New Zealand needed the Marines as much as the Marines needed New Zealand. With the bulk of its military battling the German Army in distant North Africa, New Zealand's citizens watched developments in the South Pacific with growing concern. When the victorious Japanese advanced into New Guinea, to Australia's north, and into the Solomons, little appeared able to impede a Japanese drive that most likely would end on their home shores.

Then came the 2d Marine Division. Like manna from heaven, Montague, Seng, the Meadows brothers, and the rest rushed in and restored order to a world spinning out of control. By halting the Japanese advance to the south, the Marines saved New Zealand and gave its citizens hope for the future. "We were without vitality or feeling," said one New Zealand woman. "There was no life here. And then you arrived. You gave us life; you woke us up. You brightened up the entire country."[1]

Sheila Robertson recalled the memorable image of watching the Marines arrive in her country. She later wrote, "Lambton Quay was electrified by the crowd's emotions that memorable afternoon (fifty years ago) as we Wellingtonians watched the United States Marines disembark and march eight abreast down the normally quiet thoroughfare. New Zealand would now be safe from the threats of Japanese invasion. There would be no more talk in apprehensive households of holing up in the hills; no more would my mother make lists of items we would need to take with us."[2]

The citizens of that southern nation vowed to repay their redeemers with a kindness that few had known before. Families opened their homes to the young men from faraway America; tavern owners proffered drinks; hospitals tended to the wounded and ill. Most showed no sign of injury from bullet or blade, but almost every Marine suffered from a variety of exotic diseases or from battle fatigue. Jim and Bill Meadows, along with Lieutenant Hawkins, were a few of the thousands who spent weeks in hospitals trying to recover from malaria.

"I had a lot of fever from malaria," stated Capt. J. Wendell Crain. "I went to the hospital twice. You have a terrible shaking of your body. I'd have to have four or five blankets, and when that went away, about thirty minutes to an hour, you had a terrible headache. You'd take aspirin for that, that's all they had. A lot of people were sent home."[3]

"A Land of Milk and Honey"

New Zealanders did more than simply care for the Marines' physical ailments. In a touching display of affection, the people opened their homes and hearts, and in the process restored a sense of civility to men who had just returned from the indecency of combat.

Wellington's mayor, Michael Fowler, wrote of the Marines, "Their joyous carefree natures quickly broke through the New Zealanders' native reserve and they were invited into thousands of homes and in many cases came to be regarded almost as members of the family."[4]

Charlie Montague and Gene Seng had never seen anything like New Zealand's gorgeous terrain. Snowcapped mountains and streams teeming with fish offered a different world from Texas's wide-open spaces. The people back home were friendly, but the New Zealanders vowed to stop at nothing to repay the men who saved their nation by halting the Japanese.

"It was a land of milk and honey—more explicitly, steak and eggs, friendly allies, and beautiful girls," wrote Jim Lucas, a Marine combat correspondent. "Americans were heroes, and Marines the best of the Americans, for they had saved New Zealand at Guadalcanal."[5] Lucas added that if for some reason he could not live in the United States, he would happily choose the British Commonwealth nation as his home.

A love affair blossomed between the Marines of the 2d Division and the people of New Zealand. Many of the Marines had never before left their cities or towns of birth, but they felt an instant rapport with the residents in the friendly country thousands of miles from the United States.

"Oh, I loved New Zealand," said Private First Class Muhlbach. "They were lovely people."[6] If New Zealanders spotted a pair of Marines sitting in a bar, free drinks or invitations to join them for a home-cooked meal quickly followed. The Red Cross arranged weekend retreats with families, and some towns opened five hundred homes to the Marines. The government allowed extra gasoline to residents so that they could drive the Americans about their beautiful country.

Fun became the key word for a bunch of young Americans who were about to go into battle. Wellington transformed one skating rink into a basketball court for the Americans, and New Zealand's bountiful game, including deer and wild boar, and streams bulging with fourteen-pound trout offered many opportunities to hunt and fish. The city of Rotorua, with its hotels, hot springs, fishing, and golf, was especially popular.

On one sightseeing expedition in the South Island, Montague and Seng were trekking up a glacier when snow broke loose and cascaded down on the pair. The snow pinned Charlie's leg against some rocks and broke an ankle, which put the Texan into the hospital for one month.

For a time, a concerned Gene Seng wondered if the injury was severe enough for the Marines to send Montague home, but physicians agreed that after a brief recuperation, Charlie could return to his unit. Seng wrote that while he was sad for Charlie's sake, "I am glad for mine, though."[7]

Whether or not the old adage "The quickest way to a man's heart is through his stomach" is true, there was no denying the fact that on New Zealand, the Marines ate like kings. Some needed extra nourishment to rebuild their bodies after the fighting in the Solomons. All—veterans or fresh replacements— needed relief from Marine chow. From February through October 1943, they received just that.

Marine Chaplain Willard counted six meals a day. After breakfast, New Zealanders enjoyed morning tea at 10:00 A.M. Lunch followed around noon, four hours before afternoon tea. A 6:00 P.M. dinner preceded a final meal served before bedtime. Meals included the nation's staple of steak and eggs, roast lamb, mounds of butter, and warm beer. In addition, numerous milk bars offered milk shakes and ice cream. Accustomed to a meager diet, Marines easily adjusted to the bounty. Bowen loved the steaks topped with fried eggs and tomatoes, while Montague and Seng feasted on mutton and potatoes.

In the early stages, with time on their hands, Marines turned to one of their favorite pastimes—drinking. In Pfc. Charles Wysocki's camp, cases of beer had been piled high, but within two weeks the men had depleted the supply. In town, each Marine unit quickly "adopted" its own bar, banning men from other companies unless accompanied by a Marine from the designated unit. Besides the warm beer, which took a little getting used to, Marines drank an Australian concoction they nicknamed jump whiskey because one swallow of the potent liquid made a man jump. If that was not available, shellshock—a native drink mixing port and stout—would do, as would Juarez, a Mexican liquor.

Stanley Bowen and his friends regularly hopped on the train leaving camp for Wellington thirty-five miles away, "and almost always got drunk by midnight."[8] The fun backfired one time when he consumed too much 190-proof bootleg alcohol at a party and passed out. When he awakened he found that his buddies had taped his entire body in thick tape. For the next three days he alternated between being sick from the alcohol and peeling adhesive cloth from his body.

The Marines loved the food and sightseeing, but unless they were married or accounted for back home, most of the young men had one thing on their minds—females. With so many New Zealand males fighting in North Africa, little competition for women existed. Stan Bowen, serving with F Company, 2d Battalion, 8th Marines Regiment, stared in amazement at the number of young women available. "On liberty, you'd get off the train and the whole platform would have fifteen to twenty girls, asking, 'You Yanks come to our party?' and they were such beautiful people," explained Dick Meadows. "Of course, we were checking out the prettiest."[9]

Norm Hatch enjoyed an attraction few other Marines could boast. He served in the same unit with Louis Hayward, the handsome Hollywood film star of such movies as *The Man in the Iron Mask,* who had been asked to organize the Marine combat film department. The good-looking Hatch never had much difficulty meeting girls, but when walking around Wellington with Hayward, all he had to do was wait until females recognized Hayward, which never took long, and he had his pick of the beauties.

Hundreds of clubs catered to the Marines' desire to mingle with females or to experience a touch of home—the Grand, the St. George, or the posh Majestic Cabaret. At the Cecil Club, which housed the American Red Cross, a Marine could enjoy a cup of real coffee—an amenity hard to find in the tea-drinking nation—hamburgers, Coca-Cola, or apple pie.

"We'd go into the Cecil Club and on this one wall was a large map of the United States and a ladder," remembered Dick Meadows. "You'd write your name on it and your town. It was so fascinating to find guys from close to where you lived."[10]

The most popular act was undoubtedly seven-year-old Leigh Brewer, a singer whose performances hushed hardened men and prompted thoughts of home. The little singer, called Wellington's Shirley Temple, reminded each man of a girlfriend, a sister, a daughter, or a mother waiting in the United States. Her audiences frequently lapsed into silence as men dealt with the memories triggered by the melodic tunes and grappled with the fact that an ocean of water stood between them and what they most loved. Listening to Leigh Brewer made them more determined to end the fighting as fast as possible and return to loved ones.

As a small way of returning the favors, the Marines dispatched their military bands into towns for Sunday night concerts, or hosted dances of their own. At one August dance the renowned musician Artie Shaw led his band in snappy renditions of "All or Nothing at All," a current Frank Sinatra hit, "Besame Mucho," and pieces from his own smash album, *Cross Your Heart*. Marine units organized football teams and played exhibition games for New Zealanders, and a vaudeville group called the Fourragere Follies entertained audiences around Wellington. A love affair between the Marines and New Zealand, begun in the harsh circumstances of war, deepened into a bond that has lasted to the present day, when eighty-year-old veterans happily return to revisit Wellington and other spots.

"My dream of returning to New Zealand never happened," wrote Pfc. Charles Wysocki, "but my love for New Zealand and its people will always be in my heart."[11]

"She Is a Swell Girl"

Not surprisingly, more than a few Marines fell in love. Before the transports left for Tarawa, six hundred Marines married or became engaged to New Zealand women, including Gene Seng. In his first letter home, written about one month after he arrived, Seng mentioned he had met a girl named June Mc-Dougall, "who has been awfully nice to me." Within a month, he admitted to his family, "I have a girl friend here. She is a swell girl—cute as a bug's ear and full of life as a barrel of monkeys and about the size of a half grown peanut."[12] His feelings toward June increased to the extent that Charlie began teasing his friend about falling in love. Seng, who had always preferred the attentions of many females rather than one, hotly denied the charges.

Whenever he and Charlie had liberty, the pair rushed to June's house, where they relaxed with June's family and enjoyed great food. Gene and June would head out for short walks after dinner so they could be alone, and before long infatuation turned into love. Often, when the boys did not have liberty, Gene risked the brig by going over the wall to visit June.

The pair shared their New Zealand experiences with family in Texas. Each night Charlie wrote Billie a letter, and he remained faithful to her even though the New Zealand girls provided ample temptation. After she sent him a photograph of her sitting beside a picture of Charlie, Montague wrote, "Boy Billie, you really look good and are mighty pretty. Darn it, I wish I could see you. I would give anything in the world to get back to you." He then added, "The boys have looked at the pictures and they said I have a mighty pretty girl. They aren't telling me anything that I don't know."[13]

Like many Marines existing far from loved ones and familiar surroundings, Charlie endured a few rough stretches in New Zealand. He had survived his first taste of battle, and even though the break in New Zealand provided welcome relief, he pined for home. Also like many young Marines, Charlie turned to alcohol for comfort. Gene Seng explained that Billie sent angry letters when Charlie admitted he had been doing some drinking, but stated, "If she just knew how little there is to do here she would understand a little better."[14]

Fortunately, Charlie's drinking lasted less than two weeks. Gene wrote home on September 28, "Charlie is just fine. He is settling down again—he kinda busted loose on a little spree for a little while. I didn't like to see him do it on account of Billie but don't blame him on account of the conditions we live under. In order to have a half way good time a guy has to get looped unless you are lucky enough to have someone take up your interests like I do."[15]

The Marine Forces

On July 20, 1943, opposing commanders received similar orders. As Rear Adm. Keiji Shibasaki assumed command of the 3d Special Base Force stationed at Tarawa, the United States Joint Chiefs of Staff directed Adm. Chester W. Nimitz to plan the Gilberts operation. Nimitz selected Vice Adm. Raymond A. Spruance, the victor of Midway, to head the assault. Two other capable officers assisted him. The irascible Rear Adm. Richmond Kelly Turner commanded the Fifth Amphibious Force, the naval unit transporting the men to Betio, while the equally volatile Marine Maj. Gen. Holland M. "Howlin' Mad" Smith commanded the land troops comprising the V Amphibious Corps, which included a Marine division and an Army division. While the Northern Attack Force, with Turner along as commander, hit Makin Atoll to the north, Rear Adm. Harry W. Hill would take the Southern Attack Force in against the island of Betio in Tarawa Atoll.

Facing the first attempt to assault from the sea a defended beachhead, Holland Smith turned to his best Marine division, one that had combat experience combined with amphibious training—the 2d Marine Division, led by Maj. Gen. Julian C. Smith. The men of the 2d Marine Division loved Julian Smith, who relied on persuasion and serenity to command rather than intimidation. One Marine officer said the fifty-eight-year-old Smith reminded him of a kindly old gentleman babysitting his grandchildren.

Thirty-eight-year-old Lt. Col. David M. Shoup, who became commander of the assault battalions, matched Julian Smith's calm demeanor. The officer, who frequently wrote his thoughts, often in poetic verse, in notebooks, brought an iron determination to the battlefield and a belief that he was meant to command in combat. He scribbled in his notebook, "If you are qualified, fate has a way of getting you to the right place at the right time—tho' sometimes it appears to be a long, long wait."[16] His time arrived on Betio's beaches, where his firm leadership brought organization amidst chaos.

Julian Smith commanded 19,965 men organized into five regiments—three infantry regiments (including the 2nd Regiment, Dick and James Meadows's 6th Regiment, and Major Crowe's 8th Regiment), Bill Meadows's 10th Artillery Regiment, and Montague and Seng's 18th engineer regiment. The 2d Amphibian Tractor Battalion and 2d Tank Battalion supported the five.

The Solomon Islands campaign had given the 2d Marine Division combat experience, but it also removed from division rosters many of those combat-hardened men, either through death or injury sustained on the battlefield, or more likely through malaria, dysentery, or one of the other exotic diseases contracted during their stay on Guadalcanal, Tulagi, or Gavutu. Ninety-five percent of the survivors suffered from one malady or another; doctors and medics in New Zealand treated thirteen thousand cases of malaria. Smith would have to replace and retrain half the division's strength before they would be ready for Betio, and the other half required time to recover from their wounds or sicknesses. Even the veteran troops, once they recovered, would have to learn the amphibious style of assault required by Betio, a style of combat not faced in the Solomons.

To transform the men into a crack amphibious unit, Julian Smith brought in as his chief of staff Col. Merritt Edson, who had been awarded a Medal of Honor for his leadership on Guadalcanal. Smith knew the no-nonsense Edson would soon have his men at peak efficiency.

He was not so sure about his key piece of equipment—the eighty-seven amtracs set to bring in the first three waves. Designed by Donald Roebling for use in the Florida Everglades, the vehicles with caterpillar tracks could carry twenty Marines and a crew of four at four knots in the water, handily traverse any coral reef, then once on shore speed inland at the rate of fifteen miles per hour. Negatives existed—a lack of armor on the versatile vehicles made the men inside vulnerable to enemy fire, and in the absence of a ramp, Marines had to climb over the amtrac's sides, a difficult task to execute while under fire and weighed down by extra equipment. However, the amtrac's main benefit—swift movement to shore—overshadowed the drawbacks, and the .50-caliber and .30-caliber machine guns provided some protection. Julian Smith only wished that he had more of the landing crafts.

Training

"We are back to soldiering again,"[17] Gene Seng wrote his parents on April 7. Though he would still enjoy occasional weekend liberties and generally had a twenty-four-hour pass every six days, rest and relaxation faded to the background.

Easy times ended in August 1943 when Colonel Edson arrived in New Zealand as the chief of staff for the division's commanding officer, Gen. Julian Smith. Edson carried a reputation as a stickler for intensive training and for thoroughly preparing his men. One correspondent wrote, "His pale blue eyes gleamed with the impersonal menace of pointed pistol muzzles."[18] Marines joked, somewhat wistfully, that they could kiss their vacations good-bye, for Edson was certain to keep them busy.

Edson quickly set about transforming the 2d Division into a crack outfit. He focused on three items—keeping the attack moving forward, noncommissioned officers and privates taking personal initiative in case the commanding officer fell in combat, and fire discipline during the nights, when jittery young Marines would be most likely to shoot at noises and slight movements. By the time training ended in late October, fifty-one Marines had died from overexertion or accidents, but Edson had the men in fighting trim and ready to take on the best the Japanese could offer.

Though training occurred at various locations about New Zealand, most Marines stayed at the sprawling camp near the small railroad town of Paekakariki, fifty miles north of Wellington. Replacement Marines fresh from the United States, such as Stanley Bowen and Dick Meadows, blended in with Charlie Montague, Gene Seng, and other veterans of the Solomons combat so they could benefit from their experiences. In some units, because of the losses absorbed in the Solomons, replacements comprised more than half of their total numbers.

One officer whom every Marine trusted and feared was Maj. Henry P. "Jim" Crowe. Already known throughout the Corps for his fearlessness, Crowe enhanced his legendary status during one stalled attack in the Solomons by leaping off a half-track, rushing over to a group of Marines taking cover in a shell hole, and shouting, "Damn it, you'll never get the Purple Heart hiding in a foxhole! Follow me!" He then led an attack in which he single-handedly knocked out a machine gun, an action that garnered him a Silver Star and promotion on the spot to major. One combat correspondent wrote of the major, "His men spoke about him reverently, in subdued whispers, as one worthy of the highest respect of man and God."[19]

In New Zealand, Crowe called a meeting with new arrivals, including Stan Bowen. After introducing his officers to the men, the no-nonsense major turned to the entire assembly and challenged any enlisted man or officer who thought he was better than Crowe to join him in the woods. "He'd beat the crap out of anyone who thought he was tougher to show who was the commanding officer," said Bowen. "No one ever challenged him."[20]

Major Crowe relentlessly drove the men of the 8th Battalion, pushing them to break division records for sixty-mile hikes in full combat gear, even once wagering a case of Scotch with the commander of another battalion that his men would establish a new mark.

The major shared the same discomforts as his men and occupied a front spot in the marches. During one brief stop when Crowe ordered all his men to change their socks, men near the officer noticed Crowe's boots had filled with blood. When they returned to camp, haggard and ready to collapse on a cot, the Marines encountered a group of local New Zealanders who invited the

Marines to a dance. Rather than offend their hosts, Crowe accepted and spent the next few hours on the dance floor.

"He prowled," stated one Marine of Major Crowe. "No matter where you were on the base, no matter what you were doing, no matter what time of the day or night it was, every once in a while you could look up and see him there. If you were a junior Marine, and I certainly was, it was as though God himself were coming to visit the mess hall, or the front gate, or the guardhouse at the brig—whatever." The Marine added that Crowe "had enormous presence, made up as much by respect as pure fright."[21]

Despite the grinding schedule, Pfc. Robert Muhlbach loved serving under Crowe. "You couldn't help but admire the guy," said Muhlbach. "He had a command presence about him. He'd just say something and you automatically did what he wanted. His men would follow him to hell and back."[22]

On the other hand, Muhlbach and the others had their doubts about Crowe's executive officer, Major Chamberlin. Bowen thought the studious-looking Chamberlin, who was a college professor in civilian life, lacked the fearsomeness Crowe conveyed. Bowen knew he and the other men would be in good hands with Crowe, but he wondered how the quiet Chamberlin would react under fire.

The last place anyone expected to find William Chamberlin was in the Marines, let alone on a battlefield. The quiet scholar so deftly moved through library stacks and dusty reports in his job as economics professor at renowned Northwestern University in Chicago, Illinois, that most expected the man to live his life in the blissful calm provided by the sheltered world of academia. A perfectionist, Chamberlin insisted that the most important feature a man possessed was his character. Honor, integrity, and sound morals meant more than riches. One time, when he discovered at home that a restaurant owner had given him thirty-seven cents too much in change for a dinner the family had just enjoyed, Chamberlin drove five miles back to the business to return the money.

Born February 10, 1916, in Chicago, Chamberlin enlisted in the Marine Corps Reserve in 1936 during his student years at Dartmouth. He took summer officer training classes at Quantico, Virginia, in 1936 and 1937, then received his commission upon graduation in 1938, when he was Dartmouth's valedictorian. Chamberlin then completed work at Columbia University on his master's degree and doctorate in economics in 1940, and had started teaching economics at Northwestern University in Chicago when the Marines called him to active duty on November 8, 1940.

After a brief stint as an intelligence officer stationed in Iceland, Chamberlin headed to the Pacific after the outbreak of war. He served in the Solomons in later 1942, where he impressed other officers with his intellect and supreme organization, and had been promoted to major by June 1943, two months before becoming Crowe's executive officer.

"You Can't Do Much About It"

Before leaving New Zealand, Gene Seng had some unfinished business to tend to. During an arduous training maneuver that separated Gene and June for two weeks, Charlie noticed that his friend seemed distracted and bothered. Gene confided that he had been thinking of June all the time they had been in the field and he intended to ask her to marry him once they returned.

He kept true to his word. On July 5 he surprised June with a proposal and handed her a gold and platinum ring that Charlie helped select. Three days later he wrote home with the news.

"I know it's going to be a shock to you but it is the way I thought best. I am engaged to June—it happened on July 5. I can just about imagine what you think about it but I believe that I did the right thing. I know she will make me a good wife and we love each other very very much. I was very hesitant about asking her to wait for me until after this damned war is over because of the great uncertainty which lies ahead. But she said she would wait regardless of whether we were engaged or not so I thought that we might as well have something tangible for us to base our love and trust in one another on so I asked her formally to be mine tho there already was the understanding between us."[23]

He added that Charlie and his buddies liked his choice, and stated that June had agreed to become a Catholic like Gene. Gene wished he had been able to benefit from his parents so far away, "but that can't be and it's my life to work out. I try to bear in mind the principals [sic] you have brought me up to in going into any decision and I couldn't go very wrong if I stood by them." When love hits, "I reckon that you can't do much about it—it just happens." He wrote that they would love June, who "has more life in her than a Mexican jumping bean and a personality to match."[24]

Gene provided as much information about the McDougall family as possible, including that June's sisters called him brother and called Charlie their cousin, that they always knit socks or baked cakes for them, and that when Charlie won some money playing poker, he purchased a tea set for Mrs. McDougall to repay the family's kindness.

To allay his mother's fears that June had replaced her in Gene's affections, the Marine wrote, "Don't ever think you are being slighted the most minute amount in my loving you because of my new love either. My love for you grows stronger every day—for my sweetheart of a mother. I didn't think one man could be capable of experiencing so much love at one time."[25]

Charlie and other Marine buddies threw an engagement party for Gene and June the following Sunday. Charlie toasted the couple and said that the "little flower" his friend had selected "outdid all the bluebonnets of Texas."[26]

June wrote Mrs. Seng in July, "I don't know just how you will feel about it, Mrs. Seng, but I really hope you will like me and approve of Gene's choice." Though the family was Presbyterian, she reiterated her wish to convert to the Catholic faith, that her parents heartily approved, and that she would readily leave her beloved New Zealand for Texas. "I am not afraid, though, because I love Gene enough to go where ever he wants me to."[27]

During the remainder of his stay in New Zealand, Gene saw June almost every night, usually with permission, but if that was not possible, without. He often had to walk five miles back to camp in the early morning hours, "but believe me, it's worth every step of the way." He said his buddies teased him about being love-struck, but "they just don't realize the power of my incentive. I am afraid there is going to be a couple of awful lonesome people when we do shove off."[28]

Inevitably, Gene was caught leaving camp without permission and had been "catching hell over it. I hope it blows over. But I wasn't the only one caught so I don't feel so badly about it." In any event, the punishment was worth it, for he did not know how much longer he would be able to see June, a prospect that bothered the Texan. "But even in our happiness we still have the dread overshadowing it when we know we will have to bear the hurt of parting for God knows how long. . . . I guess our absence will make us appreciate each other more, which I can't see could be possible at all, we think so much of each other already."[29]

"I Want Only Fighting Marines Around Me!"

Preparations to leave New Zealand intensified in the latter half of October. Hatch, who believed that previous battlefield film footage miserably failed to capture the essence and brutality of combat, was determined to go in with the assault waves and film amidst the troops. When he scanned the roster of officers, he stopped at one name—Major Crowe—whom he called "the whole, total embodiment of the Marine Corps, all in one man."[30] If Hatch sought action, Crowe would be the one to follow.

After arranging matters with headquarters, Hatch informed Crowe.

"Well, Sergeant, what can I do for you?" asked Crowe when Hatch entered his office.

"I just wanted to let you know that I was going to be assigned to your organization for the upcoming battle."

"What do you do?" inquired Crowe.

"I'm a motion picture cameraman," replied Hatch.

"I don't want any goddamn Hollywood Marine with me!" bellowed Crowe, determined to halt what he considered an absurdity. The last thing he needed was to babysit a noncombatant in the midst of his troops. "I want only fighting Marines around me!" he practically shouted at the cameraman.

"Sir, I already have over four years' service in the Corps, I've been through all the training, and I shot expert with the M-1."

Crowe surveyed Hatch for a few moments, then quickly made up his mind.

"All right. But stay the hell out of my way!" With that brief meeting, Hatch sealed a spot in the front waves that would hit Betio. In fact, he would ride in the same landing craft with Crowe. His chances of filming something spectacular, he thought, looked good.[31]

Robert Sherrod also knew how to be at the right place at the right time. The veteran *Time* magazine reporter competed with skilled journalists all his career, and he was not about to miss what he thought might be the biggest landing of the Pacific War to date. Sherrod and the other war correspondents had one goal when they wrote their accounts—to be as accurate as possible in conveying the death and horror of war, not to embarrass the government, but to educate the public to the sacrifices required to win the war. Their accounts would be the first to describe what unfolded, so the writers felt a duty to be precise in conveying the emotions and drama of what they observed.

None sought to uncover conspiracies or secret deals that might make the Allies appear less than noble, for World War II offered what few wars since have provided—clear-cut villains in both Europe and the Pacific who had to be destroyed before American soldiers could return home. The correspondents' job was to inform the American public so they could vicariously share the experiences of the fighting men and bond with them in a campaign to stem fascism.

The government recognized that newspaper and magazine correspondents helped fashion public opinion, so unlike World War I, where correspondents rarely reached the front lines, men like Sherrod and Ernie Pyle enjoyed near-unfettered access to combat. Sherrod was not embedded with one unit for the duration. He shifted his assignments as needed—from Attu in the Aleutians to Tarawa to Iwo Jima—and within a campaign moved about the battlefield from platoon to platoon. Consequently, it was not unusual for ten or more correspondents, representing magazines like *Time* and newspapers such as the *Chicago Tribune* and *New York Times*, to head in with the troops in Pacific assaults. They faced the same risks as the men they covered, ate the same rations, experienced the same anguish.

The mighty conglomeration of military strength in New Zealand and the rigorous training pointed to one thing—the opening act of a lengthy drive toward Japan through the Central Pacific. In September, Sherrod left New Zealand for the ten-thousand-mile journey back to New York to convince his editors that he should cover the next offensive, which was expected to commence soon.

After gaining his editors' permission, Sherrod returned to Pearl Harbor, where he used his influence with high-ranking naval officers to arrange an assignment to Betio. Along with combat correspondent Keith Wheeler and combat artist Gilbert Bundy, Sherrod would now go in with the Marines at Tarawa. A public relations officer told Sherrod on his way out, "You don't know how lucky you three are."[32] Sherrod was not sure how to interpret the remark, but he left with the satisfaction of knowing that when the fighting started, he would be where his instincts told him to be.

"Such Brave and Lovable Sinners!"

Reverend Willard wanted to be in the thick of the fighting, but for different reasons than Hatch or Sherrod. When informed that he would land with later waves, instead of with the assault units as he wished, Willard requested a switch in assignment from Maj. Lawrence C. Hays Jr., the commanding officer of the 1st Battalion, 8th Marine Regiment. The front, with the men who faced the deadliest dangers, was where he belonged.

"I'd never forgive myself if anything happened to you," replied Major Hays. He then asked the chaplain why he wanted to be placed in the most dangerous spot.

"The Marines would more readily accept my message of Christ," answered Willard. "I want to do more than conduct funeral services."[33] The answer im-

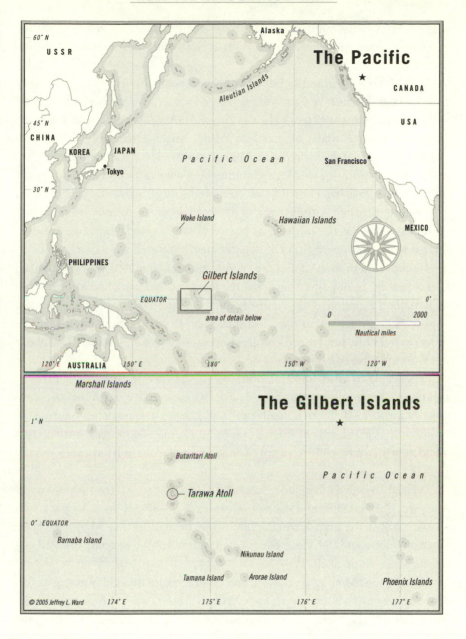

pressed Hays, who realized that nothing he said would probably deter the chaplain anyway. He agreed to let Willard go in with the initial waves of his battalion.

Willard always wanted to be where he was needed most. When the Japanese hit Pearl Harbor, Wyeth Willard seemed ancient in comparison with the young Marines he would tend. He was also one of the last people one might expect to find in the midst of a violent Pacific battle. Born July 12, 1905, in Massachusetts, the deeply religious Willard detested war and announced himself a pacifist during his theological studies at Brown University. After graduating in 1927, Willard earned a master of divinity degree from Princeton Theological Seminary, then turned down high-paying offers from Boston churches to accept the position as pastor of the Forestdale, Massachusetts, Baptist church, a congregation of twenty-one that offered ten dollars per week.

He expected to spend a lifetime serving his flock, but December 7 knocked him onto a different path. Angry that the Japanese had launched a surprise attack, Willard abandoned his pacifist beliefs. One day later, on December 8, he applied to be a chaplain in the Naval Reserve. He could not willingly take another person's life, but he could at least bring comfort and God to those about to close with a barbaric enemy.

"According to Christian tradition, we are opposed to wars," Willard later explained. "Yet in most rules of the law, there are exceptions. When the Japanese unannounced dropped bombs on Pearl Harbor, I immediately shifted my position."[34] Willard still considered war to be a heinous endeavor, but one that a nation sometimes had to accept, just as an individual must at times defend himself from assault.

Willard attended Chaplain's School at Norfolk, Virginia, then was assigned to the 2d Marine Division. He brushed aside one comment made by the senior chaplain when the man learned Willard was headed for the Marines. "Have you made out your will? Have you paid all your bills? You're going out and you may not be coming back."[35]

While Seng, Montague, Bowen, and other recruits flooded into one of San Diego's bars during boot camp leaves, Willard visited Baptist churches. At one, he met an official from the Gideon Society who told Willard he had 2,400 Bibles. When he asked Willard how many he could use in his ministry to the Marines, Willard gladly accepted them all. He then arranged with his commanding officer to interview every man he could. Starting in San Diego and continuing until the day before the Tarawa landing, Willard chatted with more than one thousand Marines of all faiths and handed each a Bible.

The action in the Solomons confirmed Chaplain Willard's suspicions that he ministered to as decent a group of men as he could find, and of the righ-teousness of their mission. "I must confess that I am very fond of the marines, even if some are sinners," the minister later wrote. "Oh, they're such brave and lovable sinners!"

The popular chaplain shared the same dangers and discomforts endured by the Marines. He endeared himself by attaching to his vest "Mike" and "Ike," two old, powderless hand grenades. He may have looked fierce, but Willard was as gentle as a kitten.

When an officer asked him how he, a man of peace, could be involved in something so deadly, Willard unhesitatingly answered, "I would not needlessly hurt a worm, to say nothing of a human being. The enemies of our nation pre-ferred war to peace. There was nothing left for us to do after Pearl Harbor but to fight. The enemy started the war. We must end it."[36] Willard realized that tough fighting on unknown islands lay ahead, action from which he might not return, but he knew one thing—wherever the action was hottest, that was where he would be. He would do God's work in the midst of the most ungodly actions imaginable.

"I'm Getting Ants in My Pants"

Gene Seng turned more introspective as he and Charlie sensed that the time to again engage the enemy neared. He claimed that the war had changed his outlook on life, that he was now more serious about matters than before, and determined to make a good life for June. "Being out here has surely made me realize the terrible injustice in the world today." He added that the hardships he faced were nothing compared to the good that could occur. "It's not much of a sacrifice to be out here if you figure that some of the multiple wrongs of this world are being righted."[37]

Since he could not begin that part of his life until the war ended, he was ea-ger to jump into the next campaign. "I hope we shove off soon so we can get this job over again," Seng wrote his parents, "though I know that I will wish we were back here whenever we do get to some hell hole again."[38]

Seng read that some of his pals back home envied his presence in the Pa-cific and wished they could join him, an idea Seng tried to deflate. "They just don't know how lucky they are, do they? Because they would wish to God they had never left if they were. Believe me, I am ready to get back into it again but it's just for the simple reason that it looks like we are going to have to win the war before we get back home and I sure want to get to it."[39]

He explained that everyone figured the next operation would be tough, and that they were trying to guess where the fighting would occur. "I'm getting ants in my pants," he stated to his father. He was delighted that events in Europe seemed to be going well, because "then we can turn the full brunt on these yellow monkeys. That's the day I am waiting for and I hope I can be right in the great big middle of it." He added later, "But I wish the Japs could be catching more of the hell than they are. I think they are getting too much of a break on this time to prepare to defend what they already have, the dirty little rats."[40] Seng did not realize how prophetic his words were, as the Japanese were at that moment strengthening the very Betio defenses that he and Montague would be assaulting.

"All Too Soon the Halcyon Days Were Over"

Events moved more rapidly in the middle of October. Capt. J. Wendell Crain attended a meeting where he received details of the upcoming battle and studied maps of the target. In the interest of maintaining secrecy, however, the speakers divulged neither the precise name nor location. With a few basic investigative skills, Crain quickly filled in the missing details.

"The map had to be fifteen feet long and fourteen feet wide," said Crain. "Nobody was told where it was, but I noticed the markers for latitude and longitude were still on there. I noticed it was right on the equator, and the longitude one still had the number there. I mentally put that down and I went back to my ship and had a Pacific map from *National Geographic* and traced it to Tarawa."

With that sensitive information in hand, Crain took no chances of accidentally revealing the final destination. "I never went ashore again because I didn't want anyone to think that I had the word and was passing it around."[41]

Shortly before leaving New Zealand, Sergeant Hatch attended a meeting conducted by the head of his unit, the Hollywood star Louis Hayward. Hayward told the group that cameramen in other theaters of the war had so far received all the acclaim, but this was about to change. "I know all of us are fed up with hearing about the 'marvelous' photography coming out of the European war," said an animated Hayward. "This time, let's really give 'em something to talk about—from the Marines in the Pacific."[42] Hatch had no idea how crucial a role he would play in making these words come true.

* * *

For many Marines, their New Zealand vacations terminated way too soon. While on a liberty Dick Meadows and a friend met two young New Zealand girls. They hit it off and agreed to spend the next weekend together, but when the pair of Marines returned to camp to obtain a forty-eight-hour pass, they learned the Marines had other plans.

"We went back to camp," said Meadows, "and they told us to strike our tents and that we were moving out. To this day I wonder if those girls are still waiting for us."[43]

Not only Meadows, but every Marine in New Zealand received orders to pack his bags and prepare to depart. Gene Seng, who wrote on the day he boarded the troop transport bound for Tarawa that June "has come to fill a place in my heart that I didn't believe could be filled so completely,"[44] could not break away for a last good-bye before steaming out of Wellington. Gene, June, and other couples would have to wait for romance until after the operation.

For the people of New Zealand, the months-long love affair with the men of the 2d Marine Division also came to a sudden end. Some received an inkling that the departure neared during a scheduled airing of the John Ford documentary *The Battle of Midway*. Instead of a depiction of the recent major naval clash that saw the United States Navy sink four Japanese aircraft carriers, a training film was erroneously sent. The hushed crowd sat in silence as a film titled *Kill or Be Killed* showed graphic ways of maiming an enemy, including knifing and gouging out eyes. Little did anyone in the room know how accurate was this foreshadow of the Tarawa fighting-to-be.

Instead of Marine-packed pubs and souvenir-happy Americans filling store cash registers, quiet returned. Troop transports left the docks of New Zealand, taking with them not only the young men, but the gaieties and delights they had infused into a nation weary of war scares.

"All too soon the halcyon days were over," explained New Zealander Sheila Robertson. "The troop transports lined up at Aotea Quay, and the Second Marine Division Marines, in full battle gear, boarded to leave. Then they were gone, gone to Tarawa, that hell of underwater barbed wire where so many lost their lives. The many months that those wholesome, valiant young men spent in our country left an indelible mark on our hearts. We shall never forget the debt of gratitude owed them."[45]

Years later the men of the 2d Marine Division mounted a plaque at the Aotea Quay Gates on Wellington's wharves to show their appreciation for what the country had meant to them. The plaque's words, though few, conveyed a volume of emotion and meaning. TO THE PEOPLE OF NEW ZEALAND: IF YOU EVER NEED A FRIEND, YOU HAVE ONE.[46]

Newspaper correspondent Jim Lucas, who later wrote a vivid account of his time in the Pacific, felt a similar sense of loss as he boarded the transport. "Vacation was over for the combat correspondent, but he was never to forget New Zealand. He was leaving behind promises to return as a civilian." Lucas then added one other thought.

"Ahead was hell."[47]

4

"A MILLION MEN CANNOT TAKE TARAWA"

"A Treasure Trove of South Sea Island Beauty"

The beauty and mystique of the Pacific Ocean have long fascinated people. One can travel thousands of miles without seeing anything but water, when suddenly land, sometimes so minuscule it seems to exist solely at the whim of the vast ocean, materializes on the horizon. In the Central Pacific, luscious atolls offer beaches fringed with swaying palm fronds, and crystal blue lagoons nestle inside protective coral reefs. They provide a beauty surpassed by few places, and their sand and foliage fashion thoughts of romance or high-seas adventure.

Famous novelist Robert Louis Stevenson, who discovered a tropical paradise in the Gilbert Islands in his travels through the Pacific, wrote that the islands throughout that part of the Pacific were a "treasure trove of South Sea Island beauty."[1] War, the brutal, savage type as seen in the conflict with Japan, is out of place on the serene, idyllic isles that populate the Gilberts and the other atolls of the Central Pacific. Yet that is precisely where one of the most savage clashes of the Pacific War unfolded.

The Gilbert Islands consist of sixteen atolls straddling the equator 2,100 miles southwest of Hawaii and 2,900 miles southeast of Tokyo. One, Tarawa Atoll, contains thirty-eight islands forming a reverse L along two arms eighty miles north of the equator. A surrounding coral reef opens into an imposing lagoon teeming with tropical sea life.

Betio, the most important island of Tarawa Atoll, anchors the southwest corner. Two miles long and seven hundred yards at its widest—less than half the size of New York City's Central Park—the flat isle contains no point higher than ten feet above sea level. Betio's shape resembles a parakeet, with the bird's head and beak at the western end, its tail to the east, and a long wharf on the northern side forming the bird's leg. Resting along the isle's spine is the reason for Betio's importance to both the United States and Japan—its airfield.

In 1788 an English captain named Gilbert gave the islands their name. Fifty-four years later the first American to visit the atoll, Navy Lt. Charles Wilkes, stopped during an expedition to map Pacific islands, but the location remained under British control until December 10, 1941, when the Japanese occupied Tarawa and seized control of the two thousand native inhabitants. The Japanese intended to use the Gilberts as a place from which to scout American movements in the South Pacific.

Without the 1,500-yard-long airfield on Betio, the war would have passed by Tarawa Atoll. Once the Japanese constructed the airfield, the Americans could no longer ignore Betio's strategic value, for in the vast reaches of the Central Pacific, which holds few spots capable of housing an air squadron, a single airstrip on a solitary island controls thousands of square miles of water.

In April 1943, while Montague, Seng, and the other Marines of the 2d Division trained in New Zealand, Adm. Ernest J. King, the commander in chief, U.S. Fleet and chief of naval operations in Washington, D.C., ordered Rear Adm. Raymond A. Spruance, his chief of staff, to examine the prospects for an assault in the Central Pacific. King mentioned the Marshall Islands as a possibility.

Spruance and his staff soon realized that a deep thrust into the Central Pacific against the Marshalls was unrealistic for this stage of the war. Since the Japanese had closed the islands to foreigners in 1919, American military planners possessed little intelligence on the Marshalls. Besides, their close proximity to the Japanese stronghold at Truk, with its abundance of ships, men, and supplies, bothered Spruance.

Spruance substituted Tarawa. American aircraft and submarines could easily reconnoiter the atoll, the Japanese had not had the time to build defenses as they had in the Marshalls, and Tarawa stood within range of American land-based air power in the Ellice Islands. In addition, seizing Betio would eliminate the Japanese threat to Samoa, protect the American lines of communications to the South Pacific, hand the United States an unsinkable carrier from which to strike against the Marshalls, and provide valuable experience in amphibious assaults for the Marines and Navy.

Spruance convinced King of the Gilberts' value. King then persuaded the Joint Chiefs of Staff to let him use the landing craft originally earmarked for

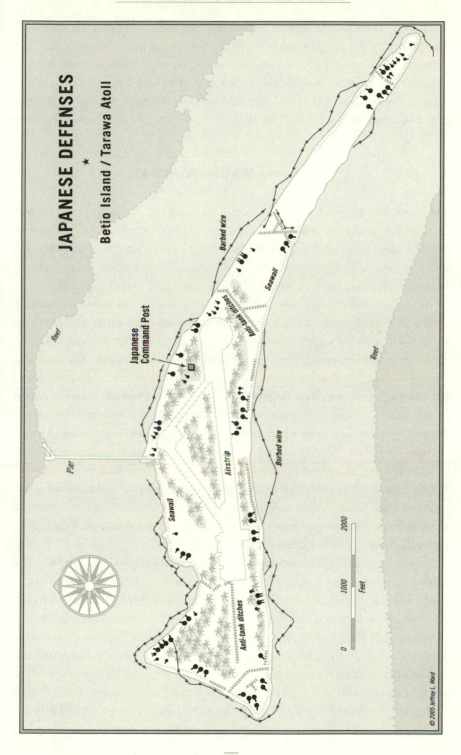

JAPANESE DEFENSES

★

Betio Island / Tarawa Atoll

Reef

Barbed wire

Seawall

Anti-tank ditches

Japanese
Command Post

Pier

Seawall

Airstrip

Barbed wire

Reef

Anti-tank ditches

0   1000   2000

Feet

© 2005 Jeffrey L. Ward

the European cross-channel attack, which had been postponed until 1944. The assault against Betio would thus be the first major use of landing craft, especially the amphibious tractors—amtracs—in an assault against a well-defended beachhead. Should the attack fail, it would not only impede the Central Pacific drive but would cast doubt on the ultimate success of the proposed landings in Normandy. Much therefore rode on the invasion of Tarawa.

"To Land Where We Did"

"Up until that time, I had never heard of an island in the Pacific by the name of Tarawa,"[2] said Gen. Julian C. Smith, the commander of the 2d Marine Division, when told in an August 1943 briefing the name and location of his target. The best maps available offered little help, as nothing had been drawn to improve upon the charts constructed during the 1842 Wilkes expedition.

Intelligence gleaned from military intercepts and other sources quickly added to Smith's pool of information. American analysts broke the Japanese naval code, which enabled them to read many messages sent to and from the Japanese commander on Tarawa. In particular, they learned the size and makeup of the Betio garrison. Aerial photography delivered stunning images of the buildings and of certain defenses on Betio; the submarine *Nautilus* added hundreds of periscope photographs during an eighteen-day September patrol offshore; and sixteen former residents of the atoll provided much useful information.

By the time the Marines boarded the transports that would take them to battle, their leaders possessed abundant information about their enemy. They estimated the Japanese garrison to be between 2,500 and 3,100, and believed the enemy mounted an impressive array of guns, from mammoth 8-inch guns and antiaircraft guns to machine guns.

What they did not know about the Japanese defenses, though, was the problem. Intelligence could analyze what rested on Betio's surface, but it could not peek underneath the camouflage or gaze through the sand to see how solidly constructed and cleverly designed were the Japanese defenses.

Above all, their intelligence could not reveal an accurate image of what Betio's erratic tides would do and how deep the water would be over the protective coral reef on November 20, the day of the assault. The landing craft in the first three waves, all amtracs, could climb over an exposed reef, but should there be insufficient water covering the coral on November 20, the larger landing craft in the following waves, which required a minimum of three and a half feet of water, would be unable to cross it. Should that frightening prospect occur, the Marines would be forced to abandon their craft and wade ashore from as far as seven hundred yards out—directly into enemy machine gun and rifle fire.

November 20 occurred during what is called a neap tide. Neap tides happen during the first and third quarters of the moon, and generally feature less water at high tide than the other two quarters. Some residents informed Julian Smith that five feet of water should cover the reef on the assault day. They hedged their statements, however, by adding that Betio sometimes experienced a phenomenon called dodging tides, an unpredictable event that left much of the coral reef exposed.

Maj. Frank Holland, a New Zealander who had lived on and sailed about Tarawa for fifteen years, at first agreed that five feet of water should be present, but when he learned the assault's exact date, he argued that Betio's unpredictable tides at that time of the month could spell disaster. He claimed he never thought anyone would be foolish enough to land on a neap tide and contended that less than three feet of water could greet the invasion force.

Staring at the specter of his unprotected Marines walking straight into withering enemy gunfire, Julian Smith pondered a delay in the operation, but two factors ruled against it. A majority of former residents disagreed with Holland's assessment, and Admiral King, anxious to commence the Central Pacific drive, pressured Admiral Nimitz to disregard the objections.

The position of the moon ensured that most of the Marines would have to wade ashore. Tides are affected by the proximity of the moon—the closer the moon's orbit to earth, the higher the tide. On November 19, the moon would be at its most distant. That, on top of the neap tide, guaranteed insufficient water over the reef. Montague, Seng, and the others steamed toward a potential disaster.

Col. Merritt A. Edson, the 2d Marine Division's chief of staff, and Col. David M. Shoup designed a simple plan to seize Betio—land along its northern beaches, drive straight across the narrow island, and kill the defenders. They selected the northern (lagoon) side rather than the southern (ocean) side beaches as the site for the landing because even though the southern beaches offered better landing conditions—a relatively straight beach with few places for the Japanese to mount cross fire—the Japanese had placed their sturdiest defenses along that stretch of sand. Shoup and Edson figured that the lagoon side would be calmer than the ocean-side beaches, which absorbed the harsher ocean currents, and they assumed that the Japanese would delay completing the lagoon defenses until all else was finished, as they needed to use the long pier stretching from the northern beaches to the reef to bring in supplies.

"The question was what you would do if you were on the island," Shoup later explained. "Chances are you would mine everything but the place you use daily—that would be the last place to be sewed up. This conclusion was a very definite factor in our decision to land where we did."[3]

The landing zone contained three adjoining five-hundred-yard sectors stretching from the bird's beak at the extreme west end of the island to just beyond the pier in the middle. After Lieutenant Hawkins and his scout-sniper platoon eliminated the Japanese positioned along the lengthy pier, the assault waves would crash ashore at three spots. On the far right, at the bird's beak, Montague and Seng would land at Red 1 along with the rest of Maj. John F. Schoettel's 3d Battalion, 2d Marines, cross the bird's head toward the southern beaches, then swerve down the bird's spine to the eastern tip.

At the same time Lt. Col. Herbert R. Amey Jr.'s 2d Battalion, 2d Marines, with Hawkins and Chaplain Willard, would crash ashore to the right of the pier at Red 2, seize the airfield a short distance inland, then turn east and head down Betio's middle. To the left of the pier, Major Chamberlin, Private First Class Muhlbach, and Staff Sergeant Hatch would come in at Red 3 with the 2d Battalion, 8th Marines under Maj. Henry P. Crowe and defend the left flank from Japanese attacks originating from the tail.

Reserve forces, including Maj. Wood B. Kyle's 1st Battalion, 2d Marines, Maj. Lawrence C. Hays Jr.'s 1st Battalion, 8th Marines, and Maj. Robert H. Ruud's 3d Battalion, 8th Marines, waited to exploit any breakthrough. The 6th Marine Regiment, containing the Meadows brothers, formed the Force Reserve under Gen. Holland Smith's control. He could send them into battle either at Betio, if needed, or against Japanese forces at nearby Makin Atoll to the north.

The straightforward plan contained drawbacks. The Marines had to attack heavily defended beaches against superbly trained soldiers waiting in camouflaged, reinforced bunkers, all situated on a confined area. The tiny island, unlike the larger Guadalcanal, offered little room for maneuver. No diversionary force could draw enemy attention from the beaches, and once the Marines landed, they lacked the space needed for major flanking attacks.

That left one tactic at their disposal—simple and brutal. They had to storm the beaches through heavy machine gun and mortar fire, scratch out a toehold, repel probable counterattacks, then take Betio in the toughest of ways—yard by yard, absorbing potentially horrifying losses until every pillbox, every bunker, every Japanese, had been eliminated. On Betio, brute force and savage fighting overshadowed finesse. This would be a bloody slugfest of heavyweights standing in the middle of the ring, not two fast-moving foes landing quick jabs.

One part of the plan—the brief length of the preinvasion bombardment—bothered Shoup, Edson, and Gen. Julian Smith. The trio argued that the scheduled three-hour naval blasting of Betio would have little impact on the Japanese defenses, and instead recommended a several-day lambasting of the island.

Colonel Edson reminded those who felt Betio would be a simple operation that in December 1941, the Japanese believed that in a few hours they would seize Wake from the five hundred American military manning the island's defenses. Instead, for more than two weeks they battled a badly outnumbered foe before finally overwhelming the tiny garrison. If the men of Wake could mount such a noble defense, what might Tokyo's best on Betio do? A protracted bombardment could reduce enemy opposition.

When superiors rejected their suggestions, Julian Smith demanded that the record reflect his disagreement over inadequacy of the bombardment's length. In a letter to historian Joseph Alexander, Julian Smith's wife, Harriotte, explained that her husband asked for the clause's insertion because "if the assault proved unsuccessful he didn't want to wind up the scapegoat and become known as the general most responsible for the slaughter of his own troops."[4]

The amazing request illustrated the depth of Julian Smith's conviction that the preinvasion bombardment would accomplish little. It also proved to be a remarkable foreshadow of things to come for Montague, Seng, and the other young Marines slated to assault Betio's beaches.

"Dye the Sands with Their Blood"

Warrant Officer Kiyoshi Ota would hate to assault this place. Ota enlisted as an airman in the Imperial Japanese Navy on June 30, 1936, and served four years aboard aircraft carriers. In 1939, during the fighting in China, he joined the *Hiryu* as a machinist's mate, and two years later steamed with the carrier as it headed deep into the Pacific for the December 7, 1941, attack against the U.S. fleet at Pearl Harbor. When he stepped onto Betio in March 1943 with the other members of his 7th Sasebo Special Naval Landing Force from Japan and observed what had already been done to transform the little island into a fortress, he knew any opposing force would face nearly insurmountable obstacles.

Betio had not always been the scene of such feverish activity. Life had been tranquil for the Japanese garrison stationed on Betio after occupying the atoll in December 1941. The soldiers constructed pillboxes and bunkers, but they also enjoyed the benefits that tropical isles bring—a lagoon filled with an inexhaustible supply of fish, luxuriant beaches and swaying palm trees, and gorgeous sunsets that painted the Pacific in luscious hues of reds, blues, and golds. The men could swim, play cards, and feast on decent rations and sake.

They barely thought about their American foe, who, at this stage of the war, posed no threat in the region. The Japanese on Betio worried more about the sharp coral reef surrounding the island or about hungry sharks than they did about the United States.

That abruptly changed in August 1942 when an American raid against Butaritari Island in Makin Atoll to the north, led by Col. Evans F. Carlson, ignited shock waves that reached Tokyo and awoke the Japanese from their somnolence. Within one week of the raid, Fleet Adm. Meinichi Koga, who would succeed the slain Adm. Isoroku Yamamoto as chief of the Imperial Combined Fleet, ordered the Gilbert Islands reinforced and dispatched thousands of troops and Korean laborers to the region.

Lieutenant Murakami, commander of the 111th Pioneers, took charge of turning Betio from the luscious isle of lore into a bastion bristling with guns and death. Expecting any assault to come from Betio's ocean side to the south, he ordered his men to first mine and emplace bunkers and pillboxes along that shore. Other Japanese constructed the runway, a command post, and other fortifications.

Work intensified when the forty-nine-year-old Rear Adm. Keiji Shibasaki assumed command in August. A 1915 graduate of Japan's naval academy, Shibasaki served in a number of posts before Betio, including command of a ship, a naval station, and service in China. A superb officer who studied at the University of Tokyo, Shibasaki's skills at fortifying Betio would confound and haunt the Marines of the 2d Division.

Under Shibasaki, the garrison constructed defenses for most of the day, followed by military drills the rest. Shibasaki not only wanted his men to fight from behind the best-constructed defenses, but he intended that his young warriors would know what to do once the Americans appeared.

Shibasaki sent Warrant Officer Ota and other soldiers to cut down coconut trees on Tarawa's other islands so he could use them in strengthening Betio's defenses and in constructing a three- to five-foot log seawall along the isle's likely invasion beaches. He blasted coral rock out of the reef to make concrete for shelters and pillboxes.

Nothing for which the Marines had trained in New Zealand prepared them for what Shibasaki planned. A typical Japanese pillbox—and hundreds dotted Betio's landscape—featured a series of concentric walls, including a twelve-inch reinforced concrete wall, around a three- to five-foot concrete floor. Soldiers packed alternating layers of sand, coconut logs, and sandbags on top until the desired thickness for both walls and roof had been achieved, then tapered the sand to eliminate the presence of shadows that might be observed by American surveillance aircraft. Shibasaki fashioned angled trenches as entry points to the pillboxes so that direct fire into the positions would not reach his soldiers, and partitioned interiors added extra shelter from explosions. Shibasaki situated his defenses so that whenever the Marines attacked any pillbox, they came under withering fire from other Japanese emplacements.

After a September American aircraft carrier air raid, Shibasaki started work on a large bombproof shelter, complete with concrete walls several feet thick and reinforced with steel beams, to serve as his communications and command post. The triple-tiered bunker housed three hundred men. Machine gun nests surrounded the bombproof shelter, and hundreds of soldiers manned pillboxes and bunkers nearby to defend it.

Shibasaki hoped he would not have to rely on his land defenses, however. In an attempt to halt the American assault before it reached the beaches, he emplaced a series of antiboat obstacles in the waters surrounding Betio. Enemy landing craft would first encounter underwater barriers, including mine-laden concrete tetrahedrons, cunningly placed in the lagoon to channel landing craft into the path of point-blank fire. Barbed wire and log barricades waited under the water to trap intruders.

Other frightening weapons added more punch. Large guns, including mammoth 8-inch naval cannon and 3-inch and 5-inch antiaircraft and antiboat guns, would lob shells into the enemy's midst at long range, while machine guns and mortars would open up from closer distances. Should any Marines make it onto the beaches, a three- to five-foot-high coconut log seawall would halt their progress while field guns, machine guns, and rifles tore into their ranks. Marines could crouch behind the seawall for protection—practically the only shelter they would find on the island—but Shibasaki intended that the respite would be only temporary. As one Marine described it later, "An American helmet reared above this seawall would be as clear and helpless as a fly walking down a windowpane. And, if the Americans crouched beneath it, Betio's mortars would dye the sands with their blood. The mortars had the beaches registered—and they were behind a formidable array of machine guns and light artillery interlocked to sweep the lip of the seawall."[5]

Shibasaki peppered that array of guns about Betio, and since no point on the island stood more than three hundred yards from a beach, most of his weaponry could be targeted on an invading force. Shibasaki entrenched the guns in hexagon-shaped pillboxes of double-tiered coconut logs hooked together with railroad spikes. Sand had been poured between the tiers for reinforcement, and on top, half-inch steel roofs lay underneath three feet of sand.

Larger, sturdier blockhouses with five-foot-thick concrete walls stood between the pillboxes. A network of trenches connected this formidable system, which Shibasaki had designed so that each position would be safe from any but a direct artillery hit or a close-in, costly assault by invaders. Shibasaki intended that the Americans would have to eliminate the five hundred fortified positions and fourteen light tanks sprinkled about the small isle in the most brutal of ways—hand-to-hand combat.

An official U.S. Army history later concluded that, other than Iwo Jima's, Betio's beaches "were better protected against a landing force than any encountered in any theater of operations throughout the Second World War."[6] Okinawa, the Philippines, the Solomons, New Guinea, or Omaha Beach, the scene of fighting so memorably and graphically depicted by Steven Spielberg in *Saving Private Ryan*—none would offer as frightening a reception as Betio would to the young men of the 2d Marine Division.

"We Were Not Overly Worried"

Warrant Officer Ota was as impressed with the garrison as he was with the fortifications. Tokyo had dispatched 5,000 of its finest troops to the island, anchored by the superbly trained 1,559 men of his own 7th Sasebo Special Naval Landing Force (SNLF), commanded by Comdr. Takeo Sugai. Often compared to U.S. Marines, SNLF selected and drilled top physical specimens. The 7th Sasebo dispelled the errant notion, held by young Americans like Stanley Bowen, that their Japanese enemy was small in stature and suffered from poor eyesight, as some of its men stood much taller than six feet in height. More than 1,100 men of the 6th Yokosuka Special Naval Landing Force, 1,250 combat engineers from the 111th Pioneers, and 970 men of the 4th Fleet Construction Department Detachment joined the 7th Sasebo in providing Admiral Shibasaki with a formidable fighting force.

Shibasaki enjoyed a powerful combination of new recruits blended in with veterans of the China conflict. Ota, for instance, had been involved in a 1940 attack against the Chinese on Hainin Island. He and the other veterans brought considerable experience to their tasks.

Other than a few nuisance bombing raids, the war had pretty much skirted to the north and south of Betio and left the garrison alone. Ota wrote later that, "we were relaxed and not overly worried"[7] in the late summer and early fall of 1943. After performing their daily duties, each evening the Japanese faced Tokyo and recited the words of the Imperial Rescript that reminded them of their duties to Emperor Hirohito and of the glories of death in battle. Little did they know that soon they would be fighting for their lives in a brutal contest for the luxuriant island.

As Admiral Shibasaki realized, the Gilberts existed as a part of Japan's outer ring of defenses. An inner ring, standing closer to Japan, consisted of the Philippine Islands and other areas containing essential resources. An expendable outer ring existed to shield the inner one from attack as long as possible, and to draw out the American fleet so the Imperial Japanese Navy could destroy it in a massive ocean engagement. The Japanese did not intend to waste reinforcements on the outer ring. They would defend it as long as possible with the forces on hand until the fleet arrived to deal with the American Navy.

It thus became crucial to halt any American assault at the beaches before the enemy seized a foothold. An October 1942 order, issued by Shibasaki's predecessor, stated as much. "When the enemy is assembling for a landing, wait until the enemy is within effective range, direct your fire on the enemy transport group and destroy it. If the enemy starts a landing, knock out the landing boats with mountain gun fire, tank guns and infantry guns, then concentrate all fires on the enemy's landing point and destroy him at the water's edge."[8]

Colonel Edson, who had earlier fought against the Japanese on Tulagi and Guadalcanal, harbored no doubts about the quality of the men his Marines were about to engage. When asked by reporters to summarize their abilities, he answered, "Imperial Japanese Marines, [they're] the best Tojo's got."[9]

The coming battle thus pitted two superb foes, testing each other's skills in a confined arena offering no room for regrouping or retreating. Once the battle started, they would have to charge straight at each other, kill their opponent before they were killed, and stop only when the final enemy was slain. Unlike the larger Guadalcanal, where Marines enjoyed relatively safe areas, Betio would be, as one correspondent at the time wrote, an "assault from the beginning to the end." He added, "On a barren atoll you come in and the foe is right there. He meets you with all his firepower as you come ashore. He must stop you there or never. Water provides no foxholes in which to hide."[10]

Admiral Shibasaki felt confident he had done all he could to prepare his men. He still had some work to complete, especially on the lagoon side of Betio, but he liked his progress. The efficient officer had installed what one prominent historian, Samuel Eliot Morison, has called "the most complete defensive system . . . that could have [been] devised . . . Corregidor was an open town by comparison."[11]

Shibasaki agreed. He was so confident in his men and his preparations that he boasted, "A million men cannot take Tarawa in a hundred years."[12]

"Broken Hearts and Broken Dates"

Julian Smith insisted that an air of secrecy shroud the 2d Marine Division's departure from New Zealand to Tarawa. He had seen what happened when the 1st Marine Division left Wellington fifteen months before on its way to combat in the Solomons, when headlines in New Zealand newspapers loudly proclaimed the move. He was not going to hand the enemy such helpful information.

As a ruse, Smith's headquarters planted a story that the men were embarking on another landing exercise along New Zealand's coast, but that the men would be back in Wellington in time for a scheduled dance with the local lovelies. To eliminate the risk that one of his Marines might learn the real reason for leaving and pass on that information to a civilian, he restricted all Marines to their ships that final night.

Late on October 31, the eve of the departure, after the entire division had boarded the transports in Wellington Harbor, General Smith visited New Zealand's governor-general, Sir Cyril Newall, and informed him his Marines would not be coming back. Newall, disappointed that the men his nation had so freely adopted would soon be gone, wished Smith luck on his mystery voyage, "wherever it takes you and your splendid lads."[13]

Stanley Bowen, Norm Hatch, and Majors Crowe and Chamberlin accompanied the 2d Battalion, 8th Marines, onto the *Heywood*; the men of F Company and Robert Sherrod headed onto the *Zeilin* with the 2d Battalion, 2d Marines; Montague and Seng piled onto the *Middleton* with the 3d Battalion, 2d Marines; while the Meadows brothers headed up the gangways to different vessels—Jim and Dick Meadows boarded the *Bell* with the 2d Battalion, 6th

Marines, while brother Bill stepped onto the *Feland* with the 1st Battalion, 6th Marines.

On November 1 the collection of ships steamed out of Wellington Harbor, veered to the north, and began its nineteen-day voyage to the Gilbert Islands. When a screen of cruisers and destroyers appeared, most Marines realized that they would not return quickly, if ever, to New Zealand.

"With regard to the dance," stated Julian Smith, "one of the division wits remarked that maybe we didn't leave many broken hearts in New Zealand but we certainly left a lot of broken dates."[14]

Gene Seng was only one of the many men who were now separated from New Zealand sweethearts. Seng also knew that some of the veteran Marines had not seen their wives or girlfriends back home in more than a year. When a soldier goes to war, family and friends go with him: not physically, but spiritually and emotionally. They suffer the same pains of separation. They endure their own forms of fear and worry. Casualties of war occur not only on the battlefield, but in the living rooms and kitchens of loved ones in San Antonio, Texas; Beverly Hills, California; or Watertown, South Dakota.

As Seng and others coped with the abrupt parting, rumors about their final destination raced through every transport. Most wagered that they would head north and retake Wake, which had been lost to the Japanese in the war's first month.

Bowen, Montague, and the rest of the 2d Division were not the only ones talking about their destination. As always seemed to happen, news filtered back to the enemy. From her base in Japan, propagandist Tokyo Rose taunted the Marines almost as soon as they left New Zealand waters. On November 3 she smugly broadcast, "There are a hundred ships under way from New Zealand, and Japanese submarines have a torpedo waiting for every one of them."[15] Some of the Marines wondered not only how she knew they had departed, but how accurate her threat was.

"Love of Country, Love of the Corps"

Five days after leaving New Zealand, the convoy pulled into Efate in the New Hebrides Islands southeast of the Solomons for two final landing rehearsals. Following the second rehearsal on November 9 the commander of the assault regiment on Tarawa, Col. William Marshall, suffered a heart attack. With less than ten days remaining before the Marines crashed ashore at Tarawa, Julian Smith could not afford to name a new commander who would be unfamiliar with the men and plans. He turned to his operations and training officer, Lieutenant Colonel Shoup, who had played a vital role in developing the assault plans for the operation. As his substitution would create the fewest disruptions, Shoup was promoted to colonel and ordered to lead the Marines into Tarawa. By that quirk of fate, one of the most capable leaders now controlled a key portion of the invasion.

"He was an interesting character, this Colonel Shoup," wrote Robert Sherrod. "A squat, red-faced man with a bull neck, a hard-boiled, profane shouter of orders, he would carry the biggest burden on Tarawa. On his judgment and ability would depend the lives of several thousand men and, ultimately perhaps, whether or not we won the battle."[16]

The studious Shoup combined the intelligence of a genius with the calmness of a Greek stoic. In many ways he did not fit the usual image of a warrior. He had pored over the plans for the 1915 British amphibious assault at Gallipoli in preparation for Tarawa, and the quiet officer filled notebooks with his private thoughts on subjects ranging from war to romance, from friendship to honor. Along with a handful of other officers on Tarawa, he would provide needed stability in the early hours of chaos.

Shoup concluded that the men of the 2d Division would exceed expectations, for he had long been proud of what made his Marines so special. Someone once asked him why the Marines possessed such great esprit de corps; Shoup replied, "Love: love of country, love of the Corps and its tradition, and love of the man to the right and left of you."[17]

By the time the invasion force left Efate on November 13, one week before the landing, all that remained was to tell the Marines the piece of land for which they would be asked to risk their lives. This could now be done, as the convoy's next stop was also its last—Betio.

"We Sweated Without Pause"

Correspondent Robert Sherrod walked around his transport, *Zeilin,* observing the young men heading toward an unknown destination. He had to agree with those who said that the worst part about a battle is waiting, for it seemed that was all the men did—they waited for food, they waited for showers, they waited for word of their objective, they waited only to wait a bit more. Making matters worse was that no one, at least among the enlisted, knew where they were headed and what they were expected to do. All they knew was that each moment took them closer to combat and farther from loved ones.

The heat compounded the problems. On a tropical isle, at least they could head to the shores and water, but the transport offered nothing but narrow confines and cramped quarters. "We lay in bed and sweated without pause all night long," wrote Sherrod. "Then, in the daytime, we swallowed many salt tablets to restore the salt we had lost through perspiration through the night."[18] Little alleviated their discomfort in the equatorial sun, where the men labored, day and night, in uniforms soaked with sweat. As the long day unfolded, few places provided shelter from the blistering heat. Belowdecks, where the men slept, was unbearably hot. Above, on deck, was little better in the hundred-degree temperatures, but at least some of that humid air circulated.

"Most of the transports had these four- and five-tiered racks for bunks, a metal frame with a mattress on it," said Private First Class Muhlbach. "It was very uncomfortable. It was hot. You couldn't get much air in the troop holds. It smelled. There was seasickness. The heads [bathrooms] were inadequate—you had a seawater pump in a trough with a board put on top. That wasn't very nice."[19]

Stan Bowen, who so loved the outdoors, could barely navigate the passageways and decks jammed with Marines, and he might not have minded waiting for hours in line for the chow if he had considered it edible. The food especially paled in comparison to what the Marines had recently feasted upon in New Zealand, where they enjoyed steaks, eggs, and ice cream to their hearts' content. Then, at night, he lay in his bunk in the quarters designated for his platoon and stared at the bunk above him—so close that it almost touched his head.

Bowen could not even count on a freshwater shower to cool down. Saltwater showers were available, but they did little to cleanse the sweat and grime off his body or to wash his clothes—only freshwater showers did that. To conserve the precious commodity, however, fresh water was turned on for one hour in the morning and one in the evening. Bowen and hundreds of others scampered for a good spot in line, but most left disappointed. At least they could laugh at the hapless men who were caught when, in the midst of lathering their faces to shave or soaping up to wash their bodies, time expired and they stood there, without water, covered in suds.

One other malady plagued the Marines as the transports headed north toward the equator. Now steaming in tropical waters, the dramatic rise in temperature aggravated the malaria many had picked up in the Solomons. Men shivered in their bunks with chills and high fevers or headed for medical treatment in the ship's infirmary.

"Cruised Our Way Across the Pacific"

Montague, Seng, and the other Marines gradually fell into a loose schedule as the transports headed to parts unknown. Other than attending daily mandatory instructional classes with their units, the men passed the hours in a variety of ways. They exercised every day to maintain their physical edge, cleaned their equipment, and sharpened their knives and bayonets, but at first did so without any sense of urgency.

One Marine kept a record of his activities during the nineteen-day voyage from New Zealand to Tarawa. He played 215 consecutive games of gin rummy, smoked six cartons of cigarettes and one box of cigars, drank ninety-three cups of coffee, got a haircut, washed the same pair of socks and underwear eleven times, read *The Pocket History of the United States*, read two religious essays and 19 mystery stories, and read a book titled *The Haunted Pajamas*.[20]

Among the myriad activities, a few dominated. The men loved to watch the teeming sea life that accompanied the force as it wound through the Pacific. Magnificent whales, graceful dolphins, and millions of flying fish captivated them, while the ever-present sharks that circled behind in wait of the daily garbage dump filled the Marines with equal amounts fascination and fear. Each night young men, many from prairie farms and lands distant from the sea, leaned over the railings to obtain a clearer view of the strange fluorescent glow that coated the water's dark surface in the trail of each transport.

They slept, day and night, and when awake, they watched movies—a new one arrived every other day—or sat down with one of the hundreds of pocket books and magazines that made the rounds of each unit.

Above all came letter writing. In their bunks, stretched out on the deck, or any other place they could find, Marines took out pencil and paper to scribble a brief note to loved ones. Stanley Bowen wrote romantic letters to Marge McCann, and Gene Seng penned thoughtful expressions of what he and June would do when all this was over. "I don't know what I would have done without her letters to look forward to over those long and lonely months,"[21] Bowen later stated of his correspondence with Marge. One Marine drove the censor, Lt. Adolph Norvik, crazy with his antics. "I wouldn't mind [reading such a large volume of mail] so much if that damned corporal didn't write five identical letters to five different girls every day."[22]

Gene Seng wrote his mother that, "life aboard this 'pig iron' isn't exactly a bed of roses. There is not much else to do besides sit around topside and read and think. About the main thing that [I] think about is getting back home with June. I get all mixed up when I start thinking of all the uncertainties staring me in the face—I truly get lonesome."[23]

Seng and Montague avoided the other prime activity—gambling—but Bowen loved wagering a few dollars in a hot game of poker or craps. Some played for hours, wagering everything they had, figuring they had little to risk anyway on the eve of a battle which they might not survive. On November 18, only two days before the landing, Marines aboard the *Zeilin* staged a winner-take-all epic that lasted much of the day. One lucky Marine wired home $16,000 in winnings, with which his wife purchased their first home.

At least he had his rum, thought Sergeant Hatch. Thank God for that. Always a farsighted individual, Hatch had purchased from a New Zealand sailor his six-month ration of rum, about the same as a fifth of alcohol. When he boarded the transport, he quickly finagled an arrangement from a friendly boatswain—the boatswain provided Coca-Cola and lemons, Hatch provided the rum. Then, each night Hatch, Pvt. William Kelliher, and the boatswain sneaked into a boat hanging alongside and enjoyed nightly cocktails. As the sun set over the broad expanse of water, gradually losing its luster in the twilight, a breathtaking array of colors illuminated the horizon—orange, crimson, mauve, gray blue. Finally, puffy clouds materialized, each marvelously stained by the setting sun, making one think he witnessed a new Michelangelo painting in the making. The trio "cruised our way across the Pacific sitting there with the beautiful sunset drinking the rum."[24] If ever a peaceful way to war existed, this had to be it.

Sometimes they marveled at the assembled might of which they were a part. Each transport carried a battalion of Marines, while others conveyed the machinery of war—weapons, artillery, tanks, and a hundred other items needed to subdue the foe. One man said, "You felt the muscle, the pent-up power, ready to be hurled against that spit of land which was our target, and you felt that nothing on earth could resist the momentum of this vast seagoing war machine."[25]

Hatch and his friends were not the only ones contemplating their surroundings. Robert Sherrod wanted his readers to understand these young men who headed into battle, so as he made his way about the transport, he closely observed their actions and listened to their words. The first thing that struck him was their diversity. "The range of their background was as broad as America: farmers, truck drivers, college students, runaway kids, rich men's sons, orphans, lawyers, ex-soldiers."

Sherrod wondered whether these boys could handle the extreme demands of battle. In the spring of 1943 he had accompanied troops fighting in the Aleutians and seen evidence of both courage and fright. "I thought I learned a lesson on Attu which probably applied to all armies: not all soldiers are heroes—far from it; the army that wins, other things being fairly equal, is the army which has enough men to rise above duty, thus inspiring others to do their duty."[26]

He concluded that some of the young men simply lacked the mental preparation required to cope with the horrors they faced. Accustomed to years of peace, they now had to switch into a wartime mode. Would the young Marines walking about him now on the *Zeilin* be ready? What about all the men aboard the other vessels? No one could possibly know until the moment of truth arose.

He and Major Crowe discussed this issue shortly before arriving off Betio. The major fretted that so many of his young Marines had never experienced combat and told Sherrod, "They were soft, not tough like us older Marines."[27] The sole consolation was that Crowe had utilized every moment in New Zealand training and drilling and marching the men. Hopefully, that would carry them through when the time came.

At least the men knew what they fought for, and that comforted the veteran correspondent. When he asked what compelled them to risk their lives, they gave similar answers. "It was inconceivable to most Marines that they should let another Marine down, or that they could be responsible for dimming the bright reputation of their corps."[28]

Thus reassured, Sherrod believed most men would make a good accounting when the firing started. Besides, why worry? Officers told him that, following what was expected to be a devastating preinvasion bombardment, little would be waiting for them.

"Don't Be a Boy Scout"

On November 14, Stan Bowen and the entire complement aboard the *Heywood* wound their way in groups of fifty through the sweltering confines to meetings with their commanding officers. Sweat poured down everyone's faces and arms, even though most were stripped to the waist. It didn't help that just about every Marine chain-smoked, but few minded. Cigarettes were considered almost as much a necessity as were shoes and socks.

Suddenly a captain entered and started talking. For the first time, Bowen and the other Marines were to learn the object of their intense training, why they had been in New Zealand for so long, and whose rumor was correct.

"Gentlemen," asserted the captain, "we are going to soon be killing lots of Japs at a place called Tarawa. The Japs claim it can't be taken, but they don't know about the 2d Marine Division!"[29]

"Tarawa?" thought Bowen when he heard the atoll's name. "I had never heard of it. Up until the time they told us on the ship, we knew nothing about it."[30]

Using a huge relief map detailing what American intelligence had uncovered about Tarawa's defenses, the captain explained that once the island was in their hands, the United States could advance to stronger enemy bases in the Marshalls and Marianas. This operation, therefore, was important in establishing a foothold in the Japanese defensive perimeter and in proving that an amphibious assault against a heavily fortified island could succeed.

The officer then handed out two contrasting items. A booklet provided information on the native inhabitants and their customs and spoke of the Gilberts, with "waving palm fronds and a lapis lazuli lagoon," as if the troops were headed on a vacation. The second gave Bowen pause. The mimeographed sheet listed every trick the Japanese had used in the Solomons and admonished the men, most in their late teens and early twenties, "Don't be a Boy Scout. Kill or be killed is their creed."[31]

Bowen and the other young Marines, many of whom had only months before attended high school proms, became pensive as they listened to the explanations. The blunt talk momentarily jarred them out of their revelry and forced them to ponder just where and into what they might be headed.

Along with the Marines of the 2d Battalion, 8th Marines, Bowen would be going in on Red Beach 3, the landing area resting on the left (eastern) flank. The forces at Red 3 were to dash inland to the airstrip, reduce enemy defenses on their left, and hold the line against likely Japanese counterattacks that would come from the eastern end of the island. If they could not maintain a secure line, the Japanese could smash through Red 3 and threaten the Marines on Red 2 and Red 1. Along with fellow corpsman Johnny Snyder, Bowen would land with the second wave, only minutes after the first wave, containing his close friend, corpsman Howard Brisbane, crashed ashore.

The captain gave the men another incentive for doing well at Red 3. Major

Crowe, never one to back down from a challenge, had wagered a case of whiskey with his counterpart on Red Beach 2, Lt. Col. Herbert R. Amey, commander of the 2d Battalion, 2d Marines, that his battalion would rush across and reach the ocean side of Betio before Amey's. "Now, we're going to win that whiskey for the major and here's how." The captain ended by stating that everything depended on a simple formula—the goal for each Marine rifleman was to "get on shore, move forward, kill Japs and secure the island." Bowen listened avidly, but still wondered how things would fare for him and the other corpsmen, whose job was to treat the wounded. Since Bowen and many others had never treated men under fire, he had no clue what lay ahead. "For us pharmacist's mates it wasn't so simple—we knew not what to expect."[32]

Bowen was not worried, however. He and the other men had one thing in mind. "I was very anxious to get going," Bowen recalled. "All of us wanted to kill Japs."[33]

Bowen noticed one unnerving detail, though. While he and the other newcomers to the division cheered the captain's words and enthusiastically looked forward to the coming battle, the Guadalcanal veterans remained strangely silent. "Everyone was anxious to get into action, except the guys who had been on the 'Canal. They never said much, but they weren't excited like the rest of the kids were, and we were just kids then, ages 17–19. I was 20, a little bit older than the average Marine. The veterans were calm, and the rest were excited to get going."[34]

His unease increased later that day when Howard Brisbane walked up to Bowen, a look of concern masking his otherwise jovial countenance. "Stan, I'm scared. I'm not going to make it. I know it."

"Bullshit, Howard," retorted Bowen, a bit taken back by his friend's unexpected pessimism. They had spent many happy hours on liberty in New Zealand, and Howard's gloomy outlook angered Bowen. "We're all gonna make it. I know it,"[35] added Bowen in an attempt to comfort his buddy.

"Maybe We'll Walk Ashore"

While Bowen listened as the plans for Red 3 unfolded aboard the *Heywood*, in similar stifling rooms aboard the *Zeilin* the men of F Company, Lieutenant Hawkins, and Chaplain Willard learned from Lieutenant Colonel Amey what they were to do at Red 2 in the middle of the landing zones. The tall, black-mustached, popular commander who wagered a case of whiskey with Major Crowe explained that after leaving their amtracs, the men were to dash across the island as quickly as possible, cut off the Japanese in the western half of Betio from those fighting in the east, then swing eastward and gradually eliminate enemy fortifications all the way to the island's tail.

Cpl. Noal C. Pemberton, Pfc. Robert R. Twitchell, and the other men of the 2d Battalion listened as Amey, sweating profusely, explained that the Navy would blast the island from the air and sea and that aircraft would keep the surviving defenders pinned down until the Marines could kill them. "I think we ought to have every Jap off the island—the live ones—by the night of D-Day," he stated in a tone that made believers of his men. "We are very fortunate. This is the first time a landing has been made by American troops against a well-defended beach, the first time over a coral reef, the first time against any force to speak of." Then, gaining momentum as he spoke to the hushed gathering, he declared, "And the first time the Japs have had the hell kicked out of them in a hurry. Maybe we'll walk ashore. I don't know."[36]

Before departing, Amey reminded his men to drink water sparingly in the opening hours, as no one knew how long it might take for supplies to reach them once the fighting started, to quickly hit the enemy as they would probably be punch-drunk from the shelling, and to remember that no matter how optimistic the outlook, to be on guard as the bombing and shelling might not kill every enemy. "Don't expect all of the Japs to be dead just because they have been bombed and shelled. There is always some dumb jackass that doesn't get the word and will still be shooting."[37]

Also paying attention was a group of newsmen who had been scheduled to land in the fifth wave with the battalion. Eager to reach shore and cover the action, one correspondent had misgivings, though, upon learning he would be going in with the Marines heading toward the middle beach. He turned to a fellow reporter and remarked that they would get shot at from both sides.

"Until Hell Wouldn't Have It"

Montague, Seng, and the Meadows brothers heard similar information about Beach Red 1, standing on the right flank of the invasion beaches. Assaulting Betio's western edge, they were to drive across the western shoreline—the bird's head—then swerve east and push down the ocean beaches—the bird's spine—and reduce Japanese defenses until the enemy had been forced into the tail. Dick Meadows liked what he heard. If true, he and his brothers would face nothing more than minor inconvenience. "Tarawa was so little," he said. "We didn't expect a lot of the trouble, with the Navy shelling and all."[38] Who knew? Maybe after a simple landing, Gene Seng could rejoin June McDougall back in New Zealand.

A common thread connected the briefings. Aboard almost every troop transport, officers issued optimistic assessments of the coming assault—the men would land against little opposition, secure a largely demolished island, then return to transports for a trip back. Rear Adm. Harry Hill asserted, "Before we land on the place, we're going to pound it with naval gunfire and dive-bombers. We're going to steamroller that place until hell wouldn't have it." Rear Adm. Howard F. Kingman, commander of the fire support group, agreed. "Gentlemen," he told Marine officers, "it is not our intention to wreck the island. We do not intend to destroy it. Gentlemen, we will obliterate it."[39] Officers told Sherrod, Hatch, and other correspondents to expect such light casualties that they might be surprised.

Lt. Col. Raymond L. Murray, commander of the 2d Battalion, 6th Marines, listened to Admiral Hill explain the preinvasion bombardment and wondered what would remain for his men. He stated later, "We actually began to think—certainly I did—'My God, there is not going to be anybody left to fight when we get on that island. We're just going to be able to walk over it.'"[40] Some men even wondered if the Japanese might pull out of Betio before the troops arrived, as they had recently done at Kiska in the Aleutian Islands.

Here and there, a few signs indicated that the optimism might be unwarranted. Colonel Edson explained to a group of correspondents that, unlike his fellow officers, he harbored doubts about an easy operation. He questioned whether any naval bombardment could significantly reduce enemy defenses and said that the Marines should not "count on taking Tarawa, small as it is, in a few hours." He added that the fighting could be difficult, in part because "these Nips are surprising people."[41] The *Time* magazine reporter looked about and saw that every correspondent's reaction mirrored his—astonishment over Edson's pessimism.

Colonel Murray also remembered his Camp Pendleton days, when a group of important politicians and officers were invited to observe an aerial bombing. After a series of five-hundred-pound bombs supposedly obliterated the target area, the host officer stated to the visitors, "As you can see, nobody could live through a thing like this."[42] Just as he uttered the words, a deer jumped out from the target area and ran away. If a deer could survive in the open, what might the Japanese do from beneath fortified positions?

"Please Leave Enough Japs"

Though hundreds of rumors abounded aboard every transport, few men who served under Major Crowe doubted the veracity of one. According to scuttlebutt, Major Crowe had gone to the mat to ensure his battalion occupied a crucial spot in the assault waves. If he obtained his wish, it meant that his men would land with the first three waves to crash against the Japanese defenses. They would be the first to attack the enemy, the first to suffer casualties.

Colonel Shoup denied his request, but the forty-four-year-old Crowe, replete with stunning red hair and waxed handlebar mustache, refused to take no for an answer. He insisted that his men had earned the honor with their superb training in New Zealand, where they had set records for cross-country marches. Shoup finally relented and positioned Crowe's men at Red 3. Crowe's stubbornness meant that Major Chamberlin, Sergeant Hatch, Private First Class Muhlbach, and the other men of 2d Battalion, 8th Marines, would churn toward shore directly against what American intelligence claimed was Shibasaki's sturdiest defenses.

Fellow battalion commanders joked with Crowe when they learned the Marine legend had wrestled his way into the assignment. Lieutenant Colonel Murray, somewhat disappointed that his 6th Marines missed out on a similar spot and had instead been designated as the reserve unit, teased his friend, "Please leave enough Japs so that when the 6th Marines get ashore, we'll have a few to shoot."[43]

Some, including Staff Sergeant Hatch, worried whether Crowe's executive officer, Major Chamberlin, would be up to the task. Chamberlin's first impression certainly left much to be desired, and Hatch found it hard to believe that he had been paired with Crowe, a bulldog of a battler who led with profane words and aggressive deeds. Here, aboard the troop transport where he first spotted Chamberlin, Hatch dismissed him as a bookish sissy who employed few words, and those few seemed to be used in nagging the men.

"He was very quiet and self-effacing," said Hatch of Chamberlin. "The troops called him Old Maid because he used to run around insisting that the guys put on shirts on deck."[44] The Marines hated to wear their shirts in the tropical heat, but Chamberlin insisted on it. Anyone caught without a shirt received a reminder from Major Chamberlin, who waited until the offender had donned his shirt.

Behind Chamberlin's back, the Marines griped about being henpecked and expressed serious concerns that such a man could be effective once the fighting commenced, when their lives depended on Chamberlin's ability to make split-second decisions. Hatch said, "All the guys were really teed off at him. . . . Everyone kept saying, 'Jesus, what an old maid,' you know, 'what kind of guy are we going to get into a fight with?' "[45]

Chamberlin had more of a reason to pester them than they realized—sunburn. If they headed into battle with that malady, he worried that some, in order to alleviate their pain, would discard the backpacks and other equipment they so badly needed.

"We Are Entering Enemy Waters"

Funny thing, thought Chaplain Willard. It happened each time, though. One would guess that the assault would dominate their thoughts from the moment they boarded the transports, but that was not so. During the first half of the voyage, at least until they learned of their destination and exact mission, the men joked, sang, gambled, read—anything except talk about the attack. "Seldom, very seldom," he said, "the men would talk about the coming battle."[46]

That changed with the November 14 briefings. Now, with their mission clearly in mind, joking and fun, while still present, diminished. Willard sensed a quiet seriousness, an urgency to prepare that had been missing. The men knew they had to get ready for a battle.

The mood deepened on November 17, three days before the scheduled landing, when the men received orders to don life jackets and carry a canteen of water in case an enemy attack required them to abandon ship. If that were not sufficient to jar the young Marines out of their complacency, loudspeakers blared an unsettling message. "Now hear this. We are entering enemy waters. You will exercise every precaution to avoid disclosing our position: you will take care to throw nothing over the side. The smoking lamp is out at sunset."[47]

Suddenly, as if a brisk breeze had chilled the tropical air, little was the same as it had been the day before. The zigzagging, done to make a submarine attack more difficult, now carried more import, and alarms to "Man your battle stations!" that sent sailors scurrying to their battle posts and Marines tumbling belowdecks could no longer be assumed to be just another drill. Montague, Seng, and the rest could do little during these times as the watertight doors slammed shut behind them. They sometimes felt that they rested on a floating bull's-eye. Some muttered nervously that they preferred to be fighting on land, where, if you were attacked, you at least had a foxhole to jump into. Where do you go in the middle of an ocean?

Optimism, always a necessary ingredient before an assault, soared on November 18 when word spread that B-24 bombers attacking Betio reported no signs of enemy activity and faced minimal antiaircraft fire. One surgeon, feeling more confident as the force edged closer to Betio, predicted to Robert Sherrod there would not be "a damned Jap on Tarawa," then added, "Why in the hell don't we just take this force and keep going to Tokyo and get the goddam war over with?"[48]

Sherrod took an informal poll of Marines and found that, while most expected the naval bombardment to pulverize the one square mile of Betio, not everyone predicted an easy show. One sergeant believed the preinvasion bombardment would make things easier, "but something in the back of my mind tells me there's going to be a lot of shooting Japs left when we start going ashore." The sergeant stated that once on land, the Marines would have a tough nut to crack, because the enemy was "the damnedest diggers in the world. It's like pulling a tick out of a rug to get one out of his hole."[49]

Stanley Bowen stared at Major Crowe's orders with a combination of disbelief and optimism, precisely what the officer had intended. Major Crowe wanted his men to head into battle with a sense of confidence and hope, yet tempered by the reality that a nasty job awaited them. Thus he ordered them to continually check and clean their weapons, to carry four hand grenades in their pockets, to promptly obey orders to avoid confusion, to delay loading weapons and fixing bayonets until ordered, to keep their minds focused on their jobs instead of watching air strikes or other ships, to be aggressive once ashore, to fire only when they had a target in sight, and to remember that since their grenades had only three-second fuses, to toss them quickly after releasing the safety lever.

Crowe also referred to a problem that had plagued commanders for hundreds of years. "Bear in mind at all times that we are here to kill, not to hunt souvenirs." He said they would have plenty of time after the battle to collect whatever they wanted, but until that time, they had a dangerous job to complete.

He ended with stirring words that were meant to instill spirit and fire in his men. "All the help possible has been furnished you prior to your landing. After landing you are the ones who take over. It is your show from here to the south beach. Make it a good show by being a MARINE [capitals Crowe's]."[50]

Every man figured that if the Japanese survived the bombardment, the Marines faced a rough fight with a barbaric foe. Numerous stereotypes reinforced the image that the Japanese opponent was little more than a savage beast with rape, pillage, and death on his mind. The 1943 U.S. Naval Institute manual, *Hand-to-Hand Combat*, warned the men what to expect from their Oriental foe.

"The daily story of the war emphasizes again and again the fact that we are facing an enemy which is careless of life because they are so steeped in a fanatical nationalism. The common rules of war mean nothing to a desperate enemy." The manual added that in the present barbaric war, "the code of sportsmanship is suspended 'for the duration,'" and admonished, "You do to the enemy exactly what he would like to do to you—only, you do it first!"[51]

"Would You Plant a Rose for Me?"

Chaplain Willard enjoyed few moments of rest. By his count, since November 1 he had held twenty-two divine services attended by 5,141 men, given 426 communions, converted 44 men to the Baptist faith, baptized another 62, conducted 781 interviews with the Marines aboard ship, and handed out 366 of the Gideon Bibles he picked up in San Diego.

However, nothing compared to the few days immediately prior to the invasion. With each mile the transport steamed closer to Betio, Marines increasingly turned to their faith for succor. As exhausted as Willard might have been, he could reject no one, for he had been placed aboard ship precisely to bring comfort to men about to enter battle.

Already, the men devoted less time to playing cards and sunbathing and more to sharpening knives and cleaning rifles. Many penned last letters to loved ones or made final arrangements for their belongings should they be killed. Gene Seng asked Fred Ellis to send his mother carnations each Mother's Day should anything happen to him. Staff Sergeant Bordelon wrote his sister, "Don't know when this will reach you. Just a little remembrance of my love for you. Would you somewhere, in some garden, plant a rose for me?"[52]

Willard knew his cohorts from other faiths experienced the same. Fr. F. W. Kelly, a Roman Catholic priest, heard confession almost nonstop. Father Riedel, beloved equally by the Marines for his religious convictions and for his tendency to swear, told conglomerations of young men, most stripped to the waist in the heat with both dog tags and religious medals dangling from their necks, "It takes guts for a man to meet his obligations to God."[53] Men wound along the starboard side and filed back along the port side to receive Communion.

On the eve of the battle, Lieutenant Hawkins and Robert Sherrod discussed the coming operation. Hawkins was proud of his scout-sniper platoon and boasted to Sherrod, "I think the thirty-four men in my platoon can lick any two-hundred-man company in the world." Hawkins related that his platoon would head in before any other unit, clear out opposition at the pier, and hold until men arrived. Despite being placed in the vanguard, not one volunteered when Hawkins asked for a man to stay behind to guard their equipment. "My men are not afraid of danger," he told Sherrod.

The correspondent walked away believing he had just talked with "the bravest man I have ever known" and that "there were no Marines who hated Japs more than the scout and sniper men. Through bitter experience they had learned that men who hate most, kill best."[54] He wondered how this man Hawkins, who talked with equal fondness of his mother and his men, would fare.

Sherrod then headed over for a chat with Colonel Shoup, the man who had planned much of the operation and would lead it once ashore. Unlike his fellow officers, Shoup believed that fewer than seven hundred of the three thousand Japanese would be dead by the time his Marines had to land. "What worries me more than anything else," Shoup stated, "is that our boats may not be able to get over that coral shelf that sticks out about five hundred yards. We may have to wade in. The first waves, of course, will get in all right on the 'alligators,' but if the Higgins boats draw too much water to get in fairly close, we'll either have to wade in with machine guns maybe shooting at us, or the amtracs will have to run a shuttle service between the beach and the end of the shelf."[55]

Shoup's words bothered Sherrod, but the correspondent took comfort in knowing that men like Hawkins and his platoon led the way.

"Let Us Make Up Our Minds to Die"

In his underground bunker on Betio, Warrant Officer Ota enjoyed no such comfort. For the last week, American long-range bombers had lambasted Betio, killing 35 soldiers and wounding another 169. The final two days had been especially rough, for American carrier aircraft continually bombed the island in an attempt to reduce the Japanese defenses and daze the defenders, while on November 19 three American cruisers hurled 1,941 shells in two hours. He understood why most warriors claim that aerial, naval, or artillery bombardments rank at the top of the most feared aspects of modern warfare, for they leave the defender little to do other than hope the next bomb or shell does not crash down on him. After forty-eight harrowing hours, Ota and his comrades regrouped and prepared for the expected land assault.

Ota emerged from his bunker to find that the damage could have been worse. Some heavy guns and antiaircraft guns had been destroyed, but most of their machine gun positions and many larger guns survived intact. With the large amounts of ammunition, rifles, and hand grenades that remained, Ota felt confident he and his comrades could mount an honorable defense, but he doubted they could be victorious.

"But there were our collapsed and shattered buildings, the fallen coconut trees, the raging fires, and the choking smell of powder smoke," Ota later wrote. "Many of our men had been killed and about 300 were wounded. Our men could not speak. Their faces were pale. We were surrounded by an overwhelming force of the enemy, with no hope for outside support or assistance. It was like the lonely song of an insect. We knew that we would die, one after another, as cherry blossoms fall or autumn leaves are scattered."[56]

Rear Admiral Shibasaki shared Ota's gloom. A Japanese airman had spotted the American force and radioed back the disheartening information, ENEMY CONTACT REPORT . . . FLEET SIGHTED . . . SEVERAL CARRIERS AND OTHER TYPES TOO NUMEROUS TO MENTION. He had informed his superiors that the United States was on its way and that he required assistance, but he had received a disheartening reply—he and his men should be prepared to die for the emperor. A Japanese airman scribbled in his diary, "What terrible news. It seems the enemy has more ships than is possible. And his planes are everywhere."[57]

On the night before the American landing, every Japanese unit gathered and vowed to die for the emperor. They recited the Imperial Rescript to Soldiers and Sailors and stated they would select suicide over surrender to the Americans. Officers then reminded their men, "Let us settle our affairs and make up our minds to die in the battle."[58]

Fortunately for the Japanese, their beach defenses had been only lightly damaged, so this final night before the Americans landed, Shibasaki ordered every man to dig more rifle and machine gun pits facing the lagoon side. After Ota and the thirty men he commanded finished reinforcing the already-sturdy machine gun position close to the water's edge just to the west of the pier—

directly where Private First Class Pemberton and the men of F Company would land—they cleaned their weapons, discussed how best to repel the invaders, and made sure they had sufficient ammunition.

Upon finishing, Ota stretched out on coconut frond mats under the open sky and attempted to get a little rest. Ota pondered a hundred different details before settling on two important items—his family and food. He had enjoyed little food the past two days, and he wondered if he would ever again see his loved ones in Japan. He wrote, "We felt little hope for a successful outcome."[59]

"Padre, I Want You to Pray for Me"

As the night of November 19 approached, in the humid, suffocating holds, men in the assault waves collected what they needed to take ashore—weapons, ammunition, water, and one day's rations. They reviewed their missions and studied maps, cleaned rifles and sharpened knives. Then, when all appeared ready, their thoughts drifted to home. "Just remember I'll be O.K. and be home soon so don't worry,"[60] wrote Pvt. David S. Spencer to his parents in Michigan.

In the moist stillness of their ship's hold, Stan Bowen spent his final preinvasion hours with Marine buddies. He and Johnny Snyder agreed to stick together during the battle to help each other tend the wounded. Tippy West, a Guadalcanal veteran, warned Bowen that the first man he treated under fire would be the worst. Bowen was not sure why, but did not think to question his more experienced friend. "I wasn't worried at all," explained Bowen. "I honest to God didn't think the Japs would be shooting back at us."[61]

Gen. Julian Smith's November 19 message to the men heading in to Betio contained a mixture of pride, encouragement, and determination. He stated that the division had been selected because of its excellence, both in training and on the battlefield, and "their confidence in us will not be betrayed. We are the first American troops to attack a defended atoll. What we do here will set a standard for all future operations in the Central Pacific area. Observers from other Marine divisions and from other branches of our armed services, as well as those of our Allies, have been detailed to witness our operations. Representatives of the press are present. Our people back home are eagerly awaiting news of our victories.

"I know that you are well-trained and fit for the tasks assigned to you. You will quickly overrun the Japanese forces; you will decisively defeat and destroy the treacherous enemies of our country; your success will add new laurels to the glorious traditions of our beloved Corps."

He ended with: "Good luck and God bless you all."[62]

Robert Sherrod, whose writings would earn him the reputation of being one of the war's most accurate, vivid reporters, waged a mental battle between what he hoped and what he feared might be reality on the morrow. He wanted to believe that the Japanese had pulled out; he knew he should be more cautious. That night, he scribbled in his notebook, "If there are a lot of Japs on Tarawa, I'll be utterly unprepared psychologically."[63]

That evening, priests and ministers held the final preinvasion services. In sweltering holds, with the heat battling the stench for dominance, men about to go into battle struggled with their emotions. Father Kelly ended by turning toward the Marines, blessing them in Latin, then proclaiming loud and strong, "God bless you, and God have mercy on the Japanese."

Later, Colonel Shoup, a Protestant, visited Father Kelly to make a request. "Padre, I want you to pray for me," the officer burdened with command over so many young men asked. Father Kelly wondered what kind of prayer Shoup wanted, and was surprised that it was not for victory. "I want you to pray that I don't make any mistakes out on that beach; no wrong decisions that will cost any of those boys an arm or a leg or a hand, much less a life. I want you to pray for that, Padre."[64] The Catholic chaplain watched Shoup depart, impressed that the officer could feel such empathy toward his young men.

As the night waned and midnight approached, men settled in their bunks and tried to catch a few moments' rest. Bowen fell into a calm sleep, confident that the next day would unfold smoothly. Sherrod put a roll of toilet paper inside his helmet, filled two canteens with water, and placed in his dungarees some rations, two morphine syrettes and a two-ounce bottle of medicinal brandy given him by a surgeon. Like the other thousands of men aboard the transports, he placed his personal belongings into a barracks bag to be brought ashore after the battle or held until he returned.

The final thing he did before falling into his bunk was replace his reporter's notebooks with two unused ones. Should he die or be captured, he did not want the Japanese learning anything helpful from the copious notes he had already taken. At 8:30 P.M. he turned out the light, hoping to enjoy some rest before the expected wake-up call at 11:45. "We all half believed, and I nine-tenths believed, that the Japs would be gone."[65]

Should the Japanese still be waiting for them in Betio's bunkers and pill-boxes, Marines like Montague and Seng could be walking into a disaster. As Gen. Julian Smith warned his overly optimistic officers who claimed the bombardment would obliterate the opponent, "Gentlemen, remember one thing. When the Marines land and meet the enemy at bayonet point, the only armor a Marine will have is his khaki shirt!"[66]

"COMMENCE FIRING—
THE WAR IS ON"

"Lambs Being Fattened for the Slaughter"

Gene Seng arose shortly after midnight on Saturday, November 20, after spending fitful hours alone with his thoughts. Few men around slept much either on a night like this, the night before a scheduled battle.

The inferno heat added to his discomfort. Seng had yet to put on his uniform and battle gear, and already sweat rushed down his face. Surprisingly, though, his mouth was dry, a phenomenon caused by the anticipation he and the other young Marines felt about the imminent assault.

Pfc. Albert Gilman attributed his lack of sleep to nerves and the activity about him. "We were always checking our equipment to make sure it was ready and to get rid of excess material,"[1] he explained. "Officers were going all over the place."

Nearby, Charlie Montague had little time to think of Billie. That might occur later, after he had eaten and readied his battle gear. For now, he and Gene had to rush to the galley with their unit to eat breakfast. Already, the lines were forming.

"Jesus, that will make a nice lot of guts to have to sew up—full of steak,"[2] cursed a surgeon when he saw what the Marines consumed for breakfast that morning. Having grown accustomed to such breakfast feasts in New Zealand, it seemed appropriate that a similar meal be prepared for invasion day. Surgeons, though, thinking ahead to the possibility of operating on full stomachs ripped open by shrapnel, held a different opinion.

Some Marines joked about sitting down to their "Last Supper," and Gilman felt he and the other Marines were "like lambs being fattened for the slaughter."[3] Most probably could have had toast and cereal and been just as satisfied, for their minds roamed far from the breakfast table. "You got up early and had some sort of chow your stomach wasn't interested in,"[4] said 1st Lt. Tyson Wilson, who would later head into Red 2. Somehow, light banter and joking seemed inappropriate that morning. A quiet mood had replaced the normal level of mealtime jocularity.

Pfc. Charles Wysocki wondered how some of the men could hungrily devour the steak and eggs when he did not want to even think of food. He figured that, with the impending action, he had better consume something, so he forced a few morsels into his mouth and hoped they would stay down.

After eating, Wysocki, who served in the same unit with Charlie Montague and Gene Seng, noticed a surreal atmosphere surrounding the preparations for battle. Nothing seemed normal, as each man handled things in his own way. Most, he observed, did so quietly.

"We packed our stuff away, and then packed our regular packs with what we would take with us," Wysocki explained. "We made sure our rifles were clean and operational. Breakfast was quiet. Everybody was keeping to themselves and preparing themselves for what was to come, or praying. I had no idea of what it would be like."[5]

Following breakfast, men gathered their battle gear and waited until boatswain mates piped them to the landing craft. Most carried ninety pounds of equipment into battle, including ammunition clips, field dressings, water canteens, a KA-BAR knife, a field pack containing rations and extra clothing, a bayonet, a helmet, a spade or shovel to dig foxholes, hand grenades, cigarettes, and candy. Some, like Montague, carried photos of girlfriends or other loved ones.

Even though corpsman Stanley Bowen would supposedly do no fighting, he took no chances. Besides his medical kit, which contained battle dressings, sulfa powder, cloth tourniquets, and morphine, he packed socks, blankets, an ammunition belt, a carbine, and a knife. "People don't think that corpsmen carried arms, but we did," explained Bowen. "They learned on Guadalcanal the Japs would pick off anyone with an insignia, like an officer or a corpsman, with a Red Cross. Nobody wore insignia."[6] If he had the chance, Bowen vowed, he would kill the first Jap he saw rather than let the enemy kill him.

* * *

Dirty and hot, the men gathered in the holds for their final moments before heading to deck and the landing craft. Most sported beards, whiskers, or other facial hair, but they donned clean uniforms to reduce the risk of infection from wounds. Surprisingly few men reported to sick bay to avoid the coming battle.

Some chatted with the men around them, but most retreated to an inner sanctuary where, free from the distractions, they could think of home or of what lay ahead. "You'd polish your bayonet, look at your rifle or pistol and stuff. Make sure the canteens were filled. You try to occupy your mind so you don't think of what's ahead,"[7] stated 1st Lt. Tyson Wilson.

"It wasn't the movie situation where the sarge talks to the recruits and here is what you're supposed to do, son. Nobody really said much at all," said Private First Class Muhlbach. "Normal conversation. Everybody was alone with his own thoughts. I was anxious to get into battle. I really wanted to get in there and get some Japanese in my sights."[8]

Chaplain Willard may have been the busiest man aboard ship in those early morning hours. He maneuvered from man to man, offering words of encouragement to some and reciting prayers with others. One chaplain handed out a sheet titled "Spiritual Ration for D-Day," containing biblical quotations to soothe the men's tension, while others heard hasty confessions.

Interested in how the Marines prepared for battle, Robert Sherrod meandered belowdecks. He found that most approached battle with optimism and boastfulness. "How many are you going to kill, Bunky?" one Marine shouted to his buddy. Another, no older than nineteen and obviously trying to sound tough despite the fear etched across his face, told Sherrod, "Oh, boy, I just want to shit in a dead man's face. Just open his mouth and let him have it."[9]

Pfc. James E. Peavey had less militaristic thoughts on his mind. After breakfast he gathered in a prayer group on the ship's fantail. The men prayed for success, but added the desire that "we may be taken instead of some that may not be ready to meet their maker."[10]

Stanley Bowen's eagerness bubbled to the surface. Pearl Harbor instilled hatred in him for the enemy, and now he had the opportunity to avenge what he considered a cowardly sneak attack. "It got to the point when we were actually going into battle, I couldn't wait to get in," he explained. "We were going to kill Japs right and left, and I never even pictured that they'd be firing back at us. I had a feeling that we were just going in and shoot those damn Japs."[11]

Only one item bothered him—his friend Howard's insistence that he was going to die.

"Man Your Tractors"

From the middle of a faint golden ring that surrounded the moon, a solitary star glittered in the darkness, lending a serene mien to an enterprise that would be anything but peaceful. The quarter moon provided enough light for onlookers to discern the shapes of ships as they waited to disgorge their contents toward shore. Aboard one transport, a Marine spotted boats in the swells below and worried that their engines made so much noise that the enemy would hear it.

The initial stirrings of action occurred around 4:30 A.M., shortly after 1st Lt. Wallace Nygren, platoon leader in the 2nd Amphibian Tractor Battalion, had eaten breakfast. As a member of the amtrac crews that would shepherd the Marines of the first three waves ashore, he faced a potentially difficult assignment should any significant opposition greet them at the beaches. Each amtrac contained a .30-caliber and a .50-caliber machine gun mounted at the front, but the lack of protective armor exposed both gunners to enemy fire.

When Nygren heard the command, "Tractor crews, man your tractors," he led his men deep into the lowest level of the LST (landing ship tanks), where seventeen amtracs were stored. A driver, assistant driver, and crew chief stepped into each amtrac, while Nygren and his maintenance sergeant, T. Sgt. Morris Wilmer, boarded the lead tractor.

Suddenly, as if on cue, the hold filled with fumes and reverberated with noise as the seventeen amtracs kicked to life. Nygren looked forward to emerging from the LST into the open air, where he could both dispense with the noxious fumes and avoid the ear-shattering engine sounds.

After the ship's engines halted and the anchor chain settled downward, the LST's bow doors slowly swung open. Though darkness covered everything in the early morning, Nygren spotted ocean swells and greedily whiffed the equatorial breeze that, while humid, provided welcome relief in the hold.

Nygren waited until every amtrac was ready, then gave the signal to begin. Nygren's amtrac lumbered up an approach ramp, slid down the main ramp, and successfully splashed into the dark, swelling water.

When all seventeen amtracs had safely exited the LST, Nygren led them toward the ship containing the men of the second wave he was to transport to Red Beach 2. Above, thousands of stars filled the tropical night. So far, all had gone according to schedule. Maybe this would be a simple operation, hoped Nygren.[12]

Aboard another transport, Major Crowe gathered his amtrac crews and emphasized that no one was to stop once the boats started heading toward shore—not at the reef, not to avoid explosions, not at the seawall. The boats were to keep going until they had crossed the island and reached Betio's southern shore. He gave his boat commander permission to shoot any driver who balked. In Crowe's mind, you faced two choices in an amphibious operation—move forward or die.

"Land the Landing Force"

While Nygren churned through the Pacific with the other amtracs, Stanley Bowen and the Marines of the first three waves waited in their sixteen transports eleven miles from the lagoon for the signal to climb down the rope nets—always a tricky feat in ocean swells—into landing boats that would take them to their rendezvous with Nygren and the amtracs.

At 3:30 A.M., bugles sounded the call to quarters for Marines, while Navy personnel shouted the orders "Away all boats" and "Land the landing force." The calls varied slightly from transport to transport, but they conveyed the same message to Marines—leave your thoughts behind, focus on what is ahead, and prepare yourself for battle.

Boatswain's whistles shrilled through the night as winches gently lowered landing boats over the sides. Already, noticed some of the Marines, boats circled in the waters below, reminding one correspondent of circus elephants going round and round.

Lt. Stacy C. Davis, who commanded a platoon of the 8th Marines leaving from the same ship as Staff Sergeant Hatch, tried to ease the nerves of his untested Marines. "Okay, men, now for those of you who were not with the 8th on Guadalcanal, I don't want you to feel cheated when this one is over. What we're really doing is just a little police work. We'll all be coming back right after we secure the place. We probably won't see a single Jap." He then added, "But don't worry. There's plenty of islands left and you'll get your share of combat."[13] Sergeants and lieutenants muttered similar thoughts aboard other transports in the dark morning hours.

Lt. George D. Lillibridge's calm words to his platoon as they lined up along the transport rail belied the feelings that rumbled inside. He claimed that "if everybody obeyed orders, did what he was told, did not try to play the hero, etc., we could, I was sure, get through with no one getting killed."[14]

Pfc. C. Don Jones, a member of F Company heading toward Red 2, wondered about the accuracy of the announcement that blared over the ship's public address system that the island would be secured before noon. The men around him seemed to be in good spirits. Nearby, Pfc. Paul R. Evans heard his officer bark, "Keep your eyes open, and your head and your ass down. Good luck to you all."[15]

Sergeants took final roll calls to ensure everyone was present, and reminded their men, "Be sure to correct your elevation and windage [of your weapons]. Adjust your sights."[16] Men, having been told they would be brought ashore once the assault ended, placed their bedrolls and personal belongings on deck, took a deep breath, and moved to the rail.

Slowly, and with precision, men climbed onto the rope netting draped over the transport's sides. As he stepped toward the rope, Pfc. Albert Gilman peered down at the water, which seemed so far below, and took his first step.

"Getting into the landing craft in the dark from the net seemed impossible. The hardest part of going over the side and down the landing net with such high seas was that one minute you were hanging on to the net over the side of the ship, flat on your back yet still clinging to the rope, and the next minute you were lying on the bottom of the landing craft. From them we transferred to amtracs, which again was a difficult and tricky job because of the high seas and huge waves. I now realized, 'This is war.' It made your heart skip a beat, and you begin to wonder whether this is it."[17]

"That was really spooky," stated Stanley Bowen. "You're loaded down with your pack and rifle, a first-aid kit in my case, and the ship is swaying back and forth."[18] They had been trained to seize the vertical rope lines and step onto the horizontal ones, for if they did not, they risked having their hands crushed by the Marine above. In the swaying seas, packed down with ninety pounds of hand grenades, ammunition, and other gear, no one wanted to lose his grip and plummet to the water. Once at the end of the rope netting, each Marine had to carefully time the final jump into the craft, for the landing boat could be at his boots when he released his hold but twenty feet lower by the time he fell.

The frightening reality of what they were about to do impressed Staff Sergeant Hatch and Private Kelliher as they stood on the deck of the *Heywood* and peered over the side. The men filtering into the boats carried rifles, grenades, pistols, bayonets, and knives, yet they were about to go into battle armed with cameras.

"The fact really struck me for the first time that I was going to be doing something that had never been done before. First I was going to be photographing an amphibious attack against a heavily fortified beachhead. And this [an amphibious assault] was something that had not been accomplished in most of history. Most of them had failed—Gallipoli, Dieppe. This was uppermost in my mind. I had trained for most of four years to do this, so I felt there was a lot of weight on my shoulders to be able to document what went on so that people coming afterwards could see it and understand it and maybe learn something from it and it could be used for training and whatever. That was in my mind, and of course I had no knowledge of whether I was going to be hit or knocked out, and where the other cameramen of the division might be or might not be."[19]

Hatch prayed that he would not let his buddies down, that he would uphold the honor of the Corps, and that he possessed the courage to do his job the way he was supposed to do it, which in this case meant leaving the island with an accurate film version of the fighting. He then climbed down the net into the landing craft, followed by Kelliher. Determining that the engine cover, an exposed position on the forward portion of the boat, provided the best view of the proceedings, the filmmaker sat on that spot and prepared to film what unfolded.

"Let Us Exhibit Our Samurai Spirit"

Reveille sounded at 2:00 A.M. on Betio, at which time Japanese officers notified their men that the United States fleet had been sighted off the lagoon entrance and to expect an attack at daybreak. Officers burned secret documents, then reported to headquarters to receive last-minute instructions. "We stood about in the darkness," wrote Ota later, "sweating in the tropical heat of the night, uncertain as to what lay ahead of us."[20]

Comdr. Takeo Sugai, the commanding officer of the 7th Sasebo SNLF, burned the headquarters flag, then turned to his men. Warrant Officer Ota listened intently as Sugai depicted what the next few hours might bring. "The rise or fall of our motherland may well rest on our last decisive battle," asserted Sugai. "Let us exhibit our Samurai spirit and try our best."[21] Ota and the other men vowed to die in battle if need be.

After Sugai finished, Ota collected the thirty men in his charge and led them to the lagoon side of the island, the beaches selected by the Americans as their landing site. He placed the soldiers in the reinforced machine gun and rifle positions dug in close to the water's edge west of the long pier, directly where Corporal Pemberton and the men of F Company intended to rush ashore. Ota liked his position, situated close to the borders of Red 1 and Red 2, because the beach veered back on his left flank. If the enemy tried to land near him, they would face a decimating enfilading fire from his machine guns and riflemen.

At 4:41, as Montague and Seng descended the ropes into their landing craft, a red star cluster from Admiral Shibasaki's command bunker, just inland from the eastern edge of Red Beach 3, bathed the nighttime darkness in an eerie red tint and signaled his commanders to fire their own flares when their beach positions were manned and ready. Smaller ribbons of light soon sliced the sky from multiple spots on the island, creating a festive atmosphere while informing Shibasaki that his forces were prepared for the enemy. Shibasaki then sent runners to each post granting permission to fire at their own discretion whenever they spotted a target.

"How Could Anybody Live Through That?"

Strong currents and winds disrupted the landing operation and forced Gen. Julian Smith to twice delay H-Hour, first to 8:45 and then to 9:00 A.M. Montague and Seng shook in their tiny landing craft, battling their preinvasion nerves as well as the ocean sways that doused them in water and lobbed the boats up and down. Many could not keep down the steak and eggs they had consumed a few hours earlier. Before long, dawn would bring a blazing equatorial sun and 110-degree temperatures. Drenched, apprehensive, and far from home, the uncomfortable Marines faced at least five hours in the buffeting boats before they hit the beach, but at least they took comfort in officers' reassurances that the Japanese would mount, at best, minor opposition. They could handle five to six hours aboard a miserable landing craft if it ended in a brief shoreline skirmish.

Staff Sergeant Hatch stated that he and the others believed the whole thing would be nothing more than a "walk ashore and that would be it."[22] Stanley Bowen doubted he would even have to use his medical skills and, in a strange way, anticipated the assault. "I was just looking forward to it. I was young and dumb."[23]

Action started at 5:05 when a scout plane from the USS *Maryland,* Julian Smith's command vessel, catapulted into the air. The Japanese spotted the red flash from the liftoff and fired a few shells in its direction.

The mighty American fleet immediately opened a thundering bombardment. Battleships and cruisers had formed an arc off Betio's beaches so their big guns could either rain shells directly at the enemy or weave a deadly cross fire. Now, for more than thirty minutes, the lumbering behemoths belched devastation on the enemy.

"Commence firing. The war is on,"[24] ordered the *Maryland*'s gunnery officer. Marines and sailors watched the potent exhibition with mouths open and thanked God they were not on the receiving end. A naval officer aboard the *Maryland* declared he had never seen anything like it. "The big ship flinched as though a giant had struck her with a hammer. Old trouper that she was, she quivered in every corner, dust filtered down from the overhead fixtures in flag plot. Several lighters were jarred out in that first blast, and I thought several of my teeth had been jarred out. Then the forward two turrets let go in unison, and then they alternated, forward four and after four, WHAM! WHAM!"[25]

Capt. Earl J. Wilson, a Marine press officer, watched from his transport as the combatants exchanged fire in the darkness. "First there would appear a big flash at sea," he later recalled, "then the graceful slow moving arc of twin red balls with bright flashes when they hit. Then would come a rumble like distant summer thunder." Wilson hated to admit it, but "it was beautiful to watch."[26]

One 14-inch shell smacked directly into the magazine for a Japanese 8-inch gun and produced a spectacle of pyrotechnics that rivaled any Fourth of July fireworks display any man had witnessed. Unfortunately, the concussion from the *Maryland*'s guns so severely shook the battleship that it knocked out her ability to communicate with the forces ashore. In the early hours of the battle, Julian Smith's difficulty in contacting his commanders on Betio would play a significant role.

Men in landing craft and aboard the battleships and cruisers cheered the awesome spectacle. Pfc. Jeremiah Hanafin, part of the reserve force, stood on his troopship and watched the nighttime sky brighten from the muzzle flashes and explosions. Streams of fire hurled large shells from each gun in clearly visible paths toward the island as the explosives sped toward their designated targets. "Fires burned from one end of Betio to the other," stated Hanafin. "As I watched the destruction I couldn't help thinking, 'How could anybody live through that?' "[27]

Robert Sherrod, scheduled to land with the fifth wave, rushed to the *Zeilin*'s deck for a front row seat. "There was a brilliant flash in the darkness of the half-moonlit night," Sherrod later wrote. "Then a flaming torch arched high into the air and sailed far away, slowly, very slowly, like an easily lobbed tennis ball. The red cinder was nearly halfway to its mark before we heard the thud, a dull roar as if some mythological giant had struck a drum as big as Mount Olympus."

As other ships added their fire, Sherrod thought that the sky had to be as bright as noontime. So many shells raced toward the hapless island that Sherrod compared the sight to a hail of cinder. Each time one struck Betio, Marines on the *Zeilin* cheered. "Now the Jap, the miserable, little brown man who had started this horrible war against a peace-loving people, was beginning to suffer the consequences. He had asked for this, and he should have known it before he flew into Pearl Harbor that placid Sunday morning."

Marines near Sherrod shouted that this would stifle any opposition and make their assault a simple operation. Sherrod agreed. "Surely, I thought, if there were actually any Japs left on the island (which I doubted strongly), they would all be dead by now."[28]

Warrant Officer Ota, one of those left alive, stared at the enemy ships as the initial gleams of daylight illuminated the scene. He counted thirty-six warships in the distant waters, majestically maneuvering "like floating castles." When they opened fire, Ota felt that every enemy gun must have made him its target. "We could do nothing but wait and to try to control our fear." Direct hits splintered palm trees into hundreds of pieces, rocketed entire trunks hundreds of feet into the sky, and heaped sand and dirt onto soldiers who tried to shield their ears from the numbing noise.

"This bombardment was violent beyond expression!" wrote Ota afterward. "A frightening and horrifying experience! It went on and on, without ceasing; the shriek and rumble of heavy shells and the terrific explosions. Numberless coconut palms were broken off, burned down, or shattered into splinters. My position received a direct hit but none of us were wounded; we were only buried by sand which we quickly dug away. I still marvel that so many of us escaped with our lives during this period when heavy shells were falling on the island like rain."[29]

One group on the island welcomed the thundering bombardment. The Japanese had forcibly transported Korean laborers from their homes to build Betio's defenses. Twelve-hour days combined with treatment as a second-class, inferior people intensified the hatred the Koreans felt for their overlords. "When we saw the bombs fall," said one Korean when interrogated after the battle, "we were happy, though some of us were being killed."[30]

"That's What Hell Must Be Like"

Across the waters, the young Marines and veteran correspondents were about to receive the shocks of their lives. The nighttime bombardment, brilliant in its display of sheer destructiveness, for a time lulled them into passivity, as if they were fans viewing a spectacle. That abruptly changed when they realized the show could bite back.

Private First Class Hanafin was standing on the transport *Harris*, leisurely smoking a pipe while he watched the bombardment, when suddenly an enemy shell splashed within fifty yards of the vessel. The occurrence so startled Hanafin that he accidentally bit his pipe in half. Veterans of the Solomons fighting chuckled when newer recruits ducked, as if they could somehow evade the darting missiles.

Robert Sherrod concluded the shell that splashed near his ship, *Zeilin*, must have been an errant shot from a nearby destroyer. When a second shell splashed even closer, producing "a vertical stream of water high into the air, like a picture of a geyser erupting," he turned to Maj. Howard Rice standing next to him and muttered, "My God, what wide shooting! Those boys need some practice."

Major Rice stared at Sherrod as if the correspondent had temporarily lost his sanity. "You don't think that's our own guns doing *that* shooting, do you?" he half asked, half barked at Sherrod.

Sherrod, reacting as if water had been tossed in his face, pondered what the words meant, for him and for all the young men in the landing craft below. "Then, for the first time, I realized that there were some Japs on Betio. Like a man who has swallowed a piece of steak without chewing it, I said, 'Oh.'"[31]

Elsewhere throughout the American assault force, other men absorbed the same dramatic reality—live Japanese inhabited Betio, Japanese who intended to make them pay dearly for seizing the island. They had somehow survived a bombardment that left most Marines speechless, meaning that instead of big naval guns finishing the job, men, many like Montague and Seng barely out of high school, would have to go in and pry them out. Men in khaki shirts would have to do what the Navy's mammoth guns could not.

Troop transports weighed anchor to move out of range of Betio's guns, while amtracs and Higgins boats trailed after. "Our little group of tractors bobbed up and down as we lay dead in the water, watching our ships flee," wrote First Lieutenant Nygren of his time in an amtrac. "Dark shapes loomed up out of the night and cut across our bows. We were in danger of being run down by our own ships."[32]

Nygren stared ahead, trying to find the transport carrying the men he was to take into Red 2's second wave, but in the confusion he could not locate the ship. Like many others, he improvised and boarded a group of Marines designated for the third wave, then followed the guide boat that corralled the amtracs into an uneven line and veered them toward the island.

* * *

At 5:42, according to plan, Admiral Hill ordered a cease-fire so the expected carrier air strikes could blast the Japanese defenses. Since his communications systems aboard the *Maryland* had been knocked out by the guns' concussion during the bombardment, he did not receive word that the air strikes had been delayed thirty minutes so the aviators could benefit from daylight. Admiral Hill, growing angrier as the minutes passed, fumed about the aviators' absence, while across the waters his opponent, Admiral Shibasaki, took advantage of the unexpected lull to switch more men and ammunition from the ocean side of Betio to the lagoon side.

After waiting vainly for twenty-three minutes, Hill resumed the bombardment at 6:05, then again halted it at 6:10 when the fighters and bombers from the carriers *Essex* and *Bunker Hill* abruptly arrived. The aircraft bombed and strafed Betio for ten minutes, hardly sufficient to inflict great damage, then disappeared. The one weapon Marines most wanted to see, potent two-thousand-pound daisy cutters designed to shred Shibasaki's shoreline positions and kill the Japanese manning them, were never used because the bombers from Funafuti failed to appear at all.

At 6:27 Hill again ordered the naval bombardment to commence. This time, rather than focusing on targets that had fired on the American fleet, the bombardment systematically raked every yard of Betio. Mighty guns boomed from battleships and cruisers, while destroyers moved closer to shore to blast the Japanese with their smaller batteries. For two hours the Navy hammered Shibasaki's defenses with three thousand tons of shells.

Again, the effect stunned onlookers. Rear Adm. Howard Kingman, aboard the battleship *Tennessee*, said, "It seemed almost impossible for any human being to be left alive on the island." A sailor aboard the destroyer *Ringgold* watched the island practically disappear in clouds and smoke, broken only by giant pillars of flame that shot heavenward. A man near him quietly viewed the operation and gushed, "Mate, they need firemen in there—not Marines."[33] The sailor silently agreed and thought that the Marines now heading toward shore would find nothing but dead Japanese and blazing foliage.

On the cruiser *Indianapolis*, Adm. Raymond A. Spruance's chief of staff, Capt. Charles J. Moore, said, "Fires were burning everywhere. The coconut trees were blasted and burned, and it seemed that no living soul could be on the island . . . the troops approached the beach, and it looked like the whole affair would be a walkover."[34]

A sailor on the battleship *Tennessee* claimed, "I couldn't see anything but black smoke and flames from one end of Betio to the other, and figured that's what hell must be like."[35]

The description fit the image. In three hours, ships pounded Betio with 1,436 shells, ranging from 14-inch and 16-inch giants to the smaller 5-inch shells. The island absorbed such a ferocious blasting that after the battle, Marines found American shell fragments on almost every yard.

The appearance belied the actual damage. The bombardment knocked out Shibasaki's lines of communications with his subordinates, forcing him to rely on using runners, a less reliable system in the heat of battle. It also destroyed almost every aboveground installation and many of Shibasaki's large weapons, such as the three 8-inch guns and many antiboat guns, but the hundreds of smaller beach defense guns, machine guns, and pillboxes emerged intact. The Japanese had so sturdily reinforced them that no shell, large or small, could obliterate the target.

"They put a lot of stuff out about big naval gunfire, and the Navy pronounced that you will walk across the beach and wipe out everything," said 1st Lt. Tyson Wilson. "They did the best they could, but this was the first time the Navy had used gunfire and close air support against fortified positions. The Japanese pillboxes and bunkers were reinforced steel concrete, coconut logs, and sand, so whenever the Navy shot into this stuff, it would eat 16-inch shells and they [the shells] went poof. It didn't do anything. So you had to get up on the bunkers and get in the ports to destroy them."[36]

Ironically, as the bombardment continued, explosions hampered the effectiveness of subsequent shellings. A heavy pall of dirt hovered over the island, making it difficult for naval observers to detect where shots landed and how much adjustment was needed to hit their targets.

Some ship commanders erred on the safe side to ensure their shells hit land rather than splashing into the water. The overcautiousness, however, caused more of the projectiles to hit inland and fewer to blast the strong fortifications standing along the island's shoreline.

Consequently Montague, Seng, Bowen, and the other Marines would not, as many expected, approach silent bunkers filled with dead Japanese. The Marines would instead be welcomed by alert defenders with fire in their eyes—eyes that already were peering over gunsights aimed directly at khaki shirts.

The Navy Clears the Way

An unlikely force of two small minesweepers and two destroyers formed the vanguard of the assault. While the amtracs churned toward the line of departure, at 6:20 the destroyer *Ringgold* hoisted battle colors and, accompanied by her sister destroyer *Dashiell*, headed inside the lagoon. Their mission was to suppress enemy fire and enable the minesweepers *Pursuit* and *Requisite* to clear a three-hundred-yard-wide channel through which the amtracs would follow. Though the vessels found no mines to destroy, they maneuvered directly under the eyes of the Japanese and within point-blank range. Exposed to the enemy's guns while they completed their dangerous task, *Pursuit* and *Requisite* marked the path toward Betio for Montague, Seng, and the others.

The destroyers *Ringgold* and *Dashiell* fired almost six hundred 5-inch rounds at enemy locations in support of the minesweepers. Fortunately for all four ships, inaccurate Japanese gunfire left them largely untouched. At 7:11 one shell crashed through the *Ringgold*'s starboard side but failed to explode. Immediately afterward a second shell punctured amidship, passed through the sick bay and emergency radio room, and wounded two men, but it, too, proved to be a dud.

Crewmen had to take fast action, however, to repair a hole nine inches wide and twenty-four inches long below the *Ringgold*'s waterline. Lt. Wayne A. Parker earned the first of many Navy Crosses to be awarded for Betio when, like the Dutch boy in the famous child's story, he plugged the hole with his body until other men rushed up with mattresses and timbers to stem the flow of water gushing into the aft engine room. Parker and a few other men then gingerly removed the unexploded Japanese shell from the ship's switchboard, carried it topside, and tossed it over the side.

Warrant Officer Ota witnessed this strange duel from his position near the beach with fascination and incredulity. The American destroyers drew within one thousand yards as they steamed back and forth supporting the gallant minesweepers. "With the naked eye we could clearly see the American sailors on the destroyers' decks,"[37] he remarked in astonishment.

Not far from Ota, Petty Officer Tadao Oonuki attempted to start his tank when the four enemy vessels entered the lagoon, but the engine refused to turn. When a second tank lumbered over and nudged Oonuki forward, the engine coughed to life, but the action created so much smoke that an American destroyer immediately rained shells on the area, "a move that we found most terrifying,"[38] Oonuki told interrogators later. Oonuki steered the tank toward the airfield until he reached a concealed position commanding the western section of the beaches. Oonuki decided he would fight out the battle from that spot.

At 7:15, after completing their initial task in the lagoon, *Pursuit* and *Requisite* marked the line of departure, the point in the water where the landing craft veered in toward the beaches, for the approaching amtracs. The first three waves, containing Montague, Seng, and the rest of the assault forces, soon came into view.

Toward Betio

The amtracs held the key to the entire operation, for they had the capability of traversing any type of terrain Betio offered. They would transport the assault waves beyond the beaches into Betio's interior; they would first taste the fury of Shibasaki's defenses; they would first pit Marines against the Special Navy Landing Force.

The landing craft bobbed up and down in the Pacific swells like pieces of cork, matching the turbulent feelings with which many Marines struggled that early morning hour of November 20, 1943. Soon the tiny craft, each carrying up to twenty Marines, would sever the ties with their troop transport, churn through the waters to the rendezvous point with hundreds of other landing craft, and then head toward the beach, scores of armed tentacles reaching from the mammoth troop transports and battlewagons toward what was hoped would be an undefended beach.

Standing in his amtrac, First Lieutenant Nygren faced a long, hard journey before even touching Betio's sands. After collecting his men and heading to a rendezvous point between the transports and lagoon, Nygren had to travel three and one-half miles to the line of departure just inside the lagoon. From there he and the other amtracs would swing toward the island, then start the six-thousand-yard run-in that ended on Betio.

Forty-two amtracs containing eighteen Marines each constituted the first wave. One hundred yards behind came the second wave of twenty-four amtracs, each holding twenty Marines, and another one hundred yards to the rear the third wave of twenty-one amtracs, each ferrying twenty men. Eight empty amtracs waited behind the first wave and five behind the third in case any boat sustained damage or stalled in the choppy waters. The fourth through tenth waves, comprising the Higgins boats that required at least three feet of water over the reef, would then land at five-minute intervals. If the operation proceeded according to plan, three thousand Marines would be ashore within thirty minutes, followed by another six thousand by noon.

Robert Sherrod worried that if the rest of the day continued like the start, they were headed for trouble. Before his Higgins boat had moved one-half mile from the transport, the ocean spray doused every man aboard with surprisingly cold water. Drenched and shivering, Sherrod took out a small bottle of brandy given him by a doctor and shared it with the Marine next to him, thinking both how odd it was to be quaffing shots before 7:00 A.M. yet how appropriate under the circumstances. "My only memory of the first hour and a half of the ride toward the beachhead is sheer discomfort, alternating with exaltation," he later wrote. "Our warships and planes were now pounding the little island of Betio as no other island had been pounded in the history of warfare."[39]

Sherrod needed the brandy. As the waves headed closer, Japanese shells burst directly above the open boats, but fortunately for the Americans, the Japanese had placed so much powder into the shells that when they exploded, the shrapnel was pulverized. Instead of spraying deadly metallic shrapnel on the defenseless Marines and causing numerous casualties, the missiles dusted the young Marines with powder.

By 8:20 the amtracs waited at the line of departure. Marines glanced at one another, each wondering if he looked as nervous as the man next to him.

At a signal, the three long lines of amtracs executed a ninety-degree turn, and for the first time the men stared directly at Betio's shores. With each yard of water the amtracs progressed, the island drew closer and closer.

"WE HAVE NOTHING LEFT TO LAND"

"The God of Death Has Come!"

At 8:24 the first wave of amtracs crossed the line of departure and churned toward Betio, still six thousand yards away. Even though they had received fire, the amtracs and the Higgins boats that followed sustained little damage, leading the Marines to cling to their hopes for a quick operation. They faced an open stretch of water to the reef, the reef itself, and a final run-in of seven hundred yards to what, hopefully, would be a quiet beach.

Warrant Officer Ota had other ideas as he silently watched his enemy draw nearer to the reef. Fortunately for the Japanese the waters at the reef had receded, exposing the hard, sharp coral in some spots. The unpredictable tides had worked in their favor—a happy omen—and Ota squinted straight ahead and waited for the American landing boats to grind to a sudden stop on Betio's protective reef. Stuck at that vulnerable position, the Americans would be sitting ducks for the Japanese guns that would tear into them while still seven hundred yards from shore. The enemy would suffer dearly for their gamble, mused Ota.

At 8:55, fifteen minutes before the first American touched Betio's sands, Rear Admiral Hill halted the naval bombardment. He feared that the excessive amount of smoke that draped Betio would blind his naval gunners and that shells would fall into the Marines heading to shore. General Smith and Colonel Edson argued against the cease-fire, which they thought would allow the enemy to operate unimpeded while the exposed Marines drew closer, but Hill refused to alter his order.

The Japanese again used the respite to shift troops from other places on the island to the landing sites. "Because the naval bombardment had ceased," Ota wrote later, "we took advantage of the opportunity to position ourselves carefully, to emplace our machine gunners and riflemen in the best spots, and to rearrange our ammunition supplies to the best advantage."[1] He confidently stared out across the lagoon toward the reef, cradling the gun with which he intended to kill the enemy. Montague, Seng, Muhlbach, and the others would have to advance the final leg of their journey, an almost mile-long stretch where Japanese guns could most horribly punish the Americans, without naval gunfire shielding them.

The first wave of amtracs split into three groups. On the American left, Major Crowe's 2d Battalion, 8th Marines, including Gilman, Hatch, and Muhlbach, headed southeast toward Red 3. In the center, Lieutenant Colonel Amey's 2d Battalion, 2d Marines, the unit containing the men of F Company, churned southwest to Red 2. The group on the right flank, Major Schoettel's 3d Battalion, 2d Marines, containing Montague, Seng, and Captain Crain, veered toward Red 1.

Ota's heart almost stopped when he witnessed the next development. Instead of stalling at the reef, the American landing craft rammed into it, churned up and over, and continued toward the island, "like dozens of spiders scattering over the surface of the water. One of my men exclaimed, 'Heavens! The God of Death has come!'"[2] In his long military career, Ota had never seen landing craft with that capability, but here was the enemy, brushing aside the reef as if it were a mere pebble. If every enemy landing craft could so easily cross, he and his fellow defenders faced a trying morning.

Hawkins Moves In

If one had a death wish, the assault waves were the place to be. The amtracs had to ignore the defenses lining the shores, hit the beaches and, without pausing, advance inland before dropping off their Marines. Men in the following waves would eliminate the beach pillboxes and bunkers, but the assault waves were to ram a lodgment as deep as possible into Betio. That meant that Montague, Seng, and the other 1,500 men of the first three waves would storm ashore first and would kill—or be killed—before the battle was one hour old.

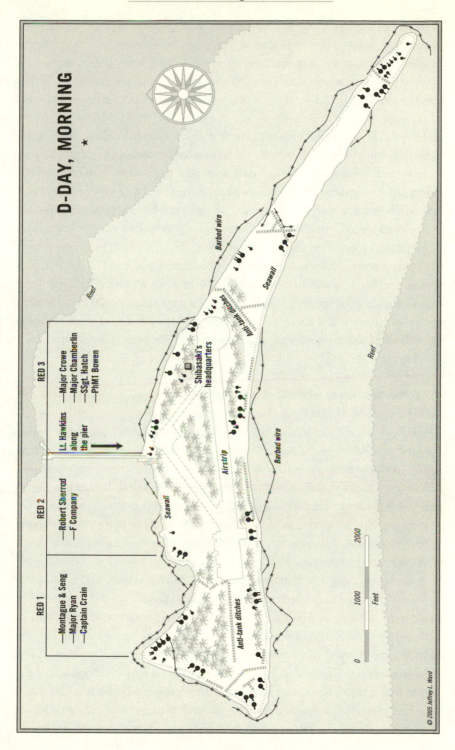

D-DAY, MORNING

RED 1
—Montague & Seng
—Major Ryan
—Captain Crain

RED 2
—Robert Sherrod
—F Company

RED 3
—Major Crowe
—Major Chamberlin
—SSgt. Hatch
—PhM1 Bowen

Lt. Hawkins
along
the pier

Shibasaki's
headquarters

Reef

Reef

Reef

Barbed wire

Barbed wire

Barbed wire

Seawall

Seawall

Seawall

Airstrip

Anti-tank ditches

Anti-tank ditches

0   1000   2000
              Feet

© 2005 Jeffrey L. Ward

Those in the assault waves who dared look at Betio quickly pulled back. Thick black smoke, interrupted in many spots by immense pillars of flame, blanketed the island. Once-luscious palm trees, now little more than twisted charcoal splinters, resembled burned sticks, devoid of all foliage. Machine gun bullets clanked off the amtracs' sides and mortar shells agitated the water yards away.

Despite the natural inclination to seek shelter, the men could do nothing but wait in the wet misery of the amtrac, shivering in the cold even though the temperature on the equatorial island would soon soar to near one hundred degrees, and try to block out the noise, the smoke, and the fear. Once on land they could fight back, but out here in the lagoon, Marines could only hope that the next mortar shell would not obliterate their landing craft. Every yard through the choppy waters intensified their fears, for it brought them closer to Japanese guns.

As each amtrac hit the reef, sudden jolts rattled the craft and shook each man out of his stupor. Drivers gunned the engines to propel the machines over, further jostling the men inside before the amtracs landed with a splash in the lagoon. Enemy fire increased a hundredfold, as machine guns, mortars, and rifles opened a thundering greeting for the Americans who dared enter their lagoon.

While the first wave was still 1,500 yards from shore, a Higgins boat containing Hawkins and his scout-snipers detached from the main force and churned toward the end of the 700-yard pier that extended from the boundary of Red 2 and Red 3 to the reef. Hawkins's job was to clear the wooden structure of Japanese soldiers, both to eliminate enemy opposition and to provide a path along which to bring in men and supplies. If he failed, Japanese machine guns would mount a devastating cross fire against either Red 2 or Red 3. Depending on what happened in the first few minutes of the battle, the pier could either be a lifeline of support to the men fighting ashore, or an avenue of death.

At 8:55, just as Admiral Hill halted the naval bombardment, Hawkins and five other men, armed with flamethrowers, KA-BAR knives, and small arms, leapt onto the seaplane ramp that extended from the pier's end. Hawkins killed four enemy soldiers by tossing a grenade into their position; then he and his scout-snipers, reinforced by a squad of combat engineers, steadily moved down the pier toward shore, ducking behind gasoline drums or crates as they scampered along. The vicious hand-to-hand fighting that unfolded at the pier set the tone for the remainder of the battle—Betio would be no walkover as some had projected. Rifles and mortars and machine guns would not inflict all the damage. Knives, bayonets, and bare hands would contribute their share.

Hawkins and his men knocked out at least six Japanese machine guns and killed twenty-five men before he ordered everyone back to the reef, but more Japanese reoccupied the structure after he left. His action only temporarily cleared the pier. For much of the battle, Marines faced sporadic enemy fire from that location.

Back at the reef, Hawkins searched for an amtrac so he could go in with the first waves, but the man who most wanted to fight was to be denied. Pinned down by enemy fire, an angry Hawkins would not reach shore until mid-afternoon.

PART I: APPROACH TO RED 1

"Annihilation Beach"

The soft-spoken Capt. J. Wendell Crain maintained the same calm demeanor in battle that he did during training, a phenomenon that reassured the younger men under him. During frightening nights on Guadalcanal, Crain visited each foxhole and offered words of encouragement. He figured if his men noticed his coolness, they would react in a similar manner.

The Solomons appeared placid compared to the holocaust unfolding ahead. "I don't recall how far we were from shore when all hell let loose," stated one Marine, who was in Captain Crain's K Company as his amtrac approached Red 1. "The amtrac started getting hit and our first reaction was that the tractors on our flanks had lost control of their guns. The sudden realization that there were Japs still alive on the island and capable of resistance snapped everyone out of their joviality. I remember a violent, turbulent trip shoreward—explosions, detonations, bodies slumping and bloody, and finally crunching to a stop; somebody screaming, 'Get the hell out, fast!'—throwing equipment out and scrambling over the side onto the beach."[3]

An amtrac near Captain Crain exploded and spun in the water from a direct hit. Machine gun tracers raced at them from shore, while flanking fire ripped into their ranks from the cove on their right and from a series of defenses called the Pocket to their left. Crain knew if he did not land his men fast, they might never make it. He tried to communicate via walkie-talkie with his lieutenants aboard other amtracs, but the water-soaked devices failed to work.

To avoid the devastating fire coming from the Pocket to their left, most of the amtracs veered toward the western, or right, end of Red 1, including the boat carrying Montague and Seng. That maneuver only took the Texas pals and everyone else directly into the four 75mm antiboat guns manned by Petty Officer Matsuo Chuma and his crew. Those Japanese guns pumped round after round into the vulnerable amtracs as they navigated their way shoreward from the reef. Montague and Seng crouched low in the amtrac to offer smaller targets, even though that mattered little in the case of a direct hit. Machine gun bullets smacked off the thin metallic sides or screeched close overhead.

As occurred at the other beaches, the cleverly camouflaged men commanded by Warrant Officer Ota inflicted terrible punishment on the Marines coming ashore, who advanced in the open against a hidden enemy. The cautious Ota reminded his men, "Keep quite cool! Do not shoot until they come within range!" Ota did not want to waste ammunition by having his men fire before the guns could be effective. Once the enemy drew within 150 yards of his guns, Ota could not miss.

"All our positions [at all beaches] opened on the enemy landing craft with a tremendous volume of machine gun and rifle fire. The Americans appeared to be surprised and confused." Before Ota's eyes, amtracs collided with each other and Higgins boats ran up on the reef, while Marines leapt out of blazing craft. "We took advantage of this opportunity and directed a great volume of fire at the enemy troops struggling in the water."[4]

"An antiboat gun stopped our craft about thirty yards from shore," stated Pfc. Richard M. Larsen of his approach to Red 1. "We were in the midst of all kinds of fire. We jumped out into the shallow water and ran around to the back of the craft. A bullet hit me in the left side of the back of my neck. There were four of us behind the tractor, and we were trapped there. They threw mortar shells, machine gun bullets, and rifle bullets at us."[5]

One of Captain Crain's cohorts, Capt. William E. Tatom, commander of I Company, peeked over the top of the amtrac's side, looked at Red 1 for a moment, then collapsed onto the deck. "He just sort of grunted when he was hit," a Marine nearby said. "He'd taken a bullet directly in his forehead. He was dead before he hit the deck."[6]

As Cpl. Norman Moise's amtrac tried to reach land, he spotted two Marines in the water. He ordered his driver to swing over and retrieve the men, but they signaled Moise away. "No, get that damned thing away from me!"[7] one shouted to Moise. They wanted nothing to do with what they considered such an obvious target to the Japanese gunners ashore. Some Marines clung to one of the pyramid-shaped concrete obstacles that dotted the waters off Betio, frozen in fear, rather than advancing to the beach.

In another amtrac bound for Red 1, Warrant Officer John Leopold tried vainly to reach shore, but could locate no safe route through the hail of fire. Leopold recalled, "The tracers and bullets cracked through the air like pistol shots, coming so fast it was like popcorn. The tracers crisscrossed, and the whole area was a pattern of thin red lines of flame. Every now and then an amtrac would go up in flames."

Leopold stared straight ahead, wondering where to go and how to land the Marines. It seemed that no other boat had successfully reached shore, let alone driven inland to deposit its men. "We swore everyone on the beach was dead. We thought no one was alive because we didn't see how any got in." Leopold had been told the night before that more than a thousand men would hit the beach in the assault waves, but he doubted even three hundred still breathed. Of Red 1 Leopold said, "The beach should have been called Annihilation Beach. It was red with blood."[8]

Pfc. Newman M. Baird's amtrac, with twenty-five men of I Company, took its first hit one hundred yards from shore. A lieutenant yanked the lifeless form of the driver away, but he was killed before he drove the boat much farther in. When a third shell incapacitated the amtrac thirty yards from shore, Baird shouted, "Let's get the hell outa here!"[9] By the time Baird reached the relative safety of the seawall, only he and three others of the twenty-five had survived.

Pfc. Edward J. Moore drove his amtrac, which he called My Delores, to the Bird's Beak, aiming to power it right over the seawall. The amtrac stalled in an upright position at the wall, however, forcing Moore to hastily abandon the craft as bullets punctured through the bottom.

Montague and Seng's amtrac somehow coursed through the gauntlet of shells. Nearby explosions drowned out the engine noise and numbed their ears. Only yards from shore a terrifying shriek, followed by an explosion, disabled their amtrac and forced the survivors into the water. Montague and Seng leapt over the side, sagging under the burden of carrying their .30-caliber machine guns and ammunition as they waded toward shore. They kicked up water dyed red by the floating bodies of dead comrades. Stifling the urge to cry out, the pair battled their way through a barbed wire entanglement that snared some of the others, then stumbled onto the beach as bullets peppered the waters about their feet.

"I could have stretched my arms out and lost them at the elbows, there were so many bullets splashing around me," said Cpl. Henry Duke, who waded ashore near Montague and Seng. "I was trying to stay low in the water and save my butt."

Duke collapsed, exhausted from the ordeal and doubting he could move another inch, but when bullets hit near him, "I made about twenty feet in three steps. I found I wasn't tired at all!"[10]

"A Kaleidoscope of Destruction"

While Captain Crain's K Company swarmed ashore on the left half of Red 1 at 9:10, the remnants of the now-deceased Captain Tatom's I Company hit the right half. "At each step I marveled at still being alive," explained one survivor of the chaos at Red 1. "By the time I had reached a point where the water was only knee deep I felt that surely I would reach the sanctuary of the sea wall— I had cried like a baby and prayed aloud, and somehow felt that I was receiving divine assistance at that moment."[11] The man looked around from the seawall and saw men dropping to the beach and amtracs smoking in the water.

Still in his Higgins boat with the fourth wave outside the reef, Maj. Michael P. Ryan watched a disaster unfolding before him. Flames from body-draped amtracs blazed out of control, and the men on land hugged the seawall. "Ahead of us was a kaleidoscope of destruction," he said later. "Many of the amtracs were burning with the shimmering heat of burning diesel fuel. Two Marines crawled out of a burning tractor with their clothing on fire; they stood erect on the side of the tractor, outlined against the smoke for a few seconds; then slowly, ever so slowly, they fell face down into the water."[12]

Disaster did not occur because, at crucial moments such as this, men risked their lives for those behind. A young Marine, one of only four of twenty men in his unit to reach the security offered by the seawall, knew that if someone did not destroy the machine gun that had killed his buddies, it would inflict similar bloodshed on following waves. The Marine, already bleeding from a shoulder wound, rose to his feet and leapt over the log barricade.

Other men heard a collection of voices beyond the seawall shouting in both Japanese and English. Suddenly, a hand grenade exploded just as machine gun fire erupted. When Marines advanced to the spot, they found two dead Japanese, obviously blown apart by the grenade, plus the body of the young Marine, almost cut in half by the machine gun fire that riddled him a split second after he tossed his hand grenade. The Marine sacrificed his life to make it easier for his buddies. One less machine gun meant a reduction in enemy gunfire, which meant less resistance for those following.

Eventually, men from I Company poured over the seawall and moved about fifty yards inland, where they destroyed some of the antiboat guns. However, they soon became pinned down and could neither advance nor retreat. Unfortunately, their brethren in K Company fared no better.

"We Couldn't See Them"

Captain Crain's amtrac safely made it to the beach, where he jumped out and led his men onto the left half of Red 1. His senior corpsman tumbled out of the amtrac immediately, and when he let out a terrible yell Crain looked back to see that his corpsman had been hit badly in the hip. Crain rushed back and administered one of the morphine syrettes he carried, then gave the corpsman some medicinal brandy.

"Doc, this is all I can do for you right now," shouted Crain. "I'm gonna come back in half an hour and see if I can't do more."

Crain returned to his men to organize an advance, but he never forgot about the young corpsman. True to his word, Crain returned in half an hour, but the corpsman had died. "He'd lost a lot of blood. A young guy about twenty-one or twenty-two, real sharp, who wanted to become a doctor after the war. He would've made a fine one."[13]

Japanese fire wiped out much of Crain's K Company before they had a chance to fight. As they left their amtracs, the men stepped directly into the paths of several Japanese machine guns. "We were raked from all directions," stated one member of K Company. "People were getting killed wholesale; those of us who could leapt into shell craters, holes and whatever for cover. Every once in a while someone would attempt to return fire with whatever he had, but if exposed would be immediately killed."[14]

With bullets kicking up sand on all sides, Crain prepared the survivors for an advance inland. If he did not lead his men off the beach, the waves coming in would have no place to land, so it was imperative that he do something. Some already looked as if they would not budge, for even though the enemy fortifications that killed so many of their brethren had to be within grenade range, strangely, the Japanese soldiers manning those fortifications could not be seen. This phenomenon occurred throughout the three-day battle. The combatants on Betio frequently stood yards, even feet apart, yet the Marines rarely spotted the enemy soldiers.

"We couldn't see them, and they were still firing at us," explained Crain. "We were on a sandy beach with absolutely no protection. You start scrambling to try to get away from the fire, and try to get in a shell hole. You're desperate for cover, and people are scattered."[15]

Captain Crain had been at sporting events and other functions that produced noise, but nothing matched the voluminous crack of machine guns, the *pop-pop* of rifle fire, and the plaintive cries of the wounded. "I was shouting at the top of my lungs to communicate with my men,"[16] said Captain Crain later.

Even worse was the ear-shattering sound emitted by strafing American fighters. Whenever they dived toward the beach, which was almost every minute during the first few hours, Crain wanted to scream back at them, not just to remove the terrifying sound but to tell them that they strafed his Marines as well. In the furious melee that was Betio, with the Japanese and Americans shooting and killing from feet apart, American aviators were bound to accidentally hit American Marines.

Of Crain's five lieutenants, in the early moments Japanese fire badly wounded one and killed three more. His unit absorbed more than 50 percent losses before heading inland, with much of the battle yet to be fought. Though death and danger surrounded him, the moment he stepped onto the beach Crain felt that he would be safe. "I've made it to the beach," he told himself. "I'm gonna make it through this fight."[17]

"Stark and Heroic Stories"

Meanwhile Admiral Hill and Gen. Julian Smith waited for word from shore. Did the landing succeed? Were the men rushing inland and freeing space for the later waves of Marines? Before the first amtrac returned, an initial message came through. HAVE LANDED. UNUSUALLY HEAVY OPPOSITION. CASUALTIES 70 PERCENT. As if that were not disheartening enough, the final two words indicated the seriousness of the first few moments ashore. CAN'T HOLD![18]

The early moments at Red 1 had gone to the Japanese. Admiral Shibasaki hoped to prevent the first waves from penetrating inland, which would delay the landings of the following waves and tie up the American assault at the reef. With nowhere to go, the Marines and boats in the water would be easy targets for his longer-range guns and mortars. Once he destroyed those troops, he could then destroy the forces stranded on the beaches.

* * *

From his Higgins boat at the reef, Major Schoettel fretted about the situation ashore. He had lost contact with I Company and had no way of knowing if they controlled any portion along the right flank of Red 1. At least Captain Crain on the left side managed to radio him, but the message was not encouraging. Crain indicated that his men had moved approximately fifty yards inland, but had become pinned down and could not advance due to heavy gunfire.

At 9:59 Schoettel sent a message to Colonel Shoup. BOATS HELD UP ON REEF, RIGHT FLANK RED 1. TROOPS RECEIVING HEAVY FIRE IN THE WATER. When Shoup ordered Schoettel to land his reserve troops on Red 2 and have them attack west toward Red 1, Schoettel replied, WE HAVE NOTHING LEFT TO LAND.[19]

The impact of Schoettel's stark words stunned Shoup and other commanders. If it was true that Schoettel had nothing left to land, what might be happening on the other beaches? Unless Captain Crain at Red 1 and his cohorts on Red 2 and Red 3 could keep the attack going and move the assault waves off the beaches, the prognosis appeared bleak. So far, at Red 1, the assault had collapsed into sporadic uncoordinated movements by one or two men.

The outcome of battles often depends upon good or bad fortune. In the course of swerving from the heavy fire to the right, Montague and Seng's platoon turned directly into the complex of pillboxes and bunkers anchored by Petty Officer Chuma's four 75mm antiboat guns two hundred yards east of the Bird's Beak. A deadly arsenal of antiboat guns, machine guns, rifles, and hand grenades ripped into the Marine ranks as the men sloshed ashore, wet and weary. Since the Japanese had not completed the four-foot seawall at this spot, the Marines had no place to hide and were caught out in the open. A slaughter ensued.

As bullets kicked up sand about them, Montague and Seng quickly set up their machine guns and started firing at the nearest Japanese pillboxes less than twenty yards away. The pair and the other survivors destroyed a handful of enemy positions, but the Japanese had too much firepower. In a few ghastly moments, thirty-one men out of forty in the platoon perished. None had advanced farther than one hundred feet.

Among the bodies littering the beach were those of Charlie Montague and Gene Seng, lying side by side on Betio's hot sands. One could trace the route taken by the men of Montague and Seng's platoon by following the trail of bodies—some lay grotesquely mangled in the amtrac, and others bobbed in the water, still appearing in death as if attempting to escape the barbed wire that trapped them. Some rested on the beach, half in the water and half on the sand, while a few, like Montague and Seng, lay on the sand next to their weapons.

The boys who had been inseparable since high school, who wanted nothing more than to finish the war so they could return to Billie and June, died together, vainly trying to mount an answer to the Japanese weapons that sliced through their fellow Marines. The San Antonio schoolboys perished before the battle was thirty minutes old. They died before most Marines, including four who earned the Medal of Honor, even stepped foot on Betio, and like many others who died on the beaches of Betio, their exact feats will never be known. Those who might have testified in their behalf could not, for they, too, died in the opening moments.

"There were stark and heroic stories in those first three hours of attack, many of them never to be written because the principals and witnesses are dead,"[20] wrote newspaper correspondent Jim Lucas, present to cover the fight for readers back home. Montague, Seng, and hundreds like them on Betio received no honors, but their deeds matched those of any medal-winner—they died fulfilling their duty for their country.

PART II: APPROACH TO RED 2

"My God, What the Hell Am I Doing Here?"

Second Lieutenant Joseph J. Barr could not say much for his luck. He had not even reached shore, yet he had already been wounded twice. About four hundred yards out he had risen in the amtrac to take a peek at the beaches when an explosion hurled shrapnel in his face and neck. A few moments later a shell knocked out his amtrac, and as he climbed out one side he was hit in the right shoulder. "I was convinced that every Jap on the Island [sic] was shooting at me,"[21] Barr wrote. Once on the beach he lay still for a moment, then hastened to the seawall.

Barr's experience typified what the men of F Company, 2d Battalion, 2d Marines, faced when the amtracs brought them in at Red 2. A vicious cross fire from the Pocket, which stood to the right of Red 2, and from the pier on the left tore into their ranks. Barbed wire and other underwater obstacles funneled the landing craft toward approaches that the Japanese had already presited for their guns. Once reaching shore, survivors faced numerous pillboxes, rifle pits, and antiboat emplacements.

Cpl. Noal C. Pemberton expected an easy affair until an explosion rocked his amtrac and drenched everyone inside. "It dawned on me—someone is shooting at us!" he recalled. The assault quickly turned into a frightening ride through cascading water and loud noises. "Shells were exploding all around us, bullets were zinging and bouncing off the amtrac, and the closer to shore we got the louder and faster it went."

A man near Pemberton could not avoid the temptation to look over the side at the tempest. "My God," he muttered when he slumped back down, his face now ghostly white, "I just saw an amtrac get blown up right next to us!"[22] Pemberton peered out and spied an amtrac tipped on its side, burning furiously, with a collection of bodies floating facedown beside it. Nearby, Marines waded to the beach from other damaged amtracs. Sadly, Pemberton noticed, some Marines fell into the water without rising.

Navy Lt. Comdr. Patrick Grogan, assigned as the beachmaster for Red 2, the man who directed boats in and out, felt as if he were in a surreal world as he rode in his amtrac. "It was like being completely suspended, like being under a strong anesthetic; not asleep, not even in a nightmare, just having everything stop except pain and fear and death. Everyone was afraid. No one was too proud to admit it. Our voices sounded like the voices of complete strangers, voices we had never heard before."[23]

Nineteen-year-old Pfc. C. Don Jones of F Company watched breathlessly as huge water geysers erupted around his amtrac and large shells skipped across the water, tumbling end on end in their maddening path. In rapid succession, the American manning the starboard machine gun slumped backward into the amtrac with a hole through his forehead, and a bullet hit and killed the Marine next to Jones.

First Lieutenant Wallace Nygren's amtrac hit the reef, chugged over in lurching movements, then splashed into the calmer waters beyond. Japanese mortars and machine guns quickly churned the water to foam. Nygren and another man tried to answer with their machine guns, but the feeble response barely made an impact. Nygren spotted a barrier of concrete blocks protruding from the water, each sporting iron spikes, with barbed wire filling the gaps between the blocks.

"The surface of the water ahead looked like rain was falling on it," said Nygren of the intense gunfire in front of them. "A shower of steel was sweeping the barbed wire. The gaps were fire lanes for the enemy guns which had now opened up."[24]

As another amtrac neared Red 2, Japanese soldiers from behind the seawall tossed hand grenades toward the invaders. The athletic Cpl. John Spillane, who had been scouted by the St. Louis Cardinals baseball team because of his outstanding throwing arm, caught four grenades and quickly hurled them back over the seawall before they exploded. The fifth grenade, however, erupted in his hand, transforming the appendage into little more than mangled bone and torn tendons. For Spillane, the battle and his sporting career ended in the early minutes of fighting, but not before his baseball skills saved the twenty men in his boat.

"Heads down, we're heading in," the driver shouted to those who could hear in Pfc. Robert R. Twitchell's amtrac. "Make sure you have everything with you because you can't come back for it—get ready to jump when I give the word." Twitchell noticed some boys were praying, while others stared straight ahead, alone with their thoughts. As they drew closer to shore the enemy fire intensified. Bullets clanged off the armor plating and mortar shells erupted close by. In the final moments before he jumped out of the amtrac, Twitchell wondered to himself, "My God, my God, what the hell am I doing here?"[25]

Second Lieutenant Paul DuPre thought he had never seen such a disgusting sight. Marine bodies, all facedown, floated in the waters off Betio as he inched closer to shore, but what caught his attention was a slight movement among the bodies. "There were a lot of Marine bodies floating," DuPre later explained. "Some had their intestines about five to six yards following them, and a fish would be nibbling at the end. When I got to the beach I asked another officer where the front lines were and he said, 'Get down! You're standing on it!' That was my introduction to Tarawa."[26]

The amtracs' safest move was to head straight for the beach and hope for the best. Nygren's boat churned through the barbed wire off Red 2, dragging fifty feet of mangled wire as it continued toward shore, then hit the beach with a sudden jar. A bullet smacked into Nygren's right hand, and another killed a sergeant who had jumped onto the gun platform to take over the .50-caliber machine gun from the wounded Nygren.

Nygren looked at the Marines, surprised they remained inside the amtrac when they should have been leaping to shore. He shouted for them to jump out, but still they crowded together inside the boat, frozen in fear. "I cursed and swore at them," wrote Nygren. "They wouldn't budge. I was semihysterical screaming every name at them I could think of." When that failed to budge the young Marines, Nygren shamed them into action. "I finally told them they were not Marines, and belonged in the Army."[27] Slowly, the men rose and left the boat.

Many of the men from F Company, trapped in the water, sought the shelter of the pier. Partially shielded by the wooden supports, the men inched step by step toward the beach. As Pfc. James Peavey waded in chest-deep water, a photographer standing on the pier snapped his image from above. A look of concern dominated his face, which had already witnessed more than he expected. Plus, Peavey fretted about an additional concern—he had never learned to swim and being in the water made him more than uncomfortable.

Close by, Pfc. Jack Preston Jr. jumped into the water near the pier when his amtrac's engine quit. Preston walked straight toward shore as he had been trained, passing through bullet splashes that increased in number as he neared the beach. Upon hitting the sand, Preston ran to the nearest shell hole, jumped in, and saw that he had halted directly beside the body of one of his friends. Upon seeing his first dead, Preston said, "Then I knew it was real."[28]

"His Own Private War"

Along with E Company to its right, F Company landed on Red 2 at 9:22, twelve minutes after Seng and Montague landed at Red 1. In its efforts to expand the beachhead, F Company suffered losses of more than 50 percent.

First Lieutenant Wayne F. Sanford, the executive officer of F Company, and Second Lieutenant Barr, the commanding officer of F Company's 3d Platoon, typified the course of events at Red 2. In the absence of their superior officer, in this case the wounded Capt. Warren Morris, junior officers like Sanford or Barr assumed command and, for much of the next two days, led the charge.

The men of F Company and other Marines at Red 2 had made it ashore, but they held on by the slimmest of margins. Most waited at the seawall, yards from the waterline, where a peculiar pattern had already formed in the sand— five or six dead Marines fanning out in front of enemy pillboxes. If the hellish reception was that bad, how much worse would the fighting become beyond the seawall? Pfc. C. Don Jones said later, "Nobody pretended he wasn't afraid. Every man there had fought his own private war to reach that hole."[29]

Each man blessed his lucky stars. If he did not feel fortunate, he had only to look around at the bodies of the fallen Marines to change his tune. "Some of my friends died within two minutes of leaving the landing craft," said Second Lieutenant DuPre. "Luck and my guardian angel got me through."[30]

The situation at Red 2 appeared serious. The troops had to leave the beaches and move inland, an action certain to cost many lives, but little choice remained. MEETING HEAVY RESISTANCE,[31] summed up the first message Shoup and General Smith received from Red 2.

Commanders at both Red 1 and Red 2 had now radioed the gravity of their conditions. If the same held true for Red 3, on the far left of the invasion beaches, the entire operation could collapse.

PART III: APPROACH TO RED 3

"I'm Losing My Beachhead!"

The landing operations on the far-left sector, Red 3, enjoyed better success than the other two beaches. Two destroyers, *Ringgold* and *Dashiell*, lent support, while the lengthy pier provided protection against enfilading enemy fire from the right. Most amtracs at Red 3 landed their men, backed away from the beach to keep the metallic front between them and enemy gunfire, and returned to the reef for more men and supplies. Though two amtracs managed to reach as far inland as the airstrip, the Japanese quickly isolated them and negated their usefulness.

Like his fellow commanders at Red 1 and Red 2, Major Crowe waited with the fourth wave before heading ashore at Red 3. He sent in his executive officer, Major Chamberlin, with the assault waves, knowing the men were in superb hands until he arrived.

While wading in, Chamberlin watched as machine gun bullet splashes approached him from shore, abruptly stopped at his feet, and then started again to his side. Apparently the enemy gunner had momentarily taken his finger off the trigger to prevent his gun from overheating, and this lull saved Chamberlin's life.

Chamberlin stood upright, fully exposing himself to the fire from shore, in an effort to encourage his men. The tactic worked on most, but whenever he saw a Marine drop low to the water and refuse to budge, Chamberlin, certain that they would soon be cut to ribbons by the hundreds of bullets that flew out from Betio, took out his .45 pistol, waded over to the man, and threatened to shoot him if he did not move. Every Marine thus confronted, most likely wondering what had become of the nit-picking officer from the transport, stood and advanced through the fire.[32]

Like everyone else, though, Crowe had not counted on the significant opposition encountered along Betio's north shore. The irascible officer stood in his Higgins boat, watching the chaotic developments ashore, and uttering a string of expletives that Staff Sergeant Hatch, riding in the same boat, easily heard.

"Jesus Christ! I'm losing my beachhead!" Crowe yelled when he observed the amtracs veering toward the right half of the beach to distance themselves from heavy fire from the left. Crowe feared that the following waves would be disrupted unless he did something fast, so he shouted to the driver, "Coxswain, put this goddamn boat in right now! I've got to get in and straighten out that beachhead or there won't be any place to land!"[33]

Crowe had every reason to be concerned, as his men had stepped into an inferno. Corpsman Stanley Bowen's confidence that the attack would be quickly over dissipated with the first shell that whistled close by his amtrac in the second wave at Red 3. "My God, they're shooting at us!" he thought. His fears deepened when the amtrac to his immediate left suddenly exploded and disappeared. "It blew out of the water and killed everybody on it, and arms and legs were flying through the air."[34] At that moment Bowen realized the Marines were not just going to walk ashore, shoot a few dazed Japanese, and celebrate a victory.

The coxswain in Crowe's Higgins boat revved the engine and headed inland. Everyone else stooped low to stay out of harm's way, except Crowe. He stood, glaring ahead, as if his gaze could itself destroy every Japanese machine gun now killing his men. Hatch sat near him, fidgeting with his camera, while Kelliher did the same.

Like the other Higgins boats, Crowe's landing craft rammed into the coral without crossing over. An already impatient Crowe fumed as the coxswain attempted to free the craft, then bellowed, "All right, men, we're wasting too much time here. Let's go over the side!"[35]

The men had to use the side instead of the boat's ramp, which had become stuck in the collision with the reef. Hatch and Kelliher waited for the Marines to leave, then followed with their ninety pounds of equipment, including a combat pack, a .45 with five clips of seven cartridges each, a camera, and a canister of film strapped to each shoulder. The burdensome equipment made it awkward to climb over and drop down into the surf, but once in the chest-deep water, Hatch and Kelliher found that the material provided balance and made it easier to remain upright in the salt water.

In the lagoon, Hatch and Kelliher stood in plain view of the enemy, but unlike the other Marines, they had no choice. Should they fall into the water or lower themselves to make smaller targets, they would ruin the cameras and film, and thus negate their reason for being at Betio. Hatch looked at Kelliher and warned, "Kelly, if you fall down I'm going to kill you!"[36]

Hatch and Kelliher looked around and thought that they provided the only target for the enemy. The other men had dropped to the water's surface, with little but their helmets showing, and Hatch had no idea how he and Kelliher would ever survive four hundred yards through that watery gauntlet. Before they had moved twenty yards, Hatch saw several men wounded or killed and observed hundreds of bullets splash near him.

"I felt about as foolish as one can get," wrote Hatch, "knowing that I made a perfect target and especially when I saw men ahead of me get hit even though they were submerged. The temptation to lower myself into the water was overpowering, but the discipline of doing one's job, in this case preserving my camera and film, was stronger."[37]

Hatch and Kelliher finally made it to the beach, exhausted from the ordeal of wading against the water flow while burdened with so much equipment. The pair collapsed into a shell hole, weary, delighted, and wondering how they avoided injury while offering the enemy such an easy target.

After Hatch caught his breath, he looked over and saw, three feet away, a Marine bleeding profusely from a buttock that was nearly ripped off. This, he knew, was no training film. Suddenly the response that a sergeant in New Zealand had given him flashed to mind. When Hatch asked why he had not received a rifle, the sergeant told him he did not have to worry. If he wanted one, once the battle started he would have his choice. All he had to do was bend over and pick up the rifle of a slain Marine.

While Crowe headed in, Major Chamberlin took over onshore. He freely moved among the bullets and eruptions as if they did not exist. Once he shepherded the men toward the seawall, Chamberlin began organizing an advance. He regretted one thing—he had placed his pack containing a box of his favorite cigars in the amtrac, which a Japanese shell demolished when it struck the boat. He would have to lead without a cigar protruding from his mouth, at least until he could bum one off Crowe.

"All Hell Broke Loose"

Like so many Marines approaching Betio in midmorning, Pfc. Albert B. Gilman of E Company expected an easy operation. Other than sporadic gunfire, his amtrac neared the reef without significant opposition, and Gilman felt better about his chances of eventually seeing his Connecticut home.

He and the other occupants held their breath as the amtrac climbed the reef near the pier's end. A lurch forward and a loud splash indicated they had arrived inside the reef. "Then all hell broke loose." Bullets whistled by and mortars screeched, as Gilman and the others tried to manage their fears at the surprise greeting. By navigating in the shadows of the wooden pier, the amtrac safely made it to shore before lodging on the seawall. "The amtrac just hung there, tipping back and forth," recalled Gilman. "Someone yelled, 'Everyone get out!' so we piled out and headed inland. There was fine sand everywhere, and we could see the ocean on the other side of the island. Ten of us went quite a ways inland but in a short time realized we were all alone. The rest had gone back to the seawall."[38] Connecticut seemed strangely farther from his reach than it had moments before.

When Bowen's amtrac hit the beach, he and the others jumped out and sought shelter. Bowen glanced toward the seawall, but suddenly a large Japanese soldier, stripped to the waist, stood twenty feet away swinging a saber as if threatening to chop off someone's head. "He must have been six feet two inches. I couldn't believe it. They were supposed to be small."[39] Before the giant inflicted any harm, a Marine gunned him down. Bowen continued racing ahead, but wondered what all the tiny sand piles were as he passed each. He learned later that these seemingly harmless mounds, which reminded him of a schoolyard sandbox, were Japanese pillboxes.

At the seawall, Warrant Officer Leonard A. Booker was leading the Marines from E Company out of his stalled amtrac when a Japanese soldier rose and shot him between the eyes. The image momentarily immobilized those who witnessed it until Sgt. Melvin McBride, an imposing spectacle at six feet four inches and 225 pounds, scurried from man to man at the base of the seawall, glared directly into each man's eyes, and said, "When I say go, we go!"[40] McBride leapt over the seawall and led the men inland to the airfield.

In the early moments of the landing at Red 3, while the vast majority of men hugged the seawall, about ninety men from E Company proceeded inland to the airstrip. It was the deepest advance of the morning at any beach, but one that would only be temporary.

As Crowe walked ashore, a lieutenant joked that if things did not work out, they could all swim back to the transports and enjoy a hot cup of coffee. Crowe smirked, then added, "They'll have to work out today, and damn soon, or not at all."[41] Crowe took heart, though, that he and other Marine officers were there to create organization out of chaos. "It came to me that this was what I had spent my life for, learning to lead these kids,"[42] he said later of the young Marines on all sides of him.

In fact, one of those youthful-looking Marines encouraged the crusty warrior, who had earlier expressed doubts about the younger generation of fighting men. As Crowe stepped ashore a Marine, who looked no older than eighteen, was hit in the cheek by shrapnel. Crowe reached over to steady the teenager, but the Marine said, "Major, turn me loose. Those dirty bastards,"[43] and headed into the fight. Crowe then knew that, with men like that, they would win the battle.

He could not put that into an official communiqué, however. Crowe's first message to General Smith indicated the severity of the situation, just as did similar messages from Red 1 and Red 2. HEAVY OPPOSITION,[44] he curtly informed his superior, even though in the journey to shore he had lost only 25 out of 522 men.

He could have added that the perilously low water levels at the reef had little impact on the assault waves. Those first three waves, all employing amtracs, readily churned over the coral toward shore and deposited 1,500 Marines on the three beaches in fifteen minutes. In fact, had there been a full tide, the assault might have been worse for the men in the amtracs. Marines would have landed directly against the Japanese machine guns and pillboxes rather than using the seawall as shelter, and most of the wounded would have drowned in higher waters.

The initial waves at all beaches came in against much stiffer opposition than expected, yet the Marines, many not yet out of their teenage years, kept coming. When one fell, another took his place, and that courage in the face of frightening opposition was what secured the beachhead, fragile though it was.

In the battle's first hour, the Marines in the first three waves scratched out a tiny toehold on Betio's northern shore. In most places it was merely a dent in the Japanese line—a few yards in from the waterline—and any sort of determined push by the enemy would toss the American assault back into the lagoon. It would be up to the men of the assault waves and their reinforcements filtering in to expand that beachhead before the Japanese could mount a serious counterattack.

The low tides wreaked havoc on the invading Marines for the remainder of D-Day, however. The exposed reef proved to be no impediment for the agile amtracs, but it was a formidable barrier blocking every Higgins boat, and that spelled trouble for both supplies and men. After being transferred at the reef, supplies would have to be ferried to shore by amtracs. The men of the fourth and following waves would either have to hitch a ride on an amtrac after it delivered its first load of troops, or, more ominously, have to wade to shore from distances as great as seven hundred yards, all the time walking directly into enemy fire. As badly as the assault waves suffered, their losses paled in comparison to the slaughter that now ensued in the waters between the reef and Betio's sands.

PART IV: SLAUGHTER IN THE WATER

"Oh, God, I'm Scared"

Robert Sherrod had never felt such exhaustion. He and the occupants of his Higgins boat had been waiting for hours in the heaving ocean, anticipating the ride to Betio. The correspondent had seen action before—at the front lines with troops in the Aleutians—but he could not get a handle on the situation. The sounds coming from shore gave no clue how the operation unfolded.

Shortly before 9:00 his boat reached its rendezvous point and waited along with the other landing craft for its turn to go in. In the lull, Sherrod gazed shoreward, and through the smoke and haze glimpsed an unsettling sight.

"For the first time I felt that something was wrong. The first waves were not hitting the beach as they should. There were very few boats on the beach, and these were all amphibious tractors which the first wave used. There were no Higgins boats on the beach, as there should have been by now."[45]

His concern multiplied when a command boat pulled alongside. An officer yelled for the occupants to transfer to an amtrac as no Higgins boats could pass over the reef.

"This was indeed chilling news,"[46] wrote Sherrod. It meant that instead of smooth-flowing landings by Higgins boats, amtracs would have to shuttle in the men and supplies of the later waves, a more laborious and time-consuming process. Besides, what happened when they ran out of amtracs? Already, the number had diminished since the landings began, and Japanese guns knocked out more each minute. The unspoken fear was that the Marines ashore would be annihilated before additional men and supplies reached them. Would the Marines be able to hold the slim beachhead?

A gruff command interrupted Sherrod's thoughts. "Quick! Half you men get in here," shouted a Marine commander in an amtrac that came over to get them. "They need help bad on the beach. A lot of Marines have already been killed and wounded."[47]

As Sherrod transferred to the waiting amtrac, he saw Japanese shells splashing into the water not far away, and the Marine next to him brushed pieces of shrapnel off his lap.

"There we were: a single boat, a little wavelet of our own, and we were already getting the hell shot out of us, with a thousand yards to go."

As another boat off to their side was shattered by a direct hit, the amtrac officer said to Sherrod, "It's hell in there. They've already knocked out a lot of amtracs and there are a lot of wounded men lying on the beach."[48]

The amtrac took them halfway to shore, where an officer ordered everyone over the side. He told them the amtrac was too valuable and he could not risk losing it by heading in all the way to the beach. "That meant some seven hundred yards of wading through the fire of machine guns whose bullets already were whistling over our heads."[49]

The officer had, in effect, ordered Sherrod and the other occupants to take a route toward shore he considered too dangerous for his amtrac. With the unnerving thought that they were less important than a boat, they leapt into the water, now turned to a froth by hundreds of bullets and shells. "Oh, God, I'm scared," mumbled a Marine to Sherrod. Sherrod tried to force a grin to help calm the boy, but he was too frightened himself and could not stop shaking. All he could muster was a feeble "I'm scared, too."[50]

His fears were justified. He now realized that Betio held hundreds, if not thousands, of breathing foes, each willing to die in an effort to kill him and the Marines near him. Sherrod had studied previous military engagements and knew that analysts considered what he was now a part of—a landing from the sea directly against fortified enemy positions—the toughest of all operations, even if it was superbly organized. From the looks of this, though—amtracs and Higgins boats burning on the waters, men struggling ashore, dead and dying floating all about—he faced a worse predicament.

He and fourteen other men jumped into neck-deep water, and before they took one step, the Japanese had found the range. "No sooner had we hit the water than the Jap machine guns really opened up on us. There must have been five or six of these machine guns concentrating their fire on us—there was no nearer target in the water at the time—which meant several hundred bullets per man."[51]

Sherrod moved forward, a difficult feat in the swirling waters. He battled the natural instinct to flee in the opposite direction, mainly because he did not want to be embarrassed. "I'd look like a damn fool! Everyone else is going to the beach, and I would be headed the other way." Sherrod, who had been around the military long enough, kept going because he did not want to abandon the other men. Besides, as Pvt. William Kelliher explained, the men had little choice. "The only way we went was forward or down [from being hit]. The water was red, and bodies were everywhere."[52]

As he slowly edged toward shore, Sherrod recalled his request to be transferred from Makin to Tarawa because he thought he would see more action. "Now, with all the Japanese fire, I thought maybe I'd made a mistake!"[53]

The physical and mental ordeal of wading such a lengthy distance taxed every fiber of Sherrod's body. Any moment could be his last, but he had to shove that thought out of his mind and focus on the task at hand—making it alive to the beach. "It was painfully slow, wading in such deep water. And we had seven hundred yards to walk slowly into that machine-gun fire, looming into larger targets as we rose onto higher ground. I was scared, as I had never been scared before."[54]

Bullets in bunches smacked six inches on either side of him. "I could have sworn that I could have reached out and touched a hundred bullets."[55] As he moved within four hundred yards of shore, he swerved toward the pier for extra safety. Crawling alongside the pier, Sherrod noticed that with each motion of the surf a thousand dead fish, from as small as six inches long to as large as three feet long, killed by the tremendous concussions that rattled the waters, washed against the structure.

Sherrod headed toward a group of Marines on land to his left. He asked one of the men who huddled on the beach how things seemed to him. "Pretty tough. It's hell if you climb over that seawall. Those bastards have got a lot of machine guns and snipers back there."[56]

A quick survey by the reporter confirmed the grim outlook. On this portion of Betio, the beachhead was only twenty feet deep from the water's edge to the seawall and about one hundred yards long. The enemy controlled everything else.

Sherrod's walk through the watery gauntlet typified what every Marine faced as he waded ashore that deadly, humid morning. More hardships loomed ahead, but Sherrod saw something that made him more optimistic. "The beginning at

Betio did not look bright. But several hundred Marines had gone over that sea-wall to try to kill the Japs who were killing our men as they waded ashore. They went over—though they knew very well that their chances of becoming a casualty within an hour were something like fifty percent."[57]

The Marines' bravery deserved praise, but for it to have an effect, that courage had to be matched by others on every beach. If not, Shibasaki and his defenders would triumph.

The first round—the amtracs bringing in the assault waves—ended with harried Marines barely holding on to slim sections of beach. Round two—the long wade toward shore from Higgins boats stranded at the reef—was about to begin. Its horror surpassed that of the assault waves.

"A Shooting Gallery with Human Targets"

On Red 3, the Marines on land watched the men in the later waves struggling to wade ashore and wished they could do something to help. "It was a shooting gallery with human targets," said Pfc. Albert Gilman. "None of them knew where all the fire was coming from, since it came from everywhere. The lagoon was littered with hung-up boats and the dead and the wounded."[58] Staff Sergeant Hatch saw men rush out of their Higgins boats at the reef and step directly into enemy shells that left nothing but mangled bodies and twisted boats.

At Red 1, machine gun bullet splashes stitched a deadly path directly toward Pfc. Robert Libby, then swerved feet away and felled other Marines next to him. "The water around me, blood red, was a churning mass of spouting geysers through which those of us still able to continued to make our way shoreward," he remembered. "Bodies were floating on the surface everywhere we looked; here a man moving along nearby was suddenly no longer seen, and there the faltering steps of another told the story of a wounded man determined to reach dry land."

Walking wounded filtered in the opposite direction, hoping to meet a landing craft that could take them to a transport, while screaming shells, the crack of rifle fire, explosions, and the moans of those hit made Libby feel it was only a matter of time before a bullet found him. "One moment I was among a group of advancing men, the next I found myself alone with my own thoughts and prayers; we had no answer to what was taking place around us—we were live targets in a shooting gallery. . . . Every step of the way was a life and death situation; how anyone ever reached the shore is still a mystery to me as the enemy fire seemed to cover every inch between the reef and shore—there was no hiding place, no protection, our only armor was the shirt on our backs."

Libby discarded all thoughts of being a hero and "while I was still chin deep in the waters of the lagoon I asked myself what the hell I was doing here." He did not think of home or country or family. Inside the reef at Betio, "survival became the most important thing."

Libby collapsed on the beach, ecstatic over escaping the torturous walk he had just endured. He did not know what horrors waited in hell for the unjust and evil, but he concluded he had just received a preview. "If anyone can think up a picture of hell, I don't think that it would match up to that wade in from the reef to the shore at Tarawa, with the floating bodies and bits of bodies, the exploding shells and burning landing craft."[59]

Lt. Aubrey Edmonds of E Company, embroiled in his own battle ashore, could do nothing but watch and grow frustrated. He called it "a tragic sight. As the boats let down their ramps [on the reef], the Japs opened up, wiping out a large percentage of the incoming troops. Only a few made it."[60]

Petty Officer Tadao Oonuki witnessed the carnage from his tank in the middle of Betio, and while he could sympathize with his enemy's plight, he and the other Japanese were doing their jobs. "Under roaring fires, enemy craft wrecked, American soldiers went down one after another, went falling into the sea."[61]

One of those men, Private First Class Muhlbach, could barely move against the water off Red 3. Weighed down by his rifle, ammunition, and other equipment, the scout-sniper doubted he could keep his head above the water that splashed against his face. He used his rifle as a prop, hitting the coral bottom to keep him above water so he could take in another gulp of air before again sinking below the surface. Despite the rigorous training that had sculpted his body into trim form, Muhlbach labored to move forward against the swirling tide, an exercise that quickly exhausted him. He felt as if he were trapped in one of those nightmares he had experienced as a youth, the kind where he frantically tried to run away from something in pursuit, only to find that his legs would not move.

"I was almost sure I was going to drown," he later explained. "I was trying to move in, but it was difficult to move toward the beach. At one point where I couldn't quite get enough air, somebody pushed me from behind. I didn't know there was somebody behind me. He pushed me, and that was enough to get me up a little bit to get a gulp of air. There was a guy in front of me, and as I lurched forward I pushed him and I think the same thing happened with him. It saved him from drowning."

By the time Muhlbach moved halfway down the length of the pier, enemy fire burst from underneath. The marksman fired from the hip toward the area and killed two Japanese soldiers. He continued moving and came upon a series of Japanese outhouses that had been constructed alongside the pier. Muhlbach did not know whether to laugh or scream as he waded through the feces and endured the grimy water that splashed into his face.

Muhlbach shoved aside more than human waste. "There were the guts of your comrades getting hit from those guns, which would take off their heads. I saw that happen once. There was a lot of blood being spilled. [The water] was sort of a dark crimson. Not the whole thing. You'd run across it every once in a while. There'd be a guy floating there, and he's pretty well shot up, and he's had a lot of bleeding and a lot of guts and stuff floating around there."

So many bullets splattered the water near him that it reminded Muhlbach of raindrops in a barrel. Whenever he dropped below the water's surface, he was surprised that he could not see. In a tropical paradise, should not the water be crystal clear?

"The coral sand had been churned up by the amtracs and the shelling and the bombing and all that, and it was not only salt water but it was mixed in with this coral sand. If you were down below the water you couldn't see."[62]

When the weary Muhlbach finally splashed onto the beach, he counted himself among the lucky ones of the fourth wave. Many, he saw, had not made it, and he had no idea how he survived the trek inward.

"A Nightmarish Dream"

Off Red 1, when Maj. Michael P. Ryan realized his Higgins boat would never make it over the reef, he ordered everyone into the water. Ryan had warned them that they might have to walk in, but he did not expect anything as hideous as this.

Someone in another boat shouted to him, "Hey, Mike, what do you want to do?"

"What I wanted to do was turn around and go back to the ship, but I couldn't think of a good explanation," said Ryan. He ordered the men to move away from the heaviest fire, which came from their left, and head over to the Beak on the right.

Ryan recalled, "Our move into that beach seemed to take forever, just as in a nightmarish dream, and the shore seemed to be a haven that kept moving further away."

When he reached the Bird's Beak, Ryan turned to the lagoon to see how his men fared. Most were crawling on hands and knees in the water, offering smaller targets to the enemy. With only their helmets visible above the water, they reminded him of tiny turtles battling against the current.

Major Ryan required more than one hour to lead L Company seven hundred yards ashore in the Beak's region. By the time he arrived he had lost one-third of his men, but the remainder, supported by two Sherman tanks, were ready to strike back. The major, who would restore order and keep the attack moving at Red 1, could not wish for better men than the Marines who followed him onto Betio.

"Looking back, I saw that the men were leaving the boats without hesitation; the courage of these young men, many of them not out of their teens, still is a source of pride to me," he said years later. "These were not fanatical and seasoned troops as the Japanese were, but ordinary young people faced with an unimagined horror, but determined not to let their fellow Marines down."[63]

No matter how lofty the rank, no man was safe anywhere, not only in the water, but during every moment of the three-day battle. Lt. Col. Herbert R. Amey, commander of the landing team at Red 2, conveyed a sense of humor and coolheadedness when his amtrac boat became entangled in barbed wire two hundred yards off Red 2. Just before leaping into the water, Amey grinned and said to Associated Press correspondent William Hipple, "I guess you got a story. Guess the Japs want a scrap."[64]

Everyone tumbled out of the landing craft and quickly fell to their hands and knees as bullets hissed nearby. Amey raised his pistol and shouted encouragement to the men: "Come on, we're going to take the beach. Those bastards can't stop us!"[65] Almost as soon as the words left his mouth machine gun bullets shredded his throat and instantly killed the officer. His lifeless body splashed into the water and quickly coated the surface with his blood.

Ashore with F Company, and himself wounded, Second Lieutenant Barr witnessed Amey's death. "That was a real morale downer!"[66] he recalled of the shocking event. The fighting at Red 2 would have to go on without its commander. Shoup ordered Lt. Col. Walter I. Jordan of the 4th Marine Division, accompanying Amey as an observer, to take temporary command.

When Pfc. Dirk Offringa of L Company jumped out of his landing craft, a sailor inside handed him a mortar baseplate to use as a shield. All the way in

Offringa held the plate in front, which deflected the numerous bullets that pinged off the metal. Pvt. Dwayne Rogers used a different shield. As he stepped along the lagoon, he muttered Bible verses and recited prayers until he safely made it to the seawall.

To move faster, men discarded what they considered unnecessary equipment to lighten their burden. Extra changes of clothing, blankets, haversacks with forks and knives, mosquito netting, sandbags, and wire littered the water and the shoreline. Along the pier, meanwhile, other Marines struggled to rush in essential equipment, such as artillery. If they could have freely used the pier, the men could have brought the guns in with ease, but Japanese snipers made it too dangerous. Instead, the men had to push and pull the artillery through the water.

Pharmacist's Mate First Class Robert E. Costello stared at the injured and dead Marines lying about the tiny beachhead at Red 2, so thick that he could hardly move without stepping on a Marine. He and the other corpsmen, including Stanley Bowen at Red 3, faced a hectic day. They would have to mend the wounded out in the open and ignore the bullets.

"I Wanted to Cry"

Betio offered a smorgasbord of horrors. Montague and Seng lay in mute testimony to the frightfulness of what the assault waves faced, and Muhlbach, Bowen, Jim Meadows, and Chamberlin would soon experience the carnage of days two and three. However, what the Marines of the fourth and later waves experienced is one of Betio's distinguishing features. Seven months before Army infantry waded ashore at Omaha Beach in Normandy, France, Marines engaged in their own equally ghastly walk. Correspondents such as Sherrod and Lucas wrote movingly of the men wading through chest-deep water directly into incredible Japanese gunfire. Though the lines wavered, the men never faltered, despite the large numbers of Marines whose lives ended at this moment. The sheer drama and the stunning courage of the young Americans impressed observers.

Adding to the potency of the moment was that most of the men wading in the lagoon wanted nothing to do with a full-time military career. They had halted their professions and left families for one reason—to fight an obvious foe and end the war as quickly as possible so they could return home. Like Montague and Seng, many would never receive the chance to marry, raise families, or grow old watching their grandchildren.

From his observation aircraft circling above Betio, Lt. Comdr. Robert A. MacPherson forgot that enemy soldiers fired shots at his plane. He was much too taken with what he saw below, of those Americans, most half or more submerged, who labored to reach land before an enemy bullet ripped into them. "The water seemed never clear of tiny men, their rifles held over their heads, slowly wading beachward," he later wrote. "I wanted to cry."[67]

Pfc. Jeremiah Hanafin of the 3d Battalion, 6th Marines, listened to a ship-to-shore radio description of the fighting offshore in his transport as part of the reserve forces. He and others wanted to grab their rifles and dash in immediately. "My God, those guys are getting slaughtered," thought Hanafin, certain that his regiment would be sent in soon.

Hanafin walked to the ship's rail when he learned that wounded were being brought aboard ship. Sailors gently lifted the stretchers bearing the injured Marines as streams of blood poured from the stretchers into the water. "I could see they were mostly young kids. My heart went out to them. I didn't want to think about the possibility of that happening to me."[68]

One Marine in the fifth wave, Pfc. Louis Mendel, told a correspondent he had battled the Japanese for eight months on Guadalcanal, but he was more scared now than at any moment in the Solomons. Another occupant of the same boat, Cpl. Clyde E. Legg, said of the Marines walking into the torment, "They haven't got a chance. Those Japs on the beach are giving them hell!"[69]

Only one of the three landing team commanding officers, Major Crowe on Red 3, made it ashore with the early waves. Colonel Amey was dead in the waters off Red 2, and Major Schoettel had been unable to join his troops at Red 1. A pattern appeared that remained constant throughout the brutal three-day fighting—junior officers, sergeants, corporals, and privates taking command of groups of Marines in the absence of slain officers.

At this stage of the battle, those men had to spur the Marines up and over the seawall. The slim beachhead could not hold every man scheduled to land that first day, which made it imperative for the first waves to move inland as far as possible to make room for the latter waves. To do so in those early phases, however, required a man to be willing to risk almost certain injury and likely death from the many Japanese pillboxes and guns that waited for any head to peek above the coconut log wall.

"I WAS UNPREPARED FOR THIS"

"A Long, Hard Job"

The Marines who gathered at the base of the seawall felt they occupied the safest place in the world, at least in comparison to what they had just gone through in the lagoon. Now, officers wanted them to abandon their refuge, leap over the seawall, and engage the enemy in his own territory. For frightened young men who had seen Marines eviscerated from direct hits on the way in, this was a trying moment, as they had to battle the natural urge to remain where they were.

The last thing they needed was Capt. George Wentzel, who brazenly stood on top of the seawall, bare head fully exposed to enemy fire, smoking his pipe and shouting for the men to follow. He swore and called some of them cowards in an effort to prod them on, and tried to show with his example that enemy bullets were not to be feared. Some men begged him to be more careful, but Wentzel remained at his post, shouting, cussing, and prodding. Here and there a few Marines responded to his call and slid up and over the logs, but many remained frozen. Suddenly, Japanese machine gun bullets riddled Wentzel's throat and head. The sight of the lifeless Wentzel slumping to the sand only magnified the horrors of what lay beyond the seawall and reinforced the relative security of the beach.

Up and over is exactly where they had to go, however. A battle had to be won, and the only path to victory lay in rushing forward and taking land from men who did not want to give it up, land that, at this moment, reminded some of the crater-filled lunar landscape. Twisted and shredded palm trees, many shorn of their tops, lay at tortuous angles. The littered sands contained thousands of palm fronds and charred logs intertwined with pieces of metal and portions of fortifications, from foot-long chunks to slivers. Fires raged everywhere, and above hung a thick blanket of dark smoke that, combined with the stifling equatorial heat and humidity, made breathing a laborious process.

The battle raged on every square foot, most often against unseen opponents. Snipers hid in hundreds of spider holes scattered about the island and strapped themselves into palm trees, so that no matter where on Betio a Marine stood, he could not feel safe. A unit might clear a position only to find it reoccupied later, or might think that a pillbox housed nothing harmful because of its quietness when, in reality, a Japanese soldier hid patiently among the ruins for the right opportunity. On Betio, no such thing as a safe place behind the lines existed—the back lines were, for all intents and purposes, the front lines. Japanese and Americans squatted mere yards from each other.

Strong commanders—Ryan at Red 1, Crowe and Chamberlin at Red 3— rallied the men at two of the three invasion beaches. Fortunately, individuals or small groups of Marines at all three beaches filled the void created by the death or absence of a superior officer.

At 10:36 Gen. Julian Smith radioed his superiors a preliminary summation of the situation. SUCCESSFUL LANDING ON BEACHES RED 2 AND 3. TOEHOLD ON RED 1. AM COMMITTING ONE LT [LANDING TEAM] FROM DIVISION RESERVE. STILL ENCOUNTERING STRONG RESISTANCE THROUGHOUT.[1]

The Marines now had to leave the beach and take the fight inland.

PART I: INLAND AT RED 1

"Take Him Out with the Bayonet"

When he finally reached shore at Red 1, Major Ryan consulted with Captain Crain and Lt. Samuel Turner to evaluate the situation. Since no one knew where Major Schoettel was or even if he was alive, Ryan assumed command and led the charge over the seawall.

With confusion and fear rampant, the coolheaded Ryan collected the Marines near him and started the nasty, deadly job of knocking out the hundreds of Japanese pillboxes on Betio. Some would die and others would be wounded during the laborious process, but sooner or later the point would come when the Japanese simply lacked the strength to prohibit the Marines from pushing forward.

"You had to take him out with the bayonet," explained Private First Class Muhlbach of the tactics he and others used to eliminate each Japanese position. When Muhlbach approached an enemy pillbox, he first determined the enemy's field of fire, which meant how far right and left the Japanese could shout. Muhlbach or someone else in the group stood up to draw fire, quickly ducked down, moved to the side a few yards, and repeated the process. When Muhlbach rose without incurring fire, he knew the enemy could not hit him from that angle and he could approach from that side.

"Then you would get a grenade at him. As soon as the grenade went off, you'd jump in to where you thought the fire was coming from and run your bayonet into that spot. If you didn't get a Jap, you could get his weapon and disable it, then try to get the Jap or his loader. Usually they had two guys in there, one firing and the other loading."

The problem Muhlbach faced was that because the pillboxes contained such a small entry hole, he could rarely toss in a grenade that killed both Japanese. He usually could hurl it in far enough to kill at least one, and maybe destroy the weapon, but rarely did he eliminate both foes. He had to jump in as soon as his grenade exploded and struggle hand-to-hand with the survivor. At times, both Japanese soldiers survived the initial blast, which meant that bayonets, bare hands, and knives became the prime weapons.

After eliminating a position, Muhlbach moved to the next one, usually not far away, and started again. "I repeated it over and over for three days," he explained.

Muhlbach always had to worry about receiving fire from an adjoining Japanese pillbox. "Once you realized their field of fire, you could get out of that field of fire and you'd be able to attack. Of course, they had their emplacements cross-fired. They had another guy covering him, so when you'd jump up to throw a grenade you might get fire from the other position."[2]

Larger enemy positions required more weaponry. A group of Marines laid down suppressing fire to keep the enemy pinned down, while one or two other Marines—flamethrowers or demolitions men—rushed forward and blasted the spot.

Major Ryan, assisted by Captain Crain, controlled the situation the first two days at Red 1. Ryan's calmness under fire and his steady leadership inspired the other Marines to head over the wall and take the fight to the enemy.

It was far from easy. Ryan led a ragtag collection of men from various units, some of whom should have landed at Red 2 to the left. He quickly fashioned them into a cohesive force, then penetrated inland to widen the beachhead that perilously clung to the Bird's Beak and a slim stretch of beach that meandered to the left. Since he lacked flamethrowers and demolitions men, Ryan could not worry about destroying every pillbox. He had to move inland as fast as possible, killing as many Japanese along the way, with the realization that enemy soldiers would most likely be shooting at them from the rear. "We never came close to our objective the first day," said Captain Crain. "We took so many casualties and were so screwed up."[3]

Ryan had one advantage—two of the six Sherman tanks that had attempted to land at Red 1. Four sank in shell holes when they backed off the congested beach to avoid crushing Marines, but 1st Lt. Edward Bale's and one other came ashore to the right of the Bird's Beak.

Supported by Bale's pair of tanks, Ryan led his men off the beachhead and, accompanied by Crain's group, headed along Betio's west coast toward the south shore. Bale and the other tank blasted enemy bunkers and pillboxes from short range, while Marines on foot followed to eliminate any survivors.

Like Ryan, Crain had to find out what forces were at his disposal, then send them against the Japanese. Crain zigzagged his way to a shell hole containing twenty Marines and one of his company lieutenants. The fiery officer had a reputation for acting first and thinking later, so when Crain saw him firing his carbine, while the men he commanded crouched motionless, he asked him, "Lieutenant, what are you doing?"

"I'm winning the war, sir."

"Let me see that carbine," ordered Crain. The officer handed over his weapon, which Crain threw a distance away.

"My God! What did you do that for?" shouted the stunned lieutenant.

Crain admonished his impetuous subordinate. "Your job is to get these people organized. If I ever see you firing like that while the other men are sitting around not knowing what to do, I'll knock the hell out of you."[4] Crain explained that while the officer could inflict harm with his carbine, he would be far more effective if he instead brought the twenty Marines into the battle.

The fighting took a toll. In one shell hole containing a lieutenant and a badly wounded Marine, Crain told the officer that he would drag the wounded Marine back for medical assistance, and then would return. In the meantime, the officer was to remain in the shell hole.

Crain helped the wounded man to an aid station fifty feet toward the shore, then headed back to the hole. He found nothing but a smoldering ruin where the shell hole used to be. A direct hit from an enemy shell had disintegrated the officer. "I said to myself, 'You tried to help this other guy, and you saved your own life.' It was a blessing I didn't expect."[5]

Crain finally heard from his stranded commander. At 10:50, Major Schoettel radioed Crain from the reef about sending air support to his unit. Crain rejected the offer because he had not yet established a solid line and he feared the aircraft would fire into his men. DO NOT CALL FOR AIR SUPPORT UNTIL I HAVE GIVEN YOU THE WORD WHERE OUR LINE IS.

At 11:15 Schoettel again radioed, CAN WE GIVE YOU AIR SUPPORT NOW? Crain tersely responded, DO NOT WANT AIR SUPPORT.

Despite Crain's clear rejection of air support, fifteen minutes later Schoettel informed Crain he was sending in the fighters.

STOP AIR STRAFING. HITTING OUR OWN MEN,[6] begged an irate Crain at 11:40. Finally, five minutes later, the frustrating exchange ended when Schoettel halted the air attack.

"A Photographer's Paradise—in Hell!"

In small groups and by individual efforts, little by little men at Red 1 punctured holes in the Japanese defenses. Some paid with their lives. Pl. Sgt. Fred Farris attacked one machine gun that had killed and maimed many Marines. Sickened by the carnage, Farris dashed across open ground, tossed in a hand grenade, and jumped over for cover. As he flew through the air, the Japanese shot and killed him, but his hand grenade destroyed the gun and killed four enemy soldiers. His action allowed his squad to move inland.

Pfc. Robert Libby lay with the other Marines at the seawall, trying to avoid the plague of bullets that ripped into the coconut logs. No one could locate an officer, so when the fire diminished slightly, Libby and a few other men leapt over the wall and moved inland. "Few men knew each other, but this mattered little at this stage," said Libby. "We banded together and made up an attacking force of our own."

In the heat of the action Libby became separated from the rest. Approaching a tank trap, Libby heard voices coming from inside, but he could not tell whether the words were English or Japanese. "Heroes are said to be born, not made, and I felt that this was no time for me to find out which was true."[7] Libby carefully crawled the other way until he joined some other Marines.

Pfc. Milton Mayer fell with a foot wound early in the action. The smallest man in the platoon, Mayer outworked everyone else to prove he could keep up with his bigger cohorts, and he now objected to being evacuated. His buddies urged him to leave and stated that he had proven his worth many times over. A reluctant Mayer agreed and climbed into an amtrac waiting to ferry him to the reef. As the amtrac pulled away, an explosion destroyed the amtrac and killed everyone aboard.

Moments after killing a Japanese with a hand grenade, Pvt. David S. Spencer felt a bullet pass in one side of his jacket and out the other. Figuring a sniper had him in his sights, Spencer collapsed and lay as if he were dead for fifteen minutes, then bolted up and dashed for a nearby hole as bullets nipped at his heels. When he checked to see if he was wounded, the unharmed Spencer noticed the letters on his uniform, USMC, had been ripped apart by the bullet.

"I never prayed so hard in all my life as about noon the first day," he wrote his family the next month. "There was [sic] about 15 of us guys in a shell hole and it seemed to me we were all alone. Snipers were shooting from all sides, our planes were strafing them and coming so close to us that you could almost feel them going over our heads and they were getting our range with mortars. It was real hot and there was a dead Jap in the hole with us and a badly wounded Marine. I prayed for you all & Barbara and all my friends like I never prayed in my life."[8]

Like Norm Hatch at Red 3, Marine photographer John F. Leopold had no trouble finding subjects and events to capture on film. So much hectic activity occurred that all he had to do was point his camera in any direction and he would be certain to film something remarkable. "It was a photographer's paradise—in hell!"[9] he later stated.

Cpl. Emory Ashurst left the bodies of Montague and Seng at the beach to head inland. He had already seen enough killing and heard enough terrifying sounds for one day, but what he listened to in the foxhole made him feel both pity and irritation. The guy with whom he shared the hole explained that his wife was expecting their baby any day, and that he was worried about dying and never seeing his son or daughter. "I want to see my baby! I want to see my baby!" he kept crying as Japanese fire nipped about the foxhole.

Ashurst feared that the wailing would draw attention to their hole and decided that he had to be blunt for both his own welfare and the good of the grief-stricken father-to-be. "Look, if you don't shut up, I can promise you that you won't live to see your baby."[10] Ashurst's strong words temporarily silenced the man, but the unfortunate Marine had to be evacuated the next day due to mental strain.

* * *

Meanwhile, Major Schoettel still had not landed. At 2:58 P.M. he radioed General Smith that he had lost contact with his forces. DIRECT YOU LAND AT ANY COST, REGAIN CONTROL OF YOUR BATTALION AND CONTINUE THE ATTACK,[11] answered an irritated Smith.

Historians and military analysts have examined Schoettel's difficulty reaching shore. Many conclude that simple fear kept him at the reef. Others suggest incompetence or poor luck. Major Ryan, the officer who assumed command in his absence and thus had the most at stake in the battle, never blamed his commander. Ryan maintained after the war that both he and Major Schoettel faced similar situations at the reef. Ryan claimed that he veered to the right to avoid heavy fire coming from the left, while Schoettel decided to stay at the reef with his wave until a beach cleared. "My decision was no better than his—I was just luckier."[12]

Ryan's gracious attitude toward Schoettel typified the gentleman, but masks the hard truth that at a time when his men needed him ashore, Major Schoettel remained one thousand yards away. No official action report censured Schoettel, but his reputation suffered irreparable damage.

By midafternoon Ryan's men, superbly supported by Bale's two tanks, had established a loose line running 150 yards in width and penetrating 500 yards into Betio. During the afternoon advance, Marines reached a tank trap only 300 yards from the south shore. Ryan, though, concerned that enemy soldiers remained to his rear, pulled his men back closer to other friendly forces. He had learned at Guadalcanal that enemy positions assaulted by only hand grenades and rifles instead of flamethrowers and demolitions men would inevitably lead to problems later, so "we had to pull back the first night to a perimeter that could be defended against counter-attack by Japanese troops still hidden in the bunkers."[13]

Ryan withdrew to within three hundred yards of the Bird's Beak and ordered his men to prepare for the night. As dusk fell at Red 1, Ryan commanded a tight perimeter along Betio's northwest tip, but the rest of the area remained solidly in Japanese control.

PART II: INLAND AT RED 2

"We Were Just Trying to Stay Alive"

At Red 1, Major Ryan stepped in for an absent officer. Red 2, however, relied on the aggressiveness of small units like F Company to make minor gains.

The company's executive officer, 1st Lt. Wayne F. Sanford, assumed command at the seawall when his superior, Captain Morris, could not be found. Orders called for the units at Red 2 to move toward the airstrip to free space at the beaches for following waves, and to give the Marines room to maneuver against the probable nighttime counterattack, so Sanford set to his task.

So far, not many men had left the seawall. One Marine said, "If you were foolish enough to put your hand above the seawall during those first few hours, you would draw back a stub."[14] Facing a difficult predicament, Sanford turned to a man he trusted to get the ball rolling—2nd Lt. Joseph J. Barr.

"Move out!" Barr shouted to his men. Not one Marine moved a muscle. Barr, already wounded twice, looked at Sanford, whose fierce eyes related the impatience he felt toward the reluctant warriors. "My command presence didn't seem to be working too well," Barr explained of that trying moment, "and I looked at Lieutenant Sanford and he looked at me, and I figured that if we didn't move out that he'd shoot me before the Japs did."

Barr tried a different tactic. "Follow me!" he bellowed, and headed over the seawall with his runner, a Marine named Jenkins. After he had rushed twenty-five yards, Barr anxiously asked, "Are they coming, Jenkins?"[15] The Marine looked back, and to his relief saw eight to ten men following after.

One of those men, Corporal Pemberton, fired randomly as he rushed ahead, figuring that since he came in with the first wave, anything ahead of him was the enemy. "We were just trying to stay alive,"[16] he stated of the mad dash over the seawall. Some engaged in hand-to-hand combat, while others, braving the bullets that zipped close by, headed from hole to hole a few yards at a time. Fortunately, the heavy American bombardment had punctured numerous cavities in Betio's landscape.

Pfc. James E. Peavey had moved about thirty feet in from the seawall when a sniper's bullet smacked into the sand at his feet. Peavey tried to back up, but the bullets followed closely behind, so he collapsed and rolled onto his back as if hit. An excellent marksman since his boyhood days, Peavey spotted the foe above him and quickly fired and killed the sniper, although the sniper's body, attached by a cord, remained lifeless in the tree. "It brought back memories of squirrel hunting in Kentucky, when I shot a squirrel and it hung in the branches and never fell out,"[17] explained Peavey.

Corporal Pemberton zigzagged from shell hole to shell hole, taking momentary refuge in each one to gather his strength and courage for the next leg. Two Marines named O'Hare and Bailey ran a few feet, and then a machine gun ripped into them. Both young men spun around from the bullets' impacts so that they faced Pemberton, who watched from a hole a few feet behind. "I will never forget the bewildered looks of amazement on both their faces as they crumbled apart and fell in a hail of bullets,"[18] recalled Pemberton, who shortly after helped knock out the machine gun.

Pemberton next encountered a large bunker with multiple machine gun openings. He waited until a flamethrower arrived; then he and several Marines provided cover while the flamethrower crept close enough to blast fire into one of the apertures. Given an opening, Pemberton and others rushed ahead and dropped hand grenades down the air vents.

By midmorning, still not having heard from Captain Morris, Lieutenant Sanford left the seawall and joined Barr in his forward position. His ragtag unit of men leapfrogged their way to the airstrip, with one or two Marines providing cover while another moved ahead to the next foxhole.

Lieutenant Barr and Lieutenant Sanford sought refuge in a deep trench situated in the triangular section of land separating the taxiways from the main airstrip. When they received fire as they approached, one Marine crawled to within two feet of the trench and tossed in a hand grenade, but a Japanese soldier tossed it back. The subsequent explosion wounded the Marine.

Barr and Sanford scurried up and joined the wounded man. Barr peeked into the depression to assess the situation and spotted an enemy soldier with his back to Barr. "I had never killed anyone before, and hesitated," stated Barr. "He seemed to sense my presence and started to turn and I got over my buck fever in a hurry."[19]

After Barr killed the soldier, a Marine bayoneted another Japanese directly below Barr whom the lieutenant had not seen. The Japanese had pointed his rifle straight at Barr's stomach and was preparing to fire when he died.

By midafternoon F Company rested in a trench three to four feet deep, thirty feet wide, and sixty feet long. The location provided excellent shelter from small-arms fire, and the lack of palm trees nearby removed the fear of snipers, but F Company sat in a precariously exposed position. They represented the vanguard of the Marine advance that first day. While most Marines remained in the vicinity of the invasion beaches, F Company's bold plunge to the center of Betio planted an American presence in the midst of Shibasaki's defenses.

Sanford took a head count to determine his strength for the night and the expected Japanese counterattack. About fifty Marines, some from F Company and some from other units, manned the trench. Besides their rifles, the men had one hundred hand grenades, a few BARs (Browning Automatic Rifle), two light machine guns, and one mortar. Sanford possessed little with which to withstand an attack, but it would have to do.

Sanford sent a runner back to the beach to inform Colonel Jordan of his location about 250 yards inland, then prepared to defend his position.

"I Never Saw Such a Man"

The men of F Company may have been in the vanguard at Red 2, but elsewhere on the beach other individuals moved inland and, by their actions, helped carve out a small toehold. By themselves they did not win the battle; combined with similar moves by other men, the individuals led to victory.

S. Sgt. William J. Bordelon, like Montague and Seng a graduate of Central Catholic High School in San Antonio, was one. After leading survivors of his smashed amtrac to shore, Bordelon ignored the heavy fire that came from close by, stood up, and hurled two dynamite charges into pillboxes that pinned down the Marines. Though he was wounded in his left arm and cut in the face by shrapnel, Bordelon knocked out both positions.

When another Japanese gun continued to confine the Marines to the beach, Bordelon crawled over the seawall to the Japanese gun, shoved a third charge through its firing slit, and silenced the position.

Bordelon, now wounded a third time, returned to the wall and grabbed more dynamite. As he prepared to throw it, the charge exploded and mangled his hand, but Bordelon refused treatment. Bordelon told other Marines that since he was the highest-ranking man on that sector of beach, he had a duty to be an example to his men.

After sprinting into the water to help pull an injured Marine ashore, Bordelon attacked and destroyed a fourth Japanese position, in the process dragging another wounded Marine back to safety. As he rose to fire yet another grenade launcher, Japanese fire cut Bordelon down.

"Bill was the bravest Marine I ever saw," stated one man who fought at his side. "He was also the finest leader of men in and out of combat."[20] Bordelon's actions inspired other men to leave the seawall and head inland. For his hero-ics, Bordelon earned the Medal of Honor, becoming the first enlisted man to be so honored. The battle's first three hours had taken three of Central Catholic High School's boys.

Not far from the scene of Bordelon's exploits, 1st Lt. Phillip J. Doyle climbed on top of the seawall, charged a pillbox, tossed in a hand grenade, then jumped in the pillbox and killed four dazed Japanese with his bayonet.

"In those hellish hours, the heroism of the Marines, officers and enlisted men alike, was beyond belief," wrote news correspondent Richard Johnston. "Time after time, they unflinchingly charged Japanese positions, ignoring the deadly fire and refusing to halt until wounded beyond human ability to carry on."[21]

After leading his scout-snipers in the opening action along the pier, Lieu-tenant Hawkins spent the rest of the day in a landing craft at the reef off Red 2, vainly trying to commandeer an amtrac to take him ashore. Finally, around 4:15, the frustrated Hawkins found an accommodating amtrac. As the craft moved from the reef, Hawkins manned one of the machine guns and fired to-ward shore, completely exposed in the unshielded amtrac. "I'll never forget the picture of him standing on that [LVT], riding around with a million bullets a minute whistling by his ears, just shooting Japs," said a Marine who witnessed the spectacle. "I never saw such a man in my life."[22]

The amtrac brought Hawkins and his men halfway to shore; then it had to turn back for the reef. Hawkins jumped out, waded in and finally joined the Marines on Betio more than half a day after he left his transport.

In the midst of the fighting Fr. F. Kelly, a Catholic priest, and his aide, Cpl. Dan Goetz, walked among the carnage littering the beach at Red 2. Bodies lay everywhere, and Kelly knew that, both out of health considerations as well as for morale—no man wants to go into battle with the sight of dead comrades in his mind—he faced an urgent task.

With the fighting raging close by, Father Kelly and Corporal Goetz plotted out a cemetery and started the gruesome process of identifying and burying Betio's dead.

"Then I Came to My Senses"

The early moments of battle were just as confusing for the Japanese. After the immense bombardment, Warrant Officer Ota and his men waited in pro-tected emplacements near the junction of Red 1 and Red 2—the sand hills

Bowen referred to—five feet inland from the seawall. They fired at the Marines as they waded ashore or left their landing craft, but once the Americans reached the seawall, the coconut logs protected them from Ota's fire.

A flurry of grenades flew over the seawall and landed near Ota, but all missed their mark. Ota answered by shouting to his men, "I order you to follow me!" He leapt onto the beach, sword in hand, before realizing he stood alone in the midst of the stunned enemy. "For some reason, perhaps because they were startled, the Americans did not shoot at me. I waved my sword at the Marines as if to cut them down. Then I came to my senses, jumped quickly back over the barricade and returned to my position."

Ota continued to fight from his pillbox into the afternoon. A few Americans jumped over the seawall, but Ota and his men cut them down before they advanced very far. Ota's main worry was the constant stream of enemy hand grenades that arced across. The grenades gradually reduced the force he commanded.

Weary, hot, and hungry, Ota decided to again jump onto the beach and perish in hand-to-hand combat rather than wait for a grenade, but his decision came too late. As he started to move, a grenade explosion badly wounded him in the head and knee and killed two men near him. Stunned and bleeding, Ota crawled back to his shelter, where he fainted from his injuries.

Ota regained consciousness when American aircraft zoomed low overhead, but what alarmed him was that a group of Marines (F Company) had penetrated to his rear and reached the airfield. Now surrounded and almost pinned to the seawall, Ota summoned his strength and organized the fifteen survivors for an attempt to reach their own forces. The Marines quickly spotted the group and killed several of Ota's men, but Ota and the survivors crawled to an unoccupied trench, where they remained until sunset.

"My whole body was now aching with pain. One side of my face and head, where I had been hit by a grenade splinter, was terribly swollen and it felt as if my eye would burst."[23]

At about the same time, Petty Officer Oonuki drove his tank past both Ota and F Company on a journey along the airstrip to Admiral Shibasaki's headquarters inland from Red 3. When he arrived, Oonuki waited while the admiral and his staff burned official documents and prepared to move to a secondary command post on the southern shore. Shibasaki wanted to use his two-story command post as a temporary hospital for his wounded.

When the admiral completed his tasks, he explained his plan. While

Oonuki mounted a diversionary attack to draw the Americans' attention from Shibasaki's headquarters, the admiral and his staff would rush outside and head south. Oonuki would then remain near the bunker as a rear guard for Shibasaki's fleeing group.

Shibasaki read a message from Emperor Hirohito congratulating the men on their admirable defense. "You have all fought gallantly," read the note. "May you continue to fight to the death. Banzai!"

At that moment another officer dashed into the headquarters. He brandished a bloody samurai sword and shouted to the assembled crowd, "I've just killed a dozen Americans! I'm going back out to kill more. Who will come with me?"[24] A few men followed him, but Oonuki and most of the other Japanese defenders remained at the headquarters.

When all was ready for the shift to the new command post, Oonuki climbed into his tank and drove toward the enemy. Oonuki leapt out when the engine stalled, and barely avoided death from a destroyer salvo. As he scurried out of the tank, "one shell from an enemy ship came and exploded with a tremendous sound, and two of my friends who got out of the tank before me disappeared, blown up by the shell. I could not find their remnants."[25]

The body of a soldier—he could not tell whether it was Japanese or American—slammed to the ground at his feet. Oonuki dashed for the closest fortification, which he found packed with wounded Japanese.

Marines quickly surrounded the bunker. Mortar shells crashed against the structure and machine gun and rifle fire chipped away at its foundation, but Oonuki's greatest terror came when the enemy tossed hand grenades down an air vent. Frantic Japanese stuffed a blanket into the opening to muffle the explosion, but it was a temporary remedy at best. With only one exit, and that one covered by the Americans, Oonuki could either rush outside and face death from bullets, or remain inside until grenades or, worse, flamethrowers finished him. A searing bolt of flame inundated the bunker, instantly engulfing some men and almost completely sucking the air out of Oonuki's lungs. The tank officer mercifully collapsed as flames, smoke, and plaintive wails filled the bunker.

Meanwhile, Admiral Shibasaki's group tried to flee while Oonuki executed his diversion, but the men never arrived at the alternate command post. About 3:00 P.M., an American shell, probably fired by a destroyer stationed in the lagoon, scored a direct hit on the Japanese as they advanced in the open and killed every member, including Admiral Shibasaki. The Japanese would have to fight the rest of the battle without their commanding officer.

PART III: INLAND AT RED 3

"Why Do You Think They Can Hit You?"

While F Company punched a narrow avenue into the Japanese defenses at Red 2, and Major Ryan clung to the Bird's Beak at Red 1, at Red 3 the Americans ran into a stone wall. Over the next two days they assaulted a complex of pillboxes and bunkers that, bolstered by a steady stream of reinforcements coming from Betio's tail end, checked every Marine advance.

Red 3 would have been far worse without the indomitable Major Crowe, who provided a steadying force to his men. While his executive officer, Major Chamberlin, led the troops inland, Crowe remained at the beach, where he organized the men at the seawall and funneled additional Marines toward the fighting.

"Our toes were in the water and our weapons faced inland but we were making no headway at all,"[26] recalled an officer with Crowe. The major grabbed men almost as soon as they sloshed ashore and sent them forward. He filtered his men in two directions beyond the seawall—some units he sent straight off the beach, and others toward the right.

Crowe seemed oblivious to the fire as he walked around in plain view barking out orders. Snipers killed five men standing near him during one part of the morning, but nothing deterred him from organizing the attack. His booming voice could be heard admonishing men to "get off your asses and over that goddamn wall!"[27]

The sight of Crowe, his leathery face ensconced in a scowl, both petrified and energized the Marines. He chomped on a cigar that protruded from his angular waxed mustache, and brandished his favorite shotgun in one hand and his swagger stick in the other. A Marine claimed that he dared not think of running from the battle because "I figured if I tried to, that old tiger would beat me to death with that cane of his."[28]

Staff Sergeant Hatch had many chances to observe Crowe during the battle and concluded he saw few men as brave. While everyone else gladly hugged the seawall to avoid the bullets that zipped through the air, Crowe stood tall and proud. In the midst of the heat and the dust and the noise, he walked along the seawall, encouraging the men to move out.

Hatch stated of the officer, "Nine times out of ten he didn't have his helmet on, holding his gun in his hand and once again clenching a cigar in his teeth

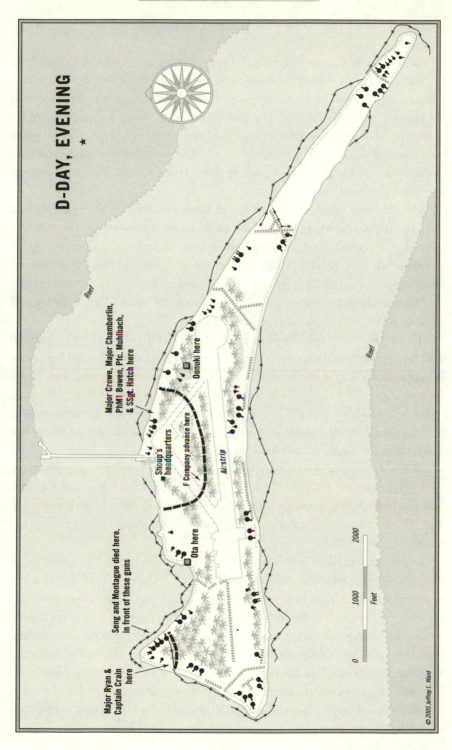

D-DAY, EVENING

Major Ryan &
Captain Crain
here

Seng and Montague died here,
in front of these guns

Major Crowe, Major Chamberlin,
PhM1 Bowen, Pfc. Muhlbach,
& SSgt. Hatch here

Shoup's
headquarters

F Company advance here

Oonuki here

Ota here

Airstrip

Reef

Reef

Feet
0   1000   2000

© 2005 Jeffrey L. Ward

and saying, 'Look, the sons of a bitches can't hit me, why do you think they can hit you? Get moving. Go.'"[29]

As fearless as Crowe was, he did not expect his men to be as foolhardy as he felt he had to be. Robert Sherrod, who spent the first half of the day at Red 3 before walking over to Red 2, observed a Marine walking about five feet from the water when a rifle cracked. The shot damaged the man's helmet without injuring the Marine, but Crowe let everyone know they could consider no place on the island secure. "All right, gad damn it. You walk along out there standing up and you're sure as hell going to get shot. Those bastards have got snipers every ten feet back there."

About fifteen minutes later a second Marine walked by Sherrod. Again, a sniper's rifle sounded, but this time the Marine spun around dead to the ground. Sherrod said that the boy's eyes bulged, "as in horrific surprise at what happened to him, though it was impossible that he could ever have known what happened to him." He ignored Crowe's instructions and paid with his life.

"Somebody go get the son-of-a-bitch," shouted Crowe. "He's right back of us here, just waiting for somebody to pass by."

Three Marines grabbed a few blocks of TNT and a flamethrower, jumped over the seawall, and destroyed an enemy pillbox resting only fifteen feet away. A Japanese soldier ran out, directly into the flamethrower's stream, and "flared up like a piece of celluloid. He was dead instantly but the bullets in his cartridge belt exploded for a full sixty seconds after he had been charred almost to nothingness." Sherrod and everyone else in the area ducked for cover, as "nobody wanted to be killed by a dead Jap."[30]

Sherrod observed several events in his brief time near Crowe that morning. Men went over the seawall to rescue a wounded Marine who cried for help, and an officer told Sherrod about another Marine with part of his thumb missing. "He just looked down at it and laughed and kept going. That damn fool has plenty of guts."[31]

Crowe benefited from two powerful weapons. To counter Japanese tanks that threatened the Marines beyond the wall, Crowe's men lifted nine-hundred-pound 37mm guns over the seawall. Even more impressive was Crowe's employment of the two destroyers that had been on duty in the lagoon since early in the morning. Unlike commanders at other beaches, who lacked workable radio sets in the crucial first hours, Crowe was able to communicate with the *Ringgold* and the *Dashiell* and direct fire at the most threatened spots.

Crowe's main concern was that the destroyers' shells would fall short and kill his men. At one time, the *Ringgold* radioed, WE HAVE SEEN THOSE GUN FLASHES, CAN WE FIRE?

HELL YES! said Crowe of the twin 5-inch mount that had cost him dearly. The destroyer moved so near the reef that Crowe felt he could throw rocks and hit it, then knocked out the Japanese weapon with a single salvo. When the *Ringgold* asked whether the shells had hit their mark, Crowe answered of the shells that crashed only twenty-five yards ahead of him, FINE, BUT DON'T GET ANY CLOSER.[32]

"He Was Like a Wild Man!"

One other officer equaled Crowe's fortitude. Major Chamberlin, the man who worried many of the Marines aboard the transport, continued his impressive lagoon performance with more strong leadership beyond the seawall. Crowe sent his capable executive to the most vulnerable spot at Red 3—the eastern flank to the left, where three of Shibasaki's sturdiest defenses stymied the Marines. Crowe told Chamberlin to collect as many men as he could and form a line along the airfield's edge to prevent a Japanese flanking maneuver.

The economics professor walked up and down the left side of the beach telling men to "get the hell over that seawall!" Pharmacist's Mate Bowen, more accustomed to the stolid officer he had seen aboard the transport, said of Chamberlin, "When he got ashore, he was like a wild man! He was not afraid to jump up and lead his men."[33]

As Chamberlin rose above the seawall to observe the situation, he felt something nip his shoulder that he thought was a bee sting. A sniper firing from a palm tree fifty feet away had hit him in his right shoulder. The bullet passed clean through, leaving a three-inch scar, but after a corpsman applied a bandage to the wound, Chamberlin returned to his men as if nothing had happened.

The Marines Chamberlin hoped to assist had been at the airfield since the opening moments. For five hours Lieutenant Edmonds and E Company, including Private First Class Gilman, held ground near the main runway, but they were vulnerable to an attack in their dangerously exposed position. Fire from both the enemy and from friendly aircraft, thinking that troops standing so far ahead of the assault waves had to be Japanese, pinned down E Company, and Japanese tank assaults imperiled their fragile hold.

Private First Class Gilman had seen action for months on Guadalcanal, but "this is when I knew what war was all about." As he lay in a shell hole with three other Marines, Gilman spotted a Japanese soldier in a coconut tree drawing a direct bead on him. The enemy sniper was above and to his rear, and Gilman realized he had to shoot first before the sniper shot him. He and three other Marines fired in unison, killing the sniper, "but not before I was shot in the back of the head. The bullet went around in the lining of my helmet, a direct hit but not powerful enough to penetrate both the helmet and my head. It burned the side of my neck and ear, went in high up on the left side of my chest and emerged near my left armpit.

"Wow, did my ears ring! You know you've been hit but in the excitement of battle you don't truly realize it. As long as you're breathing you feel you are O.K."

Gilman and the other Marines huddled in the bomb crater. A Japanese soldier emerged from a small building to shoot at them, but one of the Marines tossed a grenade into the building that, as it turned out, contained a large supply of gasoline. "An enormous blast threw us into the air, then dropped us back in the crater. There was water in the bottom of the crater, and for a time I thought I had been thrown clear out to the ocean."

Gilman was alive, but shrapnel from the blast tore into his right leg, inflicting a more serious wound than the first one. "I noticed the blood, so I tied up the leg and tried to walk. I could move O.K. At these times you tell yourself you've got to go on until you can't because you've got a job to do."[34] The battle was only hours old and already Gilman had been hit twice.

"You Don't Think About the Danger"

Human nature and instinct dictate that people will defend themselves when threatened. Every battle, however, offers examples of men who plunge into the thick of the fighting, but instead of a rifle, they carry a medical kit, a camera, a Bible, a pen. These men brave the horrors of war, not to shoot and kill but to carry out a different obligation.

Corpsmen like Stanley Bowen played a prominent role in saving lives in the brutal Pacific campaigns. Realizing that a great number of casualties would occur in the opening moments of amphibious operations, and understanding that speedy treatment would save lives, American medical staffs intended to bring basic treatment to the men right on the front lines. Experience showed that if a severely wounded man received care within one hour of his injury, he faced a 90 percent chance of survival. The odds plummeted to 25 percent after eight hours.

Corpsmen would administer morphine or sulfa and stem blood flows to stabilize the wounded Marine, then make a preliminary diagnosis of the injury for medical staff at an aid station a short distance from the front. Physicians at the aid station would dispense additional treatment, which might include surgery, before sending the wounded on to a hospital ship.

As soon as Stanley Bowen stepped ashore at Red 3, he plunged into the thickest of the fighting to treat the wounded. Bowen rushed to a man from his platoon who was lying on his stomach with his feet twisted skyward. He and Johnny Snyder thought the man had a broken leg, but when they turned him over, "I lifted up and my hand came through his pants. His leg was blown off. I had blood and tendons and bone, and I couldn't believe my eyes."

Bowen stared at Snyder in shock, then fought the urge to vomit as he helped this first casualty. He removed the man's belt and strapped it around the upper portion of his leg to stem the blood flow, then administered a shot of morphine to dull the pain. Bowen did not have the heart to tell the obviously dying Marine how serious his injury was, so he told him he had a broken leg. Though Bowen later treated more hideous wounds, he called his first casualty "a shocker. I was unprepared for this."[35] Tippy West's prediction that his first patient would be his roughest had proven true.

Bowen and Snyder moved from man to man, doing what they could with sulfa powder, morphine, and bandages to treat wounds that obviously needed more than they could administer. After the first hour, the pair split up because so many casualties needed help. The stomach injuries bothered Bowen more than any other, but the quiet courage of the wounded Marines impressed him.

"There was no panic. They'd say, 'Thanks, Doc,' then most of them got back up and resumed fighting. I was patching guys up all over."[36]

The first day Bowen remained mostly at the seawall, as so many men required help just off the lagoon. As the later waves came in, bringing the men who had to abandon their Higgins boats at the reef and wade in, Bowen knew his work would intensify. Smoke from shells and fires enveloped the island, and the constant noise of combat caused a ringing that remains in Bowen's ears to this day.

"Oh God, the noise was unreal! Hand grenades, Navy planes dive-bombing and strafing would come down real low. You had to shout to communicate most of the time."[37]

Bowen knew he could be killed or wounded as he bent over to treat a man, but he had a job to do and never dwelt on being maimed or killed. "I never gave it a thought. I just did what I was trained to do. You don't think in a situation like that. You just do it. I knew damn well they were shooting at me, but you don't think about the danger. I never thought I was going to get hit and I didn't.

I think for a guy to have the feeling they were going to get hit would be a dangerous thing. If you're afraid, you can't do what you've got to do."[38]

Sometimes, men do more than duty calls. That first afternoon a Marine came up to Bowen as he treated another injured man.

"Doc, there's a guy out in that amtrac that's hurt."

Bowen looked toward the amtrac, which rested about twenty-five yards from shore, grabbed his medical gear, and ran out to see what he could do. He quickened his pace when bullets splashed the waters at his feet, and reached the amtrac without being hit. "I remember distinctly thinking as I ran out to that amtrac with the little plunks of water jumping up that the Japs were zeroing in, and I zigzagged and ran as fast as I could." The former high school and college track star utilized every training moment and running talent he possessed to get those men to safety.

Four Marines hid behind the damaged amtrac, each man bleeding, but they brushed aside their injuries and told Bowen that a badly wounded Marine inside needed his help more. Bowen climbed into the amtrac. When he bent over the young Marine, who had remained at his machine gun to provide cover for the other Marines as they left the vehicle, and noticed the gaping hole in the man's chest, he knew the man was beyond saving. "He had hung on the amtrac when it was hit bad and stayed at his machine gun and kept firing. He took a hit right in the chest. He had a hole right through him. You could practically see clear through him."[39]

Bowen administered a shot of morphine, then spent a few moments with the youth. "He was dying and he knew it and so did I. He was calm and asked me to stay with him. I did for a few minutes but then told him to hang on, I had to go—all hell was breaking loose." Years later, the incident still bothered Bowen. He hated leaving the Marine in his final moments, but he had a duty to other men as well, "so he died by himself."

With enemy fire intensifying, Bowen scurried over the side to check the four Marines in the water, who could not wade in without help. He had to assist them ashore where an aid station could give them better care.

"Drop everything and put your arms around my shoulder!" Bowen ordered two of the four men. When they had done so, he shouted, "Now!" and the trio headed toward the beach twenty-five yards distant. Bullets converged on the three from everywhere, inflicting an additional wound on one of the Marines.

Bowen dropped the first two men on the beach, then rushed back into the lagoon to the amtrac, picked up the final two Marines, and again made his way though heavy fire to safety on the beach. As he neared shore, admiring Marines at the seawall cheered his efforts and urged him onward. "Good job, Doc," they said to Bowen when he arrived. Then, in maybe the finest compliment a combatant can give a noncombatant, the Marines added, "You're O.K.," meaning that he had earned their respect.

Only when he was at the relative safety of the seawall did Bowen realize that both Marines had again been wounded. In two trips through heavy fire Bowen had rescued four men, three of whom were hit in their arms while leaving him untouched.

"Talk about God being on my side," wrote Bowen. "I never got hurt on Tarawa. I had guys hit while I was patching them up. I had guys hit when I was helping them back to the aid station. I got sunburned real bad, got scratches on my hands, but never got hurt until we were in Hawaii about a month later."[40]

Bowen later received a letter of commendation signed by Secretary of the Navy Frank Knox. The honor cited him for "heroic performance of duty" and explained, "When the fighting was most desperate and some of our men in a tractor in front of our lines were severely wounded, Bowen, with utter disregard for his own safety, made his way through to the tractor and, although continually exposed to enemy rifle and machine-gun fire, rendered first aid to the victims."[41]

Bowen continued to treat a variety of maladies, including sunburn, which few ahead of time realized would be a problem. The burning sun cracked everyone's lips, and without protection, burned to a deep red the tips of noses and tops of heads. Bowen noticed that Major Chamberlin ignored a serious facial sunburn while he commanded his troops, and the wounded men lying on Betio's sands not only endured the burning sand from below but the blazing sun from above.

Later that afternoon, Bowen headed back to the aid station to replenish his medical kit. Enjoying a temporary lull from his duties, Bowen looked toward the lagoon, where men still struggled to make it to shore. The numerous bodies that lapped at the shoreline attested to the continued massacre that played itself out on Betio's beaches for much of the three days.

Never known for shyness, Bowen took advantage of the lull to fire his carbine and even throw a few hand grenades. If someone intended to kill him, Bowen planned to shoot back. If the enemy rushed him while he tended the wounded, he would have a surprise waiting.

Bowen also used the lull to relax for a few moments. He sat with his back to the seawall while a friend faced him, both enjoying some coffee. Suddenly the friend's face twisted with a surprised look. The man slumped forward, dead from a bullet that passed directly above Bowen and into his forehead. Bowen grabbed his carbine, spotted a sniper in a tree, fired three or four rounds, and shouted when a body dropped out.

Crowe cut short his jubilation. "Stop that Goddamned shooting! You'll draw fire. If you want to kill Japs, go out and get them, but not here!"[42] Crowe's reprimand irritated Bowen, who had just lost a friend, but the corpsman knew better than to object.

Bowen spent the next three days moving forward with the Marines and treating their wounds. The Marines' ability to withstand pain without complaint and their eagerness to rejoin their buddies in battle never ceased to amaze the corpsman. A correspondent commented, "Men with gaping holes in their stomachs, almost certainly fatal, begged doctors to fix them up so they could return, and one captain, shot through both arms and legs, sent his major a message apologizing for 'letting him down.'"[43]

Bowen and the other corpsmen risked their lives to aid those who needed help, applying bandages and administering morphine under the heaviest of fire. One corpsman, shot in the cheek while treating a wounded man, simply placed one hand on his face to hold in the blood while he finished patching up the Marine. At Red 2, Lieutenant Barr cautioned a corpsman against helping a Marine felled in the open by machine gun fire. Stating he had a job to do, the corpsman ran to the wounded Marine, but died from Japanese fire as he knelt over the man.

Out of admiration for what the corpsmen did on the battlefield, Marines called each of them Doc. They developed such deep affection for Bowen and the other corpsmen, who were actually Navy personnel, that they considered them Marines like themselves rather than members of the "hated" Navy.

Bravery exists in more than charging an enemy position. Bravery comes with giving comfort to men while bullets fly about you.

"You Can't Get Emotionally Involved"

On the other hand, Staff Sergeant Hatch wanted detachment from the Marines. He had to record the actions of men as they fought, and undoubtedly some of these Marines would be killed. Thus he had to film as if in a plastic bubble, immune to whatever occurred. This attitude actually provided Hatch a sense of security. For three days he stood and filmed various parts of the battle, yet tricked himself into believing he would not be harmed since he was only filming the action instead of being a part of it.

"You can't get emotionally involved in your stories. If we did we'd never get anything done. We were reporters on what was going on. You'd see people hit. Those twelve men in a squad were completely dependent on each other and are emotionally tied to guys they worked with and trained with. We go into battle as one or two, and we go all over the place. We don't know what happens to the other cameramen."[44]

The rule for photographers was to cover everything they could, but never to show the faces of the wounded and dead. Superiors in Washington did not want loved ones to learn a harsh fact in such an impersonal manner.

Both Hatch and Kelliher carried weapons, although they rarely used them. Hatch fired his .45 pistol once, when he saw a Japanese soldier taking aim at Kelliher. He missed the startled Japanese soldier, but the sound alerted nearby Marines who quickly killed him. "It's the only shot I fired during the whole war, and I just aimed it in the general direction."[45]

Hatch and Kelliher wondered what the other men, or the enemy for that matter, thought of two guys who walked around filming combat instead of seeking shelter. To obtain decent images, both had to stand upright and ignore the bullets. Hatch remarked, only partly in jest, that the courageous men shot the Japanese and the crazy ones shot the film.

Some Marines may have regarded Hatch as crazy, but not because of his filming. One time he sat down to reload his camera, but thought the sand felt harder than it should. When he brushed away the debris, he uncovered a wooden carton of Kirin beer that the Japanese garrison had meant to consume. He and Kelliher opened two bottles, sat back, and enjoyed a refreshing beverage as the battle raged. Until the supply ran out, Hatch and Kelliher loved to attach two bottles to their belts, approach Marines during lulls, and ask if they would like a beer. Incredulous looks were quickly replaced by grateful welcomes when Hatch and Kelliher handed over a bottle of beer.

With night approaching, Crowe set up his defensive perimeter. Marines at Red 3 had enlarged the toehold to about 150 yards inland. Edmonds and E Company defended a line stretching from the seawall to the northeast edge of the airstrip, while other companies manned a makeshift line swinging to the right, where the stubborn series of three Japanese strongholds had denied any gains to Crowe's men.

"Just Say, 'Follow Me' "

While the battle raged at all three beaches, the assault's commander, Colonel Shoup, had difficulty reaching land. At the reef he commandeered an amtrac returning with a load of wounded Marines, but when he jumped into the craft, he saw that most of the Marines were dead. He ordered the crew chief and gunner to help him toss the bodies overboard, then returned to the reef to transfer the wounded and pick up his staff, including the regimental surgeon, an artillery commander, and observer Lt. Col. Evans F. Carlson.

When Shoup's amtrac churned near the Higgins boat, Shoup waited for his staff to join him, but none budged, preferring the safety of the Higgins boat.

"All right, who's coming with me?"[46] demanded a disbelieving Shoup. Instantly Colonel Evans, the famed warrior from Guadalcanal, stepped across to Shoup's amtrac, but Shoup had to individually shout out the name of each staff member to prod them over.

As the amtrac headed toward shore around 10:30 A.M., heavy Japanese fire damaged the craft. Shoup ordered everyone to jump into the lagoon and veer toward the pier. Shoup encouraged every Marine near him and chastised those he felt were holding back. "Are there any of you cowardly sons of bitches got the guts to follow a Colonel of the Marines?" he challenged one group clinging to the pier. Shoup turned away, hoping his words made an impact, and took heart when most of the men left and headed in. "The Marines are coming in and will be okay!"[47] he thought.

The final one hundred yards to the beach proved to be the most dangerous for Shoup. A shell concussion knocked him to the water and wrenched his knee, but the gutsy colonel rejected help and splashed onto the beach around noon.

As he arrived, another close explosion hurled shrapnel into Shoup's legs and killed two men next to him. He again refused help from his staff and moved a short way inland to set up his command post behind an air raid shelter. A dangerous Japanese cross fire threatened the path to the command post, but at least Shoup had a place to set up and begin contacting his subordinate officers. When a bodyguard warned Shoup that live Japanese had fled into the shelter not long before, Shoup ordered it destroyed.

"We can't, Colonel—without blowing you up,"[48] answered the Marine. As a temporary measure, Marines shoved debris into the shelter's openings and Shoup posted guards to watch for Japanese, then turned to contacting his commanders at the three beaches.

Shoup tried to evaluate what had occurred to this point in the battle. He obviously had suffered heavy casualties, especially among the officers. From the sparse information at hand, Shoup concluded that the amtracs had saved the day in the first few hours, but that he stared at a difficult time in the hours ahead because he could not shuttle in fast enough those men and supplies waiting in Higgins boats at the reef. He faced a trying race against time— would the dwindling number of amtracs ferry in reinforcements and ammunition to enable his men to repulse the expected counterattack, or would they be destroyed first?

Shoup, whom one Marine officer called "the brainiest, nerviest, best soldiering Marine I have ever met," turned to a correspondent who waded ashore with him and said, "If we don't secure a piece of this island by nightfall, we're in a spot!"[49]

The dynamic Shoup alternately encouraged some men and chastised others, depending on their performances. One time he slapped a pair of legs protruding from a pile of rubble. Shoup continued to smack the legs until finally a young, frightened corporal peered out.

"I'm Colonel Shoup. What's your name?" he asked the corporal. When the man responded, Shoup asked where his mother lived, and added, "Well, do you think she'd be proud of you, curled up in a hole like that, no damn use to anybody?"

The corporal agreed she would not. When Shoup, chewing on his ever-present unlit cigar, inquired about his squad, the Marine informed him they were all dead.

"Well, why don't you get yourself another squad?" asked Shoup. The corporal said he did not know how, so Shoup, with the pressing responsibilities of a commander confronting him, took time to explain. He pointed to groups of Marines hugging the seawall, not moving at all, and said, "Pick out a man, then another and another. Just say, 'Follow me.' When you've got a squad, report to me."

The corporal nodded and disappeared down the beach. Shoup returned to other matters, never expecting to see that man again, but a short time later, the corporal returned.

"I got me a squad, sir," said the Marine. When Shoup asked where his new squad was, the corporal pointed to two shell craters not far away. Shoup wondered if they were ready to fight and the corporal, a young man who overcame near-paralyzing fear to do his duty, answered in the affirmative. Shoup handed him a mission and sent him on his way.

Colonel Shoup never learned the name of this corporal or whether he survived the battle, but long after the war he stated that this was one of his proudest moments as an officer. He helped a frightened young man realize what he needed to do, and then under the most dangerous conditions, the corporal carried out his duties. That, in his opinion, was how you win wars.[50]

If Shoup were to win this one, though, he had to have more men and ammunition. When he asked for a volunteer to leave the beachhead, return to the fleet, and report to General Smith, Colonel Carlson volunteered. Shoup told

Carlson to inform the general that he had set up a command post on Red 2, that he needed men and material fast, and to land them at the end of the pier at Red 2 rather than trying to force them into the more bitterly contested beaches at Red 1 and Red 3.

Shoup then added a final message. "You tell the general and the admiral [Hill] that we are going to stick and fight it out."[51]

After walking toward shore through harrowing gunfire, Carlson now repeated the trek in the opposite direction. The charmed officer made it safely and delivered his report to General Smith, who turned to shake Colonel Edson's hand in triumph.

"They've done it!" said a buoyant Smith.

"I'd rather wait, sir."[52] Edson, like Carlson a veteran of the harsh fighting in the Solomons, knew that nothing had yet been decided. The contest ashore could easily swing either way, and much depended on whether the Marines survived the nighttime counterattack.

The Reserves Come In

Edson had many reasons to be cautious. The unexpectedly harsh fighting had refuted the previous chatter about the "simple" operation. Before the battle was three hours old, Colonel Shoup asked General Smith to send in reserve troops to buttress the depleted forces ashore.

Two regiments arrived almost simultaneously. Less than one hour into the battle, Shoup requested that Maj. Wood B. Kyle's 1st Battalion, 2d Marines, land at Red 2, drive against the Pocket to the west, and join with Major Schoettel's men vainly trying to expand a slim beachhead at the Bird's Beak. Kyle landed at 11:30, directly into the same fire that greeted every other Marine that bloody morning. The Japanese machine guns split Kyle's men into two groups, one heading toward Red 2 and the other wading away from heavy fire toward Red 1.

At the same time, General Smith ordered Maj. Robert H. Ruud's 3d Battalion, 8th Marines, into Red 3 to bolster Crowe's stalled left flank. The waves of Marines approached Red 3, but stepped into a maelstrom of enemy fire. Some mortar shells exploded just as Higgins boats lowered their ramps at the reef, leaving burning hulks and mangled men. After a Navy coxswain witnessed two boats disintegrating from direct hits, he yelled in hysterics to the Marines inside, "This is as far as I go!"[53] The Marines jumped over the side into deep water, where their heavy equipment dragged them beneath the surface and drowned them. Marines along the seawall cursed as they watched Ruud's men meander through what seemed even worse fire than they had endured.

Fewer than one-third of Ruud's men survived the ordeal, forcing Ruud to send a message cautioning against dispatching further troops into Red 3 until the waters could be better secured. Many of his survivors huddled at the pier's end and did not arrive at Red 3 until midafternoon.

While these two battalions battled ashore, General Smith prepared a third. The 1st Battalion, 8th Marines, under Maj. Lawrence C. Hays Jr., formed his last reserve unit, but if he committed those troops to battle, he would have nothing remaining to aid in any future emergency. As a remedy, he asked Admiral Turner to release to him the corps reserve, the 6th Marines, that waited aboard transports to assist at either Betio or Makin. When Turner approved his request, Julian Smith quickly sent in Hays's unit, knowing he could also bring in the 6th Regiment if needed.

From 2:00 P.M. on, Hays waited with his men at the line of departure for orders that would send him into Red 2. Minutes turned into hours, and still the final orders failed to arrive. Chaplain Willard, sitting in one of the landing craft, shouted to an officer, "What are they saving us for, the Junior Prom?"[54] He was anxious to reach land where injured and grieving men needed him.

Confusion caused their delay at the line of departure. Hays did not receive the order that first day because his superior officers thought he had already landed. An observation aircraft spotted a group of Marines heading for shore and, assuming the men to be from Hays's unit, relayed that information. It was not until midnight that the misidentification was remedied and Hays received word to head in at first light the next morning.

"A Day of Dreadful Carnage"

By 4:00 P.M. all three beaches faced the same situation. Mainly because the exposed reef held up the flow of men and supplies, Marines were forced to retrieve badly needed ammunition and other material from the dead. Boats waited at the reef and line of departure all day to move in and assist their fellow Marines, but in the congestion off the three beaches, and with the number of serviceable amtracs rapidly diminishing, supplies and men moved slowly. Anguished Marines watching from Higgins boats knew the men ashore needed them, and begged to be taken in. "For Christ's sake, let us in!" implored one Marine. "What can those people be thinking in there, seeing those boats in the water, needing our help, and us sitting here like we was [sic] back home?"[55]

An observer flew overhead late in the afternoon and reported that although he knew thousands of Japanese still manned the defenses, he saw not one in the cleverly hidden pillboxes and dugouts. He could detect the advances made throughout the day at the three beaches and, as far as he could determine, most Marines remained either at the seawall or close to it. A few groups had made inroads of up to 150 yards, but otherwise the Americans clung to the shoreline. By now, he knew, the Marines should have been well inland.

Capt. Earl J. Wilson, who worked with the press corps, watched a boat loaded with casualties pull alongside his transport late that afternoon. The sight made him fear the worst. "I stood at the rail and looked down into the small boat. Fatigue was written on the faces of the men and the three casualties were on stretchers. One had his face covered, with a corpsman holding a tourniquet on his arm. Bright fresh red blood was on the white sheet. It brought home the battle to me more clearly than anything else and I felt a little sick."[56]

At Pearl Harbor, Admiral Nimitz fretted over the lack of progress in the opening Central Pacific drive. He had assembled every possible resource for his commanders, yet by evening of the first day the Marines had barely made a dent in Shibasaki's defenses. He feared the worst lay ahead, as a concerted nighttime counterattack by the enemy could easily shove the Americans into the lagoon and inflict a stunning loss on the formerly optimistic invaders.

Shortly after 7:00 P.M. General Smith sent a message to Colonel Shoup telling him to dig in and prepare for a likely night counterattack. Officers and enlisted alike wondered whether they could hold against a disciplined foe determined to wipe them out.

"What we had won, in a day of dreadful carnage, heroic endeavor and selfless sacrifice," wrote correspondent Richard Johnston, "was less than one-tenth of a square mile of stinking coral, blown to useless bits and stained with great draughts of American blood."[57]

Of the 5,000 Marines who crashed Betio's beaches that first day, 1,500 were dead, wounded, or missing by nightfall. The survivors clung to thin beachheads, weary, undermanned, and worried about survival. Major Ryan, Captain Crain, and the men of the 3d Battalion scratched a tiny toehold around the Bird's Beak at Red 1; a six-hundred-yard gap then separated them from the forces at Red 2, where F Company had rammed a thrust toward the airfield; and Crowe held a thin line stretching from the pier, along the airfield, and on to the complex of Japanese bunkers that stalled them to the east. Because Crowe's units faced the eastern end of Betio, from where most of

Shibasaki's reinforcements would come, Red 3 stood in the most immediate danger of attack. No commander enjoyed a defense in depth. In some places the shoreline stood only yards from the so-called front lines, where Marines hugged the coconut log seawall. Any concentrated effort by the enemy would nudge the Marines into the debris-filled lagoon, where bodies floated amidst palm fronds and shattered equipment.

Officers issued orders to maintain strict silence. Crowe, who feared that his jumpy troops might accidentally shoot at American reinforcements being shunted into line, banned the use of firearms that first night and told his men to instead use their bayonets against suspected infiltrators. Some officers established schedules—two men to remain awake for every one that slept, or one man awake for two hours while his buddy slept. Officers tried to sprinkle in the Guadalcanal veterans with the rookies to act as a calming influence, and commanders supervising Marines at the seawall stationed Marines in foxholes a few yards inland to serve as pickets.

At the airstrip, Lieutenant Sanford placed his automatic weapons and machine guns to cover the front, while Marine riflemen guarded the flanks. He put half the men on alert while the other half rested, then switched them every two or three hours so he had relatively fresh troops guarding against an assault.

Julian Smith's apprehension about this first night ashore was justified. The Japanese matched the Marines in sheer numbers, occupied stronger positions, and had the advantage of knowing the terrain better than their foe. Should Shibasaki mount any kind of concerted counterattack, Smith doubted he could hold with what he had. If his Japanese counterpart refrained from ordering a large-scale attack and instead opted for a concentrated artillery barrage, Smith's Marines along the seawall and on the beaches, including many already wounded, would be trapped.

At 10:00 P.M. Colonel Shoup summarized the predicament in a message to General Smith. HAVE DUG IN TO HOLD LIMITED BEACHHEAD,[58] Shoup reported.

"They Knew It Was Suicide"

Marines faced fears, real and imagined, throughout that scary first night. Vivid imaginations, fueled by what they had heard of Japanese atrocities in the Solomons, the Philippines, and other places, made many Marines wary of what lurked in the yards near their foxholes, now shrouded by night's darkness.

Sand crabs slithering across Betio's beaches magnified into enemy soldiers; wounded men inching their way back to the seawall became groups of Japanese.

Numerous men heard plaintive cries for aid. "Come help me," or "Help, I'm wounded," rent the stillness, but Marines remained at their posts as ordered. No one was to move around in the darkness. Private First Class Twitchell could not sleep that first night because of what he described as the many sounds that turned "one's blood to ice. That is, if you were lucky enough to still have any blood left."[59]

Some momentarily allowed their thoughts to drift to home and family, but Private First Class Muhlbach kept his focus on the task at hand—being ready to repel the enemy. "If you're dreaming about something, you're not paying attention to what you're supposed to be doing," he said. "I don't understand guys in movies that are dreaming about home or whatever. I'd hate like hell to have to count on a guy who's dreaming. You have to count on them being aware and being able to do their thing. Every little sound and everything was so critical, that you were aware of what was going on. In battle, every little sound has to be identified and everything depended on you identifying it."[60]

Nighttime firing, with its colorful tracers, mesmerized Robert Sherrod, until he realized that some of the fire coming at the Marines originated from the lagoon. Apparently, Japanese soldiers had swum out to machine guns left in damaged landing craft and turned the Americans' guns on the Marines ashore. Other Japanese swam to a ship that had beached along the reef so they could shoot at the Marines from the rear the next morning, or hid among the pier pilings and waited for daylight.

"Clever, courageous little bastards!" wrote Sherrod of the Japanese. "They knew it was suicide, but they knew they might kill some Americans before they themselves were killed."[61]

Farther inland, Warrant Officer Ota wondered what he should do. Rumors circulated that the Americans held Betio's western end, but he had no way of knowing for sure. He could see that the enemy occupied four hundred yards of beach on either side of the pier, but other than that, he was in the dark about either the American situation or his own. Most likely Admiral Shibasaki would order a counterattack, but so far he had received no order from his commander.

"We did not know what to believe or what to do because we had practically no communication with our command centers or with the rest of our Japanese garrison forces."[62] Ota felt as isolated as some of those Marines must have felt.

"God, Were We Exhausted!"

All night long, one group of men never ceased working. While the Marines guarded the thin perimeter that defined the American-controlled sliver of beach, Bowen and the other corpsmen treated hundreds of wounded. Working out of seized pillboxes and bunkers, the corpsmen operated by flashlight and ignored snipers' bullets. As Pharmacist's Mate Second Class James R. White-head worked in one bunker, Marines killed a Japanese soldier who had hidden underneath debris in the corner. "We were so busy we didn't notice the Jap until one of the wounded Marines fired a shot into a corner," Whitehead told a correspondent. "It's a wonder we didn't ruin the lad we were working on, we were so startled by the rifle report."[63] A further search unearthed one more Japanese soldier, whom a Marine clubbed to death with his rifle butt.

Marines who had been ripped apart by bullets and mangled by mortar shells patiently waited in shell holes outside the bunkers while Bowen and other corpsmen worked on others. Once inside, some faced painful operations performed by naval physician Lt. Herman R. Brukhardt, who recalled that even when his anesthesia supply ran out, few Marines complained.

Stanley Bowen spent much of that first night braving enemy fire at the pier, where he made numerous trips carrying out wounded men and bringing in water and ammunition. "That first night, God, were we exhausted!" said Bowen. "We were under fire all the time." One correspondent wrote that Bowen and the unloading crews at the pier "worked on a bull's-eye that night but they never faltered," and added that the bright moon hampered their labors. "Back home it might have been beautiful. Out here we cursed it, for it made us perfect targets."[64]

Staff Sergeant Hatch and Private Kelliher dug a hole large enough for the two of them at the seawall's base. Hatch decided to use that spot as his personal command post and covered his extra film and equipment with sand. He had learned his lesson. Earlier, he had inadvertently left a camera out in the sun, and when he picked it up later it failed to work. He opened it to find that the blazing sun had melted the film.

Private First Class Gilman rested along the seawall not far from Hatch.

Weakened from his wounds, Gilman tried to concentrate on the dangers that might lurk in the night, but he did not find it easy. "This was the first chance I had since the battle started to let the fear in. I thought I was safe, but there were always the mortars. You always thought of water. It was amazing how intense your thirst was during lulls or at times you felt secure."[65]

The philosophical Captain Crain also could not sleep—hardly anyone could—and attempted to discern a reason to the killing. Why did he survive and others standing next to him die? He could see no logical pattern and concluded that he remained alive because of simple luck or fate. After his daylong ordeal at Red 1, Pfc. Robert J. Reder prayed much of the night and promised, "Get me off this island alive, God, and I'll never miss Sunday Mass again."[66]

Lieutenant Hawkins was one of the few Marines to leave his foxhole. After spending a frustrating day in the landing craft, watching helplessly while other Marines bled on the beaches, Hawkins slipped out during the night to eliminate one bunker with hand grenades and determine the location of three Japanese machine guns, which other Marines destroyed.

All along the beaches, Marines huddled low in their foxholes or hugged the seawall, waiting for what they thought was a certain Japanese counterattack. The men had already walked through a gauntlet of fire and death simply to reach the shore, then rose from the sands and plunged toward an enemy they rarely spotted. Now, darkness hid more horrors.

"This is the damnedest crap game I ever got into," Colonel Shoup stated to another officer as they shared a foxhole. After a harrowing nighttime trek toward shore along the pier, correspondent Jim Lucas collapsed near the seawall. A sergeant smiled at the reporter and said, "Take your rifle." Then, remembering where they were and what they faced that night, the sergeant added, "You'll probably never get to use it, but you might." Lucas and another correspondent moved a short distance inland, where they dug a foxhole behind the wreckage of a Japanese steamroller. When they completed their hole and had a chance to lie down, the other correspondent muttered to Lucas, "I'll give you odds that we're both dead tomorrow."[67]

Robert Sherrod and William Hipple chose to dig their foxhole directly beneath the seawall, less than ten feet from the bodies of four dead Japanese, who, Sherrod noted, had already begun to smell. So many Marines congested this portion of the beach that they lacked enough room to dig foxholes for every man, and he feared that if the Japanese counterattacked, they could do nothing except fight from the seawall until the Japanese overwhelmed them.

"For the first time since morning, I was really scared—this was worse than wading into the machine-gun fire, because the unknown was going to happen under cover of darkness."

Sherrod vainly tried joking to ameliorate his concerns. "Well, Bill, it hasn't been such a bad life."

"Yeah," answered Hipple, "but I'm so damned young to die."

Sherrod lapsed into thoughts of home and family. He knew he had been a decent man and had provided for his family in the event of his death, but he feared his absence would be hardest on his children. He took comfort that his wife would ably take over the reins, and that his children would have "the satisfaction of knowing that their father died in the line of duty."

Sherrod thought of the dangers that lay over the seawall and hoped he could face the end with dignity. "I was quite certain that this was my last night on earth."[68]

"A FIGHT IN A RING BETWEEN TWO BOXERS"

The Second Morning

After a restless night, Robert Sherrod awoke at 5:30, surprised that the Japanese had not launched their expected counterattack and relieved that he had survived the night. When he peered seaward, he noticed the receding tide left behind an imprint of the first day's carnage, as the lifeless forms of Marines sprinkled the beaches and lagoon. Sherrod counted at least fifty men, some already partially covered by sand. Here and there, a few still grasped their rifles. "Some have bloodless faces, some bloody faces, others only pieces of faces."[1] Sherrod prepared for another long day.

On a transport off Betio, the wounded 1st Lt. Wallace Nygren also awoke. Doctors informed him that, while they would not have to operate on his hand, the battle was over for him. "I realized with sudden relief that I didn't have to go back to that nightmare island."[2]

Relief was the common emotion in the second day's early moments—relief that one had made it through the first day, and relief that the Japanese, for some astounding reason, had failed to launch a night attack that most likely would have shoved the Americans into the lagoon.

The Japanese failed to attack during that crucial first night because they lacked two necessary items—a commander and communications. Admiral Shibasaki's afternoon death removed a capable leader from their arsenal, one who most assuredly would have ordered a counterattack. In his absence, command devolved to lower-ranked officers, but since the American naval bombardment destroyed the communications network connecting all segments of the garrison, they had no way of contacting each other and coordinating an assault.

Thus, while the Marines on land fought to carve out a lodgment, ships offshore delivered two of the crucial blows that first day. The destroyers, cruisers, and battleships had not only torn apart Betio and shredded the communications wire strung about the isle, but they had killed the Japanese commander.

Gen. Julian Smith called the failure of a counterattack a key moment in the battle, for it could have wiped out the perilously thin beachhead on Betio and given the Japanese a victory. The shock waves of such a failure would have spread to Europe, where American military strategists were then assembling the immense Normandy attack. Disaster at Betio would have caused many to reassess the value of amphibious assaults. If an amphibious attack failed at a tiny Pacific island, how could it possibly succeed against Adolf Hitler's vaunted Atlantic Wall that shielded much of the French coastline?

Fortunately for American strategists, they did not yet have to face that issue, for the Marines still held on at Betio. Unless Shoup could nudge his forces off the seawall and establish inland lines in depth, however, failure remained a specter. The Marines had survived the first night, but their chore of defeating the Japanese was far from over.

Colonel Shoup's main priority was to drive a wedge between the Japanese forces in the eastern half of Betio and those fighting in the western half. Thus split into two groups, the Japanese could be wiped out one by one. In a threefold attack for D+1, the second day, he ordered Major Ryan at Red 1 to push out from the Bird's Beak and secure Green Beach, the stretch of sand running along Betio's western end, while Major Crowe at Red 3 reduced the ornery series of enemy defenses facing him. At the same time, Marines at Red 2 were to provide the wedge by pushing across the airstrip and advancing to the southern shore.

Shoup's first call to General Smith came at 8:23 A.M., when he radioed, UR-GENTLY REQUEST RATIONS AND SMALL ARMS AMMUNITION LANDED ON THE BEACH.[3] After twenty-four hours in the equatorial sun, his weary men badly needed water, first-aid kits, salt tablets to combat the heat, and bullets. In the interim, Shoup resorted to sending teams of men to scavenge among the dead for such items.

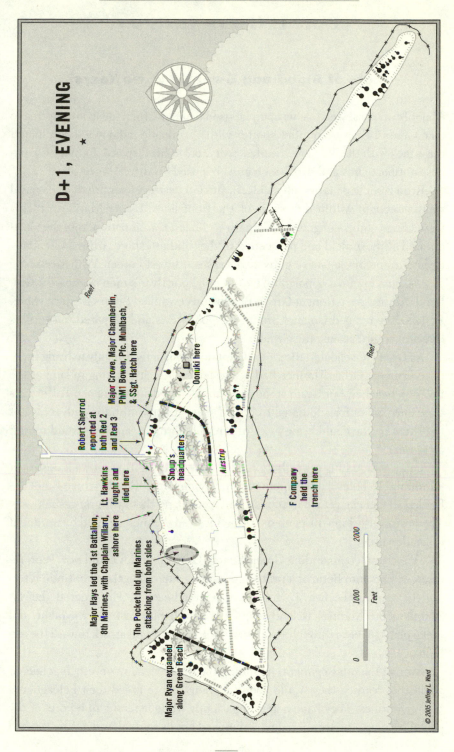

D+1, EVENING

Robert Sherrod reported at both Red 2 and Red 3

Major Crowe, Major Chamberlin, PhM1 Bowen, Pfc. Muhlbach, & SSgt. Hatch here

Oonuki here

Lt. Hawkins fought and died here

Major Hays led the 1st Battalion, 8th Marines, with Chaplain Willard, ashore here

The Pocket held up Marines attacking from both sides

Major Ryan expanded along Green Beach

Shoup's headquarters

Airstrip

F Company held the trench here

Reef

Reef

© 2005 Jeffrey L. Ward

Feet

0   1000   2000

PART I: GAINS AT RED 1

"Lots of Blood and Sweat, but No Tears"

Major Ryan possessed one weapon he used to great advantage in attempting to take Green Beach—a gunfire spotter with a workable radio who coordinated the attack with the Navy. He needed every tool at his disposal, for twelve Japanese antiboat guns and two 5-inch guns opposed his drive.

Ryan launched his assault at 11:20. Behind destroyer gunfire that the naval spotter brought within fifty yards of the front lines, Ryan's Marines quickly seized huge chunks of ground. Captain Crain led K Company across the western end of the airfield and proceeded to the southern shore, while I Company rushed to the big Japanese guns at Betio's southwest corner. With surprising ease against minimal opposition, within one hour Ryan's men occupied a two-hundred-yard-deep front at Green Beach and controlled Betio's western shore. At 12:05 he radioed Colonel Shoup the good news and prepared to send his forces eastward against the airfield.

As Ryan consolidated the gains, Captain Crain acted quickly to bring in reinforcements. Other Marines had been slaughtered attempting to land at the invasion beaches, but Crain stood at an undefended stretch of sand offering a wide entry point for additional troops. If Gen. Julian Smith took advantage of the situation, he could bring in extra forces before the Japanese could mount an answer.

Crain ordered his semaphore man to relay this information to a destroyer patrolling offshore: "I am Captain Crain. I'm on Green Beach, which is not defended. If you can get a battalion in here you'll land them with no casualties."[4] The destroyer's skipper signaled that he received the message and forwarded it to headquarters.

With Ryan commanding Green Beach, General Smith could now send reinforcements into Betio at a protected landing site rather than continue filtering them in at the heavily defended assault beaches. He ordered the 1st Battalion, 6th Marines, to land as quickly as possible, dig in for the night, and make plans to move through Ryan's men the next day and attack toward the airfield.

Men of the 6th Regiment, including the three Meadows brothers, cheered when they learned they would soon be going ashore to aid their beleaguered fellow Marines. They had waited impatiently while listening to reports of the brutal fighting, and wondered why they had not been deployed. "Why the hell are we sitting here when all the action is going on there?"[5] Dick Meadows had asked aboard his transport. Now, at last, they would soon be where they were needed.

Jim Meadows, attached to the 1st Battalion, and brother Bill, with the artillery, headed in to Betio at Green Beach. Dick, however, landed on the adjoining island of Bairiki two miles east of Betio after General Smith learned that some of the Japanese had waded across at low tide from Betio to avoid being trapped. Smith wanted to close that avenue of escape.

For his efforts in establishing order out of chaos at Red 1, Major Ryan received the Navy Cross, after the Medal of Honor the highest award that can be given to Navy or Marine personnel. The stolid leader credited his officers and men, though, whose bravery and effort kept the fight going on D-Day and widened the beachhead on D+1. "My mental pictures are of officers and noncommissioned officers reforming scattered survivors of fragmented units into disciplined groups; of unarmed corpsmen running to recover wounded men and being cut down as they hauled stretchers; of a wounded sergeant I had never seen before limping up to ask me where he was needed most; of lots of blood and sweat, but no tears."[6]

Colonel Shoup welcomed the reinforcements. Before noon he confided to Sherrod, "We are in a mighty tight spot."[7] Sherrod noticed that the colonel's hand shook as he spoke on the telephone and that he imparted information in a hurried, nervous manner. Now, with the addition of the 6th Regiment, things looked better.

PART II: GAINS AT RED 2

"We Were Seventy Versions of John Wayne"

In the middle, at Red 2, Colonel Shoup's instructions to push south and advance to Betio's ocean side reached 1st Lt. Wayne Sanford in the airfield trench. Sanford ordered his two machine gun crews to cover the riflemen while they scampered across open land to the airstrip's southern side, at which time the riflemen would reciprocate while the machine gun crews crossed. First, he had to obtain additional ammunition and learn something about the opposition he faced.

Sanford asked for volunteers to recross the airfield, pick up ammunition at the beach, then bring it back to the trench. No one budged. Corporal Pemberton thought, "He's got to be kidding, right?" for the lieutenant was asking his men to twice retrace the bloody path that had cost so many men their lives yesterday.

Finally, after what seemed an eternity, Pemberton and another man, Pfc. Bill Roberts, volunteered—"the stupidest thing I've ever done," Pemberton explained later. He and Roberts shed all equipment except their rifles and ammunition so they could move faster, then dashed out of the trench.

A Japanese machine gun opened up on them within seconds. Bullets splattered into the ground as they dodged from hole to hole, keeping as low as possible to make smaller targets. The firing halted whenever they jumped into a foxhole, then continued when Pemberton and his buddy resumed their sprint across the airfield.

When the pair finally arrived near the pier, Pemberton stated, "I could not believe my eyes at the masses of bodies lying all along the beach as far as we could see. Literally hundreds and hundreds, most of them dead, some already bloated and stinking from the blazing hot tropical sun, but a few were still alive."

After locating four ammunition belts apiece, which they crisscrossed around their shoulders, the pair again darted from hole to hole, racing a stream of bullets as they rushed across open territory. They reached one spot where, weak and hungry, Pemberton spotted a coconut dangling from a tree beside them. He shot it down, cracked it open, and in the middle of the battle, Pemberton and Roberts enjoyed a refreshing drink of coconut milk. Thus energized, the two embarked upon their final leg across and, thanks to the poor shooting of the machine gunner, reported to Lieutenant Sanford.[8]

While Pemberton and Roberts carried out their mission, Sanford asked for another person to cross the airfield in the other direction and scout the enemy's defenses. A lieutenant volunteered, and agreed to signal when he felt Sanford and the other Marines could safely join him.

The lieutenant dashed across the runway without drawing fire, but when he neared the beach a bullet grazed his mouth and knocked out his upper front teeth. Stunned and bloodied, but still conscious, the lieutenant tossed a handful of grenades into the bunker, killing the occupants, then signaled to Sanford across the airstrip that it was safe to cross.

Around 11:00 A.M. Sanford stood up and said, "Come on, boys. We can't win the war sitting here, so let's move out." The riflemen ran across first, then provided cover for the machine gunners. Nineteen-year-old Pfc. C. Don Jones

We might get to go on a ship pretty soon like this.

Charlie & I

Gene Seng often wrote to his family. He liked to include drawings to his youngest sister, Peggy, such as this one showing Charlie Montague and him aboard a troop transport. The image is another indication of how close the two Texas youths were.

Aboard a troop transport in mid-November, an officer briefs his men about the coming assault. He uses a relief map of Betio to point out their path. The long wooden pier juts from Betio's midsection to the bottom of the image. Naval Historical Center #67706.

This aerial view of Betio and parts of Tarawa Atoll clearly shows the island's resemblance to a parakeet, with the Bird's Beak to the bottom and the tail rising toward the photograph's middle. Bowen, Muhlbach, Hawkins, and F Company landed near the belly, while Seng and Montague landed on the right side of the cove. The island's airfield, the main reason for seizing Betio, dominates the midsection of the island.

Naval Historical Center #VC240309.

Marines like Pfc. Robert Muhlbach and Pfc. Albert Gilman risked falling into the seas as they cautiously inched down the nets into landing craft. The swaying ocean below made their task more difficult.

Painting by Richard Gibney. Courtesy of the Marine Corps Historical Center.

Two members of the boat's crew man machine guns on one of the amtracs (amphibious tractors) that took the 1,500 Marines of the first three waves ashore. Japanese fire killed many of the amtrac gunners, who stood exposed to bullets and shrapnel.

From the Norman T. Hatch collection.

This photograph, taken before Gene Seng (left) and Charlie Montague traveled overseas, shows the friends in Marine uniforms in San Diego. The inseparable pair enjoyed liberties together in San Diego and Los Angeles, and maintained contact with home through many letters and telegrams.

From the Seng sisters' collection.

Billie Miller sent this photograph to Charlie Montague while the Marine steamed toward the Solomons. Charlie loved the attention paid to the picture by his Marine buddies, who considered Billie a ravishing beauty.

June McDougall (middle) visits with family members and a friend in this 1946 photograph taken in New Zealand. After a difficult transition following Gene Seng's death, she eventually remarried, although June has never forgotten Gene Seng. She still resides in her beloved New Zealand.

PhM1 Stanley Bowen shortly before the battle. War interrupted the young Californian's world of sporting events and females, but like thousands of his countrymen, he readily adapted to the challenging situation.

Stanley Bowen outside his Laguna Beach home. Once a month, Bowen and a large group of friends who graduated from Beverly Hills High School gather at a local restaurant to swap tales and reminisce.

From the author's collection.

SSgt. Norman Hatch in New Zealand before the battle. The cameraman would later befriend Hollywood star Errol Flynn and help prepare him for roles in war movies.

From the Norman T. Hatch collection.

Norman Hatch in his Arlington, Virginia, office. The cameraman still maintains an active photography business, and he promotes the efforts of military cameramen through speeches and magazine articles.

From the author's collection.

Despite a Navy regulation forbidding brothers from serving in the same unit, passed after five Sullivan brothers perished on the USS *Juneau* in November 1942, the Meadows brothers (left to right, William, James, and Richard) fought at Betio. Since they were in separate units, they did not come under the new regulation, but the three were rarely more than a mile or two apart on the isle.

From the Meadows family collection.

Robert Muhlbach (left) and his close Marine buddy Steve Farrell in New Zealand shortly before departing for Betio. The two shared many experiences, both on the battlefield and off.

From the Robert Muhlbach collection.

William Hawkins displayed inner strength his entire life. He overcame physical maladies to join the Marines, and his nonstop heroics at Betio led to a Medal of Honor.

United States Marine Corps #12448.

Artist Tom Lovell captures the long wade ashore in this painting of Marines heading toward Red 3. Pfc. Rob[
Muhlbach, Pfc. Albert Gilman, SSgt. Norman Hatch, and Maj. William Chamberlin moved in along t[
route, to the left of the wooden pier. Imagine what went through the minds of the Marines as they fac[
a long walk through the surging tide, directly into Japanese machine-gun fire.

Painting by Tom Lovell. Courtesy of the Marine Corps Historical Ce[

Charles Waterhouse graphically portrays the frightful trip to the beaches at Betio in this painting. Barbed w[
has snared a few bodies, while explosions and wrecked amtracs mingle with the exhausted survivors, who y[
face the daunting task of moving forward against withering fire.

Painting by Charles Waterhouse. Courtesy of the Marine Corps Historical Cer[

This Marine fights the tide's pull, barbed wire, and the sight of mangled bodies to continue shoreward. Some men, like Pfc. Robert Muhlbach, felt as if they were moving through a nightmare, or as if they had been anesthetized.

Painting by Kerr Eby.
Courtesy of the Navy Art Collection,
Naval Historical Center.

Kerr Eby produced one of the most stunning images about the battle in this drawing of Marine dead. The artist, who also covered World War I, wrote on the back of this sketch, "In two wars this I think is the most frightful thing I have seen."

Painting by Kerr Eby.
Courtesy of the Navy Art Collection,
Naval Historical Center.

On the first day, Marines huddle at the base of the seawall while a few leap over to do battle in "No Man's Land." Pfc. Charles Wysocki Jr. (left) rests at the wall's base in a group of four Marines. From the Norman T. Hatch collection.

In the early moments of the fighting, three Marines leave the relative security of the se wall to head into the open stretch of sand and blackene palm trees beyond. As many half of these first men to charge Japanese positions were killed or wounded.

From the Norman T. Hatch collection.

From behind a wrecked amtrac, Maj. Henry P. "Jim" Crowe observes the action at Red 3 on day one. Despite being in the open for much of the battle, Crowe emerged unhurt. His good fortune did not last, however, as he suffered serious wounds at Saipan, the next Marine assault.

From the Norman T. Hatch collection.

A common sight throughout the battle was Marines comir to the aid of a wounded budd Here, two Marines risk their lives by rushing into the open to help another back to the seawall.

From the Norman T. Hatch collection.

Men help a wounded Marine to one of the few places offering shelter at Betio—the coconut log seawall. Beyond the wall was open land sprinkled with shell holes, Japanese pillboxes, and death.

From the Norman T. Hatch collection.

One Marine throws a hand grenade toward the enemy while a second pauses for a drink of water. The bayonet atop his rifle indicates the close nature of the combat on Betio, while the smoke-shrouded, denuded palm trees beyond attest to the battle's ferocity.

From the Norman T. Hatch collection.

The pier was both an avenue of death and of support during the three days at Betio. Marines rushed supplies along the structure to the men ashore, but it came with a price. In an effort to halt this, Japanese snipers made the pier a favorite target, leading some Americans to think they stood on a bull's-eye.

Painting by Kerr Eby. Courtesy of the Navy Art Collection, Naval Historical Center.

Led by Major Chamberlin (not pictured), on the third day, Marines rush to the top of the Japanese fortification that had rebuffed every attack for two days. Some peer down the other side, where Chamberlin and Hatch had first spotted the enemy. For his bravery at this location, 1st Lt. Alexander Bonnyman Jr. was awarded a posthumous Medal of Honor.

From the Norman T. Hatch collection.

In the middle, Staff Sergeant Hatch films the attack on the fortification while Private Kelliher stands to his right. Moments later, a group of Japanese soldiers rushed out of the bunker to the left, enabling Hatch to film one of the war's most memorable sequences.

From the Norman T. Hatch collection.

This photograph, taken on the third day of battle, shows the damage caused from American shells and bombs. Part of the airstrip cuts through the middle, not far from where F Company dashed across the island.

Naval Historical Center #95708.

One sign that the battle had swerved in favor of the Marines was the sight of Japanese who committed suicide rather than surrender. These soldiers pointed their rifles at their faces and used their big toes to pull the triggers.

From the Norman T. Hatch collection.

The body of a dead Marine floats near two destroyed amtracs off Red 1. High tide has covered portions of the beach upon which the Marines, including Montague and Seng, landed.

From the Norman T. Hatch collection.

Devastation, including a beached amtrac and numerous floating bodies, attests to the severe nature of combat at Red 2, where Lieutenant Hawkins and F Company fought. Betio's numerous palm trees show the effects of the fighting.

From the Norman T. Hatch collection.

The Bird's Beak stands between Beach Red 1 on the left and Green Beach to the right. Montague and Seng landed toward the upper left corner of the photograph, where the damaged craft litter the shoreline, while the Meadows brothers came ashore on Green Beach. Notice the battle's effects on Betio's once luscious vegetation.

Naval Historical Center #NH 95704.

Although Marines took refuge in shell holes and near palm trees, they quickly learned that no place on Betio shielded them from danger. Japanese soldiers, waiting in the numerous spider holes and pillboxes deftly positioned about the island's terrain, took a heavy toll.

From the Norman T. Hatch collection.

The cost of combat is graphically displayed in this photograph of one of the invasion beaches. Two Marines sit atop a wrecked Sherman tank, while others inspect the devastation.

National Archives #80-G-57405.

Scenes such as this one, picturing a landing craft filled with dead, were common. Aboard one boat, a wounded correspondent spent hours buried among the dead.

Painting by Kerr Eby. Courtesy of the Navy Art Collection, Naval Historical Center.

The debris of battle included the belongings and photographs of loved ones of one unknown Marine slain at Betio. Men like Montague and Seng gave their lives—and decades with families and sweethearts—to defeat the Japanese.

From the Norman T. Hatch collection.

Some Marines found irresistible the attraction of collecting anything Japanese, despite warnings that such activity could result in death from hidden enemy soldiers. Swords, flags, and Japanese beer were the most popular.

From the Norman T. Hatch collection.

On the third day of battle, Marines inspect one of the hundreds of Japanese bunkers that exacted a frightening toll on the invaders. The deft use of alternating layers of sand and coconut logs is shown here.

National Archives #NAVAER-452A.

Images of death and destruction covered almost every yard of Betio. Many bodies could not be identified because of the severe nature of the fighting. Here a group of charred Japanese soldiers litters one section of Betio, while the landscape beyond resembles a trash heap.

From the Norman T. Hatch collection.

Staff Sergeant Hatch pauses from filming the battle to give water to a frightened kitten. Hatch at first thought the cries he heard coming from underneath the tank were human wails, but closer inspection yielded this surprising result. Other Marines encountered a rooster, a duck, and a dog.

From the Norman T. Hatch collection.

This attempt at black humor after the battle was a grim reminder of the carnage staged at Betio, and of the cost that future operations would exact. Photographs like this, along with Sherrod's book and Hatch's film, educated the American public as to the horrors of war.

From the Norman T. Hatch collection.

From the Seng sisters' collection.

National Archives #348791.

...mple white crosses marked the Betio graves of Texas friends Gene Seng and Charlie Montague. The Seng ...mily later moved Gene's body to Texas to be closer to loved ones, while Charlie's remains rest in a Hawaiian ...metery honoring the Pacific dead.

Gene Seng's mother visits th[e] grave of her son at the milita[ry] cemetery near San Antonio. The picture visualizes the anguish felt by thousands of families who lost a loved one [in] the conflict and emphasizes that while soldiers faced tria[l] on the battlefield, family members battled their own tribulations at home.

From the Seng sisters' collection.

Maj. William C. Chamberlin (left), hero of Red 3, receives his Navy Cross from Adm. Chester W. Nimitz, Commander in Chief, Pacific Fleet. Many who fought under his command believed that the college professor deserved the Medal of Honor.

From the Chamberlin family collection.

A plaque honoring the school's former students who died in war adorns the wall just inside the main entrance of Central Catholic High School in San Antonio. The names of Charlie Montague and Gene Seng rest appropriately only inches apart, just as their bodies once lay feet apart on Betio. The third graduate who died in the battle, William Bodelon, is also honored on the plaque.

From the author's collection.

and seventy men sprinted along the airfield, yelling all the way. "We were seventy versions of John Wayne. The good guys after the bad,"[9] Jones later recalled.

The Marines reached their destination without suffering a single casualty. As most Japanese defenses in this area faced the ocean rather than the airstrip, Sanford had advanced before the Japanese had time to react and man inland defenses.

The easy journey across the airstrip served merely as a prelude to what lay ahead. Sanford led his men into a narrow one-hundred-yard-long tank trap that ran parallel to the southern beach. Heavy rifle and machine gun fire met the men of F Company from every side. Snipers hit the two men fighting next to Pemberton, one in the face and the other in the genitals, while enemy machine guns at the left end stitched the length of the ditch. "Dead and wounded fell from one end to the other,"[10] stated Private First Class Jones, who pressed his body as deep into the dirt walls as possible to avoid the buzzing bullets.

Sanford, Jones and the others dodged the fire until they finally knocked out the Japanese machine guns and eliminated the riflemen. When a sniper in a tree shot Sanford through the jaw and chin, angry Marines fired until their bullets had completely shorn the top half of the palm tree and killed the offending soldier. By securing the trench, F Company had cut Betio in half and divided the enemy into two pockets. Shoup now had Marines from shore to shore.

Additional troops from the 1st Battalion reached Sanford at 3:00 P.M., while an hour later Colonel Jordan arrived from the invasion beach and took command of the forces in the trench. Jordan and two hundred Marines held the southern shore after one of the crucial engagements of the battle's second day.

"Boys, I Sure Hate to Leave You"

Back at Red 2, Lieutenant Hawkins received orders to attack a series of enemy defenses one hundred yards west of Shoup's command post. Reinforced with a group of scout-snipers, he set out at 6:30 A.M. to register one of the battle's most heralded sequences.

Whenever the men approached a Japanese bunker or pillbox, Hawkins took the point position. Grabbing hand grenades and covered by the other Marines' fire, the officer knocked out three pillboxes in quick succession.

"Get down, Hawk, or you'll get shot," yelled a concerned Marine when Hawkins returned to the beach for more ammunition.

As he jumped back over the seawall to continue the fighting, Hawkins replied, "Aw, those bastards can't shoot. They can't hit anything."[11]

Hawkins freely moved about the battlefield, oblivious to the dangers that threatened. About seventy-five yards from the command post, Hawkins tossed a grenade into a firing slit in an enemy pillbox, but a quick-handed Japanese soldier threw it back out. The explosion sprayed shrapnel across Hawkins's chest but, although badly wounded, he stayed next to the pillbox and hurled more grenades until he had killed all its occupants.

Hawkins ignored the pleas from his scout-snipers to seek medical aid and continued to attack the Japanese. "I came here to kill Japs; I didn't come here to be evacuated,"[12] he told his men. One officer called Hawkins a "madman. He cleaned out six machine-gun nests, with two to six Japs in each nest."[13] News of Hawkins's exploits spread about the beachhead as he demolished one position after another.

Then, around 10:30, a Japanese soldier shot Hawkins in the shoulder. A stream of blood gushed into the air—the bullet had severed a main artery—as Hawkins slumped to the sand, his right armpit torn away. His scout-snipers carried Hawkins back to the beach, where Dr. Brukhardt tried to make Hawkins's final moments comfortable, but he could do nothing to save the Marine.

Had Dr. Brukhardt been in a stateside hospital with the proper tools, he might have been able to stem the blood flow, but even that most likely would have been a temporary measure. Hawkins lay near death. Lapsing in and out of consciousness, the officer died ten minutes after arriving at the aid station.

"Boys, I sure hate to leave you like this,"[14] he gasped in his final moments to his men, who cried unabashedly as they crowded around their leader. The scout-snipers, who were willing to follow their commander into any situation, now tenderly lifted Hawkins and buried him in a temporary grave behind the command post.

"It's not often that you can credit a first lieutenant with winning a battle, but Hawkins came as near to it as any man could," Colonel Shoup told Robert Sherrod. "He was truly an inspiration."[15] Gen. Julian Smith later named Betio's airfield Hawkins Field to honor the courageous Marine. Hawkins's body eventually came to rest in the National Cemetery of the Pacific in Hawaii, along with the remains of thousands of other men who gave their lives for their country.

PART III: GAINS AT RED 3

"Do They Have a Tunnel to Tokyo?"

While Major Ryan expanded the beachhead at Red 1 and F Company dashed to the southern shoreline at Red 2, Major Crowe encountered an iron wall of defenses in his sector at Red 3. Three locations especially vexed the officer—a steel-reinforced pillbox, a log and coral emplacement, and a large bombproof shelter. Each mutually supported the other, so that forces attacking one spot would be brought under fire from the other two locations. Before Crowe could push his forces off Red 3, he had to eliminate those three obstinate spots. He failed to knock them out on day two of the battle, but the small gains he registered, plus the addition of reinforcements, put men in place who would succeed the next day.

"Where the hell are they coming from?" Crowe shouted in exasperation. Every time his Marines attacked, more Japanese seemed to be defending the positions. "Do they have a tunnel to Tokyo or something?"[16]

The Marines had to wear down the Japanese—charge one spot, destroy it, then move to the next. At some places, Marines tossed in blocks of TNT and numerous hand grenades, but still enemy fire answered. They later learned that the bunkers and pillboxes were divided into compartments, requiring each one to be destroyed in order to eliminate the entire structure. The Japanese dug many foxholes in a spider pattern, with trenches extending from a center area to five or six other foxholes. After observing this and witnessing some of the primitive combat that unfolded, correspondent William Hipple vowed, "I'm asking the home office for a transfer to the European war theater the first chance I get. At least they surrender over there."[17]

Private First Class Gilman, despite being wounded, continued to fight and said that the progress was "slow, slow, slow—on my stomach from bomb crater to bomb crater, using anything to protect me from fire. I didn't see many Japanese, but I knew they were there. The Japanese bunkers were like huge anthills with a hole in the top to shoot out of. They were dug in so deeply they could have survived the bombardment forever. The Japanese soldier had a total lack of fear and a complete willingness to die. I didn't believe there were soldiers like this anywhere. We had to use flamethrowers to destroy the pillboxes, an inhumane but necessary way. It was the only way to knock them out."

Gilman, weakened from his wounds, headed to the beach to seek medical assistance. He wondered if he had made the right choice. "The beach was a gruesome place. There were dead Marines lying all over and others with wounds that made mine seem slight. I'd almost rather be back fighting than to stay here."

Corpsmen loaded Gilman on a rubber raft, which transported him to the reef. Smaller craft then took him to a hospital ship for evacuation to Pearl Harbor. Not long after the battle, the *Saturday Evening Post* published a photograph of Marines being removed from Betio on a rubber raft. Although Gilman was not in the picture, one of the wounded Marines bore a striking resemblance to him. When his mother, who had received no news of her son, saw the picture, "she thought the Marine was me. I was told that kept her going. It wasn't me, but it sure did look like me, and if it gave my parents hope that I was alive, I am grateful for that picture."[18]

"It Wasn't Dramatic with Us"

Private First Class Muhlbach's experience operating inland from Red 3 typified the bloodletting and horrors of combat during days two and three on Betio. "We jumped into the foxholes and emplacements and bayoneted them or shot them. There was a lot of bayoneting," explained Muhlbach. "The strangling and gouging is kind of movie stuff. It happened where there was occasion when we had to use our knives."

The bayoneting was not a simple move. To make sure one thrust finished his opponent, Muhlbach plunged the bayonet deep into the enemy. "You wanted to get it deep inside to make sure that it was a kill, and you'd get it in there and wiggle it around, and then extract it."

If the bayonet hit something heavy, like a strap, a cartridge belt, or the soldier's chest bone, Muhlbach quickly pulled it back and plunged again. Muhlbach learned to keep one eye out for other Japanese soldiers who might approach while he bayoneted the defender, and more than once he grabbed his KA-BAR and killed a second opponent while he labored to remove his bayonet from the first. "You'd hold onto your rifle. Just as soon as you had a chance to do it, you'd kick the body and pull on your bayonet, wiggling it a bit and loosening it, then pull it out and put it into the next guy. It's hard to explain, but you're in a fight, like a fight in a ring between two boxers. You're just thinking of trying to find an outlet where you could get a punch in or a kick in. That's what you're thinking of, damaging the other guy, and there's not much thought of anything else but trying to find that outlet to kill the other guy. Those movie versions—I guess they've got to come up with something that's dramatic. It wasn't dramatic with us. We were supposed to fight, to find a way of killing the other guy."

Like most Marines who fought at Betio, Muhlbach was shocked by the size of the Japanese soldiers. Prewar American stereotypes fostered the image of the short, bespectacled, bucktoothed Japanese, but Betio demolished those preconceptions. Muhlbach confronted Japanese who easily topped the six-foot mark. "They were defending themselves, and so we had to parry and thrust, and they were good! Those guys were so much bigger than the average Jap. They were naval landing forces, like Japanese marines, and they were larger. They were very accurate with their weapons, and good with their bayonet fighting."

One time he crawled around a bunker to a side containing a collection of little mounds. He moved to the first and poked into it with his bayonet. When the cover rose and revealed a Japanese soldier with a rifle, before his enemy could react, Muhlbach ran his bayonet through the soldier's mouth and killed him.

"A lot of soldiers would jump out of a spider hole or small bunker, out of nowhere. You'd think it was a body lying there, but it was a live Jap, so you just had to be careful. You shot the body or ran it through with your bayonet. Every time you saw a Jap you made sure he was dead, because they tended to make believe they were dead."

When Marines took enemy fire from an outhouse along the pier and from an abandoned ship on the reef, Muhlbach put the scope on his rifle, shot once toward the outhouse, then trained his rifle and fired again at the ship. A body and rifle fell from the outhouse, while a second Japanese soldier splashed into the lagoon from the ship.

"I don't know how many I killed during the three days," added Muhlbach. "It was quite a few of them. You didn't have time to count. I've seen books that have guys that say they killed 115, or 10—who counts? A lot of them you don't even know if they died or not. You hit them and don't know if they're dead. You didn't go over and ask them."

Muhlbach often teamed with another Marine, Steve Farrell, and even fought back-to-back with him at Betio. He recalls the time when he and five or six other Marines battled from a large shell hole. A unit of enemy soldiers rushed them from a bunker, but dropped one by one as Muhlbach's group laid down a withering fire. The action ended with a stack of Japanese bodies lying around the edge of the shell hole.

Not long after, an enemy grenade exploded directly among the bodies. "The explosion blew the guts of all those dead Japs right at us. We were covered with guts. One guy thought he was hit and that the guts were his, so he called for a corpsman and tried to stuff the guts back in his stomach. Finally, someone told him those were Jap guts."

Humor sometimes appeared in the midst of the fighting. One time Muhlbach's cartridge belt began slipping from his waist as he and Farrell raced across the runway inland from Red 3. He lacked suspenders to hold the heavy cartridge belt, which added one hundred rounds of ammunition to the water canteens, KA-BAR knife, and other burdensome equipment he carried. With each step, the belt slipped lower on his hips and onto his legs.

"The cartridge belt kept going down farther and farther. It got to around my knees, and I'm doing a duck waddle at high port, and I swear I could hear the guys laughing back there."

Fortunately, Muhlbach and Farrell safely crossed the airstrip, only to hear Crowe's booming voice command, "Get your asses back here, you dumb sons-of-bitches!" Crowe had not yet organized an advance at that point and wanted them closer to the seawall. Muhlbach pulled up his cartridge belt and repeated his awkward journey, this time in the opposite direction.

Crowe ordered the men to retrieve weapons and ammunition from the wounded and dead on the beach. As he walked around the shoreline, Muhlbach saw the arm of one badly wounded Marine lift up. "He was hit pretty bad and could hardly move. He saw me coming around, picking up stuff, and he lifted up his BAR [Browning Automatic Rifle] and looked at me like, 'Here. Get my BAR. You'll need that.' So I took the BAR and his cartridge belt. He laid down and I went on. I'll never forget that."

Muhlbach took few, if any, breaks from the fighting, and he ate only once when, on the second day, he cracked open a K ration and consumed a tin of meat. Sleep was an unheard-of phenomenon during his seventy-six hours on Betio. "No time for sleeping, no matter how exhausted we were, and we were pretty exhausted by the time we got to the beach." Two factors kept him going—the adrenaline rush that many combatants experience, and duty to his fellow Marines.

"You had to be a part of it. If other guys are doing things, you want to be a part of it. You don't want to hold back. You just did what you're supposed to do. The Marines are known for that. You don't think of anything else but be a part of it."

Hollywood often depicts soldiers fighting for Mom, Dad, and girlfriends, but this version is far from reality, which Muhlbach claims is not at all like the movies. "Your thoughts are of the enemy. You want to get at them and kill them. That's all I could think of. I wasn't thinking of home or anything like that, or a girlfriend. I just wanted to get out there and kill as many Japs as I could. We had to stop them from shooting our own people."[19]

"You Just Quit Worrying"

As Muhlbach's story attests, the struggle to seize Betio relied on courage and the willingness to die. Few men slept, few ate more than a morsel. They drank water that, because it had been stored in improperly treated drums that had once housed gasoline, so tasted of the fuel that Marines joked if you belched too close to a flamethrower you would explode. But they kept going, mainly because to do otherwise was unthinkable.

Capt. Carl W. Hoffman, who commanded a weapons company, concluded afterward, "It was close, hand-to-hand fighting and survival for three and a half days. . . . It was just plain old guts that carried us to victory." A correspondent depicted it more bluntly by writing that the Marines "butchered their way across Betio,"[20] destroying pillboxes and grappling with the enemy.

The unusual patterns that dotted Betio's beaches attested to the carnage. Marines thrashing about as they lay wounded or dying had twisted the white coral sand into strange configurations. The outlines looked ironically similar to the angels that children imprint in snow, but a bloodred hue to the sand reminded one that this was no youthful endeavor. Army officers in Hawaii, aghast that men willingly battled in such horrific conditions, later asked Sherrod if doctors had doped the Marines so they would more readily advance into machine gun fire.

The men needed no medication. After a time, many simply threw caution to the wind and let fate take over. "Walking along the shore with bullets all around should have been terrifying," wrote 1st Lt. Melvin A. Traylor Jr., "but after a while you figured there was nothing you could do about it, and you just quit worrying."[21]

Some tested fate in extreme fashion. Pfc. Adrian Strange walked around in clear view of the enemy, trying to bum a smoke. "Somebody gimme some cigarettes," he grumped. "That machine gun crew is out there in a shell-hole across the airfield and there's not a cigarette in the crowd."

When Strange found some cigarettes he headed back inland, with sniper bullets kicking up sand. "Shoot me down, you son-of-a-bitch," he yelled to the unseen sniper as he continued to walk back to the airfield.

After witnessing the spectacle, another Marine remarked to Sherrod, "That boy Strange, he just don't give a damn."[22]

Lt. Frank W. Plant Jr. concluded that three categories of men existed in battle. Some froze and could do nothing to contribute. For instance, he unsuccessfully tried to halt one terrorized private who dug deeper and deeper into the sand, as if in doing so he could escape the carnage. Not far from this private, two other Marines, rigid with fear, lay immobile on the ground with their arms extended at right angles.

The other extreme offered those, like Hawkins, who not only ignored every risk but seemed eager to face them. He called them "sons of guns" who inspired the men, and concluded, "Most of them probably lost their lives."[23] The vast majority, he decided, stood in the middle of two extremes, following orders and killing Japanese because that was what they were supposed to do.

Not everything was so serious. Staff Sergeant Hatch discovered a kitten in the unlikeliest of places—behind the treads of a destroyed Japanese tank. He and Kelliher had carefully approached the tank when Hatch thought he heard a noise coming from under the vehicle. At first he assumed it was a human calling for help, but when he peered underneath—taking precautions in case it was a Japanese trick—a kitten gazed back. Hatch poured out some water and enticed the cat to leave its hiding place. Kelliher snapped a photograph of the incongruous incident, which featured a man in the middle of horrifying butchery stopping to help one of nature's smallest creatures.

Siwash the duck was the darling of the press, though. The mascot of Cpl. Francis Fagan and an artillery unit, Siwash swilled beer with the Marines in New Zealand, and according to a *Time* magazine article about the battle, "in the first 15 minutes of his invasion beat the stuffing out of a Jap rooster, attacked and routed a shell-shocked Jap pig. Siwash showed no battle strain at all."[24]

Siwash garnered praise, all tongue-in-cheek. His unit recommended him for a Purple Heart, *Life* magazine ran his photograph, and a Marine wrote a poem to the duck patterned after Edgar Allan Poe's classic "The Raven."

Incidents involving animals were mere interludes in the storm. While Siwash attracted the press's attention on land, a Navy lieutenant (jg), whose name the press and the American moviegoing public already knew, performed heroic deeds near the reef during a tumultuous morning that second day.

"Not like the Movies, Eh?"

At 6:15 A.M., Major Hays's 1st Battalion, 8th Marines, waded ashore to reinforce the men at Red 2. Like every other unit that had attempted to land, they walked into a deadly greeting that had, within minutes, wiped out one-third of the battalion. "Fire from enemy positions mowed them down as a scythe cuts through grass,"[25] stated Chaplain Willard of his trek in the waters with the Marines. Muhlbach and others watched from shore, holding back tears as they viewed another slaughter, with men screaming and the water turning to red.

"The men already on the shore watched them come in and fought back tears of blind rage and cursed bitter oaths as they saw these boys go down," wrote one correspondent. "A man would fall, and would get up to stumble a few more feet before he went down again. You could see him fighting to hold his head above the water and trying to get up on his feet. Some of them crawled on their elbows. Some hung on the barbed wire entanglements that were on the reef, and drowned."[26]

Pharmacist's Mate First Class Robert E. Costello saw one Marine, weighed down by bulky equipment, hit three times before reaching the beach. When Costello asked him why he did not simply drop his huge load so he could make a smaller, faster target, the Marine replied that he had heard they needed ammunition ashore and he could not just let go of it.

Once Hays and his men gathered on Red 2, Shoup ordered him to attack westward against the tough enemy defenses in the Pocket, eliminate them, and join with Major Ryan at Red 1. Though Hays enjoyed the support of some pack howitzers, the enemy rebuffed every attempt to overrun them. Without flamethrowers and demolitions men, Hays's ability to destroy bunkers and blockhouses was greatly reduced. By nighttime, Hays's men had dug in and waited to try again on the third day.

Lt. (jg) Edward Heimberger commanded a landing craft that morning. Much of the nation knew him as actor Eddie Albert, the star of such films as *Brother Rat* and *Four Wives*, and after the war he would gain additional fame in movies and in the hit television show *Green Acres*. Aboard a Higgins boat containing several large oil drums, Albert repeatedly braved Japanese fire to rescue wounded Marines at or near the reef. Albert carefully maneuvered his boat near the stricken Marines, and often had to reach over the side to help pull them aboard.

"It was awful," he later explained. "Sometimes I think we hurt the men

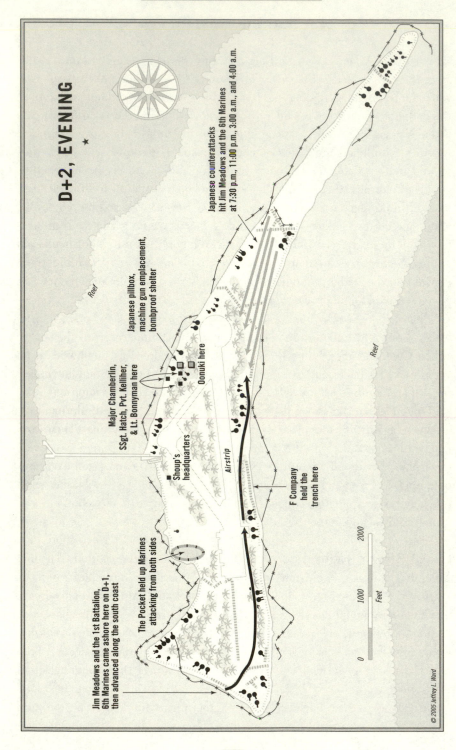

D+2, EVENING

Japanese counterattacks
hit Jim Meadows and the 6th Marines
at 7:30 p.m., 11:30 p.m., 3:00 a.m., and 4:00 a.m.

Japanese pillbox,
machine gun emplacement,
bombproof shelter

Major Chamberlin,
Sgt. Hatch, Pvt. Kelliher,
& Lt. Bonnyman here

Oonuki here

Shoup's
headquarters

F Company
held the
trench here

Airstrip

The Pocket held up Marines
attacking from both sides

Jim Meadows and the 1st Battalion,
6th Marines came ashore here on D+1,
then advanced along the south coast

Reef

Reef

Feet

0   1000   2000

© 2005 Jeffrey L. Ward

more by pulling them up by their broken arms or legs than if we'd left them in the water."[27]

On one of his runs, Albert approached a group of thirty-five Marines. They did not appear to be injured, but Albert saw they also had lost their weapons. When he offered to take them back to the transport, they declined. They wanted to join their buddies ashore and asked Albert on his next trip to bring them some rifles.

After spending the morning evacuating wounded Marines, Albert ferried supplies to the pier. When time permitted, he made his way to the beach. Johnny Florea, a *Time-Life* photographer who covered Hollywood before the war, witnessed a brief reunion that he normally would have recorded in California. "For a moment it was just like Hollywood and Vine. Lieutenant Eddie Albert, running a casualty boat, came into the beachhead and who should he run into but Captain Louis Hayward, heading the Marine photographic unit. As they passed each other, Eddie yells out, 'Not like the movies, eh, Louis?' The reply was a short, 'Hell no!' and they went about their business."[28]

Albert slept on Betio that night, but his rest was interrupted when someone jumped in on top of him to avoid gunfire. They stretched out in the foxhole, head to foot, and chatted for a time. The other man claimed he had been in the Marine Corps for thirty-eight years and he had never seen anything this bad before. The Marine removed his trousers, neatly folded them, and laid them across his chest. When Albert wondered why he did that, the Marine said there was not much he could do about the battle but he could at least look neat in the morning.

With the dawn, the Marine donned his trousers, warned Albert of a nearby sniper, then departed. Albert followed the man and asked another Marine who he was. Albert had spent the night with Lieutenant Colonel Carlson.

Chaplain Willard had stepped into a maelstrom once he reached shore. As Willard stooped low and ran toward the seawall a Marine shouted, "Hurry, Chaplain, hurry! I've seen four men killed today on the spot where you are standing!" Willard hustled over to a beached amtrac, where Major Crowe issued orders into a field telephone. Willard rose to obtain a view of the proceedings, but dropped down when Crowe yelled, "Duck, you fool! There's a sniper over there!"[29] Just as Willard lowered his head, a bullet smacked close by.

Willard, with his trademark hand grenades, Mike and Ike, dangling from his chest, joined other chaplains, such as Roman Catholic Fr. William O'Neill, in saying prayers for the dead. Time denied a proper burial for now—a shallow grave with sand heaped on top had to suffice. Willard also jumped into foxholes, offered words of comfort, carried wounded back for aid, prayed with the men, and brought comfort and peace to men existing in a cataclysmic world of violence. One correspondent observed the chaplains at work and wrote that each one was "worth as much to the boys of his regiment as a trainload of ammunition."[30]

He even indirectly saved the life of Pfc. Henry P. Clayton. Willard had given Clayton one of the two thousand Bibles he handed out in San Diego. On this day, a sniper's bullet from behind smacked into Clayton's pack, but other than being temporarily dazed, Clayton walked away unhurt. When he opened his pack, Clayton removed a torn Bible. Willard's Bible had stopped the bullet and prevented it from killing the Marine.

"You Were Dead to the World"

In the course of his work, Willard frequently encountered corpsmen like Stanley Bowen who tried to repair the ravages of battle. The men labored under the most difficult circumstances, utilizing improvised equipment at times, with little or no sleep. "All three days, all I did was treat the men," said Dr. Herman Brukhardt. "I got very little rest, and none the first night. You were dead to the world."[31]

Bowen, Brukhardt, and the rest worked on all sorts of injuries. The fine coral sand quickly filled most wounds, making them harder to clean, and corpsmen noticed that a large proportion of Marines suffered from multiple wounds. They had been simultaneously hit by different bullets, hit repeatedly as they advanced, or struck by additional bullets and shrapnel as they lay injured on the terrain.

Gunshot wounds to the legs and arms, producing shattered bones and large tissue loss, dominated the list of injuries Bowen and the others treated. The prevalence of back wounds also indicated that many Marines had been shot from behind, usually either by Japanese snipers and infiltrators, or by groups of hidden Japanese allowing the Americans to pass by before attacking. Surgeons operating aboard the transports performed numerous amputations using, according to one physician's report, "the guillotine method"[32] of removing the limbs.

Bowen could look with pride upon his work, as less than 3 percent of the men died from their wounds once they had been treated. Plasma and sulfa drugs, the new wonder drugs of the war, drastically reduced infection and led to improved chances of survival.

Along with sulfa and plasma, a third medication ameliorated injuries, at least according to the Marines. The quantities of medicinal brandy on hand did little to improve a wound or broken leg, but corpsmen and physicians noticed how an ounce or two of the alcohol improved the men's outlook. One official report after the battle concluded that while "the therapeutic value of brandy was not demonstrated . . . there is no question of its value as a morale factor."[33] One Marine, bleeding from a minor cut, said jokingly that he would have been wounded earlier had he known about the brandy.

Bowen noticed that almost every man on Betio suffered from sunburn, although the sand that hampered efforts to treat wounds now seemed to help. "It was so damn hot that sunburn was a major problem. My lower lip was split and bleeding from being burned. A lot of guys were sunburned, and you're so dirty from dust and dirt and grime, it acted like sunscreen, I guess."[34]

Unfortunately, planners had not foreseen this issue and did not think to include lip balm, so the men endured the discomfort as well as possible. Wounded men lying in the open, unable to move to shaded areas, especially suffered from the equatorial sun.

"Combat Efficiency—We Are Winning"

Despite a rough morning, Marines registered dramatic gains during day two. Ryan at Red 1 and F Company at Red 2 had consolidated their lines and expanded the beachhead, while Major Crowe at Red 3 prepared to knock out the next day the stubborn complex blocking his way.

Shortly after noon, momentum swerved to the Americans. The artillery commander, Lt. Col. Presley M. Rixey, later said that no one felt confident for the first day and a half, but that the second afternoon altered things. "I thought up until 1 o'clock today that it was touch and go," he said that second night. "Then I knew we would win."[35] Edson stated the same.

Their optimism came from different sources. Marines moving through the Japanese defenses noticed that Japanese defenders, instead of fighting, had started to commit suicide. They counted seventeen Japanese bodies in one bunker, all dead from self-inflicted wounds. Shoup took this as a sign that the Japanese spirit had been broken.

The arrival of jeeps at the pier in late afternoon reinforced the notion that the Marines had grabbed the upper hand. Up until then, Marines risked death to bring in the basics—ammunition and water. Now reinforcements had landed at Red 1, and vehicles instead of only the basics meandered along the wooden pier. "If a sign of certain victory were needed, this is it," wrote Sherrod at 6:03 P.M. "The Jeeps have arrived."[36]

Shoup felt conditions ashore had changed sufficiently that he could send a more positive assessment than his morning message. He had earlier transmitted the phrase SITUATION ASHORE UNCERTAIN. By late afternoon he felt confident enough to radio, CASUALTIES MANY. PERCENTAGE DEAD UNKNOWN. COMBAT EFFICIENCY—WE ARE WINNING.[37]

Correspondent Richard W. Johnston of the United Press agreed. He had seen Marines wade through a watery inferno and selflessly charge Japanese pillboxes, and now the effort seemed to have paid off. "Men have died around me, many lie dead up ahead and more are going in to die. The situation at one time was critical, but the valor of the Marines and the perfectly coordinated support of the navy and air force have won the battle."[38]

Colonel Shoup thought the turning point had been reached. He looked at Robert Sherrod, who had come up to ask a question, and said, "Well, I think we're winning, but the bastards have got a lot of bullets left. I think we'll clean up tomorrow."[39]

At 4:55 Lt. Col. Raymond L. Murray landed at Bairiki with the 2d Battalion, 6th Marines, including Dick Meadows. They swiftly brushed aside minimal opposition from fifteen Japanese soldiers, secured the island, and cut off that route of retreat for the enemy. With the sounds of battle raging two miles west at Betio, Dick Meadows's combat ended swiftly and peacefully, hardly what he had expected. He hoped brothers Jim and Bill were as safe over at the main island.

At 8:30 P.M. Colonel Edson arrived at Shoup's command post to take the reins from the weary officer. Shoup's firm guidance in the first two days of fighting served as the glue holding together a fragile beachhead. Now, with reinforcements and supplies pouring ashore, Edson could take over as planned and complete the operation. Though his role in the operation had ended, Shoup agreed to stay and help Edson formulate the next day's offensive.

When exhausted Marines plopped into their foxholes for the second night, more looked forward to catching a little sleep than on the first night. The Japanese had not counterattacked when they expected them to, so possibly a quiet second night loomed. Maybe they had nothing more to worry about than the hundreds of tiny sand crabs that crawled everywhere. They would later regret those thoughts.

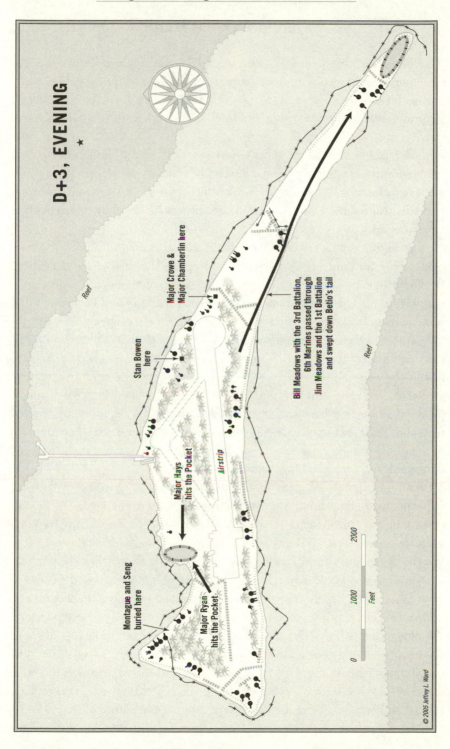

D+3, EVENING

Major Crowe &
Major Chamberlin here

Stan Bowen
here

Bill Meadows with the 3rd Battalion,
6th Marines passed through
Jim Meadows and the 1st Battalion
and swept down Betio's tail

Major Hays
hits the Pocket

Airstrip

Montague and Seng
buried here

Major Ryan
hits the Pocket

Reef

Reef

0   1000   2000
Feet

© 2005 Jeffrey L. Ward

"Hoping Against Hope"

For Billie Miller, November 21—the second day of combat at Betio—was like any other day. She awoke, prepared to go to work, and said the first of her many prayers for Charlie's safety. "I thought of Charlie every day," she said later. "I went to novenas and everything. It was all guesswork as to where he actually was."[40]

Billie did not stand alone in her ignorance. None of the families of the men fighting on Betio knew their sons, husbands, brothers, or fathers at that moment had closed with the enemy. Neither the Montagues, the Sengs, nor Mrs. Hawkins realized their loved ones had already perished on Betio's beaches half a world away.

Except for shortages in certain products, and other relatively minor inconveniences, life continued as always for these people and for the rest of the nation. President Roosevelt and his advisers, in fact, worried about the complacency that had set in. The American people had been asked to sacrifice so often that some leaders feared the nation might begin ignoring the appeals. Except for the families of the men in combat zones, who had legitimate concerns, Americans seemed content to go about their regular routines and let the military handle the war.

Nearly everyone suffered from one shortage—gasoline. Brian Montague, a local judge, wrote Billie shortly before the battle, "This gas rationing and the tire shortage have cut pretty deeply into our traveling about, for since June, we have not been to San Antonio, or away from Del Rio—except such trips as I necessarily make to adjoining counties to hold court."[41]

Rationing hampered plans for Thanksgiving, which arrived the Thursday following the Betio assault. Most families would have to spend it alone or with those who lived near them, as the gasoline crunch precluded their traveling great distances.

The Montagues faced another shortage—workers for their vast ranch. Charlie's aunt Margaret wrote Billie that George Montague looked exhausted from ranch work. "There is so much to be done and now, as time goes on and more and more boys are going to the Army or some branch of the service and the older men to the defense plants, the ranch and farm laborers are very scarce. It is getting to be quite a serious problem."[42]

Marines scoffed at such "crises." Compared to the world they inhabited, civilians back home lived a plush existence and had little reason to complain, but most men in service understood that it was human nature to gripe.

Marines refused to accept one home front feature—strikes. Men in the service detested reading about healthy Americans leaving their jobs back home, especially if the strike target was one of the industries supplying products to the military. United Mine Workers president John L. Lewis, who had already led his coal workers in three strikes against that key industry, especially earned soldiers' venom. "Damn your coal-black soul,"[43] stated the Army newspaper, *Stars and Stripes*, of the labor leader.

The toughest aspect back home, though, was waiting—waiting for loved ones to return; waiting for the war to end; waiting for word that a husband or a father was safe; waiting to hear that a fiancé or a son was still alive; waiting to see if today was the day the dreaded telegram arrived. The families of the men in a combat zone faced their own daily struggle, not with bullets and bombs, but with worry and fear.

Three stars, one for each boy, hung in the front window of Mrs. Meadows's South Dakota home signifying the sacrifice her family had contributed to the war effort. The boys' grandfather mounted framed pictures of the three boys on his living room wall. Each morning, the first thing he did was turn to the photographs and deliver a snappy salute. While it was their way of showing pride in the Meadows boys, it also indicated the deep concern they felt on a daily basis.

Charlie Montague's father avidly followed war developments on the radio—commentator H. V. Kaltenborn was his favorite—and in newspapers, but rarely culled anything helpful about his son. All he knew was that Charlie served somewhere in the Pacific. He took comfort knowing that Charlie at least had his best friend with him.

Billie assumed Charlie and Gene battled on Bougainville, an island 1,400 miles southwest of Betio that American forces had invaded earlier in November. One of their friends who had seen both Seng and Montague in New Zealand, Pfc. Lyle S. Brown, wrote to her, "First of all, I have a hunch that Charlie is on Bougainville, as I'm pretty sure that is where the 'Second Marines' are." He guessed the war would be over within one year, stated that he had met and liked June McDougall, and added, "Gene and Charlie were like brothers . . ."[44] Thinking Brown might have an inside track, Billie followed the events at Bougainville through November.

A quiet tension sometimes erupted in minor displays of irritation. The twelve-year-old George Montague loved playing the song "No Letter Today" on his turntable, but he stopped when he realized the song bothered his mother. "It didn't even strike me that this song would even touch my mother," recalled Montague. "By the time Charlie left New Zealand, the letters stopped coming. One day while I was playing that song, completely oblivious of what it might be saying to my mom, she just exploded and said, 'George, why do you have to play that awful song!'"[45] The incident made the youthful Montague realize that, while they may rarely have displayed signs, his parents lived with strain every day.

So too did their friends, the Sengs. The concern appeared in letters that the Seng family mailed to Gene while the battle at Betio raged, although they knew neither that the battle was taking place nor that their son had been killed. "No words can describe my feelings this morning son," Mrs. Seng wrote. "We are naturally very concerned for your safety and well-being, and will be most anxious until we do hear from you, and our prayers will be unceasing." She explained that another Texas boy who had been in New Zealand with the Marines was now home, and wondered "if by any chance you are going to be lucky enough to get home soon. I haven't let myself get too excited over the possibility, only hoping against hope." She ended by mentioning how fortunate he was to have the love of a beautiful girl in New Zealand and the thoughts of a wonderful family halfway around the world in Texas, "so chin up son and look for better days that are surely ahead."[46]

Near the end of November, again before learning of her son's death, Mrs. Seng sent her son a Christmas card, bearing an image of the Virgin Mother and a plea for peace. She wrote at the bottom, "With all our love to you, son, a Mass for your intention will be said on Xmas [sic] Day. May this year end with everything you wish for."[47]

Other mothers' sons would yet die before the fighting at Betio ceased. As day two wound into day three, the Japanese prepared to deliver a potent punch to the invaders, while Major Chamberlin stood poised to destroy the large bunker that hampered operations at Red 3. In the process, Staff Sergeant Hatch and Private Kelliher recorded one of the most stunning visuals of the Pacific War.

"NOTHING WAS LEFT—
NO TREES, NO BUILDINGS"

"Tarawa Was a Stinking Golgotha"

Robert Sherrod walked along the invasion beaches that third morning, astonished that even one American reached Betio. Wherever he looked, Japanese pillboxes stood every five yards along the shore. When Sherrod peered inside one fortification, where four dead Japanese lay with two dead Marines, he understood why the Marines had succeeded. Men of the assault waves had jumped into pillboxes and perished destroying their enemy so that men in subsequent waves could land and move inland. Sherrod added, "They also gave their lives for one hundred and thirty million other Americans who realize it, I fear, only dimly."[1]

Keith Wheeler, a reporter for the *Chicago Daily Times,* thought that morning that the battle had turned. On November 22, D+2, he wrote from Betio, "It looks as though the Marines are winning on this blood-drenched, bomb-hammered, stinking little abattoir of coral sand."[2] In these pre-CNN and pre–Fox News times, citizens in the United States would not read this and other comments until days later, due to the continued fighting and to military censorship, but an undeniable air of optimism blossomed at Betio.

Sherrod also realized during his walk that he had not eaten since leaving the transport. Swept up by the intense, nonstop combat, Marines and correspondents alike battled and acted without thinking. Then, when a calm moment finally arrived, hunger pains reminded them of food.

Colonel Shoup talked with another officer who had not eaten for two days. "This business kinda takes a fellow's appetite doesn't it?" mentioned Shoup.

"Colonel," replied the Marine, whose wife had recently given birth to a son, "every minute I have fed on what I feared would be the last memories of my wife and baby boy."[3]

Sherrod and anyone else who had time to observe the beaches on that third morning could not help but be struck by the hundreds of bodies that lay in grotesque forms, on land and in the lagoon. Work parties shuttling in supplies along the pier requested help—the numerous floating bodies bobbing alongside impeded their efforts at moving food and ammunition.

Lt. G. D. Lillibridge, who lost twenty-six of the thirty-nine men he commanded in the 1st Battalion, 2nd Marines, wrote of the littered battlefield he faced inland from Red 2, "Bodies were everywhere: a hand here, an arm there, a leg, a shattered torso. A head, even."[4]

John Magruder, an officer in the battle, wrote graphic descriptions of the butchery to a friend less than six weeks later. Magruder was certain he would never again see anything so appalling. "There was one stretch of beach where every foot of the barbed wire was literally draped with dead Marines who had been caught trying to force their way over it," he told Thomas Weil. "Tarawa was a stinking Golgotha, littered with destruction from one end to the other—torn to shreds by the fierce naval and air bombardment, blackened by flame throwers, explosives and wreckage and reddened with the blood of thousands of our own and the enemy's dead."[5]

Robert Sherrod stopped in his morning meanderings to witness a burial party collecting the dead, many of whom had been floating in the lagoon for two days. "Some are bloated, some have already turned a sickly green. Some have no faces, one's guts are hanging out of his body. The eyeballs of another have turned to a jellied mass, after so long a time in the water."

A bulldozer scooped a long trench three feet deep that would serve as a temporary cemetery for the Marines, whose bodies were gently placed side by side in a long row. Sherrod watched them lift one dead Marine, his head and left arm blown off and shreds of skin hanging from his shoulders, into the depression.

"What a hell of a way to die!" he said to a Marine standing next to him.

"You can't pick a better way,"[6] replied the Marine.

After a chaplain said prayers over the bodies, the bulldozer filled in the pit with dirt, then moved on to repeat the process at another location. It would be days before the burial parties disposed of what the fighting and killing had produced.

As a result, every combatant or correspondent alive on Betio had to endure the sickening odor of death that blanketed the island, a smell so pervasive and foul that it turned their stomachs. The equatorial sun blackened the corpses, and bubbling sounds emanated from the gaseous matter that built up on the insides. Millions of flies feasted on intestines and other body parts.

"The smell was inescapable," wrote a correspondent. "It was everywhere, and it was not the kind of smell one gets accustomed to. It suffused the Marines' hair, their clothing, and seemed to adhere to their bodies. They smelled it for weeks after the battle, and like all pungent odors, it evoked instant and nightmarish memories. . . . By dawn of D plus 2 all freshness was gone and Betio was nothing but stink and death."[7]

"The Day the Japs Fell Apart"

Colonel Edson's orders for day three contained no subterfuge. He ordered Jones and the 6th Marines to move through Ryan's men at Red 1, attack eastward along Betio's southern beach at 8:00 A.M., then pass through F Company and other units holding isolated pockets south of the airfield and merge with Major Crowe's line. This would create a solid wall of Marines from the beaches at Red 3 across Betio, thus confining the Japanese facing Crowe to the island's tail end. Edson called for coordinated air and naval strikes to blast targets five hundred yards ahead of the advancing 6th Marines. In the middle, Hays's depleted battalion would strike west against the Pocket, while Crowe was to subdue the Japanese defenses on the right flank of Red 3.

The Marines benefited from the increased flow of supplies that streamed in along the pier. Additional tanks, flamethrowers, and armored half-tracks could now support the offensive against a Japanese opponent whose numbers and fighting capability diminished by the hour. American material superiority overwhelmed the spirited but outclassed foe, a story that would be repeated as the American military juggernaut churned across the Pacific to Tokyo. "This was the day the Japs fell apart,"[8] summed up Robert Sherrod.

The reserve force in which the Meadows brothers served, the 6th Marine Regiment, played a key role in the day's events. The 1st Battalion, with Jim Meadows, landed on the second day, while the 3d Battalion, including Leon Uris, who later wrote a fictionalized account of his experiences, *Battle Cry,* as well as many other best-selling books, came in the morning of the third. Smoke shrouded the island and the odor of death wafted over them as they landed, providing an alarming greeting.

The first sight one Marine in the 3d Battalion observed when he hit the beach was a Japanese soldier shot in the head, his brains leaking onto the sands. Not far away rested the remains of four other soldiers, bloated and covered with flies. Only their helmets and shreds of uniform identified the four as American. A few more yards revealed a dead American and a dead Japanese lying side by side. Then a Japanese soldier, wearing nothing but a jockstrap, rushed out of his hiding spot but died in a flurry of bullets before he took many steps. "What the hell am I doing here?"[9] asked the Marine, only moments into his battle.

At 8:00 A.M., with the 3d Battalion taking positions behind in support, Major Jones and the 1st Battalion moved along the south coast against a system of defenses that had been emplaced to halt an assault from the ocean side. Every one hundred yards featured at least six machine gun pillboxes, situated so that they supported each other. Jones had little choice but to go straight at them, as the narrow confines south of the airfield left him no more than one hundred yards between the airstrip and the water in which to maneuver.

He placed one company supported by flamethrowers at the point, advancing behind three tanks, with the other two companies following closely behind. As the tanks blasted at bunkers from the front, Marines crept along the sides, moved in, and destroyed them with grenades and flamethrowers.

One pesky machine gun position confounded the Marines. No matter where they approached, thick fire halted them. Finally, in exasperation, a Marine threw caution to the wind. "You bastards, I'm coming in!" he yelled to the Japanese. The man grabbed a hand grenade and, with complete disregard for his safety, crawled directly under the machine gun's muzzle while other Marines pinned down the Japanese. After lobbing the grenade into the bunker and destroying it, the Marine pounded the ground in glee and, according to a correspondent who witnessed it, howled "with a laughter that was not quite natural."[10]

In three hours of action, Jones's battalion advanced eight hundred yards toward Betio's middle and joined with Barr and the men of F Company who had held the trench since the day before. They suffered light casualties while killing almost three hundred. "We've got 'em by the balls now!"[11] shouted Maj. Thomas A. Culhane, a regimental operations officer. Jones moved the battalion farther down the coast and eventually joined with Major Crowe's forces coming over from Red 3.

"Do You Want to Take Pictures of the Attack?"

As Jones's Marines seized control of the southwestern shoreline, Major Crowe organized the day's assault against the trio of Japanese positions that had so vexed the major at Red 3 for two days. Crowe placed his trusted executive officer, the wounded Major Chamberlin, in command in the middle, where Crowe expected the harshest resistance to originate.

Aided by mortars and the tank *Colorado*, Crowe's Marines subdued two of the three pesky fortifications in two hours. Under suppressing fire laid down by a company of Marines, the *Colorado* churned to the steel pillbox's opening and pumped several rounds into it from point-blank range. Before the stunned Japanese inside could react, Marines rushed forward and destroyed the position with grenades and demolition charges. A fortunate strike from Marine mortars ignited an ammunition supply at the coconut log bunker, which erupted in a fury of flame and smoke. By 9:30, two of the three Japanese bunkers had been eliminated.

That left the toughest—the bombproof shelter farther inland. Japanese machine gunners sat in protected holes on the shelter's top, while soldiers concealed along the sides waited to repulse any Marine unit before it reached the slopes. Blasts from tanks and howitzers had been ineffectual due to the thick layer of soft sand that muffled every explosion, and the Navy's destroyers could not chance a bombardment because of the Marines crowded so closely to the shelter. With the first two Japanese bunkers eliminated, Crowe now planned to end his frustration. He ordered Marine riflemen to pin down the Japanese with suppressing fire while engineers and flamethrowers crept toward the bunker's top to destroy the machine gun nests. With that opposition removed, the Marines could then pour gasoline and throw hand grenades down the air vents to force the Japanese into the open, where the Marines could mow them down.

Crowe left the attack's execution to Chamberlin. The college professor faced one of the battle's toughest challenges, as the Marines would have to scale the slopes under enemy fire, wrest the top from machine gunners, then kill the shelter's occupants.

Staff Sergeant Hatch and Private Kelliher were about to capture one of the Pacific War's most incredible film shots. Hatch listened at Crowe's command post as Crowe and Chamberlin discussed the morning's plans.

"We're ready to take that command post now," Chamberlin said to Crowe.

"Are you sure?" asked Crowe. "Is everything O.K.?"

"Everything's fine," reassured Chamberlin. He then turned to Hatch and asked, "Do you want to watch? Do you want to take pictures of the attack?" Chamberlin added that he thought Hatch could obtain some excellent pictures of the fighting if he was willing to accompany them on the dangerous assault.

Hatch, a staff sergeant, knew better than to decline an offer from a major and agreed to come along. He went back to his foxhole along the seawall, informed Kelliher of the morning's developments, then prepared his camera and film.

About 8:00 A.M. Hatch and Kelliher moved to Chamberlin's command post, situated in a shell crater, for Chamberlin's briefing with his platoon lieutenants and NCOs. Chamberlin instructed his men what to do, then asked, "Are you ready?" He looked at his watch and ended the meeting with "At 9:00 we'll take off."[12]

"Here Come the Japs!"

As the time for the assault neared, Chamberlin checked on the men. Hatch had observed the officer's motions for much of the two days and described him in battle as "a wild man, a guy that anybody would be willing to follow and run around with and do whatever needs to be done in a combat area."[13]

That at first did not seem to be the case with this advance. At 9:00 A.M. Chamberlin looked at Hatch and said, "Are you ready?" Hatch replied he was. Chamberlin stood, yelled, "Follow me!" and waved with his hand.

With Chamberlin in the lead, Hatch and Kelliher followed closely behind, camera and equipment dangling as they ran. They scampered up the thirty-foot hill to the top, peered over to the other side, and spotted a dozen or more Japanese soldiers looking up at them. "They probably wondered what in hell those guys were doing on top of the mound," said Hatch. "We turned around, and we were the only Marines in sight. We were the only guys standing up on top of the mound."

"Major, where's your rifle?" Hatch asked when he noticed Chamberlin did not have a weapon.

"I gave it to a guy that lost his."

"Where's your pistol?"

"I lost it in the landing."

Hatch carried his .45, but he could not reach it with all the gear he had. The Marines stood atop the position, basically unarmed, with twelve Japanese soldiers thirty feet below.

"We'd better get the hell out of here, right now!" shouted Hatch.

"I agree with you."

The scene at the bunker's crest lasted mere seconds but seemed hours. Hatch wished that he had his camera running when he saw the enemy group below, but any further delay would have meant certain death. The trio hustled down the slope and back to the shell hole, where Chamberlin castigated the men for not following him. "Now we're gonna go take that goddamn thing," he said, a sense of urgency, as well as disappointment and anger, filling his voice. "If those cameramen can do it, so can you!"[14]

Chamberlin discussed the second rush with 1st Lt. Alexander Bonnyman Jr., who would charge to the top with a group of engineers and toss grenades and TNT through the structure's air vents. When all was ready, Chamberlin shouted, "Go!" and thirty to forty men swarmed the slopes. This time Hatch, with Kelliher feet away, had his camera running.

As other Marines laid down suppressing fire, Chamberlin, Hatch, Kelliher, Bonnyman, and the rest leapt over the seawall, dashed to a wooden fence that ran perpendicular to the shelter, then headed to the slopes. "Chamberlin could give Major Crowe a run for his money as commander," stated a Marine who served under him. "He was fierce. He didn't care where he was standing. He put everything into it."[15]

Chamberlin and Bonnyman provided the needed inspiration that morning. As he braved thick fire from the defenders, Bonnyman waved his engineers toward the top, where some quickly eliminated the machine guns posted along the crest while others ran over to the air vents. In the background, they could hear Chamberlin's booming voice encouraging other Marines to the top.

Bonnyman kept encouraging men, despite the bullets that whizzed through the air and smacked into the sand. Finally, Bonnyman's luck ran out. As he rose on one elbow to tell someone to bring more charges, a bullet instantly killed the lieutenant. A flurry of Japanese grenades inundated the crest and forced one Marine to jump to the other side of Bonnyman's body and use the lifeless man as a shield to take the brunt of the explosions.

Engineers finally destroyed the thorny bunker with TNT, but not before Bonnyman and at least eight other Marines died in the brief attack. Elements of four Marine companies now enveloped the location to cut off any retreat and to guard a bulldozer that slowly moved up to shove sand into any openings and seal the Japanese inside.

More than one hundred Japanese defenders poured out of an exit to the bunker to evade certain death from fire and explosion, only to be slaughtered by the Marines posted outside. Hatch was standing on the slope filming the fighting at the crest when he heard someone shout, "Here come the Japs!"[16] With the camera still running, he veered to his left toward a log emplacement and captured a sequence of film that has subsequently been used in hundreds of documentaries about the Pacific War. In his film, a group of Japanese soldiers rush from the bunker toward open land, while a startled Marine fires.

Hatch recorded an image no other cameraman captured in the war, either in Europe or the Pacific. Hatch's film, which lasted about fifteen seconds, shows in the same frame both combatants of a battle—Japanese soldiers and the Marine are clearly viewed together.

Hatch happened to be at the right place at the right time, and as a result obtained that dream sequence people in his profession long for. "Standing there I had the camera ready, and I just pivoted myself to my left and it worked,"[17] said Hatch years later, still amazed at how the gripping shot occurred so naturally.

Chamberlin later claimed that Hatch and every other photographer should receive medals for entering battle armed with cameras instead of rifles. Although Hatch later received many awards for his fifteen-second sequence, he would not know for sure what he had recorded until the film could be processed and viewed after the battle. He felt confident, though, that he had something special. In a letter to his wife, he stated, "I think I got some Japs in the same frame with our guys killing them."[18]

Chamberlin's successful attack removed the last of the three Japanese positions that had confined Crowe to the beach area. His forces now rushed to the airfield, where Crowe halted them to avoid being shot at by Jones's battalion advancing along the south shore.

Bonnyman, whose body had been so badly mauled by Japanese grenades that only the dog tag identified the corpse, received the Medal of Honor for his bravery. Many Marines believe Chamberlin should have been so honored as well, not only for his deeds on the third morning but for the leadership he exuded throughout the battle. Staff Sergeant Hatch contended that Chamberlin has never received the proper acclaim for what he accomplished at Betio, probably because the quiet college professor declined to engage in self-promotion. "He's the guy that took the thing," said Hatch, "yet he doesn't get much credit."[19]

Chamberlin received the Navy's second-highest honor, the Navy Cross, but he probably appreciated as much the gesture made by one of his Marines. After the attack on the bunker, a Marine unearthed a bottle of Japanese beer buried in debris near the beach. He had sat down to drink it when a voice behind him commented on the good fortune he had to find the beer. The Marine turned to see Major Chamberlin, bedraggled from almost nonstop combat since D-Day. Rather than consume the liquid, the Marine offered it to Chamberlin, a man he respected above all others and who, at that moment, looked worse than anyone the Marine had yet seen.

End of the Third Day

Marines had secured much of the western half of Betio by the afternoon of the third day. Heavy fighting, not only in Chamberlin's sector but elsewhere, pushed most Japanese into the tail section to the east, but not before a tough foe mounted a deadly defense.

"They were good," said Private First Class Muhlbach, "and we were pretty good, too. So it was two of probably the best military outfits in the war." What made combat on Betio so unique was that both forces stood in a limited area, knew where the other was, and embarked on three days of nonstop maiming. "There was nowhere to hide on the island. You can't run away and hide. It was like two heavyweight boxers slugging it out. Both wanted to slaughter the other side. That's how wars are won and lost."[20]

The hellish landscape could not have helped any Marine harbor leniency toward their enemy. Bodies had already begun drifting farther out to sea, where some became entangled with ships' blades. Swarms of flies buzzed around the abundance of bodies on land, creating a health hazard for the living, and whenever a Marine opened a can of rations, ravenous flies descended in hordes.

A more pleasing sight, at least to the Marines, was the increased number of enemy soldiers committing suicide. Most opted to either clutch hand grenades to their chests, or place the muzzles of their rifles in their mouths and pull the triggers with their big toes.

The unselfish spirit exhibited by the Marines impressed onlookers. More than once, Robert Sherrod watched Marines willingly yield their only canteen of water to a wounded buddy. "What a pity Americans at home cannot display the same unselfish attitude toward each other and toward the men who fight for them!"[21] he wrote later.

Sherrod here referred to the sensitive issue of home front civilians either complaining about gasoline and food shortages or, even more irritating, going on strike. One Marine told Sherrod he regretted that union leader John L. Lewis was not present at the battle, at which another Marine instantly added, "He wouldn't be alive if he was beside me. I don't mean the Japs would kill him. I would."[22]

Sherrod had noticed the antagonism toward labor intensifying for the past year. Marines understood the mammoth amount of supplies that would be needed to defeat the Japanese, and every time a union struck, their wrath magnified. Most Marines believed the home front had no idea what occurred on Pacific battlefields, mainly because they felt the military so heavily censored written dispatches that combat's grim harshness was removed.

"The soldier wants the people back home to know that 'we don't knock hell out of 'em' every day of every battle. He wants the people to understand that war is tough and war is horrible. He thinks labor's tendency to strike is part of this misconception on the part of his own people at home—surely, no sane man would dream of striking against his own soldiers if he understood what war was like."[23]

Sherrod and Staff Sergeant Hatch were about to educate the home front about battlefield conditions—Sherrod with a moving book and Hatch with his film.

By dusk of the third day, the Marines had finally seized the upper hand. The Japanese still fought in two places—the system of defenses in the Pocket at the border of Red 1 and Red 2, and an estimated one thousand Japanese gathering in the tail end of Betio. Major Crowe's battalion, including Stan Bowen, had joined lines with Major Jones's forces, which included Jim Meadows, to create a solid wall of Marines from the northern to the southern shores. All that remained for the next day—hopefully the last—was to wipe out the two isolated enclaves.

Eager to transmit stories of the battle, Sherrod and the other civilian correspondents requested permission to return to a transport that possessed typewriters. When the reporters arrived, sailors pestered them for information and readily handed out razors, soap, toothbrushes, and clothes to the grimy reporters. One man disbursing the items said in obvious disgust, "It's the first time I've had a chance to do anything, and the battle only two thousand yards away."

After the correspondents feasted on coffee, ham, and iced tea, the ship's captain offered his quarters so they could shower. The men had long since become accustomed to the foul odor that clung to their bodies and their clothes, but hastened to scrub the dirt and smell of Betio from their bodies. Sherrod liberally applied ocean water and soap, "but it will take many baths to purge the grime of Betio from the skin pores."[24]

"It Was Just Like Hell"

Petty Officer Oonuki awoke in his nearly destroyed shelter, apparently the only man still alive. He tried to stand, but to balance himself the weakened Oonuki reached for an item that stuck out nearby. His hand slipped on the greasy matter and pulled away a large chunk of cooked flesh from a soldier's arm.

Oonuki finally freed himself from the pile of bodies. Unfamiliar voices outside caused him to remain in the bunker until dark. He then removed his uniform, crept out of the shelter, maneuvered down the tail end of Betio—at times dodging American fire—until he reached the shore and headed toward Bairiki. Sadly, he found nothing there but dead Japanese. Oonuki debated whether he should join his comrades who had already chosen to kill themselves.

Meanwhile, on Betio, a Japanese radio operator sent a message to Tokyo. OUR WEAPONS HAVE BEEN DESTROYED AND FROM NOW ON EVERYONE IS ATTEMPTING A FINAL CHARGE. . . . MAY JAPAN EXIST FOR TEN THOUSAND YEARS![25] The fighting and killing had not yet ended.

An orderly located Warrant Officer Ota to tell him to meet at headquarters. Hampered by his injured knee, Ota stumbled over for a meeting with a senior commander.

"We will make a night attack," explained the officer to the assembled officers. He added, "We will attack the enemy group which occupies the center of the island, drive them back on the sea and destroy them."[26] One group would strike from the west while a second unit charged from the east, and any soldier unable to fight was to use grenades to commit suicide.

After the meeting, Ota issued instructions to his men, but the sight of the ragtag unit shocked him—only six of his original thirty men were alive. Before handing out grenades, he told the survivors their duty this night was to fight the enemy to the death in a final charge. As Ota's men moved out, they carried so many hand grenades they had difficulty walking.

The Japanese attacks during the night of November 22–23 began as a series of organized assaults against Marine lines. The Japanese hoped to use their skill at nighttime actions to disrupt the American forces and throw their invasion timetable into disarray. Hemmed in at the tail section as they were, the Japanese had little choice but to either attack, or to wait where they were and die in their foxholes.

Across the lines, James Meadows heard the whispered instructions in the foxhole he shared with another Marine. "Everybody stay down! Anyone standing up or moving around will be shot because the Japanese are wandering around!"[27] The pair and the rest of Major Jones's 1st Battalion, 6th Marines, manned positions on the front line between the airfield and the southern shore, directly in the path of the coming Japanese attack.

The battalion's three companies established a thin north-south line facing the Japanese to the east. On the left flank, C Company dug in, while

A Company and B Company stood to its right. The weary Marines settled in for the night, hoping that the darkness would at least bring them respite from the fighting.

The first of four counterattacks occurred at 7:30 when Japanese soldiers with fixed bayonets rushed through thick vegetation east of the airfield toward Marine lines. Japanese officers waved swords while soldiers fired from the hip as they ran.

The Japanese had to advance through a five-hundred-yard artillery curtain to reach the Marines. Many died in the punishing bombardment, which came within seventy-five yards of Meadows and the other Marines, but enough still filtered through to infiltrate the 6th's lines.

Marines greeted the invaders with their own bayonets, then engaged in bitter hand-to-hand combat. The fighting at Betio, savage from the start, dissolved into the most primitive form as men clutched each other's throats, bit, gouged, and kicked one another. The fighting at some spots became so intense, especially when the Japanese drove a wedge between A and B companies, that Major Jones threw a hastily assembled reserve force consisting of cooks and headquarters personnel into the front lines. Wounded men lay untended on the ground while the battle raged about them.

Pfc. Horace Warfield moved behind a machine gun when the Marine firing it was killed. He had barely started using the weapon when a Japanese soldier jumped into the foxhole and bayoneted him in the thigh. As he fended off the soldier, Warfield grabbed a pistol and clubbed his enemy to death.

A mortar platoon commanded by Capt. Lyle Specht wiped out the last of the Japanese infiltrators when, with fixed bayonets, it collided head-on with the Japanese in the gap between the endangered A and B companies. "We pitched everything we had at them," said Specht, "and when the melee of grenade-throwing, machine-gunning and bayoneting was finished, we marched forward across piles of dead Japs. In some spots, dead bodies were stacked four and five deep."[28]

Two hours of bloody combat ended at 9:30 when the remaining Japanese fled. Marines checked on buddies and prepared for a long night. As much as they hoped for an end, they guessed the Japanese would return before long.

Their respite did not even last ninety minutes. At 11:00 a second assault hit Marine lines. The Japanese tried to intimidate their opponents by screaming, "Marine, you die!" and "Japanese drink Marines' blood!"[29], then unleashed a potent attack directly against B Company near the southern shore. Japanese, many armed only with knives or bayonets, leapt into foxholes and again grappled hand-to-hand with the Marines. Some Japanese clutched grenades with the pins drawn, jumped into foxholes, and killed one or two Marines along with themselves in the explosion.

In the frenzied excitement of the night, Warrant Officer Ota forgot about his injured knee and rushed toward the enemy's lines. "The dark night was lighted as bright as day," he recalled. "There were the heavy sounds of grenade explosions, the disordered fire of rifles, the shrieks, yells, and roars. It was just like Hell."[30] Suddenly an explosion knocked Ota to the ground, where he lapsed into unconsciousness.

The attack was quite an initiation for Lt. Norman Thomas, who only a few hours earlier had replaced a wounded officer as commander of B Company. He had reached for the field telephone in the midst of a savage counterattack to call down artillery when a huge Japanese soldier jumped into his foxhole. Thomas dodged the long bayonet heading toward his stomach, grabbed the soldier's wrist and smacked him to the sand. He then clubbed him as he lay on the ground, shot the soldier with his .45 in the chest and temple, and tossed the body out of his hole.

Not far away, Jim Meadows slept as his buddy kept watch. Suddenly, Meadows felt an elbow to his side, turned, and saw two Japanese soldiers jumping toward them. "My buddy heard them approaching and alerted me, and I turned over and saw this bayonet coming at me," said Meadows. "I reached up with my right hand and grabbed onto the bayonet. My hand slid up the bayonet and sliced the flat part of my hand. He stuck me in the left side of my throat about an inch deep, but he didn't get the jugular or I wouldn't be alive."

Meadows held on as the bayonet sliced further into his hand. "The struggle lasted maybe a minute. We were wrestling around, rolling around and around, trying to get out from underneath that bayonet. I held him off until another Marine shot and killed him."[31]

Meadows lay on the ground, bleeding and exhausted. One corpsman was killed trying to reach him, but a second succeeded and bandaged his throat and hand. Meadows, who could not move without help because of his injuries, then lay back in a state of shock and waited to be evacuated.

For a time it looked as if the 6th Regiment could be overrun. "We are killing them as fast as they come at us, but we can't hold much longer; we need reinforcements," shouted Lieutenant Thomas over the phone to Major Jones.

"We haven't got them to send you," Jones replied of his predicament. "You've got to hold."[32]

Jones understood he asked much from his subordinate, but he also grasped the gravity of the situation. After putting down the field telephone, Jones said to his staff, "If they don't hold we may lose the entire battalion."[33]

Jones pulled out every weapon at his disposal. For thirty minutes a destroyer shelled fifty yards ahead of Marine lines, while artillery emplaced at Bairiki turned their guns on the Japanese. That, along with the courage of the regiment's men and reserves, finally halted the second attempt.

"By God, We Held"

The Japanese attacked American lines for the third time around 3:00 A.M. when they opened fire with machine guns from demolished trucks about fifty yards in front. A unit of Marines crawled into the darkness, destroyed the guns, and ended what was the briefest assault of the night.

One hour later the Japanese returned in force when more than four hundred soldiers unleashed a last-gasp attempt to overwhelm the Marines. A failure for the Japanese here meant abandoning hopes of stemming the Marine advance across Betio.

Again armed with machine guns, bayonets, rifles, grenades, knives, and swords, the Japanese, some wearing only loincloths, swarmed toward the Marines in a do-or-die assault. Heavy Marine gunfire cut swaths into the Japanese ranks. Colorful tracers rent the darkness into a multicolored web—yellow streams pouring out of Japanese weapons, red, white, or pink from the Marines. Offshore, two destroyers emptied their 5-inch magazines into the charging Japanese, who vaporized in frightening explosions or screamed as shrapnel ripped apart their torsos.

Once again, combat descended to the primeval as men, many out of ammunition from the earlier charges, resorted to hands and clubs. The initial Japanese charges maintained a semblance of order, but this final offensive turned into an all-out suicidal, banzai onslaught.

Pfc. Jack Stambaugh wondered before the battle how he would react to his first taste of combat. He mentioned to a friend, "I don't know how I'll feel when I get into battle, but I don't think I'll be yellow. Maybe I'm just blowing off now, but I think I will be a fighting fool."[34]

Stambaugh backed up his words with deeds during this final counterattack when his rifle jammed as he heard a buddy cry for help. Stambaugh grabbed his bayonet, killed the enemy soldier threatening his buddy, then bayoneted three other Japanese soldiers as they ran at him one by one. As Stambaugh yanked his bayonet out of the fourth man, a Japanese officer ran a saber through his back and killed him.

Finally, around 5:00 A.M., the attack ceased. As many as five hundred Japanese bodies littered the territory immediately in front of Marine lines, while the 1st Battalion saw its ranks depleted by three hundred dead and wounded. Lieutenant Thomas praised his men for staging such a valiant defense. "The boys stood up to it, slugging it out with the Japs. They stood up to it by sheer guts alone. Every one of them's a champion."[35]

They felt that way when leaving the front lines the next morning. Some Marines walked by Robert Sherrod and remarked to the correspondent, "They told us we had to hold . . . and, by God, we held."[36]

After the fighting ended, Warrant Officer Ota regained consciousness but remained as still as possible. "I found myself lying on the ground in the darkness with the enemy coming and going, walking over me as if I were dead." He waited until all movement ceased; then, his leg so stiff and swollen that he could not stand, he crawled and rolled on the ground until he found a bunker holding other Japanese soldiers.

Conditions inside were little better than outside. Every man suffered from at least one wound, and Ota heard the moans of men who were "dying in the corners of the dugout with no one to care for them." Ota begged for water to quench an unbelievable thirst, but all that was available was a can of pineapple juice. "I drank up the juice with one breath," wrote Ota, who called it "the most delicious and satisfying drink I have had in my whole life!"[37] Ota, in pain from a badly injured leg and with blood clotting his ear, again lapsed into unconsciousness.

"Is It Over?"

The nighttime counterattacks proved to be the final gasp for the Japanese on Betio. After the Marines repulsed those four charges, two areas had to be cleared—the Pocket in the west and the remnants hemmed into the tail in the east.

Both were eliminated by early afternoon of November 23. Major Schoettel's men, including Major Ryan and Captain Crain, smashed against the Pocket from Red 1 while Major Hays closed in from the east. The two units advanced in a semicircle, converged at the airfield, and trapped the Japanese in a rapidly dwindling enclave along the beach. Supported by 75mm guns, Marines swiftly destroyed the set of pillboxes that had killed so many of their brethren and declared the western half of Betio secured at 1:05 P.M.

Marines enjoyed similar success in the east. Bill Meadows's 3d Battalion, 6th Marines, passed through brother Jim's 1st Battalion and drove toward the tail. Bill unsuccessfully looked for his brother among the haggard remnants of Marines who walked slowly back to a reserve area, weary from a brutal night repelling hordes of Japanese. One correspondent wrote, "Their faces were whipped with fatigue and their eyes were glazed. The night had been hell."[38]

Bill Meadows and his companions faced a shattered, demoralized collection of Japanese in their push to the eastern shore. Their backs had been broken the night before, and now all that remained was to sweep down the three-hundred-yard-wide tail and eliminate any final areas of resistance.

Supported by tanks, the 3d Battalion jumped off at 8:00 A.M. They encountered minimal opposition until they moved one hundred yards east of the airfield, where a set of pillboxes and bunkers slowed the momentum. One company of Marines swerved around the Japanese flank while another attacked from the front, causing seventy-five Japanese soldiers to rush into the open. From point-blank range the tank *Colorado* turned her guns on the fleeing soldiers. The ensuing massacre ended the confrontation and enabled the battalion to continue toward the tail.

Japanese resistance had obviously lessened. Marines encountered fewer interlocking fields of fire along the way, which simplified the tasks of the flamethrowers and demolitions men in destroying pillboxes. As the Japanese retreated toward the narrow east end of Betio, naval gunfire tore into their ranks from offshore while artillery and Marines emplaced on Bairiki blocked any possible escape route. The Japanese were trapped in a constantly shrinking area that was continually pounded by American forces.

By this time the Marines were in no mood to take prisoners. The savagery and blood, the fear and worry, the loss of friends shattered the thin veneer of civilized behavior that most combatants took to the battlefield. "By now we had quit even trying to take prisoners,"[39] stated one Marine.

It was in such a state of mind that a weary Muhlbach and Farrell were ordered to guard a Japanese prisoner. A lack of sleep combined with hastily devoured rations to create a foul mood that could only be alleviated with rest and decent food.

The Japanese soldier was much taller and appeared stronger than either of the two young Marines. As he stood there wearing only a loincloth, with his hands raised above his head, the prisoner looked at the nineteen-year-old

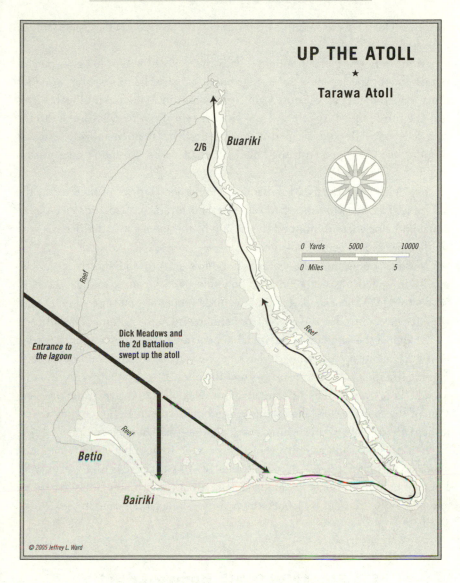

UP THE ATOLL

★

Tarawa Atoll

Buariki

2/6

Entrance to
the lagoon

Dick Meadows and
the 2d Battalion
swept up the atoll

Reef

Reef

Reef

Betio

Bairiki

0 Yards   5000   10000
0 Miles   5

© 2005 Jeffrey L. Ward

Marines "like we were a couple of children. He lowered his hands and folded them across his chest."

Muhlbach and Farrell motioned with their rifles for him to again put his hands up, but the Japanese soldier "grinned at us like he was saying, 'You kids don't have the guts to kill me.' I got furious at him," stated Muhlbach. "This was the third day—I was tired; I was mad as hell. I ran that bayonet in to the muzzle of my rifle and wiggled it around until he stopped moving. He was taunting us. He expected to be killed. In most cases, we didn't take prisoners."[40]

Besides the weariness, Muhlbach and the other Marines wanted to pay the Japanese back for what they had done to their buddies. Atrocities at Guadalcanal and elsewhere reinforced the notion of the Japanese as barbarians who neither gave nor expected any mercy.

Marines waded into the waters off Betio's eastern end shortly after 1:00 P.M. In its speedy drive, the 3d Battalion killed 475 Japanese and captured 14 while losing 9 Marines killed and 25 wounded. For the first time since D-Day, the Marines controlled the island from end to end, and the guns fell silent.

At almost the same time, the first Navy carrier-based fighter aircraft landed on Betio's airstrip, now named Hawkins Field to honor the slain lieutenant. Marine riflemen rushed forward to greet the pilot, Ens. William W. Kelly, who asked, "Is it over?"[41] The jubilant reaction was all the answer Kelly needed. One of the main reasons for asking young men to die at Betio—to possess an airfield capable of striking against the Japanese—had been accomplished.

At 1:05 Gen. Julian Smith sent the message he had hoped to relay much sooner when he notified Admiral Hill, BETIO HAS FALLEN.[42] After seventy-six hours of practically nonstop bloodshed—combat rarely matched elsewhere for savagery—the Marines had taken the two-mile-long plot of sand in the Central Pacific.

"The Stench of Death Hung over Betio"

Now that the Marines could pause, they looked around their battlefield. Gruesome sights lay in abundance, from the bodies that floated in the lagoon or lay in blackened amtracs to the mangled torsos and palm fronds that littered the ground. Many compared Betio to a junkyard, or thought of the moon when examining the hundreds of craters that pockmarked the land.

"The island was a completely devastated, garbage and litter strewn wreck," concluded the official sanitation report after the battle. "Bodies were buried everywhere on the island, and the task of burying the dead was still incomplete." It added, "Flies were everywhere <u>unbelievably</u> [emphasis the report's] dense."[43]

The smell from the bodies, which was almost universally described by survivors as a sickly-sweet odor, soaked into uniforms and permeated every pore. "The stench of death hung over Betio," wrote correspondent Jim Lucas. "We had slaughtered more than 4,000 Japanese. Their grotesquely burned, blackened corpses littered every foot of the atoll, many of them dead for three days. They were bloated and swollen. For weeks we were to taste and smell corruption."[44]

When Robert Sherrod finished filing his initial reports to *Time* magazine from aboard the troop transport, he returned to the island on the afternoon of the fourth day. He had not even completed walking in on the pier when he bent over and vomited from the scent that emanated from Betio. "What I saw on Betio was, I am certain, one of the greatest works of devastation wrought by man," he wrote. "Words are inadequate to describe what I saw on this island of less than a square mile. So are pictures—you can't smell pictures."[45]

The first successful amphibious assault against a heavily defended beach produced appalling casualties, but earned widespread acclaim. In its December 6, 1943, issue, *Time* magazine labeled a map of the location BETIO: ONE SQUARE MILE OF HELL, and compared the fighting to other heralded military struggles in American history. "Last week some two to three thousand U.S. Marines, most of them now dead or wounded, gave the nation a name to stand beside those of Concord Bridge, the *Bonhomme Richard*, the Alamo, Little Big Horn, and Belleau Wood. The name was Tarawa."[46]

Young Americans jeopardized dreams of family and future to wade through ferocious fire, leap over the seawall, and struggle with the enemy. The ultimate sacrifices of Montague, Seng, and the rest who perished, combined with the heroics of Major Chamberlin, Captain Crain, and the survivors, removed the first Central Pacific island from Japanese control and inflicted serious harm to the Japanese ability to stem the inevitable American march toward Tokyo.

Counting casualties from both combatants, 6,000 men died in three brutal days at Betio. On the American side, 1,027 Navy and Marine personnel lost their lives, 2,292 were wounded, and 88 were recorded as missing in action. The losses to seize tiny Betio were three times higher than what it took to land in North Africa, twice the cost of the operations at Sicily, and almost equal to the casualties incurred during two weeks of vicious combat at Salerno. The hard fighting at Guadalcanal produced similar casualties, but that campaign lasted six months compared to Betio's three days. The 2d Division's 3,300 killed and wounded earned it the dubious distinction of registering the highest casualty rate for a division in the war. In the history of the Marine Corps, no battle produced a greater loss per ratio of men involved than Betio.

Two factors most illustrated the savage nature of combat at Betio, where hand-to-hand fighting and killing at short ranges were the norm—the number of men killed, and the astounding number of bodies that could not be identified. More than one-quarter of the dead were never identified, either because a direct hit disintegrated the man or multiple hits so riddled the body that little remained but an arm or a hand. One battalion lost more than 300 dead of the 750 who landed, including 15 of its 39 officers. Only one-third of the gallant men of F Company who swept across Betio's midsection emerged unhurt— the rest either died or suffered wounds.

"Gentlemen, it was our will to die,"[47] answered Maj. Gen. Holland Smith to reporters who wondered how the Marines had succeeded.

"Tarawa Recruitin' Office"

Marines who battled nonstop for seventy-six hours now had their first opportunity to lay down their weapons and relax. S. Sgt. George Stutsman organized a post exchange in a Betio hangar and handed out cigarettes, candy, soap, and razor blades free of charge to the weary Marines. Someone gave Lt. G. D. Lillibridge a canteen of hot water, chocolate, coffee, and sugar, a repast the Marine later stated "was the best meal I ever had."[48]

Pfc. Charles Wysocki tried to eat, but after the horrors he had endured, and what he now saw, he could not keep any food or water down for eight days. Private Kelliher felt little fear during the entire battle, despite standing side by side with Staff Sergeant Hatch, but now that he could think about the battle, his knees began shaking.

"God, I was tired," explained Stanley Bowen, who marveled at the sudden stillness that settled over the isle. "I walked all around the island and really couldn't believe the destruction—nothing was left, no trees, no buildings and, oh God, how the place smelled from dead Marines and Japs." Bowen searched for his buddy, Howard, who had predicted his own death, and found his friend's body slumped on the beach near the water. "He never even got thirty yards. He had been machine-gunned. He was all bloated up." Bowen only recognized the corpse as his friend's by the little pointed ears and a high school graduation ring. "All those bodies lying there, bloated in the hot sun, plus the bodies that floated in the water. The place was really a mess. The smell was horrible." The corpsman, who later went into combat with the Marines at Saipan, Tinian, and Okinawa, stated of Betio, "I never ran into anything like that."[49]

The initial wounded had been evacuated during the first day, when corpsmen placed them on rubber boats and Marines pulled them to the reef. Landing craft then ferried them to transports, where surgeons performed operations and readied them for the long trip to Hawaiian hospitals. Now, on the fourth day, the flow of wounded continued, as sporadic gunfire still shattered the calm.

Men tried to restore a semblance of normalcy amidst the most abnormal of circumstances. Some erected makeshift signs identifying their foxholes as SHANGRI-LA and HOME SWEET HOME, while one Marine turned macabre. Attached to a battered palm tree, that former symbol of beauty and South Seas romance, was a gruesome reminder of his hellish experience—a skull resting atop a sign proclaiming, TARAWA RECRUITIN' OFFICE.

Many stripped their uniforms, reeking from sweat, blood, and the odors of three days of battle, and donned clean white Japanese naval uniforms in hopes of at least feeling more civilized. Some collapsed into the nearest foxhole and quickly fell into a deep sleep. Pfc. Robert L. Kinley was awakened when he felt his body being dragged along the bottom of the crater—a burial party mistakenly thought he was dead and had started to take Kinley to a temporary cemetery.[50]

On November 24, the day after the fighting at Betio ended, Marines proudly hauled two flags to the tops of palm trees, both denuded of fronds from the battle—the Stars and Stripes on one and, as Tarawa had been a British possession before the war, the Union Jack on the other. Pfc. James Williams, the bugler, had been inside a tank for most of the battle and had replaced his filthy uniform with a clean Japanese outfit, but when he marched up to sound Colors, Gen. Julian Smith yelled, "Get those clothes off and keep them off!"[51] The general quickly issued orders that no Marine was to wear the uniform of their enemy, both out of decency to the American dead and from concern that they could be mistaken for the enemy and shot.

The sound of Williams's bugle deeply moved men who, only hours before, had been scratching and clawing for the very plot of dirt upon which the palm trees rested. One correspondent wrote, "Men turned from digging foxholes, from unloading boats, from burying the dead. They stood at attention, with their dirty, tired young hands held at salute. Some of the wounded managed to stand up, too, while the more seriously hurt could only turn their heads as they lay on their litters. The assault troops paused in their shuffling toward the end of the pier."[52]

With Marines looking up and seeing the Stars and Stripes snapping in the breeze, Betio at last belonged to the Corps. They had fought and killed and maimed for precisely this moment, the time when a Japanese-controlled possession had been taken from the enemy. As Captain Crain, Stanley Bowen, and the other weary assault troops headed to the pier to depart on the transports, they could hold their heads high knowing they had triumphed on a nightmarish battlefield.

"The Flowers of the Pacific"

While the assault troops left Betio, reserve Marines remained to clear out the remaining enemy pillboxes and bunkers. The battle had officially ended, but sporadic killing continued for the next few days.

Men approached supposedly cleared positions at their own peril. A Korean laborer, nicknamed by the Marines as Tojo the Earbanger, pointed out the different hiding spots of eighty-one Koreans as well as a smaller number of Japanese. All eighty-one laborers surrendered and survived, but most Japanese either rushed out of their concealed position and were killed or committed suicide.

Of the more than 4,800 Japanese and Koreans on Betio before the battle, 146 survived, of which only 17 were Japanese soldiers. The near-total devastation wrought by the fighting made the task of intelligence officers nigh impossible, for the combat destroyed most Japanese documents, and few officers remained for them to question. Admiral Shibasaki's body, lying somewhere near the airfield off Red 3, was never recovered.

Back in Japan, accounts of the battle differed from reality. Radio Tokyo claimed that the Imperial Japanese Fleet sank three American aircraft carriers and three troop transports, which took five thousand Marines to their deaths, and asserted that the brave Japanese still fought at Betio. They called the men "the flowers of the Pacific"[53] and exhorted every man and woman to follow their brave example.

A December 21, 1943, headline blazoned across one Japanese newspaper declared, FOE DEALT ENORMOUS DAMAGE, and stated that the brave Japanese defenders, while they eventually succumbed, "fought most doggedly against appalling odds of more than 50,000 enemy troops." The newspaper added that even though they fought day and night, "our officers and men kept on charging upon the enemy by jumping over their comrades' lifeless bodies, wielded their bayonets if they ran short of bullets, and if their bayonets were broken, they would dash on in human bomb fashion."[54]

The string of ill fortune continued for the hapless Koreans, whose misery only started when the Japanese forcibly removed them from their homeland and transported them to Betio. After months as laborers, they then waited out the battle, hoping to avoid death from irate Japanese or from Marines who misidentified them as the enemy. Even after their capture, the Koreans endured hostility. One complained to an interpreter aboard a transport, "Look at the way the American sailors look at me. They think I am Japanese. If they only knew—I hate the Japanese as much as they."[55]

Petty Officer Oonuki and Warrant Officer Ota were two of the seventeen to survive the ordeal. The famished Oonuki became separated from a group of soldiers when he stopped to eat some shellfish. After becoming deathly ill from the raw food, Oonuki crawled into a bunker and lapsed into unconsciousness.

A unit of Marines captured him the next day. When they took him under guard to a detention area, other Marines, obtaining their first glimpse of a live enemy, stepped close to Oonuki's face to stare at the prisoner. One Marine handed him a canteen of water and some C rations. After interrogation, Oonuki was shipped to Hawaii and then on to his final wartime destination of Crystal City, Texas. Ironically, while Montague and Seng never returned to their beloved Texas, a man who spent three days trying to kill them and other Marines spent the remainder of the war in the Lone Star State, less than one hundred miles from the Montague Ranch and Central Catholic High School. Upon cessation of hostilities in 1945, authorities returned Oonuki to Japan.

Marines captured Warrant Officer Ota on November 24. Ota was huddled in a dugout with ten wounded Japanese when a flurry of hand grenades exploded in their midst, killing or further wounding many of the occupants. Ota heard one dying soldier cry, "Mother! I am painful! It hurts too much!"

The sounds of rifle and machine gun fire then filled the bunker as the Americans closed in. "Suddenly a brilliant orange-red flame roared into the dugout, with black smoke," recalled Ota, certain he was about to die. "The Americans were using a flame-thrower! I could not breathe. I was done for. I was burning and suffocating. There was a whirlpool of flame in the dugout."[56]

When the back of Ota's uniform caught fire, he thought of his mother, recited a brief Buddhist prayer, then lapsed into unconsciousness. When Ota regained his senses he was in the midst of Americans, who had found him alive, carried him to an aid station, and treated his wounds. The Marines fed him and treated him with decency, actions that confounded Ota, as he had been told the Americans were barbarians who tortured their enemy.

The Americans shipped Ota, like Oonuki, to Hawaii, then on to a Wisconsin prisoner of war camp. Also like Oonuki, he rejoined family in Japan when the war ended in 1945.

Twenty years later Ota received another surprise when a box of personal belongings from Betio made its way to his doorstep. After the battle, a Marine had taken the box, which contained some pencils, pens, a toothbrush, a pocketknife, postage stamps, a photo, and an identification card. He eventually gave the box to a friend, who sent it to an associate in Japan. A brief investigation found that Ota was still alive, and two decades after the fighting, Ota and his possessions were reunited.

Ota was far more fortunate than the loved ones of one thousand dead Marines, who were never reunited. Two of the grieving families were the Montagues and the Sengs.

"A REQUIEM FITTING
FOR HEROES SO PROUD"

"Here's Charlie Montague"

Cpl. Emory Ashurst, Cpl. Joseph Sobol, and other engineers from the 18th Regiment slowly shuffled along the beach at Red 1 the morning of November 24, looking for the bodies of their comrades cut down by machine gun fire as they landed on D-Day. The survivors were scheduled to leave Betio later that day, but before they did, they wanted to make sure the remains of those who stayed behind, including Montague and Seng, were properly buried.

Their search ended quickly, as fifteen bodies lay where they had fallen on the beach four days ago, not far from the two Japanese guns that most likely ended their lives. Corporal Sobol had to either check the man's dog tag or cut off the man's pack and read the name stenciled underneath, for Betio's sun had so bloated most of the remains that proper identification could not be achieved with a simple look.

"Here's Charlie Montague,"[1] Sobol muttered after he removed the pack from the young man's back. Yards away, also lying facedown in the sand, rested Gene Seng.

According to Corporal Ashurst, the survivors gently moved the bodies twenty yards inland to "a place we thought right for them,"[2] and placed them in shallow graves. Another man fashioned fifteen rough crosses from wooden splinters, each bearing a different man's name and date of death, and arranged them in a neat row.

Ashurst then read the Burial Service found in the U.S. Marines Divine Services book, led the men in the Lord's Prayer, and ended the service with the words, "Unto Almighty God we commend the souls of our brethren departed."

The men covered the bodies with sand, took a final glance at the crosses, and slowly turned away. "Yes, I cried, we all did and we weren't afraid to show our sorrow and respect for our fallen Marines," recalled Pfc. Charles Wysocki. "I'll remember them and that day until the day I die."[3]

Like the rest of the Marines who witnessed that private funeral service, Corporal Ashurst left Betio with a deep respect for the slain comrades that has lasted to the present day. He said of Montague and Seng in 2005, "They were a couple of very fine young men, dedicated to the Marine Corps and to each other and to their families in Texas."[4]

"Let Them Rest on Their Sun-Scoured Atoll"

Similar scenes occurred at many locations on Betio, although none conveyed the personal touch and the warmth provided by Montague and Seng's buddies. Chaplain William W. Lumpkin, the division chaplain, supervised the enormous task of burying the many dead—American and Japanese—that littered the isle.

Some wondered why they had survived while these young men died. "If God had not given me His special protection I would have been wounded or killed at least a dozen times," stated Chaplain Joseph Wieber. Chaplain Willard emerged without a scratch, even though he served in a unit that absorbed alarming casualties. Chaplains, as well as medics like Stan Bowen, suffered 78 percent wounded and killed. "But why has God taken so many of my friends, and yet has seen fit to spare me?"[5] Willard asked.

Religious affiliation mattered little to Willard or any other chaplain. Protestant, Catholic, Jew—all received tender treatment. The chaplains removed the dog tag or other item of identification, placed the body in a grave, said a few prayers, had either Marines or a bulldozer cover the remains, and then moved to the next in a seemingly endless line of deceased. In spare moments, the religious leaders wrote letters informing family members, including the Sengs and the Montagues, of their loss.

Burial teams faced one of the most unpleasant tasks, for they had to gather bodies maimed in one of the most violent struggles the war had yet seen. Marines frequently lifted bodies onto stretchers or corrugated iron only to have the corpse fall to pieces in their hands. The foul stench caused hardened Marines to vomit, and many covered their noses and mouths with a wet cloth in hopes of reducing the odor. "Body fluid bubbled through taut cloth as bodies stiff with rigor mortis were piled onto sheet metal,"[6] wrote one Marine assigned to burial detail.

Graves Registration personnel took fingerprints when possible and retrieved personal articles, such as photographs, good luck charms, or Gene's scapular medal from Sister Gabriella, from the bodies before burial, but as so many men had died violently, often little remained for them. Lists of the burial locations on Betio frequently carried the single word *Unknown*, indicating the remains had never been identified.

Chaplain Willard counted seventy-six dead Marines lying in a brief section of Red 1, the beach Montague and Seng assaulted. As he walked among the fallen, Willard suddenly understood why he had purchased a hatchet in New Zealand—with the tool he made rough wooden crosses for the fallen Marines. He marked some graves with "Just a pair of legs," or "Burned to death"[7] because he lacked enough of the body with which to identify the slain.

Willard took a card from the body of one young Marine containing a code he created to inform his girlfriend of his destination. Fifteen locations bore a coded word or phrase to elude the censor—if the Marine started his letter with "My darling," that meant he was in Australia. If the letter opened with "Violet darling," he was on his way to New Britain. "But only we could let Violet know that her friend had landed on Tarawa and would not be back,"[8] added Willard.

Five separate cemeteries had been started by the time most of the assault troops departed on November 24. Some crosses bore personal inscriptions, such as the one left by a buddy of the fallen Marine stating, U KILLED 10 JAPS, IT WILL TAKE 100 TO AVENGE YOUR DEATH.[9]

Other Marines and naval personnel, including Lt. (jg) Eddie Albert, retrieved additional bodies from the lagoon and offshore waters, but due to the circumstances, they could not afford the same amenities as the parties working ashore or even their cohorts aboard ship, where a proper burial at sea could be performed. Men in boats used bayonets to puncture the grossly bloated bodies, then weighed them down with chains so they could sink.

No matter how the Marines laid the dead to rest, they honored their memories and realized that during the fighting, but for a tilt of the head one way or a split-second delay, they might be in the ground as well. A plaque erected at one of Betio's cemeteries best conveyed the emotions most felt.

> SO LET THEM REST ON THEIR SUN-SCOURED ATOLL,
> THE WIND FOR THEIR WATCHER, THE WAVE FOR THEIR SHROUD,
> WHERE PALM AND PANDANUS SHALL WHISPER FOREVER
> A REQUIEM FITTING FOR HEROES SO PROUD.[10]

Disposal of the Japanese dead was another expression of the emotions swirling about the island. Bulldozers at first shoved groups of bodies into bomb craters and piled dirt on top, but when that used up too much land on restricted Betio, Marines tossed the bodies on boats and dumped them into the sea for the sharks.

"We Looked Like a Bunch of 'Zombies'"

Julian Smith wasted little time pulling the assault troops out of Betio. Marines boarded troop transports on November 24, less than one day after the island was declared secure, altered from the individuals they had been only four days before. Young men, boys in some cases, had traveled to Betio, but after engaging in a weekend of slaughter, they left weary, quiet, and affected. "When we left that hell-hole we looked like a bunch of 'zombies,'" wrote Pfc. Charles Wysocki, "eyes that were looking nowhere, skin that was drawn and pale and clothing that had the look of battle all over them—they would never be worn again." Wysocki thought of the buddies who would not be returning, including Montague and Seng, whom he called "the real heroes of the battle," and wondered "how or why I was spared—someday, if I go to heaven, the Lord will tell me."[11]

Some Marines passed by Japanese prisoners on their way to the pier. A few gathered enough strength and spat at their defeated enemy. Standing on the deck of his transport, another Marine peered back at the scene of such devastation and said, "I won't go there any more."[12]

Sailors who helped the filthy, ragged men board the transports stifled urges to cry as they obtained their first glimpse of the warriors, covered in the gore of battle and emitting a stomach-turning stench. Sensing that the Marines had experienced a hell they could only imagine, sailors refrained from pestering them with questions about the fighting. In time, maybe the young battlers would share their experiences, but for now, they needed calm, quiet, and rest.

If they had the facilities, ships' captains opened up their showers, issued clean uniforms, and instructed that the old ones be tossed over the side. "We were a filthy looking lot," wrote Robert Lilly. "The ship's crew stared at us as though they had never seen such a sight before—and maybe they hadn't. Apparently our appearance and the aroma of death that we brought aboard was too much for the captain—he wanted us cleaned up and into clean clothes."[13] A shower, even with ocean salt water, rejuvenated many of the Marines, but no matter how many times they scrubbed their bodies the stench followed them through the eleven-day voyage.

When Robert Sherrod flew out of Betio, the copilot courteously refrained from saying anything. After a few hours, though, he could take no more. Handing extra clothes to the correspondent, the copilot said, "All of you smelled like dead Japs."[14] Sherrod offered his dirty clothes in exchange, but the aviator politely declined and told him to bury the items. Robert Muhlbach received dungarees and underwear from the crew of his ship, but other transports lacked the shower facilities and extra clothing. On those vessels, the Marines had no choice but to remain in their grimy uniforms for the two-thousand-mile voyage.

Ships' officers willingly yielded their cabins, barbers cut hair, and messes prepared hot meals around the clock. Some of the Marines had eaten either nothing or very little since the battle opened four days earlier, but now that they could unwind, a ravenous hunger overtook them.

Even though the ships steamed away and the island receded from view, the battle accompanied each man. He retained it in his thoughts, and every time a burial ceremony occurred aboard ship at the death of a wounded Marine, memories flooded back. For these occasions the entire complement, crew and Marines, stood topside to witness the moving ceremony. Sailors rested the deceased on stretchers, sewed sailcloth around each, then draped each with an American flag. After a chaplain conducted the service, the tunes of a hymn from the ship's loudspeaker wafted above, and a Navy squad fired a rifle salute. As a bugler sounded the melodic, powerful notes to taps, the bodies went to their resting place.

"Sailors picked up each stretcher in turn, raised it to the rail, and while two of them held the flag, the others tipped the stretcher so that the body slipped off into the sea," wrote Richard W. Nash of a burial aboard the *Feland*. "The sound of the ship sloshing through the sea didn't quite cover the sound of the splash as the body hit the water."[15]

Moved by the impact of the battle, many of the Marines turned pensive about their futures. Chaplains noticed that attendance at church services soared. Lt. (jg) Jay O'Dell, a naval liaison officer assigned to a Marine battalion, chatted with the Marine in a bunk below.

"Can you see?" the Marine asked O'Dell.

"Yes," answered O'Dell.

"I can't see—I never will again," explained the Marine. "Gee, it's going to be tough, not seeing. I don't think I would mind so much but for one thing. My wife had a baby not long ago. I will never get to see my own son."[16]

Depressed and blaming himself that men died under his command at Red 2, on the transport Lieutenant Lillibridge repeatedly wrote out the names of the men in his platoon who died, then spoke their names over and over, promising never to forget their sacrifices. He also vowed that if he were to be an effective combat officer in the future, he must never again allow himself to become so emotionally attached to his men, so that when any perished, as surely they would in this lengthy war, he would not grieve as he was this November.

Lillibridge attempted to write their families, but gave up in frustration. "I know now that anything would have been acceptable, but at the time I just found myself too jammed up inside to do it." He thought he might more easily write the wife of his close friend who died on Betio, but even that task proved more than he could bear.

"Afterwards, I sat down and I must have written 20 letters to his wife but I never mailed any of them. It all seemed too futile and so tragic. I wept over it but it didn't make the words come out right. Howell and Brown [two other friends] corresponded with her for years and she must have thought I was a real bastard for not writing."[17]

The Thursday after the battle the Marines enjoyed a touch of home when each ship's crew celebrated Thanksgiving. Marines feasted on turkey, ham, potatoes, cranberry sauce, cake, candy, and pie as they slowly peeled away the emotional residue of battle. Meadows and the other men back at Betio also enjoyed a Thanksgiving meal—K rations, bouillon, coffee, and peaches eaten from captured Japanese bowls. It may not have matched what their cohorts aboard the transports enjoyed, but it topped anything since leaving New Zealand.

Whether on a ship or at Betio, Marines that Thanksgiving had much for which to be thankful. They had experienced a grueling melee that produced thousands of casualties, and while the haunting memories lingered, they at least had survived. Correspondent Richard W. Johnston tried to remind his readers back home that, whatever they were thankful for, nothing matched the good health of a family member in the service. "This dispatch is written while folks at home are sitting down to platters of Thanksgiving turkey. We share that spirit of Thanksgiving. Most of all, we are thankful to be alive. But for the chance of battle we would be in one of the five cemeteries on the island, hanging grotesquely from the barbed wire in the surf or lying among the wounded who have been taken aboard ships enroute [sic] back to hospitals."[18]

"The Most Completely Defended Island I Have Ever Seen"

Gens. Julian Smith and Holland Smith toured Betio on November 24, and what they saw astounded, and humbled, the career officers. Holland Smith, who had only just arrived after flying in to view the carnage, wrote, "No words of mine can reproduce the picture I saw when the plane landed after circling that wracked and battered island. The sight of our dead floating in the waters of the lagoon and lying along the blood-soaked beaches is one I will never forget. Over the pitted, blasted island hung a miasma of coral dust and death, nauseating and horrifying. Chaplains, corpsmen and troops were carrying away wounded and burying the dead."[19]

Upon observing one Marine body leaning against the seawall, with an arm still extended upright inches below the blue-and-white flag that it had been his task to place as a mark for the following waves, Holland Smith told Julian Smith men like that could never be defeated. The Marine had died doing his duty.

Twisted guns, destroyed bunkers, decaying bodies lay everywhere. One Japanese soldier was so badly burned that nothing remained but a charred spinal cord and a glob of flesh where his head should have been. When a Marine showed Gen. Julian Smith his helmet, dented by a Japanese bullet, the moved general asked the youth to always keep the item as a reminder of what he and his brethren had faced.

"I saw Marine dead in rows along the beach," stated Julian Smith, "and couldn't help noticing that every man had fallen face forward, some within a few feet of the Jap guns they were trying to take." Smith spotted a dead Marine with a hand grenade ring still on his finger, and four dead Japanese lying in a nest a few yards away, indicating the Marine had thrown the hand grenade that killed the Japanese just as they gunned him down. "Those men were not just going in there and dying," said Smith as tears coursed down his cheeks, "they were taking Japs with them."[20]

As the two generals continued their walk, Julian Smith remarked, "There was one thing that won this battle, Holland, and that was the supreme courage of the Marines. The prisoners tell us that what broke their morale was not the bombing, not the naval gunfire, but the sight of Marines who kept coming ashore in spite of their machine-gun fire. The Jap machine-gun fire killed many Marines in the water and on the beach. But other Marines came behind those who died. They landed on the beaches, they climbed the seawall, and they went into those enemy defenses. They never thought they would lose this island."[21]

Holland Smith added that he had served in World War I and had seen most of those horrendous battlefields, but claimed the Germans had built nothing in France remotely comparable to what the Japanese constructed at Betio.

Later, after reflecting on the stark devastation, Holland Smith summed his feelings. "I passed boys who had lived yesterday a thousand times and looked older than their fathers. Dirty, unshaven, with gaunt, almost sightless eyes, they had survived the ordeal but it had chilled their souls. They found it hard to believe they were actually alive. There were no smiles on these ancient, youthful faces; only passive relief among the dead."[22]

Near the end of the tour, Holland Smith remarked, "I don't see how they ever took Tarawa. It's the most completely defended island I have ever seen."[23] The officers could not help but notice that a full tide, complete with dead Marines, lapped against the coconut log seawall. Julian and Holland Smith stared momentarily at the water, and mused over the horrible carnage that could have occurred had a full tide allowed passage over the reef by the Higgins boats, but denied them the relative safety of the beaches and seawall. Marines in those boats would have landed directly on top of enemy guns, with no place to hide.

"Each Man Was a Hero"

Stan Bowen headed toward a troop transport for the trip away from the island. Shortly after arriving aboard, Bowen received word that the ship's doctor wanted to see him.

"Did you run out to an amtrac and pick up some guys?" the physician asked.

"Yeah."

"I heard about that, so I'm putting you in for a Silver Star."

Bowen eventually received a letter of commendation, which cited him for saving "the lives of men who otherwise might have perished" and praised his "utter disregard for his own safety" as he dashed into the waters "although continually exposed to enemy rifle and machine-gun fire."[24]

Numerous individuals received honors for their heroism at Betio. Four earned the nation's highest award, the Medal of Honor—three posthumously (Lieutenant Hawkins, Lieutenant Bonnyman, and Staff Sergeant Bordelon) and one who survived (Colonel Shoup). More than three hundred other men received medals, such as Navy Crosses, Distinguished Service Medals, Silver Stars, Legion of Merits. The Navy issued a Legion of Merit to Chaplain Willard, while Major Crowe and Major Chamberlin earned the Navy Cross for their actions at Red 3.

Chamberlin's citation praised him for reorganizing remnants from various units into an effective fighting force. "Personally directing the yard-by-yard advance of these assault units, he repeatedly exposed himself to intense enemy grenade and rifle fire" as he rushed from flank to flank. His actions "inspired his men to tremendous endeavors which resulted in the successful completion of an extremely difficult mission."[25]

Most men who fought under Chamberlin's guidance assert that the quiet professor deserved a Medal of Honor. At Betio, many unselfish efforts either went unrewarded or underrewarded. Hawkins and Bonnyman earned a deserved Medal of Honor because others witnessed their heroics, but other Marines accomplished much the same without recognition, either because no one saw their deeds or, more likely on the killing field of Betio, the witnesses perished in the same action. "The story of Tarawa is a saga in which only a few of the heroes have been or ever can be identified,"[26] stated Col. W. K. Jones.

After the fighting ended, a group of officers struggled with the issue of who should receive medals. They finally agreed to recommend no one in their unit because everyone deserved one. How could they possibly single out one man without doing injustice to another?

Pfc. Albert Gilman, twice wounded before the battle was even hours old, may have stated it best. "Those men who won the Medal of Honor were brave, but everyone was brave. Anyone who says he was not afraid on Betio is lying, but even with the fear, they did what they were trained to do. Each man who took another step forward in the water or on land was a hero."[27]

"Japs Were Lying All Around Me"

Marines faced a titanic task in removing the debris of battle from Betio. Thousands of mangled bodies, hundreds of thousands of metal fragments, shattered weapons, palm fronds, dead fish, and chunks of fortifications had to be disposed of. Robert Sherrod suggested it would be better if the Marines left for a few days and instead sent in a million buzzards. Men had to be wary about where they stepped, as bodies lay partially buried in the sand. Sometimes, a hand or a foot was the only sign that a combatant lay buried beneath. "Japs were lying all around me," said 2d Lt. Paul DuPre. "The bodies made bubbling sounds from the gasses. One guy said every time he stepped on a Jap, he saluted. His hand went up."[28]

Even though the fighting had ended, the dying continued. In the process of filling sandbags, a Marine hit a land mine with his shovel and died instantly in the explosion. Japanese stragglers emerged from places of concealment to bayonet men to death, and snipers were a constant concern. Only hours after Julian Smith passed by one spot on his walking tour, snipers killed three Marines.

Joseph Jordan was awakened from a deep slumber when he felt something crawl over him, followed by a burning sensation in his shoulder. "One of the stragglers had crawled into our area and was doing a job on my back with a bamboo-handled knife with about a 6-inch blade [which hit] the bone of the left shoulder blade and slid several inches through the flesh."[29] His terrified screams brought other Marines to his aid, who killed the invader.

After shooting three snipers, one Marine asked a question on everyone's mind. "Why don't somebody tell those bastards that the war's over?"[30]

Remarkably, as the fighting dissipated, souvenir hunters multiplied. Major Crowe had warned his battalion against looking for Japanese artifacts and weapons until after the battle but some Marines, anxious to send keepsakes back home, scoured Betio before the island had been secured. High on their list were Japanese beer and sake, swords, flags, and rifles. Staff Sergeant Hatch collected Japanese money, photo albums, and flags.

Some looked for gold, not on land, but inside their enemies' mouths. "A lot of guys took teeth," explained one Marine, who collected a few along with Japanese knives. "The Japs almost always had gold teeth, and we dug them out with a KA-BAR or bayonet."[31] Another used his rifle butt to crack open the mouth, then put the teeth in a bag draped over his belt.

Men had to be cautious about entering supposedly destroyed bunkers and pillboxes. Private Kelliher inched into one dugout hoping to find a keepsake among the many bodies piled inside, but quickly ran back outside.

"What's the matter, Kelly?" asked Hatch.

"There's somebody alive in there."

Kelliher had disturbed a wounded Japanese as he searched for souvenirs. Other Marines dragged him outside and killed him.[32]

Humorous incidents interrupted the more somber moments. Marines hurried to the aid of one man who dashed out of a bunker, expecting to kill yet another hidden Japanese soldier, only to find a dog in hot pursuit.

At another location, Marines heard movement inside a bunker and shouted for the person to identify himself. They waited a few moments, prepared to shoot, then watched a drunken Marine stumble out, clutching a bottle of sake. The sight of Marine rifles aimed at his head quickly sobered the man, who could only mutter about his close call, "Jesus Christ."[33]

"Peace on Earth"

Humor was in short supply for Dick Meadows and the men of the 2d Battalion, 6th Marines. First of all, he could not find his brother Jim. He and Bill reunited on the third day, then searched Betio for Jim, but could find no one who knew where he was or what had happened to the bayoneted Marine. The only solid information was disturbing. "I found his pack, his helmet, his helmet liner, and mosquito net in the tank trap,"[34] said Dick. Frantic for news, the pair moved about the isle in hopes of determining whether Jim was alive or dead, but met only frustration.

Dick Meadows also fumed that he faced more combat. While the battle had ended for the assault troops on Betio, Meadows's battalion received the unenviable task of sweeping up the atoll to ensure the Japanese had been cleared from the other islands. No one wanted to die in an action most considered an afterthought, but the job had to be done by someone.

The battalion first secured Bairiki, the island closest to Betio. After encountering minimal opposition, they headed toward each of the next isles in succession, gradually working their way along the atoll's eastern and then the northern arm.

"We went to all these islands," stated Dick Meadows, most of the time wading in chest-deep water from island to island by holding on to ropes stretched across. "Some had water one foot deep and some five feet deep, and a tremendous current between them. We were quite worried if we fell that we would be swept out to sea." As the smallest man in his unit, Meadows experienced the roughest time, especially at one section where he barely touched bottom as he worked along the rope. "We were wet from the first day to the last."[35]

The Japanese had fled every island except one—Buariki at the atoll's northern tip. Along the way, Meadows and the 2d enjoyed the enthusiastic welcome offered by natives who saw them as liberators from the harsh Japanese. Marines exchanged chocolate bars and cigarettes for coconuts and tried to mask their stares at the bare-breasted females who flashed furtive smiles their way.

Many of the isles featured thick brush four to five feet high through which the men had to advance. Never knowing where an enemy soldier might be lurking, Meadows maintained a constant vigilance when moving forward.

The 2d Battalion annihilated the final Japanese force and secured Tarawa Atoll on November 27, when they battled the Japanese at Buariki. A running battle, featuring hand-to-hand combat that matched anything on Betio, lasted several hours. "It was very ferocious, hot, heavy, and short," said Dick Meadows, who saw one Marine lieutenant sitting on the ground, with his rifle neatly across his knee, dead from a bullet hole between his eyes. "A lot of lead flying all over."[36] The battalion maintained pursuit until they reached the island's tip, where they wiped out the handful of survivors. Meadows's battalion killed 175 Japanese while losing 32 dead and 59 wounded.

Their assignment complete, the 2d Battalion returned to Betio, now empty of all but service and defense forces. Dick Meadows's brothers, as well as all the assault forces who had fought and bled for three days, already enjoyed the comparative comforts of the troop transports as they headed to Hawaii and much-needed rest.

Until January 15, Meadows patrolled Betio, hunting down the few stragglers still hiding. Despite the initial attempts to clear the isle of debris and bodies, Betio still resembled a trash heap. "There was a terrible stench, absolutely horrible," said Meadows, "but the sea breeze helped. We had a volleyball court we had fixed up, and in one corner this hand kept popping out of the sand. Guys shouted to chop it off, and it kept moving up out of the sand. It was obviously a Jap in a shallow grave, but we didn't think anything much about it."[37]

As Christmas neared, Dick Meadows remembered the emotional experience of the year before, when on Christmas Eve he watched the film *Holiday Inn*. He had hoped for a better Christmas in 1943, but that wish was not to be fulfilled.

Instead, on December 25, he heard "Condition Red!" as the battalion received warnings of a Japanese air attack. Meadows scrambled to a shell hole containing his company commander, Captain Leonard, and several other Marines, and waited out the bombardment.

"You know, back in the States they're singing 'Peace on earth, good will toward men,'" remarked Captain Leonard, "and we're saying, 'We've got the son-of-a-bitch in our lights,'"[38] referring to the searchlights that tried to illuminate the Japanese aircraft.

Conditions brightened on January 15, when Meadows and the 2d Battalion embarked for Hawaii. Before the month had ended, he was reunited with Bill and Jim, the latter recuperating in a hospital from his wounds.

"No One Seemed to Care"

The first transports entered Pearl Harbor on December 5. Marines eagerly lined the rails, ready to head to the nearest bar and begin a much-needed liberty, but after stretcher-bearers carried the wounded ashore, the ships weighed anchor and headed back to sea for the two-hundred-mile trip to the big island of Hawaii. A convoy of trucks transported the men sixty-five miles across rugged volcanic terrain to Camp Tarawa, their home for the immediate future.

Disappointed that they had missed the pleasures of Honolulu, Marines received a second jolt when they viewed their new residence: a camp situated between two extinct volcanoes. The men would have to live in tents until they constructed more sturdy quarters to block out the surprisingly cold winds and rain that inundated them at the higher altitude.

"They landed us and there was no camp, no nothing. Just a blanket and a toothbrush," recalled Stan Bowen. "You'd think they'd have something waiting for us." Bowen scanned the bleak setting, thought of what he and the others had just endured, and stifled the urge to cry as "it was cold and we were dirty, tired and really mad that no one seemed to care."[39] The men labored for three weeks before the camp, located sixty-five miles from the nearest store, offered even the most basic of amenities.

Though certainly not the welcome the men hoped for, authorities had reasons for placing them so far from civilization. The isolation gave men time to adjust from battle. It separated them from Hawaii's vast population of Japanese Americans, a crucial step in the emotionally charged atmosphere, where anyone bearing the slightest resemblance to a Japanese soldier might be considered an enemy. The relative coolness ameliorated the malaria from which many still suffered, and the mountainous terrain and open land offered superb training areas for the next campaign, designated to occur on the hilly island of Saipan.

The men of Tarawa thus returned to mixed signals. While Gen. Julian Smith handed out awards and praised the division as "the men who have knocked down the front door to Japanese defense in the Pacific," they returned to miserable conditions. A correspondent wrote of the time, "Thus were the heroes of Tarawa received—shelterless orphans in a strange cold land."[40]

As New Year 1944 neared, the men at Camp Tarawa had begun to mend from the battle. Conditions in the spartan camp had yet to significantly improve, but at least they enjoyed better facilities than Dick Meadows on Betio. Physical wounds and mental scars presented obstacles that many had difficulty surmounting, but others headed toward a recovery. "It always will be a source of supreme satisfaction and pride to be able to say—I was with the Second Marine Division at Tarawa!"[41] said General Smith in his holiday message to his troops.

"God Was a Little Stronger"

Early accounts of the battle hit U.S. papers and magazines shortly after the end of the fighting. Sherrod's articles appeared in *Time* magazine within a week, and in December *Life* magazine ran a series of photographs taken during the battle.

Though the public read about the general details of the fighting, family members of the men who fought sometimes waited weeks to learn specific details—had their loved ones been involved in the combat and, more importantly, had they survived? Slowly, Marine letters arrived in home front mailboxes bringing either glad tidings—or crushing news. Gen. Julian Smith wrote his wife on November 28, but refused to divulge particulars. "I'm not going into the terrible details of the fighting," he wrote. "I can't."[42]

Now that they were able to mention their whereabouts, men wrote letters describing the battle, although most omitted the more gory details out of fear of worrying loved ones. Pvt. David S. Spencer sent Japanese bills and coins to his family, and explained that he had lost twenty pounds—ten from not eating and another ten from worrying. He told them he was in Hawaii and had suffered no injuries.

In a December 8 letter he wrote, "You've probably read the papers about Tarawa so I won't bother to tell you all about it. God and your prayers must have pulled me thru [sic] because I came close to being killed several times. I've got two bullet holes in my jacket that is evidence that if I'd have been running a little faster I would have got it in the heart."[43]

Four days later he mentioned a transformation that first started on the transports. "Tarawa made me a very good Christian and church-goer. It seems as if I look forward to Church to thank God for my life and the fact that all of you are well & happy. I believe all of us that came back from Tarawa can safely say that Death had us by one hand and God the other and God was a little stronger." He later added, "I'll never understand or stop being grateful why my life was spared while other boys around me were being taken. I guess our prayers were answered."[44]

One young lieutenant who commanded a machine gun unit spared his parents the blood and violence, and instead focused on what most moved him about his men. "After the battle was over I spoke to my men and gave them my heartfelt congratulations. It was the most important incident in my life. I couldn't say much, the words just seemed to choke up, but each and every one understood. My men followed orders bravely and did their respective jobs magnificently. Each is a hero in his own right. I am proud of them . . . they may not have rank, prestige or background, but they have greater substitutes—guts, bravery and honor in facing death's danger. To me these traits are outstanding and will bring this war to an end. . . . Those that did not return fought like men and met their end bravely. Not one flinched, nor did they show any signs of pain. Theirs was the satisfaction of another job well done, one that would bring peace on earth closer to their loved ones. I find comfort in my prayers for them, in a comrade-in-arms' duty to carry on, and the honor of having been with them in our common cause."[45]

Even interservice rivalry softened in the aftermath of the battle. The *Range Finder*, an Army newspaper published at Camp Callan near San Diego, substituted praise for the Marines for its usual stories heralding the Army. On January 6, 1944, the paper stated, "But today, while 1026 telegrams from the Navy Department are being delivered to American mothers and fathers, informing them that their Marine sons were killed while taking the Pacific island of Tarawa, we most reverently dedicate this space." The newspaper explained that Tarawa was the bloodiest battle in Marine history, but "regardless, those Marines killed on Tarawa plowed forward in the face of machine gun fire and cannon blasts, fate or strategy be damned. All they knew was that they had an objective to take and all the Japs on earth couldn't halt them. They used the bodies of their own dead for sand bags as they pushed on until every Jap had been killed. Hell, those Marines waited for nothing except another shot at another Nip." The paper ended with "And so in closing let us best remember and respect those heroic Marines by considering each of them our superiors until we have had an opportunity to prove ourselves their equals."[46]

Most families learned of their loved ones' deaths either by receiving an official government telegram, or from another Marine whose letter first reached the family. Captain Crain had faced horror off Red 1, not far from where Montague and Seng died, but in many ways the task of writing letters to parents and spouses of the men killed under his command proved harder. "I was trying to do all I could do," explained Crain. "I would say I was sorry their son was killed, that he landed on the beach early in the landing, that the landing was very difficult, that we tried to get adequate cover, that I wanted them to know he died for a good cause, and that they and the nation could be proud of him."[47]

Crain never knew if his words provided much solace, for he rarely heard from the families. The one response he does remember came from the brother of a casualty. Crain had mailed the deceased Marine's ring to his brother in Missouri, but the man sent three emotional letters asserting that Crain had to be mistaken. He could not accept that his brother had died.

The reverse proved true for Mrs. Meadows in Watertown, South Dakota. The mother of three sons fighting in the Pacific twice received ominous news that reinforced any doubts she may have had. Shortly after the battle someone in town saw her at the local post office.

"Oh, you're Mrs. Meadows. You're the one who has three boys in the Marines on Tarawa?"

"Yes," Mrs. Meadows warily replied.

"Well, you know the law of averages," added the person, more than a bit insensitive. "One out of three [will be killed]."[48]

An erroneous radio report then stated that her son Jim had died on Tarawa. Fortunately, by then she had received a telegram informing her that Jim was recovering in a Hawaiian hospital.

Mrs. Hawkins was not as fortunate. After receiving the telegram informing her of her son's death, she asked Robert Sherrod to help find details about his end. "He was my whole world, all I had," she wrote the reporter. "He was a wonderful son, always cheerful, confident, sweet, kind, and thoughtful of others. . . . Please help me, if you can, to get a picture of his last days."

Happy to oblige for the mother of a man he considered a hero, Sherrod wrote Mrs. Hawkins a lengthy letter divulging what he knew. He ended by praising her son's actions as a reminder to the nation of what it needed to accomplish. "What can one say about a man who died so nobly in the service of his country? If Lieutenant Hawkins had lived a hundred years, he could not have known a fuller life. He could not have achieved more. Hawk knew what the war was about. He knew that we must crush the Japanese utterly, so that our sons will not have to fight this war again in twenty or thirty years hence. His example of devotion and unselfishness will surely serve to sustain other millions of young men who must finish the job. His name will live always in the brightest pages of those men who are proud to call themselves 'United States Marines.' "[49]

Marines who served with Lieutenant Hawkins also mailed words of praise to his mother. One sergeant wrote, "When he was a sergeant, I knew he would make a fine officer. . . . Your son was born to lead and I would have followed him anywhere." He added that " 'Hawk' loved trouble. If there was a tough job to do, he'd ask for it."[50]

Gy. Sgt. J. J. Hooper credited Hawkins's spirit for boosting the entire unit. "During the action on Tarawa, his courage and absolute fearlessness inspired each member of the platoon. This inspiration was great enough to enable the platoon to carry on even after Mr. Hawkins was critically wounded."[51]

Honors poured in for the lieutenant. The Navy christened the destroyer *Hawkins* in October 1944, and El Paso, Texas, named a street and school after the Marine.

On August 30, 1944, Mrs. Hawkins traveled to the White House, where President Franklin D. Roosevelt handed her the posthumous Medal of Honor awarded to her late son. *Time* magazine published an account, including a photograph of Mrs. Hawkins with the president, that stated, "The U.S. had many heroes last week. Some of them would never grow older than their framed photographs back home on the mantel, or the piano."[52]

"No News Is Good News"

The Montagues and Sengs had heard nothing from their sons since the first of November. They were accustomed to receiving a letter at least once a week, and Billie more frequently, but the families assumed the gap indicated that Charlie and Gene had departed toward an operation somewhere in the Pacific. They dared not let themselves think that the lack of news meant the worst—that their sons had been injured or killed.

In a letter to Billie, family member Brian Montague, a local judge, expressed the optimism that kept the family on an even keel. "You have been much in our thoughts all year, but particularly of late—since the 2d Marine Division attacked the Gilbert Islands," the judge wrote. "My optimism concerning Charlie may be wholly unfounded, but since that attack, I have felt that each day that passes without news of or concerning him, was in fact good news, for undoubtedly they must early have learned those who were fatal casualties, and since we heard nothing, we could deduce that he was still among us. That fact, however, does carry with it the possible implication that he has been more than slightly wounded, and word from him awaits developments. But, above all, I just simply live from day to day in confident faith that your prayers have reached the source from which all protection comes, and when this dirty job has been completed, he will return to you. We wish for nothing more ardently than that."[53]

Mrs. Seng clung to the same hopes. In a December 20 letter to her son, she mentioned that "we try to feel under the circumstances that 'no news is good news,' darling, but with the uncertainty of things, we are still anxious and praying fervently for your well being." She added, "Remember you are with us now and every day in thoughts and prayers and send every wish for a blessed Xmas & New Year with our love that grows ever stronger. Extend our best to Charlie too."[54]

Magazines and newspapers did not make things easier for either family. *Time* magazine quoted the Army's surgeon general, Norman T. Kirk, as cautioning the nation to expect an influx of men without arms, legs, and even faces. "Don't be callous," he advised, "and don't be oversympathetic and over-helpful. Treat him as a normal human being."[55]

These reminders only made the lack of information about Gene and Charlie harder for the parents and siblings to bear. The battle had ended over one month earlier and Christmas approached, yet they did not know if either Marine was alive. "That was the hard thing, for Mom, for all of us," said George Montague. "Why did it take so long?"[56]

On January 1, Gene Seng Sr. wrote his son that the family waited every day to learn of his safety. He explained that the entire clan had gathered at the house to celebrate the New Year, "with the one exception of that certain Marine who is the only one of the family who is undergoing the hardships and privations of war." He told his son, with whom he had shared so many happy moments fishing and hunting, that "we are honored and proud in the knowledge that you are serving your God and Country—willingly . . . the Marine way—bravely but without heroics."[57] He wished his son a happy New Year and that God grant him the hopes and dreams he held for the future.

"Well, Now We Know"

Their waiting ended on New Year's Day, 1944, the same day Gene Seng Sr. penned his letter to his son. The Montague family, including the parents, brothers George and Bruce, and sister Virginia, had just finished supper when the telephone rang. Father Strobel, the pastor of the Catholic church in Bandera, said he needed to see Mr. Montague right away. No one thought much of the call, as the priest suffered from tuberculosis and everyone assumed he needed a ride to the hospital.

Mr. Montague grabbed a bottle of whiskey, thinking it might help the ill priest, then drove away. After a few hours, George heard the family Chevrolet pulling up in the driveway. "I got up and went to the door, but my father passed on through without saying a word. He stuck his hands in his pockets, leaned back against the deep-freeze, and said, 'I've got some bad news for you.'"

George studied his father's face, normally devoid of emotion. He noticed his eyes had turned red and that he kept swallowing, as if trying to force down something unpleasant.

"Charlie was killed—killed in action," he informed the family. He took out a telegram from the War Department, then slumped against the wall as tears coursed down his face. George rushed to his mother, then cried on her shoulder while his father paced back and forth, still sobbing.

"We deeply regret to inform you that your son Pfc. Charles Montague USMC was killed in action in the performance of his duty and in the service of his country," stated the telegram. The wire gave no location, but most assumed he had been killed at Tarawa.

Finally, Mrs. Montague reacted. "Well, now we know," she said. She then stepped across the room to embrace her grieving husband, but he pulled away. Taken aback at this rejection, Mrs. Montague turned and walked into one room while her husband stumbled into another, alone in their mourning.

Billie Miller had dreaded this day since she waved to Charlie as the train whisked him away to boot camp. After taking a phone call, her father walked into the living room with the news that the Montagues had just informed him that Charlie had been killed. Billie refused to believe that her fiancé was dead, and for a long time afterward she kept thinking that Charlie was all right and living at the Bandera ranch. Family members became so concerned for Billie's health that she remained under a doctor's care for the next four weeks.

The morning after receiving the telegram, the family attended Sunday Mass, where friends and other family members stopped by to offer condolences. One uncle could only mutter, "Damned Japs."[58]

"Little Gene Seng Sleeps a Hero's Sleep"

Ralph Seng worried for his mother, especially after November 21 when she told Ralph and his three sisters, Peggy, Lorraine, and Patsy, "Something's happened to Gene, and I think he's dead." Gene's mother worried about her boy so much that the specter of his death invaded her dreams, shattering the only remaining sanctuary to which she could flee to escape her anxiety.

She explained that the night before—November 20, the day Gene died on the beaches of Betio—she had a dream in which Gene reached out his arms to her and cried, "Mother! Mother!"

"Momma was pretty upset," said Ralph Seng. "We didn't know exactly where Gene was because of the secrecy, but we knew he was going back into action."[59]

Family members wonder whether Mrs. Seng had the dream the night before, or days or weeks prior, but she related this dream on November 21, the day after her son's death. The government had not yet contacted the family. She had no news of her son, no way of knowing he had already died. She would not find out for six more weeks that her fears had become reality.

Once the Montagues learned of Charlie's death, Gene Seng Sr. figured he would soon receive similar news of Gene, for the two were always together. He did not have long to wait. Two days later, on January 3, Mr. Seng looked out the window and saw the Western Union man walking toward the door, a telegram in his hand. "Oh no, no, no!"[60] Mr. Seng cried.

The rest of the family sat in the living room, wondering what caused Mr. Seng's reaction. Once the deliveryman handed over a telegram, they instinctively knew. Ralph and his three sisters followed their parents into the bedroom, where Mr. Seng sat on the bed, opened the telegram, and read aloud the words they never wanted to hear.

"My dad took it real bad," said Ralph Seng. "My Uncle George Nelson, a tough old guy who had fought in World War I, said, 'I want to kill me a Jap.'"[61]

That their mother remained strong and steadfast did not surprise the youngsters, for she had always been the anchor at home. "Mother was a rock," said Patsy Dealy. She rarely showed emotion, and whenever she felt the need to break down, "she would cry by herself. Go into her room and cry. She never let things get her down. She held the family together more than Daddy, who was always officiating football and basketball."[62] To handle a grief he never quite mastered, Mr. Seng sometimes escaped to a hotel in a nearby town to be with his wife and little Peggy, away from things that reminded him of his son.

The city of San Antonio mourned the loss suffered by the prominent city athlete and sports store owner. Along with Charlie Montague and William Bordelon, the battle at Tarawa had taken three of Central Catholic's young boys.

"Little Gene Seng is dead with the marines on Tarawa," stated a columnist for the *San Antonio Light*. "Pride of a father known fondly by every sports follower in San Antonio for 30 years, bearer of one of the most honored names in this city's athletic history, little Gene Seng sleeps a hero's sleep on a far Pacific isle, and San Antonio is shaken by his passing as it has seldom been by a wartime tragedy."

The writer added that with these deaths, an impersonal war involving "soldiers" and "battlefields" had now become personal. "It has become a bitter, close-to-home thing, to be fought the harder and faster so that not too many others like Charley [sic] Montague and little Gene Seng shall give their lives in the winning."[63]

The same day, Gene Seng Sr. cabled June in New Zealand with the news. The younger Seng had written on Christmas 1942 of his hopes for a normal Christmas in 1943, but neither he, June, nor his family would ever enjoy that prospect.

With the bodies of their sons resting in Tarawa graves, family members attended Requiem Masses—Charlie's on January 4 and Gene's January 5. The anguish of sitting through a service for two such young men must have been trying enough, but the parents and siblings had to listen to the words and prayers with the bodies outside their reach. Charlie Montague's remains were later interred in the National Cemetery of the Pacific in Hawaii, while ten years later Gene Seng was laid to rest at Fort Sam Houston National Cemetery in San Antonio, to be closer to family.

"A Richer Dust"

The parents learned details of their sons' deaths later that January when Joseph Montague, Charlie's uncle, traveled to Washington, D.C., to query government sources. The Marine Corps gave him the exact dates and locations of their deaths, but he uncovered the rest by accident. A Texas congressman attended a speech delivered by Robert Sherrod, fresh from the battle, and afterward asked the reporter if he knew anything about a Marine named Montague. Sherrod replied he did, and invited Joseph Montague to contact him.

When they later met, Sherrod divulged that he had witnessed Montague's and Seng's burial on Betio and intended to use the scene in a book about the fighting. Sherrod later mailed a lengthy letter to Joseph, who sent copies to Frank and Ouida Montague and to Gene Seng Sr.

"This is indeed a sorrowful task," Sherrod wrote in the letter, "but I feel that if I tell you something about the manner in which your nephew Charles Montague died, it may assuage your grief." Sherrod then explained that Montague and Seng, along with their buddies, died rushing toward the enemy, and that men in their unit had carefully buried the two in Betio graves. The reporter marked the locations of their deaths on an accompanying map.

"This was unusual, because most of the Marines killed on Betio were buried by regular burial parties," Sherrod continued. "But these men from this particular company were finding the bodies of their buddies and burying them themselves. Since they were leaving by transport in a few hours, I supposed that they thought: 'Here is the last thing we can do for these boys we have known so long. We'll do it with our own hands.'"

After giving details of the burial, including the wooden crosses left by the men to mark Montague's and Seng's graves, Sherrod praised the Texas friends and the other young men who perished. "I cannot tell you what profound respect I have for these Marines who took Tarawa, the living and the dead. I do not believe any Americans ever fought more bravely or so unselfishly. It was a very difficult task—the Japs had told their men that a million men could not take Tarawa. I know what I think of the Marines. I think they gave their lives to crush an enemy who must be crushed utterly unless my two young sons must fight that enemy all over again twenty years hence. I salute those Marines, including Charlie Montague. I expect to do everything I can to see that their memory never dies."[64]

Mr. Seng thanked Robert Sherrod for honoring both Gene and Charlie and for giving both families memories of the boys' final moments. He wrote, "There is the justified pride in our hearts that these two sons of ours were surging forward with their boots on giving all their strength, their being, their minds, their hearts and their all for God and Country." Mr. Seng continued that because of the death of Gene and Charlie, "there is a richer dust in a corner of some foreign field known as Tarawa."[65]

Mr. Seng also thanked Congressman Paul Kilday for his aid in obtaining information about Gene. He expressed the pride he felt "in knowing that Gene gave his life for God and Country, so that thousands, yes, millions may live." He added, "I thank God that He gave me such a fine American son—for having him in my care for the twenty-one years of his life. I thank God for his manly Catholic character. I thank God for having given him the privelege [sic] of being ready to meet death—spiritually, mentally, and physically—to receive his Eternal Reward."[66]

Seng's father attempted to work through his grieving by writing letters. To a Mr. and Mrs. Goodwin, he expressed his happiness at being able now to "pray *to* Gene" instead of for him, "for I know he is in the sight of God, that he and others who die in action have suffered their purgatory here on earth in battle." In subsequent letters he stated that the family was trying to stop asking God why Gene's death occurred, and instead ask how they could best accept the tragedy. He mentioned to a Marine friend of Gene's the hope that they would face his death "with at least a fraction of the courage that Gene and all of you brave American boys faced death—that is the way we think Gene would have us do."[67]

Mr. Seng then turned his thoughts to the other people going through their own grief on the other side of the world—June McDougall and her family. In a lengthy letter dated March 12, 1944, he stated how close he and the Sengs felt to the McDougalls, as only they could grasp the deep feelings with which he and his family struggled. "First please accept my heartfelt appreciation of the fine sentiments expressed by you and your wonderful family about our boy Gene. By our boy Gene I mean your family's as well as my family's—It is truly an honor to share him with such a grand family. . . . The gracious, warm and sincere hospitality you good folks extended Gene has been a source of more than considerable comfort to us for we know that the last months of Gene's life were his happiest—due solely to your interest in him. For this we shall always be most grateful to you. . . . He fought a good fight and kept the faith—one can do no more even if he live a hundred years." He added of June, "She is as much a part of my family as any of my other children, regardless of what path life's journey has in store."[68]

"So Chin Up & March"

Mr. Montague never forgave himself for Charlie's death. He thought he should have talked him out of enlisting, and because he failed in that duty, his son had died. George Montague, who later became a Catholic priest, said that his father also blamed God for taking his son, and only found solace years later when he read the book *The Song of Bernadette*, about a peasant girl who supposedly had visions of the Virgin Mary.

The two fiancées—Billie Miller in Texas and June McDougall in New Zealand—suffered for years after the deaths of their loved ones. The Montagues frequently mentioned Billie's health in their letters and sent encouraging notes to help cheer her. "You are our first thought and our greatest concern right now,"[69] wrote Ouida to Billie just a few days after the Requiem Mass.

Fr. John Collins, Billie's religion teacher in 1940, sent words of comfort to the devout Catholic, telling Billie to stay close to God in those trying days. "I know it must have almost broken your tender little heart. Charlie died like a brave soldier and he was well prepared to meet his God—so his eternal happiness is secured—and I'm sure as he looks down from heaven he'd like to see his little sweetheart a brave soldier too! Remember you were Captain of the Drill

Team—so chin up & march—march on through life with its untold cruelties." Father Collins ended by writing, "I won't forget you and Charlie in my Masses."[70]

Other letters hint that a bereaved Billie received medical care during these times. Ouida Montague repeatedly invited Billie to Bandera, which she mentioned Billie should always consider home. Even the McDougalls, dealing with their own emotions in faraway New Zealand, asked Billie to "keep smiling because Charley [*sic*] would want it that way."[71]

The issue of Charlie's death came to a head in April, when Judge Brian Montague dealt with Billie's continued denial in a straightforward letter. She persisted in thinking that Charlie would one day suddenly appear, unharmed and unaltered, at which time the two would marry.

"Billie, as much as I would like to agree with you, and as much as I would love to respect your views, I feel I must tell you that you cannot longer hope or expect to see Charlie, or have him back in this world." Brian Montague mentioned that letters from other men serving with Charlie, and especially the information Robert Sherrod provided, should remove any doubts she still had. He wrote, "To my mind there is one other incident in the information available to us that forever bars any further hope, and that is in that part of Mr. Sherrod's [letter] wherein he states having seen the men from his company constituting themselves a burial party, and overhearing one of them say 'Here's Montague.' Billie, that is final, because it was identification by his buddies—those who knew him best."

He explained that he performed a similar duty as a soldier in World War I, and that it was almost impossible for them not to recognize a man with whom they fought, no matter how badly decomposed or mangled was the body. "I would rather do anything in the world than to attempt to disillusion you, or dissipate your hopes, but you have your own life ahead of you that must be lived, and out of which Charlie more than any one would want to see you carve and shape it into a life useful, helpful, and even in time one in which complete happiness will not be unknown."[72]

Though that letter nudged Billie toward accepting the obvious about Charlie, she still faced weeks and months of mourning. Charlie Montague's suffering ended on Betio; Billie's had just begun.

Half a world away, June McDougall endured a similar situation. June constantly spoke of Gene and mentioned she intended to travel to Texas following the war. "June has her good & bad days sometimes," wrote her sister, Lola, to Billie. "She cries & cries & there is nothing we can do to help her but she is really being brave. I think when her friends receive mail from their boys she feels it. I think she is about the only one out of her crowd who has lost anyone." Lola mentioned that June had written thirty letters to Gene before learning of his death and hoped they would not be returned to her. If so, Lola intended to burn them before June saw them.

"We were all very fond of Charley [*sic*]," she said when she turned her attention to Billie's loss. "He was a dear Billie and he was always talking about you. As far as he was concerned you were the most wonderful girl in the world and he really loved you with all his heart. He was just itching to go away & finish this terrible war because he said the sooner they get away the sooner he would get home to you."[73]

June handled the crisis more easily than did Billie, and even tried to comfort her companion in loss with a lengthy February letter. "Well, I am one person who really knows how you feel. The feeling is simply dreadful. Just as if it is all a horrible nightmare. I can't believe that Gene won't come around the house again and that I won't be running up the street to meet my Gene. For all that Billie I know they have both gone to a happier place somewhere where they will know peace & real happiness."

June added, "When I get really miserable as I do sometimes I think how brave our two boys were & how Gene would feel to see me behaving [this way], but Billie, I do get so unhappy I just don't know what to do with myself. Gene & I were so happy & contented with each other. We loved to sit by ourselves just planning about what we would all do.

"I wear my ring on my right hand & that was about the hardest thing I had to do. The happiest day of our lives was when we bought the ring & Charlie was with us. My family have been just broken hearted. Elgra & Nola always refered [*sic*] to Gene as their brother & as you know we always told Charlie that you were both our cousins."

June ended her missive by trying to bolster Billie's spirits for the days ahead. "My thoughts are with you all the time because I know just how much you & Charlie loved each other. It was God's will that Gene & Charlie should go. He wanted them as he had prepared their place for them—I know they will be waiting for us when our turn comes.

"Be brave Billie darling. It is a terrible blow but we have been left with wonderful memories. . . . Keep smiling."[74]

"Lots More of Us That Will Never Let Them Down"

Letters from officers and men with whom Montague and Seng served helped the two families in their grief. In the middle of January Capt. Don E. Farkas, the company's commanding officer, penned similar letters to both the families. To the Montagues, Captain Farkas wrote, "He was a member of a machine gun section who had to wade ashore under heavy enemy fire. Under terrific odds he put his gun into action before he was killed." Captain Farkas explained where Charlie was buried and that his personal effects should soon arrive. "In closing I would like to say that it is men with the dauntless courage like your son that has made the Marine Corps famous, and men like that will surely put an end to this war. Please accept my profoundest sympathies along with the rest of the officers and men."[75]

Chaplains Malcolm J. MacQueen and Joseph E. Wieber sent condolences to the families. In a letter to the Sengs they expressed sorrow over the sad news, but encouraged the family to embrace the contribution made by their slain son. "The action at Tarawa, already ranked among the memorable occasions of American history, reached its honorable outcome by virtue of such steadfast bravery as that displayed by Pfc. Gene G. Seng, Jr. You have every right to be endlessly proud of him because of his gallant obedience to the call of duty regardless of cost."[76]

Cpl. Jimmie N. May, a Marine from Gene and Charlie's unit, attempted to write a letter to the Sengs on six different occasions, but could not find the words to express his sorrow. He finally decided he had to send something, no matter how poorly written. May began by explaining, "I had lived with them in the same tent. Now I am the only one left in the company that lived in the same tent with them." He added, "I want you to know that Gene and Charlie died fighting. Gene got his machine gun set up and died on his gun. . . . If we have another chance [at an assault] which I think we will, I will try to get more of them [the Japanese] just for my friends that got it." The Marine ended by stating, "Gene & Charlie were men in every thin [sic] they done. . . . I want you to know there are lots more of us that will never let them down."[77]

Fred Ellis, a buddy of Gene's, wrote he would always "see Gene as the handsome smiling fellow he always was," and that "when it came time to go to protect the rights of our country in which each of us live, and to protect his loved ones, with never a backward step, he went forward to defend the things he had been taught in his home to cherish." Ellis, who had made the pact with Gene to send his mother flowers on Mother's Day should he die, ended, "To me you will always be part of my family and loved ones."[78]

*   *   *

Honors for the slain Marines also softened the pain. Both were awarded posthumous Purple Hearts, and Central Catholic High School placed their names, as well as that of S. Sgt. William J. Bordelon, on an impressive plaque that still adorns the main hallway just inside the front entrance.

Student newspapers at both Central Catholic and St. Mary's University acknowledged the pair in articles detailing the battle and their role in it. PALS SACRIFICE LIVES AT TARAWA, proclaimed the headline of the *Rattler*, St. Mary's publication. The article opened with "Pals in death as in life, fellow-Marines Gene Seng and Charles Montague, both 1942 ex-students, made the supreme sacrifice in the bloody landings on Tarawa last November 20."[79] Central Catholic emphasized that the two waded through thick fire before dying side by side on the beach.

While the Montague and Seng families dealt with their grief, a book and a documentary helped the rest of the United States comprehend the incredible horrors of war that had too often been hidden from public awareness.

"YOU SAY IT'S NOT ON THE MAP, MY SON?"

"There Is No Cheap Shortcut to Win Wars"

Tarawa altered the way the American public viewed the war. Before November 1943, censors heavily sanitized war news. The government, especially in the early months when the Japanese ran rampant throughout the Pacific, kept the full extent of the damage out of the press. Descriptions of Americans in retreat hardly created optimism. Stories shunned graphic depictions of combat, and photographs avoided disturbing images of mangled soldiers to shield American mothers and fathers. The fact that two oceans distanced the mainland from the fighting in Europe and the Pacific also lent an air of surrealism to the situation. The war existed elsewhere instead of on American soil, unlike the experience of the other Allied nations, where much of the fighting and devastation occurred in their cities and countryside. In 1943 the American public had little idea of war's terrible reality.

An occasional exception appeared. *Life* magazine published photographs of American dead littering the beaches at Buna in the Pacific in early 1943, but even those images—every soldier lay facedown, and no sign of injury could be seen—paled against reality.

In the middle of May 1943, President Roosevelt ordered the military to release more accurate coverage of the fighting. The sense of sacrifice that swept the country after Pearl Harbor had dissipated, and the nation had safely emerged from the desperate days of 1942, when Japan and Germany reigned supreme. Roosevelt believed that if the people were to continue sacrificing, they had to realize that bitter fighting lay ahead. When he amended the order by stating that the accounts could not be so graphic that they would offend the public, however, Roosevelt gutted his own command. Government censors and news agencies continued to deliver "clean" versions of combat.

Bloody Tarawa, with its flood of graphic coverage by correspondents like Robert Sherrod and photographers like Staff Sergeant Hatch, removed the final barriers to more accurate coverage. In the face of such frightening brutality at the tiny Pacific isle, the government relented and released the powerful depictions to a public sadly lacking in such matters.

Starting on December 6, Sherrod's potent prose in *Time* magazine and *Life*'s stunning photographs of Marine dead littering Betio's shoreline or floating in the water captivated—and shocked—the American public. People on the home front read the casualty figures for the three-day battle, which almost equaled the numbers of dead and wounded in the six-month Guadalcanal campaign, and paused. No previous operation in Europe or the Pacific had produced such horrific losses. Newspapers labeled it BLOODY BETIO or TERRIBLE TARAWA. Some questioned how such a costly operation could occur in such a brief time—a weekend, really—at such a tiny outpost. The *New York Daily News* printed an editorial with the title, WE SHOULD HAVE USED GAS AT TARAWA.[1]

The writing of Sherrod and other journalists, and the images of Hatch, Kelliher, and the team of combat photographers, would no longer permit the American public to ignore war's cost. "It was a great shock to the American people who had come to believe that wars could be won without bloody fighting," concluded Gen. Julian Smith. "Tarawa cost the lives of nearly a thousand American boys and brought sorrow to as many homes. It brought home to the American people the grim reality that there is no cheap shortcut to win wars."[2]

As most often happens after tragedies or unexpectedly high losses, people sought someone or something to blame. Gen. Douglas MacArthur called the frontal assault against Betio's beaches unnecessary, and Gen. Holland Smith, who had never objected to the plan before the operation, eventually concluded that Betio should have been bypassed for a different location.

Stories mentioned the low tides and the wade in against Japanese machine guns and wondered why the operation could not have been postponed to a later date. Supporters answered that a delay would only have handed the Japanese more time to strengthen an already formidable system of defenses on the isle, especially along the lagoon side, which would have claimed more American lives. Critics asked why the military selected the Central Pacific as an avenue of attack. Supporters responded that it was the shortest route to Tokyo. Critics wondered why the attack occurred at Betio instead of one of the other hundreds of islands scattered about the Pacific. Supporters replied that few other islands were correctly situated, like Betio, so that an airfield could be used with the prevailing winds.

Julian Smith and others answered their critics at every opportunity, for they did not want the sacrifices of more than one thousand young Americans at Betio to be forgotten. General Smith stated that any time the military embarks on a new campaign, the costs will be high, as inexperience leads to unexpected developments and to error. Such was the case at Betio. "There had to be a Tarawa. Tarawa was a battle of firsts, for which there was no precedent. . . . It set the pattern for future amphibious operation in the Central Pacific."[3]

Even Holland Smith initially defended the attack. He explained that the Marines killed almost four enemy soldiers for every American dead in an operation that should have cost more. He added that it took European nations two decades to learn how to fight Napoleon, but "it took the Marines just three days to learn how to storm an atoll fortress and dig the Japs out." He cautioned readers of *Time* magazine to brace themselves for similar heavy casualty lists. "But as long as the war lasts some of them somewhere will be getting killed. We have got to acknowledge that or else we might as well stay home."[4]

Military commanders had to educate the people to a long, hard war. The newly appointed Marine commandant Lt. Gen. Alexander A. Vandegrift said, "No one realizes more than does the Marine Corps that there is no royal road to Tokyo. We must steel our people to the same realization." Henry Keys, a reporter for the *London Daily Express*, concluded the same. "The battle for Betio, the fiercest, bloodiest and most ruthless I have seen in the two years of the Pacific War, showed how long, hard and costly the road to Tokyo will be."[5]

"Handsome Heroes and Easy Victory"

The Marines who fought at Betio, while loathing the home front's reaction to the carnage, were hardly surprised. Hollywood had, after all, made millions churning out war movies in which a hero, like Humphrey Bogart, single-handedly whips the enemy, or in which American soldiers run untouched through enemy fire. One soldier remarked that such films gave men like him "a pain in the pratt, because that kind of crap gives the folks at home the wrong kind of idea about what we are up against." One airman summarized what most every fighting man believed when he told a correspondent, "It seems to me that the folks at home are fighting one war and we're fighting another one. They've got theirs nearly won and we've just started ours. I wish they'd get in the same war we're in. I wish they'd print the casualties and tell them what it's like." A Marine sergeant complained, "If the Marines could stand the dying, you'd think the civilians could stand to read about it."[6]

Maj. James A. Donovan, a company commander with the 6th Marine Regiment, wrote a series of letters to his parents in which he shared his opinion of the home front. The illuminating notes convey surprise, astonishment, and disgust over the American public's inability to fully comprehend the Japanese and the violent nature of the conflict.

On December 22, 1943, he wrote a lengthy letter trying to answer some of the critics. "I notice the news mags [sic] gave the Tarawa [operation] lots of notice—also that there is some questioning on the part of certain parties as to why the casualties were so heavy. It makes me mad when these 'self-appointed' 'experts' and professional excuse-makers start questioning and arguing about things they know nothing about.

"Of course the casualties were heavy, and they will continue to be heavy in this type of warfare if we are going to win it.

"There was nothing wrong with our equipment, or the tides, or our plan.

"We had the best of everything, a good plan, and the men did a fine job—but the Japs also did a good job. They put up a tough fight until the bitter end.

"Anyway, we won, we learned a lot and a lot of good men were lost. That's the price we pay to win.

"I'm afraid too many people have the Hollywood conception of war; that its [sic] all handsome heroes and easy victory. Well it isn't—and I'm sorry to see that certain people want to know the 'reasons' why what should be the 'expected' happens."

Donovan continued his arguments in subsequent letters. "Hollywood's and radio's interpretation of this war gives me mostly a big laugh. We would like to have the uncut films of Tarawa shown to anyone who is interested," he wrote on January 27, 1944. Of mistakes that had been made, on March 20 he stated, "Granted, it was not perfect—very few operations are. We learned from it tho, and we won. If we have hard fights and reverses from time to time, it is because we are still paying for pre-war unpreparedness, lack of training, and blindness."

He claimed in the same letter that the men whose opinion should matter most, the Marines who closed with the Japanese at Betio, dismissed talk of casualties as a waste of time. "Nobody in the 2d Division is 'beating their chops' about Tarawa and after all we are the ones chiefly concerned. We are too busy applying what we learned to prepare us for the next one. Tarawa is a closed chapter."[7]

Melvin Traylor returned to the United States due to his injuries, and what he and the other wounded men found angered them. "Coming off our battle at Tarawa, we felt that we had won a great victory and were rightly proud of our selves [sic], and to read in the stateside papers that the whole campaign was a bloody mistake and that someone should pay for our errors made us furious."[8]

John Magruder, who fought at Betio, conveyed similar emotion in letters to friend Thomas Weil. "There has been much talk about the 'reef' and the terrific battle that took place as our boys struggled in over it," he wrote on January 8, 1944, "but there was a long, hard job of work to be done on the island itself. The battle had only begun when the beach was won, for the Japs are experts at the art of defense in depth and every single pillbox, trench and position had to be wiped out."

Magruder alluded to the idea that people at home seemed to focus much of their bitter opposition on the fact that men were stranded at the reef and forced to wade ashore. Civilians did this for two reasons. At first, no mention had been made of the amtracs, in part to keep information about their usefulness from the Japanese. Secondly, most reporters had been slated to arrive with the fourth and following waves, the waves using Higgins boats rather than amtracs. As a result, early writing of the battle centered on the walk in, reflecting the correspondents' experience. Thus the home front assumed that all the Marines were simply dropped off at the reef with a gauntlet of fire facing them. Magruder tried to counter what he saw as an erroneous point of view.

Magruder also talked about mistakes. "There's been a lot of ignorant and unfounded criticism of the Tarawa operation coming from certain sources—none of whom are qualified to pass judgement [sic]. I can't discuss what we knew and what we didn't know before we hit the beach, but I can say that there hasn't been one man who landed that has complained about the way the operation was pulled off, and after all, the men who went through the actual hell are in the best position to do the judging. You can't fight a war in a celophane [sic] case and if a place has to be taken it's got to be taken, and men are going to get killed doing it. It's about time some of the Monday morning strategists . . . back home started to realize that there's more to war than parades and USO benefits. All this unfounded criticism only causes disquietude at home and does nothing to improve the situation out here."[9]

Everyone, even the critics, had nothing but praise for the men who fought the battle. *Life* magazine touted the Marines as heroes, and the battle as a crucial point of the war. In its December 6, 1943, issue, the publication stated, "Tarawa proved, so that it never need be proved again, that American men can fight with the very best men in the world. The shame of Pearl Harbor, the shadow of doubt that lingered with the smoke on the hills at El Guettar, the slow success of Guadalcanal—these things were better than atoned for; they could now be forgotten. On Tarawa the U.S. Marines were fighting the Imperial Special Navy Landing Force, which is the Japanese way of saying Marines. The enemy was Japan's best. And yet the dead lay two-for-one in the dugouts, and sometimes four-for-one. Tarawa proved again that the famous tenacity of the Jap is not equal to the tenacity of an American roused."

The magazine emphasized a point many defenders had been making—that the American public had to realize that war costs lives. "Tarawa brought home, as it needs to be brought home again and again, the fact that there is no cheap short cut to win wars. It is a peculiarly American foible to want to do things the easy way."

The magazine also painted Betio as a threshold marking a swerve toward victory from the early days of defeat. "Tarawa was a proof that we are now on the way to certain victory. Notice the date on the cover of this issue of *Life*. Two years ago on Dec. 6 America spent its last day at peace. In two years the country, while dedicating itself to the defeat of Germany first, has nevertheless moved from the unawareness of Pearl Harbor, from the crushing loss of Guam and Wake, through the nightmares of Bataan and Guadalcanal, to Tarawa."[10]

In an effort to educate the public, the Marines dispatched Colonel Edson to the United States. In various speeches and appearances, he explained that the casualties suffered at Betio were no worse than Guadalcanal, and that the losses came not from mistakes but from a determined enemy. To counter the image that Betio consisted only of Marines being slaughtered in the water, Edson emphasized that more than three-fourths of the casualties occurred on land.

Edson warned the people to expect a long, costly campaign, possibly as long as four years, to defeat Japan. He need only refer to the *Time* article of January 3 quoting Tokyo as urging its citizens in the aftermath of Tarawa, "Step by step and moment by moment [the enemy] is approaching our mainland. . . . To support the spirit and follow the souls of the 4,500 men [on Tarawa and Makin] who preferred death to dishonor is the best way to fight. . . . The 100 million people [of Japan] must arouse themselves and must follow the glory of the 4,500 heroes."[11]

Edson said that, rather than easier campaigns, the people must expect more Tarawas as the American military slugged its way toward Japan. If the enemy could not defeat the United States on the battlefield, maybe they could so weaken morale back home that the public would demand a diplomatic solution. "I think the American people should realize the psychology of the people we are fighting—to make the campaigns as costly as possible because they don't believe we can take it. They are willing to take large losses in the hope that we will be ready to quit before we can lick them."[12]

"On Tarawa There Was a More Realistic Approach to the War"

The two products most responsible for bringing war's grimness to Americans' front doors were Robert Sherrod's 1944 book, *Tarawa*, and Staff Sergeant Hatch's contributions to the 1944 Academy Award–winning documentary, *With the Marines at Tarawa*. The powerful descriptions contained in the book, combined with the potent images of the graphic documentary, alerted Americans that this was a far more brutal war than they realized.

Sherrod decided to write his book when he returned to Hawaii on November 28 and heard complaints from civilians about the losses at Tarawa. The journalist, only days removed from the stink and grime of Betio, could hardly believe the naïveté that existed. "This attitude, following the finest victory U.S. troops had won in this war, was amazing. It was the clearest indication that the peacetime United States (i.e., the United States as of December, 1943) simply found it impossible to bridge the great chasm that separates the pleasures of peace from the horrors of war. Like the generation they educated, the people had not thought of war in terms of men being killed—war seemed so far away."

Sherrod's volume admirably succeeded in educating the American public, as few battlefield descriptions match the reporter's vivid prose. His powerful writing helped instruct the American people, both as to the horror and carnage of the battle, and as to their ignorance in general about the war.

Sherrod claimed that mistakes had been made, but that the military would correct those. In so doing, the shocking casualties of Betio would save lives in future operations. "The lessons of Tarawa were many. It is a shame that some very fine Americans had to pay for those lessons with their lives, but they gave their lives that others on other enemy beaches might live. On Tarawa we learned what our best weapons were, what weapons needed improving, what tactics could best be applied to other operations. We learned a great deal about the most effective methods of applying Naval gunfire and bombs to atolls."

Sherrod blasted those who criticized Tarawa's losses and wrote that "there is no easy way to win the war; there is no panacea which will prevent men from getting killed. To me it seemed that to deprecate the Tarawa victory was almost to defame the memory of the gallant men who lost their lives achieving it."

Sherrod wondered why Americans did not realize "that there would be many other bigger and bloodier Tarawas in the three or four years of Japanese war following the first Tarawa." He stated that the Japanese strategy was to dig in, make the Americans come to them in bloody encounters, weaken support at home because of ghastly losses, then negotiate a peace with an America hoping to avoid more bloodletting. "It seemed to me that those Americans who were horrified by Tarawa were playing into Japanese hands. It also seemed that there was no way to defeat the Japanese except by extermination."

Sherrod contended that Americans had expected modern machinery, such as airplanes, to win the war, and thereby reduce the number of casualties. Optimistic war reports in newspapers and magazines helped spread the conception that the war was not all that bad. He warned that "the road to Tokyo would be lined with the grave of many a foot soldier."

Sherrod pointed out that up until that time, the stories that filtered through military censorship to the public had shared little in common with the actions they supposedly described. He quoted one sergeant as saying, "The war that is being written in the newspapers must be a different war from the one we see." A bomber pilot said of his visit home from the Pacific, "When I told my mother what the war was really like, and how long it was going to take, she sat down and cried. She didn't know we were just beginning to fight the Japanese."

Sherrod then included his observations of home. "My third trip back to the United States since the war began was a let-down. I had imagined that everybody, after two years, would realize the seriousness of the war and the necessity of working as hard as possible toward ending it. But I found a nation wallowing in unprecedented prosperity. There was a steel strike going on, and a railroad strike was threatened."

He pointed out that when one politician warned the U.S. might incur a half million casualties in a few months, the public laughed, and when Gen. George C. Marshall complained that union strikes helped the enemy, most simply ignored him. Sherrod then ended his book with a blunt assessment.

"The truth was that many Americans were not prepared psychologically to accept the cruel facts of war.

"The men on Tarawa would have known what the general and the justice meant. On Tarawa, late in 1943, there was a more realistic approach to the war than there was in the United States."[13]

Sherrod's moving book earned widespread praise for opening the public's eyes to what unfolded in the Pacific. Lewis Gannett in the *New York Herald* called the volume "the most ghastly, graphic, factual, frightened and frightening picture of front-line battle that I have yet seen in print."[14] If the public needed any further convincing, *With the Marines at Tarawa* provided more material.

"This Is It"

Marine officers rushed the film footage shot by Hatch and Kelliher to San Francisco for processing. Normally, military censors reviewed any footage before releasing approved portions to the public, but that did not happen this time. The public affairs officer called a lieutenant in the Navy Department, and when the lieutenant learned that Hatch, with whom he had attended the March of Time school, had shot most of the film, he said, "If he shot it, it's O.K. Release it." The film was handed over to Fox Movietone News, who in turn distributed it to hundreds of theaters.

Hatch's footage first ran in theaters on the West Coast. A typical ten-minute newsreel of the time included three topics—at least one of which concerned a bathing beauty contest or some other lighthearted subject—but this one focused solely on the battle sequences from Betio. When Hatch arrived in San Francisco on his way to Washington, D.C., an officer took him to the theaters along Market Street to show him an impressive sight—a string of marquees bearing the newsreel's subjects, and Hatch's name prominently displayed alongside.

In the meantime, the Joint Chiefs of Staff asked noted film director Frank Capra, who had brought to theaters such landmark films as *Mr. Smith Goes to Washington* and *Meet John Doe,* to assemble a documentary about Betio. Capra first examined color footage from Betio, film Hatch had not shot, but dismissed its value as bearing little resemblance to combat. The footage showed Marines arriving and huddling on the beach, but lacked a sense of the nonstop action that characterized Betio.

"I can't make anything out of this! There's no combat. I can't believe it. That battle and there's no combat footage?"

A few days later one of his associates said he had just seen some wonderful material from Tarawa.

"Where?" asked Capra. "I thought I'd seen everything. Where did you see it?"

"It's on the newsreels," replied the associate.

Capra asked for a copy of the Movietone News segment. When the director previewed Hatch's grim footage, including the frame containing both Marine and Japanese combatants, he immediately realized he could turn the powerful film into an illuminating documentary. "This is it,"[15] he said to his fellow workers.

President Roosevelt balked at releasing the documentary, fearing the scenes would alarm the American public. After a December 28 White House press conference attended by Robert Sherrod, the president asked to meet the reporter to discuss the matter.

"What do you think about this Tarawa film?" Roosevelt asked Sherrod. "I hear it's pretty bloody."

"Yes, it is," replied Sherrod, who had seen the film in Honolulu on his way back from Betio.

"Do you think it ought to be shown?" Sherrod noticed the president seemed clearly uncomfortable with the notion of releasing such graphic content.

"Well, Mr. President, I think so. That's the way the war is out there, and since there is still an awful lot of fighting yet to be done, people might as well get prepared for it."[16] When top military officials, including Adm. Chester Nimitz, argued that the American people needed to be educated about the war, Roosevelt gave his assent to the documentary's release.

Warner Bros., the company owned by the stepfather of Stan Bowen's high school classmate, produced a nineteen-minute documentary from Hatch's and Kelliher's footage. The impact on audiences, unaccustomed to viewing such vivid film of war, was immediate. A critic for the *New York Times* wrote *With the Marines at Tarawa* had "all the immediacy of personal participation in the fight, and its sense of actual combat in close quarters is overpoweringly real." Another critic marveled at its realism and said, "You realize his [the Japanese] deadliness by the way the Marines inch their way up to these defenses until they can blast out the occupants with flame-throwers, grenades, and mortars."[17] One film executive, assuming the footage could not possibly have been real, even asked Hatch how he had managed to stage the amazing sequence showing the two combatants in one frame.

The Sengs attended a screening when the documentary arrived in San Antonio theaters. They had already drawn solace from Sherrod's material, but hoped to gain additional comfort from Hatch's film. They had recently received a collection of letters they had mailed to Gene in late 1943, stamped by military authorities USMC REPORTS UNDELIVERABLE; RETURN TO SENDER,[18] and the incident reopened the wounds. Possibly the film could ameliorate the pain.

"We went to see it [the documentary] in hopes we would get a chanced glimpse of our boy," Mrs. Seng wrote to one of Gene's Marine friends of attending the film, "but we were disappointed. However, it gave us some idea of the horror of the battle, and duly made us appreciate more fully the sacrifices that were made."[19]

The film won 1944's Academy Award for Best Documentary. As photographer, Hatch did not receive an Oscar or attend the ceremonies, but found comfort in Frank Capra's words, "You know, you never really got an Academy Award, but without your footage there wouldn't have been any film to put out."[20]

Moviegoers packed theaters to see the documentary, which so moved audiences that war bond sales rocketed afterward. Ironically, the only organization harmed by the film was the Marine Corps. The graphic footage so frightened young males that enlistments in the Marines temporarily plunged 35 percent.

Hatch's graphic footage from Betio subsequently appeared in almost every documentary assembled about the Pacific War. The producers of *Sands of Iwo Jima,* the Oscar-nominated 1950 film starring John Wayne, relied heavily on Hatch's work to depict the fighting at Betio.

"There Had to Be a Tarawa"

The United States benefited in a number of ways from the assault on Betio. The campaign proved that amphibious attacks against defended beaches worked, and it advanced the United States military seven hundred miles across the Pacific. In addition, aircraft stationed on the island's airfield could reach the next target on the Central Pacific route—the Marshall Islands. Even more, the campaign pointed out defects that had to be remedied for future operations. Since so many radios failed after being drenched by the lagoon water, a better system of communications had to be devised, and the Marines needed more amtracs to avoid the deadly snarl that occurred at the reef.

Alterations were made in the brief preinvasion bombardment. When Admiral Nimitz visited the battlefield shortly after Betio was secured, the sight of nearly intact defenses bothered the commander. He ordered detailed drawings made of the Japanese fortifications, then had replicas constructed on the Hawaiian island of Kahoolawe at which the Navy conducted intense gunnery practice. Every destroyer, cruiser, and battleship in the Pacific had to pass a rigorous test in bombardment against these fortifications.

The Navy concluded that instead of hours, future operations required days of preinvasion bombardment, and that they needed armor-piercing shells to crack through fortified walls before exploding inside. The military also decided to use demolitions teams to remove underwater obstacles, and to emphasize leadership training so that men could step into vacancies created by combat. Admiral Turner's official report concluded that the unexpectedly high number of casualties on Betio showed that for future operations, where similar losses could be expected, the men "must be trained and encouraged to use their individual initiative and resourcefulness. They must be imbued with confidence in their ability to prevail against the enemy, even when officers and NCOs are absent." As far as officers, Turner recommended additional leadership training in dealing with the unexpected. "They must be able to take the men and material available and do the job at hand. This might be called training in SNAFU leadership, leadership in a SNAFU situation."[21]

While victory at Betio shattered the southern Japanese flank and opened the way for the Navy and Marines to assault larger Japanese strongholds in the Marshalls and Marianas, it also illustrated that the Japanese would never yield without mounting a ferocious defense. If anyone held illusions that the war against Japan could be swift and relatively easy, those misconceived thoughts foundered off Tarawa's reef. "The Japanese will not crack," said the former ambassador to Japan, Joseph C. Grew. "They will not crack morally or psychologically or economically even when eventual defeat stares them in the face. Only by utter physical destruction or utter exhaustion of their men and materials can they be defeated."[22]

Betio served as the testing ground for the Navy and Marines in their drive through the Central Pacific. They retained the tactics that worked and modified or dropped the ones that did not, so that by the time Nimitz assembled his forces for the next target, the Marshalls, the Marines enjoyed more of an advantage. The experience from Betio assisted them in subsequent operations.

"In the flames of Tarawa was tempered the sword that would cut to the heart of the Japanese Pacific empire," wrote one Marine historian. "There had to be a Tarawa, the first assault on a strongly defended coral atoll," said an officer forty years later. "What the Marines accomplished there set a standard for future amphibious operations. It was much more than a successful battle. There untried doctrine was tested in the crucible of actual combat."[23]

The Marines dispatched Tarawa veterans to instruct other Marine units about what occurred at Betio. Congress, heeding the impact of the battle, rushed through a bill authorizing an increased number of ships for the Navy, including amtracs.

Colonel Edson, who headed the publicity effort to deal with home front criticism of the operation, later stated that every subsequent amphibious victory of the Pacific conflict, including Saipan, Iwo Jima, and Okinawa, owed a debt to the lessons learned on Betio's deadly sands. "The losses sustained at Tarawa were small when compared to the good that came out of it. While we mourn for those who brought us that victory, we revere them for the sacrifices which made it possible."[24]

The operation had one other benefit. Strategists planning the immense cross-channel invasion against Hitler's Atlantic Wall, now only seven months away, carefully observed the outcome on Betio. The Marine success at Tarawa reaffirmed their faith that assaults from the sea against heavily defended beaches could succeed.

"Still Real Heroes Alive"

After the battle, the surviving principals headed in different directions. Staff Sergeant Hatch continued as a combat photographer and participated in the invasion of Iwo Jima. Following the war, he worked in Hollywood, where, among other duties, he shared his experiences with actor Errol Flynn as preparation for the actor's appearances in war films.

Stanley Bowen continued his work as a corpsman. He saw action at Saipan, Tinian, and Okinawa, suffering only shrapnel wounds in an accidental explosion at a training camp. He subsequently married Marge McCann, worked as a successful insurance executive, and currently enjoys thrice-weekly golf outings in a happy California retirement.

Chaplain Willard returned to New England, where he started Camp Good News, a Christian camp for youth. The minister who walked around with two grenades, Mike and Ike, continued his clever naming after the war—his two sons, Peter and Paul, shared religious appellations with daughters Faith and Hope. He died in November 1999.

Eddie Albert returned to acting and enjoyed television success with *Green Acres*. Despite an outstanding film career, Albert maintained to his final day that the accomplishment of which he was most proud was his role off Betio. He passed away in May 2005.

In 1966, after serving thirty-one years in the military, including tours in the Korean War, Major Chamberlin retired from the Marine Corps. After the war he returned to the academic world in a variety of capacities.

The quiet commander spoke little to his family of Betio. His son William did not even know of his father's role in the battle until much later, when he read about the Pacific conflict. He recalled watching a war movie with his father, who said, "Our society is making actors into heroes. John Wayne was an actor during the war. There are still real heroes alive who actually did this stuff."[25]

The closest any family member can recall Chamberlin showing pride in himself was the time he took his son Henry to the theater to see *Sands of Iwo*

Jima. The film, starring John Wayne, included much of Hatch's footage from Betio. Chamberlin told his son that he would squeeze his hand whenever he appeared on screen. The low-key officer took this approach because he did not want to draw attention by saying anything out loud or by pointing to the screen. Major Chamberlin died at age eighty from a stroke.

"Greater Love Than This"

The Montague and Seng families keep the memories of their slain loved ones fresh, even though the battle occurred more than sixty years ago. Six members participated in a 1995 San Antonio ceremony honoring William Bordelon, in which Fr. George Montague celebrated a Catholic Mass.

Many of the men who served with Montague and Seng, the Marines who buried the pair on Betio's beach, maintain contact with the families. Years later Joseph Sobol returned to Tarawa, located the exact spot of burial at Red 1, said a prayer for the fallen comrades, then placed flowers in the sand. He later traveled to the Punchbowl, the cemetery in Hawaii honoring World War II's dead, to visit Charlie Montague's grave.

In the mid-1990s, Sobol fulfilled a promise he made to Montague. Charlie extended an invitation that, if Sobol ever traveled to Texas, he should visit the family in Bandera. Feeling an obligation to honor his word, Sobol arranged an extended visit with Charlie's siblings and other relatives. The battle had ended, but the love and emotional bonds continued.

Every November Emory Ashurst thinks of those men who perished at Red 1, and Fred Ellis visited both families right after the war to explain what he knew of Montague's and Seng's service careers and deaths. Until he died, every Mother's Day Ellis sent carnations to Gene Seng's mother.

Family members keep the memories burning. George Montague wrote an article about Charlie, and brother Bruce, who also joined the Marines and states that Charlie was his role model, claims, "I think about him a lot."[26]

One facet of a battle that often is overlooked is the "would have beens"— what would have happened to a person who died in the battle, what would they have become, what would life have been like, how would society and family have benefited? Montague and Seng never had the chance to live a long life as did others, and their loss, as well as the loss of so many others at Betio, leaves us wondering. They gave up sixty or more years of marriage to June and Billie and the opportunity to enjoy children and grandchildren.

Most family members believe that Charlie Montague would certainly have returned to Texas, married Billie, and started a ranch. Most feel he could have been a champion calf roper.

When asked what he would say to Charlie today if he had the chance, Fr. George Montague replied, "I would quote to him the Scripture, 'Greater love than this no one has than to lay down his life for his family.' I would say, 'Charlie, you did that and I thank you and I love you and appreciate what you have done for me.' He still moves me after all these years."

Father Montague cannot know for sure, since both are now gone, but he believes his father would tell his son, "Charlie, I'm so proud of you. Your other brothers have done great things, but you gave your life." His practical, less emotional mother would say, "Charlie, I had great dreams for you and what you might become, but my dreams were not God's dreams, and you did what you had to do. I am proud of what you did for your country."[27]

Billie, who suffered through so much anguish in 1944, has yet to forget her first love. She says that if Charlie were sitting in front of her today, she would say, "I'm sorry I didn't marry you."[28]

She married nine years later, "and I kept thinking Charlie was still at the ranch and was just not telling me. I wondered what would happen if he came home and I was married. I was still in love with him. I still am," she said in 2005, "but I have a son and a husband and I put them first, but I still pray for Charlie. I still miss Charlie."[29]

The war affected the Sengs in equal measure. Gene's father never accepted the loss of his son. He at times suffered from depression, and according to his daughters, his health suffered as a result.

Like Billie, June McDougall eventually married, but found it difficult to let Gene go. She so often mentioned Gene and the Sengs to her New Zealand husband that he finally arranged a trip to San Antonio in hopes that his wife could find closure. When he arrived in the United States, the husband said to Lorraine, "You know, I'm really glad to meet you because I'm really getting a little tired of this Gene bit."[30] The visit helped both the Sengs and June better deal with Gene's death, and June's husband returned to New Zealand a happier man as a result.

The Sengs also wonder what might have been. Lorraine claims the newer generation of children in the family would have loved Gene, as he enjoyed being around children. Patsy explained that the biggest compliment she gave her boyfriends was that they reminded her of her brother, and that Gene would have made a wonderful father. "You could always depend on him,"[31] she added.

When thinking of what they would say to Gene if they had the chance, Patsy claims she would ask him "to come on home and dance with me. He loved to dance, and I do, too." Peggy states she would like Gene to come back and be part of her life. "He was my big brother and I would have liked to have known him. I didn't have a big brother to grow up with."[32]

That one square mile of hell on Betio still reaches halfway around the world to Bandera and San Antonio, Texas. War's effects reverberate across the decades, more than sixty years distant, to disturb the lives of others.

"We All Became Older Than Our Years"

Combatants have not yet escaped the battle's residue. For a long time afterward, Stan Bowen suffered from nightmares that caused him to groan in his sleep, and he still carries the shrapnel from an injury that occurred in Hawaii immediately after the battle. Robert Muhlbach's ears continue to ring from the sounds of battle, and loud noises sometimes intensify the ringing and produce a stabbing sensation in his ears. Jim Meadows recovered from the bayonet slashing suffered during the night counterattack, but the scars serve as a constant reminder of the fighting. "Every time I look at my hand," he says, "I think of Tarawa."[33]

Jack Preston Sr., who fought at Red 2 with F Company, mulls the same thought considered by almost every survivor of that gruesome battle. "I thank God every day of my life and ask Him why I survived and others died all around me. Thank God it was over, and there isn't any way to express or tell anyone just how bad it was. At first I thought it was a dream. I still shake my head at times and say to myself did this really happen, and was I really there through it all?"[34]

Some Marines emerged without a scratch or any noticeable physical ailment, but suffered inside, an effect that can be as difficult as a physical malady. Some required counseling, and many were unable to talk about the battle until years later, if at all. Robert Libby said, "The mental side had a terrific effect which has lived with me since. . . . As a result of Tarawa we all became older than our years."[35]

M. F. Swango carries the images of Betio with him wherever he goes. "The memory that has forever altered my life is that of the assault on Tarawa, 76 hours of incredible horror, death and destruction. Even today I can close my eyes, envision the torn bodies, hear the mind-numbing sounds and smell the pervading stench of death. I will live with this until the day I die."[36]

When asked if he is a hero, almost every Tarawa veteran will answer in the same fashion as Stan Bowen. "No. I did what anybody else would do. Any of my friends would have done what I did." When reminded that he rushed into the lagoon to rescue men, and that he headed onto the battlefield, amidst bullets and exploding shells, to treat wounded, Bowen shrugs and replies, "That was my job. I was a corpsman. If a guy's hurt, you've got to go get him. That was my job."[37]

Bowen makes that remark almost as if it were an afterthought. He does not think he did anything spectacular during the battle. Few of the men do. They will tell you that they were just doing what anybody else would do under the circumstances, that they were doing what they were supposed to do.

Yet, when you think about it, doing what they are supposed to do is more remarkable than the men of Tarawa would have people believe. Today's world is replete with examples of individuals who do not do what they are supposed to do—parents who abdicate their responsibilities to children, religious leaders who betray the trust of their congregations, politicians who lie or cheat, teachers who halfheartedly instruct, students who refuse to work. Imagine what society would be like if everyone imitated the men of Tarawa and simply did what they were supposed to do.

"It Must Be on the Map, My Son!"

Visitors to Tarawa today would see few reminders that at one time, two skilled foes fought and bled on the beaches. A handful of rusty guns and other remnants stand, but no major landmark designates Betio as a crucial battle. A fish plant, ironically owned by a Japanese firm, long occupied buildings at the end of the pier that Hawkins and his scout-snipers assaulted. A 2d Marine Division war memorial was moved—by a Japanese crane—to a new location to make room for a new factory—Japanese-owned. Tarawa veterans from the Long Beach, California, area raised funds to send a beautiful granite monument as a substitute for the one displaced by the factory.

When Robert Sherrod returned to Betio to observe the twenty-fifth anniversary of the battle, a guide told him that natives often come across skeletal remains of Marine and Japanese dead, or work crews digging holes unearth bodies. If the uniform fragments indicate the soldier as American, the remains are sent for precise identification to a laboratory—in Tokyo.

Some of the men have returned to the island. They travel thousands of miles to leave flowers at a grave, like Sobol, to retrace the steps they took during the battle, or to honor their buddies who fell.

New Zealand has erected more memorials to Tarawa than one might find in the United States. Paekakariki, where many of the Marines trained, honored the Americans with a Tarawa Street. The resolution accompanying the naming stated that this was done "in memory of the many hundreds of Leathernecks who trained and camped at Paekakariki and later died in the landing. Memory of their gallantry and the name of the battle will be permanently retained on the site of their old camp."[38]

Tarawa veterans have frequently returned to New Zealand to renew acquaintances, visit families that treated them to dinner in 1943, or check on old girlfriends. June McDougall keeps in touch with the Seng family, and one of Seng's sisters traveled to New Zealand to visit June. A love affair begun in 1943 between the Marines of the 2d Division and the citizens of New Zealand has not diminished through the years.

The words of a plaque outside a New Zealand training camp location illustrate the close ties that bind people of two nations.

HALF THE WORLD DISTANT FROM HOME
THEY CAMPED HERE
THIS PLAQUE WAS ERECTED BY
THE NEW ZEALAND–AMERICAN ASSOCIATION, INC.
TO RECORD THE GRATEFUL THANKS OF THE PEOPLE
OF NEW ZEALAND TO THE UNITED STATES MARINES.
THEY CAMPED AT THIS SITE
FROM JUNE 1942 TO NOVEMBER 1943,
WHILE HELPING TO DEFEND THIS COUNTRY.
LATER THEY FOUGHT IN THE PACIFIC ISLANDS
WHERE MANY OF THEM MADE THE SUPREME SACRIFICE
AND CEMENTED AN EVERLASTING FRIENDSHIP.[39]

Tarawa veterans and the families of those who died, such as the Montagues and Sengs, wonder why the battle is not as well known as other World War II struggles. Despite their efforts, much of the nation has heard little, if anything, about a battle called Tarawa.

As early as 1948, merely three years after the war's end, Mrs. Hawkins made the point in a letter to Robert Sherrod. "I have wondered so many times," wrote Lieutenant Hawkins's mother, "why it is that when reference is made to battles that were fought in the Pacific, Tarawa is almost never mentioned. They always refer to Guadalcanal, Iwo Jima, Saipan, or Okinawa."[40]

Hollywood included Tarawa in three movies. *Sands of Iwo Jima,* starring

John Wayne, devoted a large portion of the film to the assault on Betio. Major Crowe served as technical adviser and appeared in the movie, as did Major Chamberlin in a segment from Hatch's footage. Six years later *Battle Cry*, based on a novel by Leon Uris, who fought at Betio with the 6th Regiment, hit theaters, while *Tarawa Beachhead* appeared in 1958. Since then Tarawa, which provides as much drama, courage, and emotion as any other Pacific battle, has received scant notice.

A poem unearthed in a folder at the Marine Corps Research Center in Quantico, Virginia, attests to the fears Tarawa veterans have that their efforts will be forgotten. Titled "Tarawa (A Veteran Speaks to His Son)," the poem consists of a Marine's conversation with his boy, who searches a map for Tarawa.

> *You say it's not on the map, my son?*
> *O God, it's engraved on my heart!*
> *That fringe of palm, our approach at dawn,*
> *A challenge to death, and the hellish spawn*
> *That tore loose our clay at Tarawa!*
>
> *You want me to tell you about it, my son?*
> *It's an epic of blood and tears!*
> *These sightless eyes and mangled feet*
> *Proclaim our victory and the Japs' defeat*
> *On the charnel-like sands of Tarawa!*
>
> *Lifeblood the price by which an atoll was won;*
> *Look again—it must be on the map, my son!*[41]

NOTES

Chapter 1—"Where's Pearl Harbor?"

1. Author's interview with Stanley Bowen, December 30, 2004.
2. Robert Sherrod, *Tarawa: The Story of a Battle,* Fortieth Anniversary Edition (New York: Bantam Books, 1983), p. xiii.
3. Author's interview with Fr. George Montague, January 20, 2005.
4. George Montague interview, January 6, 2005.
5. Author's interview with Bruce Montague, February 18, 2005.
6. Author's interview with Lucille Bohl, May 10, 2005.
7. Author's interview with Patsy Dealy, September 15, 2005.
8. Author's interview with Lorraine Clark, September 15, 2005; J. Michael Parker, "High School Buddies Died on Tarawa with Bordelon," *San Antonio Express-News,* November 20, 1995, p. 8A.
9. Letter from Gene Seng to his family, postmarked February 26, 1942, in the Seng Sisters Collection; undated letter from Gene Seng to his father; letter from Gene Seng to his father, June 8, 1942, in the Seng Sisters Collection.
10. Undated letter from Gene Seng to his father, in the Seng Sisters Collection; *The Buttoneer,* Central Catholic High School's yearbook, 1939, p. 19.
11. Lorraine Clark interview, September 15, 2005.
12. Bruce Montague interview, February 18, 2005.
13. Robert Sherrod, *Tarawa: The Story of a Battle* (New York: Duell, Sloan and Pearce, 1944), p. 48.

14. R. C. Darling, *Deane Hawkins: Nonpareil Texan* (Quantico, Virginia: Marine Corps Command and Staff College, 1991), p. 6.

15. Darling, *Deane Hawkins: Nonpareil Texan,* pp. 5–6.

16. Robert Sherrod, "Hawk," *Marine Corps Gazette,* April 1944, p. 28; Darling, *Deane Hawkins: Nonpareil Texan,* p. 5.

17. Sherrod, "Hawk," p. 28.

18. Martin Russ, *Line of Departure: Tarawa* (Garden City, New York: Doubleday & Company, 1975), p. 55.

19. Dick Wilson, *When Tigers Fight: The True Story of the Sino-Japanese War 1937–1945* (New York: Viking Press, 1982), pp. 72–73.

20. Bowen interview, December 28, 2004.

21. Bowen interview, December 30, 2004.

22. Bowen interview, December 28, 2004.

23. Author's interview with Dick Meadows, March 12, 2005.

24. John Costello, *The Pacific War, 1941–1945* (New York: Quill Books, 1982), p. 124.

25. Joe Garner, *We Interrupt This Broadcast* (Naperville, Illinois: Sourcebooks, 1998), p. 9.

26. Bowen interview, December 30, 2004.

27. Charles Wysocki Jr., "Day of Infamy," in the Charles Wysocki Jr. File.

28. "What the People Said," *Time,* December 15, 1941, p. 17.

29. James MacGregor Burns, *Roosevelt: The Soldier of Freedom* (New York: Harcourt Brace Jovanovich, 1970), pp. 165–167.

30. Winston Churchill, *The Second World War: The Grand Alliance* (Boston: Houghton Mifflin Company, 1950), p. 620.

Chapter 2—"Tokyo, We Are Coming"

1. W. Richardson, *The Epic of Tarawa* (London: Odhams Press Limited, [1945]), p. 5; John W. Dower, *War Without Mercy: Race & Power in the Pacific War* (New York: Pantheon Books, 1986), p. 92.

2. United States Marine Corps Announcements, in the Earl J. Wilson File, Marine Corps Research Center, Quantico, Virginia.

3. "What the People Said," *Time,* December 15, 1941, p. 18.

4. "'A Job to Do,' Bordelon Told His Father," *San Antonio Express-News,* June 18, 1944, in the William J. Bordelon Biographical File, Marine Historical Center, Washington, D.C.; J. Michael Parker, "WWII Hero Coming Home for Reburial," *San Antonio Express-News,* May 29, 1995, p. 13A.

Notes

5. Stanley Bowen, *Stan Bowen and Margie McCann's Romance and the War Between the Years of December 29, 1942 and February 3, 1946* (self-published memoir, 1991), p. 4 (hereafter cited as Bowen, *Reminiscences*).

6. Bowen interview, December 28, 2004.

7. Author interviews with Dick Meadows, March 12, 2005, and March 17, 2005.

8. Letter from Gene Seng to his family, postmarked February 3, 1942, in the Seng Sisters Collection.

9. Patsy Dealy interview, September 15, 2005.

10. Author's interview with Ralph Seng, June 23, 2005.

11. George Montague, *The Montague Press,* self-published newspaper, January 21, 1944.

12. Undated letter from Gene Seng to his family, in the Seng Sisters Collection.

13. Sherrod, "Hawk," p. 28.

14. Sherrod, *Tarawa: The Story of a Battle,* p. 48.

15. Darling, *Deane Hawkins: Nonpareil Texan,* p. 4.

16. Darling, *Deane Hawkins: Nonpareil Texan,* p. 7.

17. Author's interview with Norman Hatch, November 19, 2003.

18. Hatch interview, November 19, 2003.

19. Author's interview with Robert Muhlbach, March 5, 2005.

20. Muhlbach interview, March 5, 2005.

21. Dick Meadows interview, March 12, 2005.

22. Charles Wysocki, "Memories," p. 1, in the Charles Wysocki Personal File.

23. Letter from Gene Seng to his family, postmarked April 6, 1942, in the Seng Sisters Collection.

24. Melvin A. Traylor, "My Life and Times in the USMCR 1941–1946," in the Melvin A. Traylor File, #3857, Quantico, Virginia: Marine Corps Research Center, January 31, 2003, p. 3 (hereafter cited as Traylor, *Reminiscences*).

25. Lorraine Clark interview, September 15, 2005.

26. Undated letter from Gene Seng to his family, in the Seng Sisters Collection.

27. Traylor, *Reminiscences,* p. 4.

28. Letter from Gene Seng to his mother, postmarked February 17, 1942, in the Seng Sisters Collection.

29. Letter from Gene Seng to his parents, postmarked February 22, 1942, in the Seng Sisters Collection.

30. Author's interview with Henry Duke, June 29, 2005.

31. Letter from Gene Seng to his mother, postmarked February 17, 1942, in the Seng Sisters Collection.

32. William L. Ruch Jr., *My War Years* (self-published memoir, 1997), p. 5.

33. Author's interview with Albert Gilman, April 16, 1988.

34. Darling, *Deane Hawkins: Nonpareil Texan,* pp. 8–9.
35. Letter from Gene Seng to his mother, postmarked February 17, 1942; to his father, June 8, 1942; to his mother, postmarked April 26, 1942, in the Seng Sisters Collection.
36. Letter from Gene Seng to his mother, postmarked March 9, 1942; to his parents, June 25, 1942, in the Seng Sisters Collection.
37. Undated letter from Gene Seng to his mother, in the Seng Sisters Collection.
38. Letter from Gene Seng to his mother, May 17, 1942, in the Seng Sisters Collection.
39. Undated April 1942 letter from Gene Seng to Lorraine Seng, in the Seng Sisters Collection.
40. Letter from Gene Seng to his family, postmarked April 6, 1942, in the Seng Sisters Collection.
41. Letter from Gene Seng to his mother, postmarked March 16, 1942; to his parents, postmarked April 16, 1942; to his parents, June 1, 1942, in the Seng Sisters Collection.
42. Charles Wysocki, "I'll Remember," p. 2, in the Charles Wysocki Personal File.
43. Letter from Gene Seng to his parents, June 25, 1942, in the Seng Sisters Collection.
44. Letter from Gene Seng to his father, June 8, 1942, in the Seng Sisters Collection.
45. Bowen interview, December 30, 2004.
46. Dick Meadows interview, March 12, 2005.
47. Dick Meadows interview, March 17, 2005.
48. Letter from Gene Seng to his family, June 15, 1942, in the Seng Sisters Collection; Pvt. Gene G. Seng, "Diary of Trip to ? [sic] Aboard the U.S.S. *President Hayes,*" July 10 entry.
49. Seng, "Diary," July 26 entry.
50. Seng, "Diary," August 7 entry.
51. Richard B. Frank, *Guadalcanal: The Definitive Account of the Landmark Battle* (New York: Penguin Books, 1990), p. 73.
52. Letters from Aunt Margaret to Lucille Miller, July 19, 1942, and August 28, 1942, in the Lucille Bohl Collection.
53. Letter from the American Red Cross to Mr. Gene Seng, September 18, 1942, in the Seng Sisters Collection.
54. Darling, *Deane Hawkins: Nonpareil Texan,* pp. 11–12.
55. Darling, *Deane Hawkins: Nonpareil Texan,* p. 11.
56. Darling, *Deane Hawkins: Nonpareil Texan,* p. 12.
57. Letter from Gene Seng to his family, August 25, 1942, in the Seng Sisters Collection.

58. Letter from Gene Seng to his family, October 24, 1942, in the Seng Sisters Collection.

59. Letter from Gene Seng to his family, December 25, 1942, in the Seng Sisters Collection.

60. Letter from Gene Seng to his family, November 26, 1942, in the Seng Sisters Collection.

61. Letter from Gene Seng to his family, December 25, 1942, in the Seng Sisters Collection.

Chapter 3—"Have You Made Out Your Will?"

1. Tom Bartlett, "New Zealand Pilgrimage," *Leatherneck,* August 1978, p. 1.

2. Jack Walrad, "Prelude to Tarawa," *Marine Corps Gazette,* October 1993, pp. 2–3.

3. Author's interview with James W. Crain, March 9, 2005.

4. William Banning, ed., *Heritage Years: Second Marine Division Commemorative Anthology, 1940–1949* (Paducah, Kentucky: Turner Publishing Company, 1988), p. 39.

5. Jim Lucas, *Combat Correspondent* (New York: Reynal & Hitchcock, 1944), p. 161.

6. Muhlbach interview, March 5, 2005.

7. Letter from Gene Seng to his parents, April 26, 1943, in the Seng Sisters Collection.

8. Bowen, *Reminiscences*, p. 14.

9. Dick Meadows interview, March 17, 2005.

10. Dick Meadows interview, March 17, 2005.

11. Charles Wysocki, "When the Lights Come On Again," in the Charles Wysocki File.

12. Letters from Gene Seng to his family, March 12, 1943; March 25, 1943; April 26, 1943, in the Seng Sisters Collection.

13. Undated New Zealand letter from Charlie Montague to Lucille Miller, in the Lucille Bohl File.

14. Letter from Gene Seng to his parents, September 23, 1943, in the Seng Sisters Collection.

15. Letter from Gene Seng to his mother, September 28, 1943, in the Seng Sisters Collection.

16. Col. Joseph H. Alexander, USMC (Ret.), *Utmost Savagery: The Three Days of Tarawa* (Annapolis, Maryland: Naval Institute Press, 1995), p. 48.

17. Letter from Gene Seng to his parents, April 7, 1943, in the Seng Sisters Collection.

18. Richard W. Johnston, *Follow Me: The Story of the Second Marine Division in World War II* (New York: Random House, 1948), p. 90.

19. Richardson, *The Epic of Tarawa,* p. 3; in Michael B. Graham, *Mantle of Heroism: Tarawa and the Struggle for the Gilberts, November 1943* (Novato, California: Presidio Press, 1993), p. 176.

20. Bowen interview, December 30, 2004.

21. Maj. Robert B. MacKenzie, USMC (Ret.), "The Most Fearful Man in All the Corps," *Marine Corps Gazette,* November 1992, p. 44.

22. Muhlbach interview, March 5, 2005.

23. Letter from Gene Seng to his parents, July 8, 1943, in the Seng Sisters Collection.

24. Letters from Gene Seng to his parents, April 7, 1943; July 1, 1943; July 12, 1943, in the Seng Sisters Collection.

25. Letter from Gene Seng to his mother, August 18, 1943, in the Seng Sisters Collection.

26. Letter from Gene Seng to his parents, July 12, 1943, in the Seng Sisters Collection.

27. Letter from June McDougall to Mrs. Seng, July 25, 1943, in the Seng Sisters Collection.

28. Letters from Gene Seng to his mother, September 9, 1943; October 8, 1943, in the Seng Sisters Collection.

29. Letter from Gene Seng to his mother, October 14, 1943; to his parents, August 13, 1943, in the Seng Sisters Collection.

30. "Norman T. Hatch," Oral History, History and Museums Division, Headquarters, U.S. Marine Corps, 1981, p. 81.

31. Hatch interview, July 24, 2004; Brig. Gen. Edwin H. Simmons, "Remembering the Legendary 'Jim' Crowe—Part II," *Fortitudine,* Spring 1992, p. 4.

32. Sherrod, *Tarawa: The Story of a Battle,* p. 4.

33. Anonymous, "Combat Chaplain," *Leatherneck,* November 1980, pp. 3–4 (Internet version).

34. Trisha Currier Flanagan, "Navy Chaplain Recalls Guadalcanal," unnamed, undated newspaper, p. 10A; W. Wyeth Willard, *The Leathernecks Come Through* (New York: Fleming H. Revell Company, 1944), p. 193.

35. Anonymous, "Combat Chaplain," p. 2.

36. Williard, *The Leathernecks Came Through,* p. 193.

37. Letter from Gene Seng to his parents, June 5, 1943, in the Seng Sisters Collection.

38. Letter from Gene Seng to his parents, May 17, 1943, in the Seng Sisters Collection.

39. Letter from Gene Seng to his parents, May 30, 1943, in the Seng Sisters Collection.

40. Letter from Gene Seng to his father, June 17, 1943, to his mother, September 9, 1943; to his parents, July 25, 1943, in the Seng Sisters Collection.
41. Crain interview, March 9, 2005.
42. Peter Neushul and 2nd Lt. James D. Neushul, "With the Marines at Tarawa," *Naval Institute Proceedings,* April 1999, p. 75.
43. Dick Meadows interview, March 17, 2005.
44. Letter from Gene Seng to his parents, October 31, 1943, in the Seng Sisters Collection.
45. Walrad, "Prelude to Tarawa," pp. 2–3.
46. Banning, ed., *Heritage Years,* p. 41.
47. Lucas, *Combat Correspondent,* p. 170.

Chapter 4—"A Million Men Cannot Take Tarawa"

1. Capt. Walter Karig, USNR, with Lt. Comdr. Russell L. Harris, USNR, and Lt. Comdr. Frank A. Manson, USN, *Battle Report: The End of an Empire* (New York: Rinehart and Company, 1948), p. 79.
2. Harriotte "Happy" Byrd Smith, *But, That's Another Story* (New York: Vantage Press, 1992), p. 243.
3. Henry I. Shaw Jr., Bernard C. Nalty, and Edwin T. Turnbladh, *History of U.S. Marine Corps Operations in World War II, Volume III: Central Pacific Drive* (Washington, D.C.: Historical Branch, G-3, Headquarters, U.S. Marine Corps, 1966), p. 31.
4. Alexander, *Utmost Savagery: The Three Days of Tarawa,* p. 83.
5. Robert Leckie, *Strong Men Armed* (New York: Random House, 1962), pp. 182–183.
6. Graham, *Mantle of Heroism,* p. 57.
7. Kiyoshi Ota with Keith S. Williams, "Tarawa, My Last Battle," unpublished memoir in the David Shoup Collection, Hoover Institution on War, Revolution and Peace, Stanford University, p. 2.
8. Theodore L. Gatchel, *At the Water's Edge: Defending Against the Modern Amphibious Assault* (Annapolis, Maryland: Naval Institute Press, 1996), p. 123.
9. Alexander, *Utmost Savagery: The Three Days of Tarawa,* p. 22.
10. Capt. Earl J. Wilson, M. T. Sgts. Jim G. Lucas and Samuel Shaffer, and S. Sgt. C. Peter Zurlinden, *Betio Beachhead: U.S. Marines' Own Story of the Battle for Tarawa* (New York: G. P. Putnam's Sons, 1945), p. 158.
11. Samuel Eliot Morison, *History of United States Naval Operations in World War II, Volume VII: Aleutians, Gilberts and Marshalls, June 1942–April 1944* (Boston: Little, Brown and Company, 1960), pp. 147–148.

12. William Manchester, *Goodbye, Darkness* (Boston: Little, Brown and Company, 1980), p. 223.

13. Russ, *Line of Departure: Tarawa,* p. 31.

14. Shaw, Nalty, and Turnbladh, *History of U.S. Marine Corps Operations in World War II, Volume III: Central Pacific Drive,* p. 51.

15. Alexander, *Utmost Savagery: The Three Days of Tarawa,* p. 89.

16. Sherrod, *Tarawa: The Story of a Battle,* p. 29.

17. Banning, ed., *Heritage Years,* p. 76.

18. Sherrod, *Tarawa: The Story of a Battle,* p. 27.

19. Muhlbach interview, March 5, 2005.

20. Wilson, Lucas, Shaffer, and Zurlinden, *Betio Beachhead,* p. 20.

21. Bowen, *Reminiscences,* p. 7.

22. Sherrod, *Tarawa: The Story of a Battle,* p. 39.

23. Letter from Gene Seng to his mother, postmarked November 11, 1943, in the Seng Sisters Collection.

24. "Hatch," Oral History, p. 84.

25. Graham, *Mantle of Heroism,* p. 104.

26. Sherrod, *Tarawa: The Story of a Battle,* pp. 31, 33, 35.

27. John Stevenson, "Tarawa Veteran Tells of Heroisms," *Virginian-Pilot,* November 20, 1978, p. C3.

28. Sherrod, *Tarawa: The Story of a Battle,* pp. 31, 33, 35.

29. Bowen, *Reminiscences,* p. 21.

30. Bowen interview, January 6, 2005.

31. Wilson, Lucas, Shaffer, and Zurlinden, *Betio Beachhead,* p. 20.

32. Bowen, *Reminiscences,* pp. 21–22.

33. Bowen interview, January 6, 2005.

34. Bowen interview, January 6, 2005.

35. Bowen, *Reminiscences,* p. 21.

36. Sherrod, *Tarawa: The Story of a Battle,* p. 40.

37. Robert R. Twitchell, *One Returned* (self-published memoir, 1986), p. 61.

38. Dick Meadows interview, March 17, 2005.

39. Graham, *Mantle of Heroism,* p. 96.

40. "Major General Raymond L. Murray (Ret.)," Oral History, History and Museums Division, Headquarters, U.S. Marine Corps, 1988, p. 141.

41. Sherrod, *Tarawa: The Story of a Battle,* pp. 24–25.

42. "Murray," Oral History, p. 154.

43. "Murray," Oral History, pp. 141–142.

44. Hatch interview, July 24, 2004.

45. "Hatch," Oral History, p. 89.

46. Wilson, Lucas, Shaffer, and Zurlinden, *Betio Beachhead,* p. 14.

47. Russ, *Line of Departure: Tarawa,* pp. 43–44.

48. Sherrod, *Tarawa: The Story of a Battle,* pp. 44–45.

49. Sherrod, *Tarawa: The Story of a Battle,* pp. 42–43.

50. Derrick Wright, *A Hell of a Way to Die* (London: Windrow & Greene, 1996), p. 149.

51. Susan D. Moeller, *Shooting War: Photography and the American Experience of Combat* (New York: Basic Books, 1989), pp. 161–162.

52. Undated, untitled portion of article from the *Fort Worth Star-Telegram,* in the William J. Bordelon File, Marine Corps Research Center, Quantico, Virginia.

53. Earl Wilson, *Memoir,* undated, in the Earl Wilson File, Quantico, Virginia, p. 35.

54. Sherrod, *Tarawa: The Story of a Battle,* p. 47.

55. Sherrod, *Tarawa: The Story of a Battle,* p. 42.

56. Ota and Williams, "Tarawa, My Last Battle," pp. 2–3.

57. Karig, Harris, and Manson, *Battle Report: The End of an Empire,* p. 78; Graham, *Mantle of Heroism,* p. 98.

58. Ota and Williams, "Tarawa, My Last Battle," p. 3.

59. Ota and Williams, "Tarawa, My Last Battle," p. 3.

60. Letter from Pvt. David S. Spencer to his parents, November 1943, in the Spencer File, Marine Corps Research Center, Quantico, Virginia.

61. Bowen interview, January 6, 2005.

62. Julian Smith File, Folder 183, Marine Corps Research Center, Quantico, Virginia.

63. Sherrod, *Tarawa: The Story of a Battle,* p. 44.

64. Donald F. Crosby, S. J., *Battlefield Chaplains: Catholic Priests in World War II* (Lawrence: University Press of Kansas, 1994), p. 71.

65. Sherrod, *Tarawa: The Story of a Battle,* p. 56.

66. Johnston, *Follow Me: The Story of the Second Marine Division in World War II,* p. 111.

Chapter 5—"Commence Firing—the War Is On"

1. Gilman interview, July 30, 1988.

2. Author's interview with Robert Sherrod, October 9, 1993; Sherrod, *Tarawa: The Story of a Battle,* p. 55.

3. Gilman interview, July 30, 1988.

4. Author's interview with Tyson Wilson, March 5, 2005.

5. Author's interview with Charles Wysocki Jr., June 29, 2005.

6. Bowen interview, January 6, 2005.

7. Wilson interview, March 5, 2005.

8. Muhlbach interview, March 5, 2005.

9. Sherrod, *Tarawa: The Story of a Battle,* p. 58.

10. James L. Dent, ed., *We Were There: Fox Company Second Marines, Tarawa, November 20, 1943* (self-published, 1996), p. 92.

11. Bowen interview, December 30, 2004.

12. Banning, ed., *Heritage Years,* pp. 60–61.

13. Henry Berry, *Semper Fi, Mac: Living Memories of the U.S. Marines in World War II* (New York: Arbor House, 1982), p. 142.

14. G. D. Lillibridge, *Memoirs,* unpublished memoir in the Personal Papers Section, Marine Corps Research Center, Quantico, Virginia, p. 1.

15. Dent, ed., *We Were There,* p. 48.

16. Sherrod, *Tarawa: The Story of a Battle,* p. 58.

17. Gilman interview, July 30, 1988.

18. Bowen interview, January 6, 2005.

19. Hatch interview, July 24, 2004.

20. Ota and Williams, "Tarawa, My Last Battle," p. 3.

21. Ota and Williams, "Tarawa, My Last Battle," p. 3.

22. "Hatch," Oral History, p. 88.

23. Bowen interview, January 6, 2005.

24. Graham, *Mantle of Heroism,* p. 115.

25. Graham, *Mantle of Heroism,* p. 115.

26. Wilson, *Memoir,* p. 43.

27. Banning, ed., *Heritage Years,* p. 70.

28. Sherrod, *Tarawa: The Story of a Battle,* pp. 60–62

29. Ota and Williams, "Tarawa, My Last Battle," pp. 4–5.

30. S. Sgt. Dick Hannah, *Tarawa: The Toughest Battle in Marine Corps History* (New York: Duell, Sloan & Pearce, 1944), p. 80.

31. Sherrod interview, October 9, 1993; Sherrod, *Tarawa: The Story of a Battle,* pp. 62–63.

32. Banning, ed., *Heritage Years,* p. 61.

33. Graham, *Mantle of Heroism,* p. 137.

34. Thomas B. Buell, *The Quiet Warrior* (Boston: Little, Brown and Company, 1974), p. 198.

35. Graham, *Mantle of Heroism,* p. 137.

36. Wilson interview, March 5, 2005.

37. Ota and Williams, "Tarawa, My Last Battle," p. 5.

38. Russ, *Line of Departure: Tarawa,* p. 62.

39. Sherrod interview, October 9, 1993; Sherrod, *Tarawa: The Story of a Battle,* p. 64.

Chapter 6—"We Have Nothing Left to Land"

1. Ota and Williams, "Tarawa, My Last Battle," p. 5.

2. Ota and Williams, "Tarawa, My Last Battle," p. 5.

3. Wright, *A Hell of a Way to Die,* p. 49.

4. Ota and Williams, "Tarawa, My Last Battle," p. 6.

5. Graham, *Mantle of Heroism,* p. 157.

6. Graham, *Mantle of Heroism,* p. 159.

7. Norman S. Moise, "A Hellish Return Trip," *Naval History,* August 2005, p. 29.

8. Graham, *Mantle of Heroism,* pp. 162–163.

9. Graham, *Mantle of Heroism,* p. 158.

10. Duke interview, June 29, 2005.

11. Wright, *A Hell of a Way to Die,* pp. 50–51.

12. Wright, *A Hell of a Way to Die,* p. 53.

13. Crain interview, March 9, 2005.

14. Wright, *A Hell of a Way to Die,* p. 50.

15. Crain interview, March 19, 2005.

16. Crain interview, March 19, 2005.

17. Crain interview, March 19, 2005.

18. Johnston, *Follow Me,* p. 116.

19. Shaw, Nalty, and Turnbladh, *History of U.S. Marine Corps Operations in World War II, Volume III: Central Pacific Drive,* p. 61.

20. Lucas, *Combat Correspondent,* p. 180.

21. Dent, ed., *We Were There,* pp. 77–78.

22. Dent, ed., *We Were There,* pp. 56–57.

23. Russ, *Line of Departure: Tarawa,* p. 80.

24. Banning, ed., *Heritage Years,* p. 61.

25. Twitchell, *One Returned,* pp. 68–69.

26. Author's interview with Paul DuPre, July 5, 2005.

27. Banning, ed., *Heritage Years,* p. 62.

28. Dent, ed., *We Were There,* p. 69.

29. Dent, ed., *We Were There,* p. 37.

30. DuPre interview, July 2, 2005.

31. Wilson, Lucas, Shaffer, and Zurlinden, *Betio Beachhead,* p. 44.

32. Author's interview with Henry Chamberlin, July 26, 2005.

33. Hatch interview, July 24, 2004.

34. Bowen interview, January 6, 2005.

35. Neushul and Neushul, "With the Marines at Tarawa," p. 76.

36. Hatch interview, July 24, 2004.

37. Norman T. Hatch, "Marine Combat Photographer," *Leatherneck,* November 1993, p. 47.

38. Gilman interview, July 30, 1988.

39. Bowen interview, December 30, 2004.

40. Alexander, *Utmost Savagery: The Three Days of Tarawa,* p. 124.

41. Russ, *Line of Departure: Tarawa,* p. 78.

42. Stevenson, "Tarawa Veteran Tells of Heroisms," p. C3.

43. Stevenson, "Tarawa Veteran Tells of Heroisms," p. C3.

44. Wilson, Lucas, Shaffer, and Zurlinden, *Betio Beachhead,* p. 44.

45. Sherrod, *Tarawa: The Story of a Battle,* p. 65.

46. Sherrod, *Tarawa: The Story of a Battle,* p. 65.

47. Sherrod, *Tarawa: The Story of a Battle,* p. 66; Robert Sherrod, "Report on Tarawa: Marines' Show," *Time,* December 6, 1943, pp. 24–25.

48. Sherrod interview, October 9, 1993; Sherrod, *Tarawa: The Story of a Battle,* p. 67.

49. Sherrod, *Tarawa: The Story of a Battle,* p. 67; Sherrod interview, October 9, 1993.

50. Sherrod interview, October 9, 1993; Sherrod, *Tarawa: The Story of a Battle,* pp. 66–67.

51. Sherrod, *Tarawa: The Story of a Battle,* p. 68.

52. Sherrod interview, October 2, 1993; author's interview with William Kelliher, August 12, 2005.

53. Sherrod interview, October 2, 1993.

54. Sherrod, *Tarawa: The Story of a Battle,* p. 68; Sherrod interview, October 9, 1993.

55. Sherrod interview, October 9, 1993; Sherrod, *Tarawa: The Story of a Battle,* p. 68.

56. Sherrod, *Tarawa: The Story of a Battle,* p. 70.

57. Sherrod, *Tarawa: The Story of a Battle,* p. 71.

58. Gilman interview, July 30, 1988; letter from Albert Gilman to author, October 9, 1987.

59. Wright, *A Hell of a Way to Die,* pp. 55–56, 132.

60. Banning, ed., *Heritage Years,* p. 59.

61. Alexander, *Utmost Savagery: The Three Days of Tarawa,* p. 112.

62. Muhlbach interview, March 12, 2005.

63. Wright, *A Hell of a Way to Die,* pp. 53–54.

64. Hannah, *Tarawa,* pp. 24–25.

65. Wilson, Lucas, Shaffer, and Zurlinden, *Betio Beachhead,* p. 56.

66. Author's interview with Joseph J. Barr, November 19, 2005; Dent, ed., *We Were There,* p. 78.

67. Wilson, Lucas, Shaffer, and Zurlinden, *Betio Beachhead,* p. 38.

68. Banning, ed., *Heritage Years,* pp. 70–71.

69. News item written by C. Peter Zurlinden, cleared on December 5, 1943, in Earl Wilson File, Marine Corps Research Center, Quantico, Virginia.

Chapter 7—"I Was Unprepared for This"

1. Capt. James R. Stockman, USMC, *The Battle for Tarawa* (Washington, D.C.: Historical Section, Division of Public Information, Headquarters, U.S. Marine Corps, 1947), p. 19.

2. Muhlbach interview, March 12, 2005.

3. Crain interview, March 12, 2005.

4. Crain interview, March 12, 2005.

5. Crain interview, March 19, 2005.

6. Commanding Officer CT-2 [Shoup], to Commanding General, 2d Marine Division, "Report of Operations, Betio Island, Tarawa Atoll, Gilbert Islands, from 20 Nov 43 to 24 Nov 43," December 21, 1943, including John F. Schoettel, "Narrative Account of Tarawa Operation," pp. 4–5.

7. Wright, *A Hell of a Way to Die,* p. 68.

8. Letter from David S. Spencer to his parents, December 28, 1943, in the David S. Spencer File, Marine Corps Research Center, Quantico, Virginia.

9. Peter Maslowski, *Armed with Cameras: The American Military Photographers of World War II* (New York: Free Press, 1993), p. 221.

10. Author's interview with Emory Ashurst, July 4, 2005.

11. Stockman, *The Battle for Tarawa,* p. 20.

12. Michael P. Ryan, "Tarawa," *Marine Corps Gazette,* November 1984, p. 1.

13. Ryan, "Tarawa," p. 1.

14. Twitchell, *One Returned,* p. 79.

15. Barr interview, November 19, 2005; Dent, ed., *We Were There,* pp. 78–79.

16. Author's interview with Noal C. Pemberton, November 22, 2005; Herbert C. Banks II, ed., *Second Marine Division, 1940–1999* (Paducah, Kentucky: Turner Publishing Company, 1999), p. 64.

17. Author's interview with James Peavey, July 7, 2005; Dent, ed., *We Were There,* p. 93.

18. Banks, ed., *Second Marine Division, 1940–1999,* p. 65; Pemberton interview, November 22, 2005.

19. Barr interview, November 19, 2005; Dent, ed., *We Were There,* p. 79.

21. Alexander, *Utmost Savagery: The Three Days of Tarawa,* p. 130.

21. Wilson, Lucas, Shaffer, and Zurlinden, *Betio Beachhead,* p. 52.

22. Graham, *Mantle of Heroism,* p. 165.

23. Ota and Williams, "Tarawa, My Last Battle," pp. 6–8; "Preliminary Interrogation of Japanese Prisoners," December 22, 1943, p. 19.

24. Graham, *Mantle of Heroism,* pp. 193–195; Alexander, *Utmost Savagery: The Three Days of Tarawa,* pp. 148–149.

25. Alexander, *Utmost Savagery: The Three Days of Tarawa,* p. 149.

26. "Major General Carl W. Hoffman (Ret.)," Oral History, History and Museums Division, Headquarters, U.S. Marine Corps, 1988, p. 20.

27. Graham, *Mantle of Heroism,* p. 177.

28. Graham, *Mantle of Heroism,* p. 177.

29. "Hatch," Oral History, pp. 97–98.

30. Sherrod, "Report on Tarawa: Marines' Show," p. 25; Sherrod, *Tarawa: The Story of a Battle,* pp. 73–74.

31. Sherrod, "Report on Tarawa: Marines' Show," p. 25.

32. Karig, Harris, and Manson, *Battle Report: The End of an Empire,* p. 88.

33. Bowen interview, December 28, 2004; Alexander, *Utmost Savagery: The Three Days of Tarawa,* p. 125.

34. Gilman interview, July 30, 1988; letter from Albert Gilman to author, October 9, 1987.

35. Bowen interview, December 30, 2004.

36. Bowen interview, January 6, 2005.

37. Bowen interview, December 30, 2004.

38. Bowen interview, January 6, 2005.

39. Bowen interview, January 6, 2005.

40. Bowen, *Reminiscences,* pp. 25–26.

41. Copy of citation in Bowen, *Reminiscences,* p. 27.

42. Bowen, *Reminiscences,* p. 31; Bowen interview, December 30, 2004; Bowen interview, January 6, 2005.

43. Wilson, Lucas, Shaffer, and Zurlinden, *Betio Beachhead,* p. 52.

44. Hatch interview, July 24, 2004.

45. Maslowski, *Armed with Cameras,* p. 224.

46. Russ, *Line of Departure: Tarawa,* p. 93.

47. Alexander, *Utmost Savagery: The Three Days of Tarawa,* pp. 136–137.

48. Russ, *Line of Departure: Tarawa,* p. 95.

49. Wilson, Lucas, Shaffer, and Zurlinden, *Betio Beachhead,* pp. 53–54.

50. Russ, *Line of Departure: Tarawa,* pp. 94–97.

51. Shaw, Nalty, and Turnbladh, *History of U.S. Marine Corps Operations in World War II, Volume III: Central Pacific Drive,* p. 67.

52. Graham, *Mantle of Heroism,* p. 184.

53. Russ, *Line of Departure: Tarawa,* p. 87.

54. Willard, *The Leathernecks Come Through,* p. 214.

55. Wilson, Lucas, Shaffer, and Zurlinden, *Betio Beachhead,* p. 58.

56. Wilson, *Memoir,* p. 48.

57. Johnston, *Follow Me,* p. 128.

58. Wilson, Lucas, Shaffer, and Zurlinden, *Betio Beachhead,* p. 66.

59. Eric Hammel and John E. Lane, *76 Hours: The Invasion of Tarawa* (Pacifica, California: Pacifica Press, 1985), p. 132; Twitchell, *One Returned,* p. 84.

60. Muhlbach interview, March 19, 2005.

61. Sherrod, *Tarawa: The Story of a Battle,* p. 84.

62. Ota and Williams, "Tarawa, My Last Battle," p. 8.

63. Wilson, Lucas, Shaffer, and Zurlinden, *Betio Beachhead,* p. 87.

64. Bowen interview, December 30, 2004; Lucas, *Combat Correspondent,* pp. 186, 188–189.

65. Gilman interview, July 30, 1988.

66. Banning, ed., *Heritage Years,* p. 80.

67. Sherrod, *Tarawa: The Story of a Battle,* Fortieth Anniversary Edition, p. 192; Hannah, *Tarawa,* p. 32; Lucas, *Combat Correspondent,* p. 190.

68. Sherrod, *Tarawa: The Story of a Battle,* pp. 82–83.

Chapter 8—"A Fight in a Ring Between Two Boxers"

1. Sherrod, *Tarawa: The Story of a Battle,* p. 88.

2. Banning, ed., *Heritage Years,* p. 62.

3. Wilson, Lucas, Shaffer, and Zurlinden, *Betio Beachhead,* p. 75.

4. Crain interview, March 9, 2005.

5. Dick Meadows interview, March 17, 2005.

6. Ryan, "Tarawa," p. 2.

7. Sherrod, *Tarawa: The Story of a Battle,* p. 92.

8. Pemberton interview, November 22, 2005; Banks, ed., *Second Marine Division, 1940–1999,* pp. 66–67.

9. Pemberton interview, November 22, 2005; Dent, ed., *We Were There,* pp. 37, 49.

10. Dent, ed., *We Were There,* p. 37; Pemberton interview, November 22, 2005.

11. Sherrod, *Tarawa: The Story of a Battle,* p. 78.

12. Sherrod, *Tarawa: The Story of a Battle,* p. 96.

13. Sherrod, "Hawk," p. 29; Sherrod, *Tarawa: The Story of a Battle*, p. 96.
14. Darling, *Deane Hawkins: Nonpareil Texan*, p. 18.
15. Sherrod, *Tarawa: The Story of a Battle*, p. 108.
16. Wright, *A Hell of a Way to Die*, p. 91.
17. Wilson, Lucas, Shaffer, and Zurlinden, *Betio Beachhead*, p. 88.
18. Gilman interview, July 30, 1988; letter from Albert Gilman to author, October 9, 1987.
19. Muhlbach interviews, March 12 and March 19, 2005.
20. "Hoffman," Oral History, pp. 24–26; in Wilson, Lucas, Shaffer, and Zurlinden, *Betio Beachhead*, p. 80.
21. Traylor, *Reminiscences*, p. 37.
22. Sherrod, *Tarawa: The Story of a Battle*, p. 95.
23. Frank W. Plant Jr., "Tarawa Memoir," unpublished memoir in the Personal Papers Section, Marine Corps Research Center, Quantico, Virginia, 1986, p. 33.
24. "Quack Hero," *Time*, January 3, 1944, p. 62.
25. Willard, *The Leathernecks Come Through*, p. 215.
26. Wilson, Lucas, Shaffer, and Zurlinden, *Betio Beachhead*, p. 74.
27. Alexander, *Utmost Savagery: The Three Days of Tarawa*, p. 165.
28. Hannah, *Tarawa*, p. 126.
29. Willard, *The Leathernecks Come Through*, pp. 215–216, 218.
30. Crosby, *Battlefield Chaplains*, p. 74.
31. Author's interview with Herman R. Brukhardt, December 20, 2004.
32. Morris Fishbein, M.D., ed., *Doctors at War* (New York: E.P. Dutton & Company, 1945), p. 242.
33. Commander Fifth Amphibious Force, U.S. Pacific Fleet, to Commander in Chief, U.S. Pacific Fleet, "Report of Amphibious Operations for the Capture of the Gilbert Islands," December 4, 1943, p. 21.
34. Bowen interview, January 20, 2005.
35. Stockman, *The Battle for Tarawa*, p. 41.
36. Sherrod, *Tarawa: The Story of a Battle*, p. 101.
37. Shaw, Nalty, and Turnbladh, *History of U.S. Marine Corps Operations in World War II, Volume III: Central Pacific Drive*, p. 79.
38. Hannah, *Tarawa*, p. 47.
39. Sherrod, "Report on Tarawa: Marines' Show," p. 25.
40. Lucille Bohl interview, May 10, 2005.
41. Letter from Judge Brian Montague to Lucille Miller, September 22, 1943, in the Lucille Bohl Collection.
42. Letter from Aunt Margaret to Lucille Miller, August 28, 1942, in the Lucille Bohl Collection.

43. "Tribute to Tarawa," *Long Beach Press-Telegram,* June 26, 1988, p. 10.

44. Letter from Pfc. Lyle S. Brown to Lucille Miller, November 10, 1943, in the Lucille Bohl Collection.

45. George Montague interview, January 20, 2005.

46. Letter from Mrs. Seng to Gene Seng, November 28, 1943, in the Seng Sisters Collection.

47. Card from the Seng family to Gene Seng, November 29, 1943, in the Seng Sisters Collection.

Chapter 9—"Nothing Was Left—No Trees, No Buildings"

1. Sherrod, *Tarawa: The Story of a Battle,* p. 112.

2. Wilson, Lucas, Shaffer, and Zurlinden, *Betio Beachhead,* p. 88.

3. David M. Shoup, "Notebook," in the David M. Shoup File, Marine Corps Research Center, Quantico, Virginia.

4. Oliver L. North with Joe Musser, *War Stories II: Heroism in the Pacific* (Washington, D.C.: Regnery Publishing, 2004), p. 232.

5. Letter from John Magruder to Thomas Weil, January 8, 1944, in the Thomas Weil File, Marine Corps Research Center, Quantico, Virginia.

6. Sherrod, *Tarawa: The Story of a Battle,* p. 110.

7. Johnston, *Follow Me,* p. 138.

8. Sherrod, *Tarawa: The Story of a Battle,* p. 104.

9. Banning, ed., *Heritage Years,* p. 71.

10. Wilson, Lucas, Shaffer, and Zurlinden, *Betio Beachhead,* pp. 96–98.

11. Russ, *Line of Departure: Tarawa,* p. 153.

12. Hatch interview, July 24, 2005; Kelliher interview, August 12, 2005.

13. "Hatch," Oral History, p. 109.

14. Hatch interview, July 24, 2004; Kelliher interview, August 12, 2005.

15. Author's interview with Robert Rogers, July 2, 2005.

16. Hatch interview, July 18, 2005.

17. Hatch interview, July 24, 2004.

18. Hatch interview, July 24, 2004.

19. Hatch interview, July 24, 2004.

20. Muhlbach interview, March 19, 2005.

21. Sherrod, *Tarawa: The Story of a Battle,* p. 121.

22. Sherrod, *Tarawa: The Story of a Battle,* p. 114.

23. Sherrod, *Tarawa: The Story of a Battle,* p. 115.

24. Sherrod, *Tarawa: The Story of a Battle,* p. 120.

25. Charles T. Gregg, *Tarawa* (New York: Stein and Day, 1984), p. 155.
26. Ota and Williams, "Tarawa, My Last Battle," p. 8.
27. Author's interview with James Meadows, July 25, 2005.
28. Hannah, *Tarawa,* pp. 50–51.
29. Sherrod, *Tarawa: The Story of a Battle,* p. 122.
30. Ota and Williams, "Tarawa, My Last Battle," p. 9.
31. James Meadows interview, July 25, 2005.
32. Sherrod, *Tarawa: The Story of a Battle,* p. 122.
33. Wilson, Lucas, Shaffer, and Zurlinden, *Betio Beachhead,* p. 110.
34. Wilson, Lucas, Shaffer, and Zurlinden, *Betio Beachhead,* p. 116.
35. Wilson, Lucas, Shaffer, and Zurlinden, *Betio Beachhead,* p. 118.
36. Sherrod, *Tarawa: The Story of a Battle,* p. 122.
37. Ota and Williams, "Tarawa, My Last Battle," pp. 9–10.
38. Wilson, Lucas, Shaffer, and Zurlinden, *Betio Beachhead,* p. 118.
39. Graham, *Mantle of Heroism,* p. 289.
40. Muhlbach interview, March 19, 2005.
41. Graham, *Mantle of Heroism,* p. 295.
42. Graham, *Mantle of Heroism,* p. 292.
43. "Sanitation Report," December 3, 1943, p. 1.
44. Lucas, *Combat Correspondent,* p. 199.
45. Sherrod, *Tarawa: The Story of a Battle,* p. 123.
46. Sherrod, "Report on Tarawa: Marines' Show," p. 24; "A Name to Remember," *Time,* December 6, 1943, p. 15.
47. Hannah, *Tarawa,* p. 72.
48. Lillibridge, *Memoirs,* p. 6.
49. Bowen, *Reminiscences,* p. 32; Bowen interview, January 6, 2005.
50. Photograph in Norman Hatch File; Wilson, Lucas, Shaffer, and Zurlinden, *Betio Beachhead,* p. 144; Alexander, *Utmost Savagery: The Three Days of Tarawa,* p. 207.
51. Correspondent Jim Lucas dispatch, written November 24, in the Earl Wilson File, Marine Corps Research Center, Quantico, Virginia.
52. Graham, *Mantle of Heroism,* p. 297.
53. Russ, *Line of Departure: Tarawa,* p. 167.
54. *Mainichi,* December 21, 1943, pp. 1–3, in the Carl Henry File, Marine Corps Research Center, Quantico, Virginia.
55. Hannah, *Tarawa,* p. 80.
56. Ota and Williams, "Tarawa, My Last Battle," p. 11.

Notes

Chapter 10—"A Requiem Fitting for Heroes So Proud"

1. Author's interview with Joseph Sobol, June 21, 2005.
2. Response to author's questions, in the Ashurst Personal File.
3. Charles Wysocki, "More Memories, Rumors, Scuttlebutt & Questions," p. 10, in the Charles Wysocki Personal File.
4. Ashurst interview, July 4, 2005.
5. Crosby, *Battlefield Chaplains,* pp. 68, 71; Willard, *The Leathernecks Come Through,* p. 224.
6. Roger P. Scovill, "What Did You Do, Grandpa?" unpublished memoir in the Personal Papers Section, Marine Corps Research Center, Quantico, Virginia, 1994 p. 99 (hereafter cited as Scovill, *Memoirs).*
7. Willard, *The Leathernecks Come Through,* p. 222.
8. Willard, *The Leathernecks Come Through,* p. 222.
9. Wilson, Lucas, Shaffer, and Zurlinden, *Betio Beachhead,* p. 146.
10. Shaw, Nalty, and Turnbladh, *History of U.S. Marine Corps Operations in World War II, Volume III: Central Pacific Drive,* p. 91.
11. Wysocki, "My Life," p. 16, in the Charles Wysocki Personal File.
12. Wilson, *Memoir,* p. 89.
13. Wright, *A Hell of a Way to Die,* p. 124.
14. Sherrod, *Tarawa: The Story of a Battle,* p. 146.
15. Banning, ed., *Heritage Years,* p. 72.
16. "Voice in the Dark," *Time,* December 20, 1943, p. 30.
17. Letter from G. D. Lillibridge to Eric Hammel, June 26, 1967, in the G. D. Lillibridge File, Marine Corps Research Center, Quantico, Virginia.
18. Hannah, *Tarawa,* p. 53.
19. Holland M. Smith and Percy Finch, *Coral and Brass* (New York: Charles Scribner's Sons, 1949), p. 129.
20. S. Sgt. Fred Feldkamp, "The Man Who Took Tarawa," typewritten manuscript of an article found in the Julian C. Smith Files, Quantico, Virginia, p. 19; Wilson, *Memoir,* p. 85.
21. Sherrod, *Tarawa: The Story of a Battle,* p. 136.
22. Smith and Finch, *Coral and Brass,* pp. 129–130.
23. Smith and Finch, *Coral and Brass,* p. 130.
24. Bowen interview, January 6, 2005; Bowen, *Reminiscences,* p. 27.
25. Chamberlin Biographical File, Marine Historical Center, Washington, D.C.
26. Sherrod, *Tarawa: The Story of a Battle,* Fortieth Anniversary Edition, p. 185.
27. Gilman interview, July 30, 1988.
28. DuPre interview, July 5, 2005.

29. Wright, *A Hell of a Way to Die,* p. 113.
30. Wilson, Lucas, Shaffer, and Zurlinden, *Betio Beachhead,* p. 138.
31. Muhlbach interview, March 19, 2005.
32. "Hatch," Oral History, p. 113.
33. Wilson, *Memoir,* p. 72.
34. Dick Meadows interviews, March 12, 2005; March 21, 2005.
35. Dick Meadows interviews, March 12, 2005; March 21, 2005.
36. Dick Meadows interview, March 21, 2005.
37. Dick Meadows interview, March 21, 2005.
38. Dick Meadows interview, March 12, 2005.
39. Bowen interview, December 28, 2004; Bowen, *Reminiscences,* p. 35.
40. *Tarawa Boom De-Ay,* March 17, 1944, p. 1, in the Cheslaw F. Wisniewski File, Marine Corps Research Center, Quantico, Virginia; Johnston, *Follow Me,* p. 166.
41. *Tarawa Boom De-Ay,* January 6, 1944, p. 1, in the Cheslaw F. Wisniewski File.
42. Smith, *But, That's Another Story,* p. 245.
43. Letter from David S. Spencer to his parents, December 8, 1943, in the David S. Spencer File.
44. Letters from David S. Spencer to his parents, December 12, 1943, and December 28, 1943, in the David S. Spencer File.
45. Wilson, Lucas, Shaffer, and Zurlinden, *Betio Beachhead,* p. 150.
46. *Tarawa Boom De-Ay,* January 6, 1944, p. 3, in the Cheslaw F. Wisniewski File.
47. Crain interview, March 19, 2005.
48. Dick Meadows interview, March 21, 2005.
49. Sherrod, *Tarawa: The Story of a Battle,* p. 51.
50. Sherrod, "Hawk," p. 29.
51. Darling, *Deane Hawkins: Nonpareil Texan,* p. 21.
52. "Medals for Americans," *Time,* September 11, 1944, p. 18.
53. Letter from Judge Brian Montague to Lucille Miller, December 21, 1943, in the Lucille Bohl File.
54. Letter from Mrs. Seng to Gene Seng, December 20, 1943, in the Seng Sisters Collection.
55. "To the Nearest of Kin," *Time,* December 13, 1943, p. 17.
56. George Montague interview, January 20, 2005.
57. Letter from Mr. Seng to Gene Seng, January 1, 1944, in the Seng Sisters Collection.
58. George Montague, "The Sun Shines on Saturday," Spring 1944, pp. 1–3; George Montague interview, January 20, 2005.
59. Ralph Seng interview, June 21, 2005; author's interview with Peggy Rochelle, September 15, 2005; Lorraine Clark interview, September 15, 2005; Patsy

Dealy interview, September 15, 2005; Parker, "High School Buddies Died on Tarawa with Bordelon," p. 8A.

60. Author's interview with David Rochelle, August 20, 2004.

61. Ralph Seng interview, June 23, 2005.

62. Patsy Dealy interview, September 15, 2005.

63. Harold Scherwitz, "Sportslights," *San Antonio Light,* undated article in the Lucille Bohl File.

64. Letter from Joseph Montague to Frank and Ouida Montague, January 13, 1944, in the Lucille Bohl File; letter from Robert Sherrod to Joseph Montague, January 12, 1944, in the Lucille Bohl File.

65. Draft of a January 19, 1944, letter from Gene Seng Sr. to Robert Sherrod, pp. 1–2, in the Seng Sisters Collection.

66. Undated letter from Mr. Seng to Congressman Paul Kilday, in the Seng Sisters Collection.

67. Drafts of undated letters found in a notebook kept by Gene Seng Sr., pp. 14, 18–19, in the Seng Sisters Collection.

68. Draft of a May 12, 1944, letter found in a notebook kept by Gene Seng Sr., pp. 7–8, in the Seng Sisters Collection.

69. Letter from Ouida Montague to Lucille Miller, January 6, 1944, in the Lucille Bohl File.

70. Letter from Fr. John Collins to Lucille Miller, January 10, 1944, in the Lucille Bohl File.

71. Letter from Lola McDougall [June's sister] to Lucille Miller, January 27, 1944, in the Lucille Bohl File.

72. Letter from Brian Montague to Lucille Miller, April 18, 1944, in the Lucille Bohl File.

73. Letter from Lola McDougall to Lucille Miller, January 27, 1944, in the Lucille Bohl File.

74. Letter from June McDougall to Lucille Miller, February 2, 1944, in the Lucille Bohl File.

75. Letter from Capt. Don E. Farkas to Mr. and Mrs. Montague; undated letter in the Ashurst File.

76. Letter from Chaplains Malcolm J. MacQueen and Joseph E. Wieber to Mrs. Seng, January 21, 1944, in the Seng Sisters Collection.

77. Letter from Cpl. Jimmie N. May to the Sengs, February 15, 1944, in the Seng Sisters Collection.

78. Letter from Fred Ellis to the Sengs, October 17, 1947, in the Seng Sisters Collection.

79. "Pals Sacrifice Lives at Tarawa," *Rattler,* January 21, 1944, p. 1, in the Lucille Bohl File.

Chapter 11—"You Say It's Not on the Map, My Son?"

1. "Should the U.S. Use Gas?" *Time,* January 3, 1944, p. 15.
2. Smith, *But, That's Another Story,* pp. 247–248.
3. Smith, *But, That's Another Story,* p. 247.
4. "Some Will Be Killed," *Time,* December 27, 1943, p. 24.
5. Hannah, *Tarawa,* p. 74; "Tarawa . . . Victory's Cost High," *Marine Corps Chevron,* December 4, 1943, p. 1.
6. Maslowski, *Armed with Cameras,* p. 67; Johnston, *Follow Me,* p. 158; Moeller, *Shooting War,* pp. 205–206.
7. Letters from Maj. James A. Donovan to his parents, December 22, 1943; January 27, 1944; and March 20, 1944, in the James A. Donovan File, Marine Corps Research Center, Quantico, Virginia.
8. Traylor, *Reminiscences,* p. 40.
9. Letter from John Magruder to Thomas Weil, January 8, 1944, in the Thomas E. Weil File, Marine Corps Research Center, Quantico, Virginia.
10. "New Glory," *Life,* December 6, 1943, p. 36.
11. "New Samurai," *Time,* January 3, 1944, p. 36.
12. Jon T. Hoffman, *Once a Legend: "Red Mike" Edson of the Marine Raiders* (Novato, California: Presidio Press, 1994), p. 262.
13. Sherrod, *Tarawa: The Story of a Battle,* pp. 147–151.
14. James A. Cox, "Robert Sherrod: Where the Marines Were," *Marine Corps League,* Summer 1994, p. 18.
15. Hatch interviews, July 24, 2004; July 18, 2005.
16. Sherrod interview, October 2, 1993.
17. Neushul and Neushul, "With the Marines at Tarawa," p. 78.
18. A group of letters stamped by authorities and returned on March 24, 1944, in the Seng Sisters Collection.
19. Undated letter from Mrs. Seng to Jimmie May, in the Seng Sisters Collection.
20. Hatch interview, July 24, 2004.
21. Commander Fifth Amphibious Force, U.S. Pacific Fleet, "Additional Extracts from Observers' Comments on GALVANIC Operation," January 29, 1944, p. 30.
22. Wilson, Lucas, Shaffer, and Zurlinden, *Betio Beachhead,* p. 160.
23. Shaw, Nalty, and Turnbladh, *History of U.S. Marine Corps Operations in World*

War II, Volume III: Central Pacific Drive, p. 114; Sherrod, *Tarawa: The Story of a Battle,* Fortieth Anniversary Edition, p. 183.

24. Sherrod, *Tarawa: The Story of a Battle,* Fortieth Anniversary Edition, p. 184.

25. Author's interview with William M. Chamberlin, July 3, 2005.

26. Bruce Montague interview, February 18, 2005.

27. George Montague interview, January 20, 2005.

28. Lucille Bohl interview, May 10, 2005.

29. Lucille Bohl interview, May 10, 2005.

30. Lorraine Clark interview, September 15, 2005.

31. Patsy Dealy interview, September 15, 2005.

32. Patsy Dealy interview, September 15, 2005; Peggy Rochelle interview, September 15, 2005.

33. James Meadows interview, July 25, 2005.

34. Dent, ed., *We Were There,* p. 71.

35. Wright, *A Hell of a Way to Die,* p. 133.

36. Banks, ed., *Second Marine Division, 1940–1999,* p. 74.

37. Bowen interview, January 20, 2005.

38. Banning, ed., *Heritage Years,* p. 47.

39. Scovill, *Memoirs,* p. 85.

40. Letter from Mrs. Hawkins to Robert Sherrod, in Hawkins Biographical File, Marine Historical Center.

41. *Tarawa Boom De-Ay,* January 13, 1944, p. 6, in the Donald Minimum File, Marine Corps Research Center, Quantico, Virginia.

BIBLIOGRAPHY

The National Archives

The National Archives house the official military records pertaining to Tarawa and any other Pacific Marine clash. The most helpful records from this immense collection are listed below.

Commander Fifth Amphibious Force, U.S. Pacific Fleet, to Commander in Chief, U.S. Pacific Fleet. "Report of Amphibious Operations for the Capture of the Gilbert Islands," December 4, 1943.

Commander Fifth Amphibious Force, U.S. Pacific Fleet. "Extracts from Observers' Comments on GALVANIC Operation," December 23, 1943.

Commander Fifth Amphibious Force, U.S. Pacific Fleet. "Additional Extracts from Observers' Comments on GALVANIC Operation," January 29, 1944.

Commander Fire Support Group (53.4) to Commander in Chief, U.S. Pacific Fleet. "Action Report, period 17–22 November, 1943," December 25, 1943.

Commanding General, Second Marine Division. "Report of Operations, GALVANIC," December 22, 1943.

Commanding General, Second Marine Division. "Report of GALVANIC Operations," December 23, 1943.

Commanding General, Second Marine Division. "Special Action Report—Narrative Account," January 6, 1944.

Commanding General, Fifth Amphibious Corps, to the Commandant, U.S. Marine

Corps. "Report of GALVANIC Operation," January 11, 1944, General Holland Smith Report.

Commander Group Two, Fifth Amphibious Force, Pacific Fleet, to Commander in Chief, U.S. Pacific Fleet. "Report of Tarawa Operations," December 13, 1943.

Commander Group Two, Fifth Amphibious Force, Pacific Fleet, to Commander in Chief, U.S. Pacific Fleet. "Action Reports," January 9, 1944.

Commanding Officer [Shoup], to Commanding General, 2d Marine Division. "Combat Report," November 28, 1943, including:

Battalion Surgeon;

Office of the Chaplain.

Commanding Officer CT-2 [Shoup], to Commanding General, Second Marine Division. "Report of Operations, Betio Island, Tarawa Atoll, Gilbert Islands, from 20 Nov 43 to 24 Nov 43," December 21, 1943.

Commanding Officer, 2d Tank Battalion, to Commanding General, Second Marine Division. "Special Action Report," December 14, 1943.

Commanding Officer, 8th Marines to Commanding General, Second Marine Division. "Special Action Report," December 1, 1943.

Commanding Officer, 10th Marines, to Commanding General, Second Marine Division. "Report of Operations, Galvanic Area," December 22, 1943.

Commanding Officer, 18th Marines, to Commanding General, Second Marine Division. "Combat Reports, Tarawa Atoll," December 22, 1943.

Commanding Officer, CT-6, to Commanding General, Second Marine Division. "Special Action Report," December 20, 1943.

Headquarters Fifth Amphibious Corps. "Report by G-3 on Galvanic," December 2, 1943.

Intelligence Report, CT-6. Gilbert Islands Operation, undated.

Brig. Gen. Merritt Edson Report to Staff Officers. "Tarawa Operation," Marine Corps Schools, January 6, 1944.

The following unit or individual action reports were used.

"Report of Operations," LT 1/2 (Maj. Wood B. Kyle).

"Report of Operations," LT 2/2 (Maj. Howard J. Rice).

"Report of Operations," LT 3/2 (Maj. John F. Schoettel).

"Report of Operations," LT 1/6 (Maj. William K. Jones).

"Report of Operations," LT 2/6 (Lt. Col. Raymond L. Murray).

"Report of Operations," LT 3/6 (Lt. Col. Kenneth F. McLeod).

"Report of Operations," LT 1/8 (Maj. Lawrence C. Hays Jr.).

"Report of Operations," LT 2/8 (Maj. Henry P. Crowe).

Bibliography

"Report of Operations," LT 3/8 (Maj. Robert H. Ruud).

"Report of Operations," Weapons/2.

"Report of Operations," Scout Sniper Platoon, H&S/2.

"Report of Operations," 2d Amphibian Tractor Battalion (Capt. Henry G. Lawrence Jr.).

"Report of Operations," 2d Tank Battalion (Lt. Col. Alexander B. Swenceski).

ADC-3 Journal, 2d Marine Division, November 19, 1943, to November 23, 1943.

Lt. Col. Evans F. Carlson (Observer), November 27, 1943.

The Division Surgeon, December 12, 1943 (F. R. Moore).

"G-2 Study of the Theater of Operations: Gilbert Islands, Nauru and Ocean," September 20, 1943.

"Intelligence Lessons," Corps Training Memorandum Number 3-44, January 10, 1944.

Joint Intelligence Center Pacific Ocean Areas, "Japanese Forces in the Gilbert Islands," June 1943 (JICPOA Bulletin No. 8-44).

Lt. Col. Walter I. Jordan Report (Observer), November 27, 1943.

"Preliminary Interrogation of Japanese Prisoners," December 22, 1943.

Lt. Col. Charles D. Roberts (Observer), January 7, 1944.

The Sanitation Report, December 3, 1943 (Lt. Louis Shattuck Baer).

Brig. Gen. J. L. Underhill (Observer), undated.

Capt. R. F. Whitehead (Observer), December 2, 1943.

Maj. C. A. Woodrum Jr. (Observer), November 30, 1943.

The following Navy reports were used:

USS *Anderson* (DD 411), December 1, 1943

USS *Arthur Middleton* (APA 25), December 4, 1943

USS *Dashiell* (DD 659), December 5, 1943

USS *Doyen* (APA 1), December 3, 1943

USS *Feland* (APA 11), December 7, 1943

USS *Harry Lee* (PA 10), December 6, 1943

USS *LaSalle* (AP 102), November 28, 1943

USS *Maryland* (BB 46), December 15, 1943

USS *Monrovia* (FB 7-18), December 1, 1943

USS *Pursuit* (AM 108), December 6, 1943

USS *Requisite* (AM 109), December 5, 1943

USS *Ringgold* (DD 500), December 1, 1943

USS *Sheridan* (APA 51), December 20, 1943

USS *William P. Biddle* (APA 8), November 27, 1943

USS *Zeilin* (APA 3), December 4, 1943

The Marine Historical Center

The Marine Historical Center in Washington, D.C., contains the personnel files of many Marines, oral histories conducted with prominent officers, and artwork of Marine battles. Adjoining the building is the valuable Navy Art Collection.

Oral Histories

"Colonel Henry P. 'Jim' Crowe, USMC (Ret.)." History and Museums Division, Headquarters, U.S. Marine Corps, 1979.

"Norman T. Hatch." History and Museums Division, Headquarters, U.S. Marine Corps, 1981.

"Lieutenant General Leo D. Hermle (Ret.)." History and Museums Division, Headquarters, U.S. Marine Corps, 1968.

"Major General Carl W. Hoffman (Ret.)." History and Museums Division, Headquarters, U.S. Marine Corps, 1988.

"Major General Raymond L. Murray (Ret.)." History and Museums Division, Headquarters, U.S. Marine Corps, 1988.

"William K. Jones." East Carolina University Manuscript Collection, May 25, 1976.

Biographical Files

Alexander Bonnyman Jr. File
William J. Bordelon File
William C. Chamberlin File
Henry P. Crowe File
William D. Hawkins File
Michael P. Ryan File
Robert Sherrod File
David M. Shoup File

Art
From the Marine Historical Center:
Paintings and sketches of Tarawa by Richard Gibney, Tom Lovell, Charles Waterhouse, and Harry Jackson.

From the Navy Art Collection:
Paintings and sketches of Tarawa by Kerr Eby.

Bibliography

The Marine Corps Research Center, Quantico, Virginia

The beautiful facility on the grounds of the Marine base at Quantico, Virginia, houses the personal collections of thousands of Marines. A treasure of items awaits the researcher, from diaries and photographs to old newspapers and magazines. The collections used for this book are:

Colonel James A. Donovan Jr., USMC (Ret.) Collection, Box 2
Roger M. Emmons Collection
Televai Fati Collection
Charles Henry Jr. Collection
Colby D. Howe Collection
G. D. Lillibridge Collection
Donald Minimum Collection
Frank W. Plant Jr. Collection
Wayne S. Sanford Collection
R. H. Schneider Collection
Roger P. Scovill Collection
David M. Shoup Collection
David S. Spencer Collection
Melvin A. Traylor Collection
Robert E. Vorhees Collection
Russell B. Warye Collection
Thomas E. Weil Collection
Earl Wilson Collection
Cheslaw F. Wisniewski Collection

The Hoover Institution on War, Revolution and Peace, Stanford University

Kiyoshi Ota Collection
David Shoup Collection

Individual Collections

I was fortunate to benefit from many survivors of the battle, or from their families, who opened their collections to my inspection. I received many helpful photographs and written reminiscences. The collections used are:

Emory Ashurst Collection
Stanley Bowen Collection
Chamberlin Family Collection
Albert Gilman Collection
Norman Hatch Collection
Meadows Family Collection
Montague Family Collection
Robert Muhlbach Collection
William Ruch Collection
The Seng Sisters Collection
Charles Wysocki Jr. Collection

Interviews

The individuals listed below provided useful material during personal interviews I conducted with them. I cannot thank them enough for sharing their time and information with me.

EMORY ASHURST, corporal, Red 1. Telephone interview, July 4, 2005.

JOSEPH BARR, lieutenant, F Company, Red 2. Telephone interview, November 19, 2005.

LUCILLE BOHL, fiancée of Charlie Montague. Telephone interview, May 10, 2005.

MARGARET BOWEN, wife of Stanley Bowen. Telephone interview, December 20, 2004.

STANLEY BOWEN, pharmacist's mate. Telephone interviews, December 21, 2004; December 28, 2004; December 30, 2004; January 6, 2005; January 20, 2005.

HERMAN BRUKHARDT, physician. Telephone interview, December 20, 2004.

HENRY CHAMBERLIN, son of Maj. William Chamberlin. Telephone interviews, April 27, 2005; July 26, 2005.

WILLIAM CHAMBERLIN, son of Maj. William Chamberlin. Telephone interviews, April 27, 2005; July 3, 2005.

LORRAINE CLARK, Gene Seng's sister. Personal interview, September 15, 2005.

JAMES COEN, Red 1. Telephone interview, February 25, 2005.

ROBERT COSTELLO, pharmacist's mate. Telephone interview, December 6, 2004.

J. WENDELL CRAIN, Red 1. Telephone interviews, March 9, 2005; March 19, 2005.

PATSY DEALY, Gene Seng's sister. Personal interview, September 15, 2005.

RAYMOND D. DUFFEE, pharmacist's mate, Red 2. Telephone interviews, July 30, 2005; August 23, 2005.

HENRY DUKE, Red 1. Telephone interview, June 29, 2005.

Bibliography

PAUL DUPRE, 2nd lieutenant, Red 2. Telephone interviews, July 2, 2005; July 5, 2005.

ALBERT B. GILMAN, E Company, 2/8, Red 3. Letter, October 9, 1987. Telephone interviews, April 16, 1988; July 30, 1988.

NORMAN HATCH, Marine photographer, Red 3. Telephone interviews, November 19, 2003; January 20, 2005; July 18, 2005. Personal interview, July 24, 2004.

ED HYSON, Red 2. Telephone interview, March 7, 2005.

WILLIAM KELLIHER, Marine photographer, Red 3. Telephone interview, August 12, 2005.

JAMES MEADOWS, Red 1. Telephone interviews, March 22, 2005; July 25, 2005.

RICHARD MEADOWS, Red 1. Telephone interviews, March 12, 2005; March 17, 2005; March 21, 2005.

BRUCE MONTAGUE, brother of Charlie Montague. Personal interview, February 18, 2005.

FR. GEORGE MONTAGUE, brother of Charlie Montague. Telephone interviews, August 20, 2004; January 6, 2005; January 20, 2005. Personal interview, February 18, 2005.

ROBERT MUHLBACH, Red 3. Telephone interviews, March 5, 2005; March 12, 2005; March 19, 2005.

J. MICHAEL PARKER, newspaper reporter. Telephone interview, August 17, 2004.

JAMES PEAVEY, F Company, Red 2. Telephone interview, July 7, 2005.

NOAL C. PEMBERTON, F Company, Red 2. Telephone interview, November 22, 2005.

DAVID B. ROCHELLE, Gene Seng's brother-in-law. Telephone interview, August 20, 2004.

PEGGY ROCHELLE, Gene Seng's sister. Telephone interview, December 20, 2004. Personal interview, September 15, 2005.

ROBERT ROGERS, 1st lieutenant, E Company, 2/8, Red 3. Telephone interviews, July 2, 2005; November 18, 2005.

WILLIAM RUCH, F Company, Red 2. Telephone interview, March 7, 2005.

RALPH SENG, Gene Seng's brother. Telephone interviews, June 21, 2005; June 23, 2005.

ROBERT SHERROD, *Time* magazine correspondent. Telephone interviews, September 22, 1993; October 2, 1993; October 9, 1993.

JOSEPH SOBOL, Red 1. Telephone interviews, June 20, 2005; June 21, 2005.

RICHARD SPOONER, Red 3. Telephone interview, November 19, 2005.

MELVIN TRAYLOR, Red 3. Telephone interview, August 8, 2005.

TYSON WILSON, Red 2. Telephone interviews, March 5, 2005; March 12, 2005.

CHARLES WYSOCKI, Red 1. Telephone interview, June 29, 2005.

Newspapers

Alamo Register
Baltimore News-Post
Camp Lejeune Globe
Dallas Morning News
El Paso Herald-Post
El Paso Times
Fresno Bee
Fort Worth Star-Telegram
Long Beach Press-Telegram, June 26, 1988
Louisville Courier-Journal
Mainichi (English-language Japanese newspaper, December 21, 1943)
Marine Corps Chevron
Montague Press
New York Herald Tribune
New York Times
Parris Island Boot
Racine Journal Times Sunday Bulletin
Rocky Mountain News
San Antonio Evening News
San Antonio Express-News
San Antonio Light
San Diego Union
Tarawa Boom De-Ay
Virginian-Pilot
Washington Post
Washington Evening Star

Books

Alexander, Col. Joseph H., USMC (Ret.). *Utmost Savagery: The Three Days of Tarawa*. Annapolis, Maryland: Naval Institute Press, 1995.

Baldwin, Hanson. *Battles Lost and Won*. New York: Harper & Row, 1966.

Banks, Herbert C., II, ed. *Second Marine Division, 1940–1999*. Paducah, Kentucky: Turner Publishing Company, 1999.

Banning, William, ed. *Heritage Years: Second Marine Division Commemorative Anthology, 1940–1949*. Paducah, Kentucky: Turner Publishing Company, 1988.

Bibliography

Bateson, Charles. *The War with Japan*. East Lansing: Michigan State University Press, 1968.

Berry, Henry. *Semper Fi, Mac: Living Memories of the U.S. Marines in World War II*. New York: Arbor House, 1982.

Bevan, Denys. *United States Forces in New Zealand, 1942–1945*. Alexandra, New Zealand: Macpherson Publishing, 1992.

Bowen, Stanley. *Stan Bowen and Margie McCann's Romance and the War Between the Years of December 29, 1942 and February 3, 1946*. Self-published memoir, 1991.

Brinkley, David. *Washington Goes to War*. New York: Alfred A. Knopf, 1988.

Buell, Thomas B. *The Quiet Warrior*. Boston: Little, Brown and Company, 1974.

———. *Master of Sea Power: A Biography of Fleet Admiral Ernest J. King*. Boston: Little, Brown and Company, 1980.

Burns, James MacGregor. *Roosevelt: The Soldier of Freedom*. New York: Harcourt Brace Jovanovich, 1970.

The Buttoneer, Central Catholic High School's yearbook. San Antonio, Texas, 1939.

Churchill, Winston. *The Second World War: The Grand Alliance*. Boston: Houghton Mifflin Company, 1950.

Collier, Basil. *The War in the Far East, 1941–1945*. New York: William Morrow & Company, 1969.

Commager, Henry Steele. *The Story of the Second World War*. Washington: Brassey's, 1991.

Costello, John. *The Pacific War, 1941–1945*. New York: Quill Books, 1982.

Crosby, Donald F., S. J. *Battlefield Chaplains: Catholic Priests in World War II*. Lawrence: University Press of Kansas, 1994.

Darling, R. C. *Deane Hawkins: Nonpareil Texan*. Quantico, Virginia: Marine Corps Command and Staff College, 1991.

Dent, James L., ed. *We Were There: Fox Company Second Marines, Tarawa, November 20, 1943*. Self-published, 1996.

Dower, John W. *War Without Mercy: Race & Power in the Pacific War*. New York: Pantheon Books, 1986.

Editors of Time-Life Books. *This Fabulous Century: Volume V, 1940–1950*. New York: Time-Life Books, 1969.

Emmons, M. Sgt. Roger M. "Battle of Tarawa." Unpublished memoir in the Personal Papers Section, Marine Corps Research Center, Quantico, Virginia.

Fishbein, Morris, M.D., ed. *Doctors at War*. New York: E. P. Dutton & Company, 1945.

Frank, Richard B. *Guadalcanal: The Definitive Account of the Landmark Battle*. New York: Penguin Books, 1990.

Garner, Joe. *We Interrupt This Broadcast*. Naperville, Illinois: Sourcebooks, 1998.

Gatchel, Theodore L. *At the Water's Edge: Defending Against the Modern Amphibious Assault*. Annapolis, Maryland: Naval Institute Press, 1996.

Goodwin, Doris Kearns. *No Ordinary Time*. New York: Simon & Schuster, 1994.

Graham, Michael B. *Mantle of Heroism: Tarawa and the Struggle for the Gilberts, November 1943*. Novato, California: Presidio Press, 1993.

Gregg, Charles T. *Tarawa*. New York: Stein and Day, 1984.

Hammel, Eric, and John E. Lane. *76 Hours: The Invasion of Tarawa*. Pacifica, California: Pacifica Press, 1985.

Hannah, S. Sgt. Dick. *Tarawa: The Toughest Battle in Marine Corps History*. New York: Duell, Sloan & Pearce, 1944.

Harries, Meirion and Susie. *Soldiers of the Sun: The Rise and Fall of the Imperial Japanese Army*. New York: Random House, 1991.

Hoffman, Jon T. *Once a Legend: "Red Mike" Edson of the Marine Raiders*. Novato, California: Presidio Press, 1994.

Holmes, W. J. *Double-Edged Secrets: U.S. Naval Intelligence Operations in the Pacific During World War II*. Annapolis, Maryland: Naval Institute Press, 1979.

Howarth, Stephen. *To Shining Sea: A History of the United States Navy, 1775–1991*. New York: Random House, 1991.

Hull, Cordell. *The Memoirs of Cordell Hull*. New York: Macmillan Company, 1948.

Ienaga, Saburo. *The Pacific War: World War II and the Japanese, 1931–1945*. New York: Pantheon Books, 1978.

Johnston, Richard W. *Follow Me: The Story of the Second Marine Division in World War II*. New York: Random House, 1948.

Karig, Capt. Walter, USNR, with Lt. Comdr. Russell L. Harris, USNR, and Lt. Comdr. Frank A. Manson, USN. *Battle Report: The End of an Empire*. New York: Rinehart and Company, 1948.

Keegan, John. *The Second World War*. New York: Penguin Books, 1989.

Koppes, Clayton R. and Gregory D. Black. *Hollywood Goes to War*. New York: Free Press, 1987.

Larrabee, Eric. *Commander in Chief: Franklin Delano Roosevelt, His Lieutenants, and Their War*. New York: Harper & Row, 1987.

Lash, Joseph P. *Roosevelt and Churchill, 1939–1941*. New York: W. W. Norton & Company, 1976.

Layton, Rear Adm. Edwin T., USN (Ret.), with Capt. Roger Pineau, USNR (Ret.), and John Costello. *"And I Was There": Pearl Harbor and Midway—Breaking the Secrets*. New York: William Morrow and Company, 1985.

Leahy, Fleet Adm. William D. *I Was There*. New York: McGraw-Hill Book Company, 1950.

Bibliography

Leckie, Robert. *Strong Men Armed*. New York: Random House, 1962.

———. *The Wars of America*. Edison, New Jersey: Castle Books, 1966.

———. *Delivered from Evil: The Saga of World War II*. New York: Harper & Row, 1987.

Lewin, Ronald. *The American Magic: Codes, Ciphers and the Defeat of Japan*. New York: Farrar Straus Giroux, 1982.

Lillibridge, G. D. *Memoirs*. Unpublished memoir in the Personal Papers Section, Marine Corps Research Center, Quantico, Virginia.

Lingeman, Richard R. *Don't You Know There's a War On?: The American Home Front, 1941–1945*. New York: G. P. Putnam's Sons, 1970.

Lucas, Jim. *Combat Correspondent*. New York: Reynal & Hitchcock, 1944.

Manchester, William. *Goodbye, Darkness*. Boston: Little, Brown and Company, 1980.

Maslowski, Peter. *Armed with Cameras: The American Military Photographers of World War II*. New York: Free Press, 1993.

Millett, Allan R. *Semper Fidelis: The History of the United States Marine Corps*. New York: Macmillan Publishing Co., 1980.

Millett, Allan R., and Peter Maslowski. *For the Common Defense: A Military History of the United States of America*. New York: Free Press, 1984.

Moeller, Susan D. *Shooting War: Photography and the American Experience of Combat*. New York: Basic Books, 1989.

Morella, Joe, Edward Z. Epstein, and John Griggs. *The Films of World War II*. Secaucus, New Jersey: Citadel Press, 1973.

Morgan, Ted. *FDR: A Biography*. New York: Simon & Schuster, 1985.

Morison, Samuel Eliot. *History of United States Naval Operations in World War II, Volume VII: Aleutians, Gilberts and Marshalls, June 1942–April 1944*. Boston: Little, Brown and Company, 1960.

———. *The Two-Ocean War*. Boston: Little, Brown and Company, 1963.

Murray, Williamson, and Allan R. Millett. *A War to Be Won*. Cambridge, Massachusetts: Belknap Press, 2000.

North, Oliver L., with Joe Musser. *War Stories II: Heroism in the Pacific*. Washington, D.C.: Regnery Publishing, 2004.

Ota, Kiyoshi, with Keith S. Williams. "Tarawa, My Last Battle." Unpublished memoir in the David Shoup Collection, Hoover Institution on War, Revolution and Peace, Stanford University.

Perkins, Frances. *The Roosevelt I Knew*. New York: Viking Press, 1946.

Perrett, Geoffrey. *Days of Sadness, Years of Triumph: The American People, 1939–1945*. New York: Coward, McCann & Geoghegan, 1973.

Plant, Frank W., Jr. "Tarawa Memoir." Unpublished memoir in the Personal Papers Section, Marine Corps Research Center, Quantico, Virginia, 1986.

Potter, E. B. *Nimitz*. Annapolis, Maryland: Naval Institute Press, 1976.

———. *Bull Halsey*. Annapolis, Maryland: Naval Institute Press, 1985.

Prados, John. *Combined Fleet Decoded: The Secret History of American Intelligence and the Japanese Navy in World War II*. New York: Random House, 1995.

Pratt, Fletcher. *The Marines' War*. New York: William Sloane Associates, 1948.

Richardson, W. *The Epic of Tarawa*. London: Odhams Press Limited [1945].

Roosevelt, Eleanor. *This I Remember*. New York: Harper & Brothers, 1949.

Roosevelt, Elliott. *As He Saw It*. New York: Duell, Sloan and Pearce, 1946.

Rottman, Gordon. *US Marine Corps 1941–1945*. Oxford: Osprey Publishing, 1995.

Ruch, William L., Jr. *My War Years*. Self-published memoir, 1997.

Russ, Martin. *Line of Departure: Tarawa*. Garden City, New York: Doubleday & Company, 1975.

Scovill, Roger P. "What Did You Do, Grandpa?" Unpublished memoir in the Personal Papers Section, Marine Corps Research Center, Quantico, Virginia, 1994.

Seng, Pvt. Gene G. "Diary of Trip to ? [sic] Aboard the U.S.S. *President Hayes*," July 1, 1942 to August 9, 1942.

Shane, Ted. *Heroes of the Pacific*. New York: Julian Messner, 1944.

Shaw, Henry I., Jr., Bernard C. Nalty, and Edwin T. Turnbladh. *History of U.S. Marine Corps Operations in World War II, Volume III: Central Pacific Drive*. Washington, D.C.: Historical Branch, G-3, Headquarters, U.S. Marine Corps, 1966.

Sherrod, Robert. *Tarawa: The Story of a Battle*. New York: Duell, Sloan and Pearce, 1944, and revised edition, New York: Bantam Books, 1983.

———. *History of Marine Corps Aviation in World War II*. Washington: Combat Forces Press, 1952.

Sherwood, Robert E. *Roosevelt and Hopkins: An Intimate History*. New York: Harper & Brothers, 1948.

Shindler, Colin. *Hollywood Goes to War*. London: Routledge & Kegan Paul, 1979.

Simmons, Brig. Gen. Edwin H., USMC (Ret.). *The United States Marines, 1775–1975*. New York: Viking Press, 1976.

Smith, Harriotte "Happy" Byrd. *But, That's Another Story*. New York: Vantage Press, 1992.

Smith, Holland M., and Percy Finch. *Coral and Brass*. New York: Charles Scribner's Sons, 1949.

Smith, S. E., ed. *The United States Marine Corps in World War II*. New York: Random House, 1969.

Smith, Scott Slaughter. *Unspoken Bond of Courage*. California: Xlibris Corporation, 2000.

Spector, Ronald H. *Eagle Against the Sun: The American War with Japan*. New York: Free Press, 1985.

Bibliography

Stockman, Capt. James R., USMC. *The Battle for Tarawa*. Washington, D.C.: Historical Section, Division of Public Information, Headquarters, U.S. Marine Corps, 1947.

Toland, John. *The Rising Sun*. New York: Random House, 1970.

Traylor, Melvin A. "My Life and Times in the USMCR 1941–1946." In the Melvin A. Traylor File, #3857, Marine Corps Research Center, Quantico, Virginia, January 31, 2003.

"Tribute to Tarawa," *Long Beach Press-Telegram,* June 26, 1988.

Tully, Grace. *F. D. R., My Boss*. Chicago: Peoples Book Club, 1949.

Twitchell, Robert R. *One Returned*. Self-published memoir, 1986.

Van der Vat, Dan. *The Pacific Campaign*. New York: Simon & Schuster, 1991.

Weinberg, Gerhard L. *A World at Arms*. Cambridge: Cambridge University Press, 1994.

Wheeler, Richard. *A Special Valor: The U.S. Marines and the Pacific War*. New York: New American Library, 1983.

Willard, W. Wyeth. *The Leathernecks Come Through*. New York: Fleming H. Revell Company, 1944.

William J. Bordelon Medal of Honor Recipient Memorial Ceremonies, November 19–20, 1995.

Wilson, Dick. *When Tigers Fight: The True Story of the Sino-Japanese War, 1937–1945*. New York: Viking Press, 1982.

Wilson, Earl. "Memoir." Undated, in the Earl Wilson File, Quantico, Virginia.

Wilson, Capt. Earl J., M. T. Sgts. Jim G. Lucas and Samuel Shaffer, and S. Sgt. C. Peter Zurlinden. *Betio Beachhead: U.S. Marines' Own Story of the Battle for Tarawa*. New York: G. P. Putnam's Sons, 1945.

Winton, John. *Ultra in the Pacific*. Annapolis, Maryland: Naval Institute Press, 1993.

Wise, James E., Jr., and Anne Collier Rehill. *Stars in Blue: Movie Actors in America's Sea Services*. Annapolis, Maryland: Naval Institute Press, 1997.

Wright, Derrick. *A Hell of a Way to Die*. London: Windrow & Greene, 1996.

———. *Tarawa 1943: The Turning of the Tide*. Oxford: Osprey Publishing, 2000.

Wukovits, John F. *Devotion to Duty: A Biography of Admiral Clifton A. F. Sprague*. Annapolis, Maryland: Naval Institute Press, 1995.

Articles

"'A Job to Do,' Bordelon Told His Father." *San Antonio Express-News,* June 18, 1944.

"Alamo Honors: WWII Hero's Body Lies in State at Shrine." *Dallas Morning News,* November 20, 1995, p. 15A.

"A Name to Remember." *Time,* December 6, 1943, p. 15.

"Body of Lieutenant Hawkins to Remain in Tarawa Island Grave." *El Paso Herald-Post,* May 29, 1946.

"Bordelon's Buddy Tells of Heroism on Tarawa." *San Antonio Light,* June 15, 1944.

"Buddy of Sgt. W. J. Bordelon Arrives to Participate in Awarding of Medal." *San Antonio Evening News,* June 15, 1944.

Cox, James A. "Robert Sherrod: Where the Marines Were." *Marine Corps League,* Summer 1994, pp. 15–18.

Cutler, Thomas J. "Remembering Eddie Albert." *Naval Institute Proceedings,* July 2005, p. 26.

"Epic of 'Bravest Marine' Related by Wounded Buddy." *Fort Worth Star-Telegram,* February 26, 1944.

Feldkamp, S. Sgt. Fred. "The Man Who Took Tarawa." Typewritten manuscript of an article found in the Julian C. Smith Files, Quantico, Virginia.

"The Fight for Tarawa." *Life,* December 13, 1943, pp. 27–35.

Flanagan, Trisha Currier. "Navy Chaplain Recalls Guadalcanal." Unnamed, undated newspaper, p. 1, 10A.

Haley, J. Frederick. "A Marine's Marine." *Marine Corps Gazette,* November 1983, pp. 99–102.

Harwood, Richard. "He Told Truth About War." *Washington Post,* February 28, 1994, p. A17.

Hatch, Norman T. "Marine Combat Photographer." *Leatherneck,* November 1993, pp. 44–48.

———. "Tarawa—1943." *Marine Corps Gazette,* November 2002, pp. 111–112.

Johnston, Richard W. "Marine with Shotgun Leads Marine Battalion Thru Bloody Carnage to Victory on Tarawa." November 1943.

Jonas, Carl, U.S.C.G. "My First Day on Tarawa." In *The 100 Best True Stories of World War II.* New York: Wm. H. Wise & Co., 1945, pp. 236–244.

Jones, Don. "We Weren't Yet Afraid." *Leatherneck,* November 1993, pp. 38–43.

Kozaryn, Linda D. "Combat Photographers Risk All to Document War." American Forces Information Service News Articles, October 13, 2000, pp. 1–3, found in http://www.dod.mil/cgi-bin/dlprint.cgi?http://www.dod.mil/news/Oct2000/n10132000_200010131.html

"Letters." *Time,* December 27, 1943, p. 4.

"Letters." *Time,* January 10, 1944, p. 6.

"Lt. W. D. Hawkins Gets Posthumous Medal of Honor." *El Paso Times,* May 25, 1944.

Lucas, Jim G. "Hero's Mother Favors Military Training." *Rocky Mountain News,* November 1, 1945.

MacKenzie, Maj. Robert B., USMC (Ret.). "The Most Fearful Man in All the Corps." *Marine Corps Gazette,* November 1992, p. 44.

McLemore, David. "Alamo Opens for a Hero." *The Dallas Morning News,* November 26, 1995, p. 1A, 14A.

"Medals for Americans." *Time,* September 11, 1944, pp. 18–19.

Moise, Norman S. "A Hellish Return Trip." *Naval History,* August 2005, p. 29.

Montague, George. "The Sun Shines on Saturday." Unpublished article written Spring 1944, pp. 1–4.

Neushul, Peter, and 2nd Lt. James D. Neushul. "With the Marines at Tarawa." *Naval Institute Proceedings,* April 1999, pp. 74–79.

"New Glory." *Life,* December 6, 1943, p. 36.

"New Samurai." *Time,* January 3, 1944, p. 36.

Pace, Eric. "Robert Sherrod, 85, a Journalist and Author of 'Tarawa,' Is Dead." *New York Times,* February 15, 1994.

"Pal Says San Antonio Marine Killed on Tarawa Belongs in Hall of Fame." Unnamed, undated news clipping in the William J. Bordelon Biographical File, Marine Historical Center, Washington, D.C.

"Pals Sacrifice Lives at Tarawa." *Rattler,* January 21, 1944, pp. 1–5.

"Parents Proud of Youth Who Died Hero on Tarawa." *Alamo Register,* June 16, 1944, p. 1.

Parker, J. Michael. "WWII Hero Coming Home for Reburial." *San Antonio Express-News,* May 29, 1995, pp. 1A, 13A.

———. "High School Buddies Died on Tarawa with Bordelon." *San Antonio Express-News,* November 20, 1995, p. 8A.

———. "Hero Gets Welcome Home 52 Years after Sacrifice." *San Antonio Express-News,* November 21, 1995, p. 1B.

Pineau, Capt. Roger, USNR (Ret.). "In Profile: Robert Sherrod." *Naval History,* Fall 1990, pp. 55–58.

"Postscript on Tarawa." *Time,* January 17, 1944, pp. 28, 30.

"Quack Hero." *Time,* January 3, 1944, p. 62.

"Reef Climbers." *Time,* December 20, 1943, pp. 69–70.

"Reserve Center Named for Tarawa Hero." *Leatherneck,* July 1994, p. 40.

Sherrod, Robert. "Battle of the Pacific: Profit & Loss." *Time,* December 13, 1943, pp. 36–38.

———. "Report on Tarawa: Marines' Show." *Time,* December 6, 1943, pp. 24–25.

———. "Best-Covered Story." *Time,* December 13, 1943, p. 76.

———. "After Two Years." *Time,* December 27, 1943, p. 31.

———. "Hawk." *Marine Corps Gazette,* April 1944, pp. 27–29.

———. Video Oral History. *Time,* March 19, 1985.

"Should the U.S. Use Gas?" *Time,* January 3, 1944, p. 15.

Shultz, Herbert L. "A Memoir of Marine Esprit." *Marine Corps Gazette,* November 1994, p. 86.

Simmons, Brig. Gen. Edwin H. "Remembering the Legendary 'Jim' Crowe—Part I." *Fortitudine,* Winter 1991–1992, pp. 3–7.

———. "Remembering the Legendary 'Jim' Crowe—Part II." *Fortitudine,* Spring 1992, pp. 3–9.

Simmons, Brig. Gen. Edwin H. "Remembering Bob Sherrod." *Fortitudine,* Summer 1994, pp. 3–7.

Smith, Gen. Holland M., and Percy Finch. "Tarawa Was a Mistake." *Saturday Evening Post,* November 6, 1948, pp. 15–17, 91, 94, 96–98, 101–102.

Smith, J.Y. "Gen. David Shoup Dies; Was Marine Commandant." *The Washington Post,* January 17, 1983, p. B6.

"Some Will Be Killed." *Time,* December 27, 1943, p. 24.

Stevenson, John. "Tarawa Veteran Tells of Heroisms." *Virginian-Pilot,* November 20, 1978, p. C3.

"Tarawa Aftermath: Betio Shows the Scars of Battle." *Life,* December 27, 1943, pp. 32–33.

"Tarawa: The Marines Win New Glory in the Gilberts and Prove There Is No Cheap Way to Victory." *Life,* December 6, 1943, p. 36.

"Tarawa . . . Victory's Cost High." *Marine Corps Chevron,* December 4, 1943, p. 1.

"This Was Tarawa." *Time,* December 13, 1943, pp. 24–25.

"To the Nearest of Kin." *Time,* December 13, 1943, p. 17.

Tolbert, Sgt. Frank X. "Crowe's Feats." *Leatherneck, Pacific Edition,* October 15, 1944.

"Voice in the Dark." *Time,* December 20, 1943, p. 30.

Walrad, Maj. Jack, USAF (Ret.). "Prelude to Tarawa." *Marine Corps Gazette,* October 1993, pp. 48–49.

Wise, Capt. James E., Jr., USN (Ret.), and Anne Collier Rehill. "From Tarawa to Hooterville." *Naval History,* July/August 1997, pp. 57–59.

Zurlinden, Pete. "'Scout-Sniper' Outfit Wrote Heroic Chapter at Tarawa." *Racine Journal Times Sunday Bulletin,* December 19, 1943.

The following articles came from the Marine Corps Association's archives Web site, http://pqasb.pqarchiver.com/mca-marines/doc, containing a library of articles from *Leatherneck* and from *Marine Corps Gazette.*

Anonymous. "Combat Chaplain." *Leatherneck,* November 1980, pp. 1–6.

Bartlett, Tom. "New Zealand Pilgrimage." *Leatherneck,* August 1978, pp. 1–10.

Bibliography

Johnson, J. E. "My First Look at a Dead Person." *Marine Corps Gazette,* February 1991, pp. 1–2.

Ladd, Dean. "Reliving the Battle: A Return to Tarawa." *Marine Corps Gazette,* November 1983, pp. 1–5.

Richardson, Herb. "Colonel Jim Crowe." *Leatherneck,* November 1980, pp. 1–5.

Ryan, Michael P. "Tarawa." *Marine Corps Gazette,* November 1984, pp. 1–2.

Sherrod, Robert. "Who Is This Marine?" *Marine Corps Gazette,* January 1976, pp. 1–4.

Swango, M. F. "Assault on Tarawa." *Marine Corps Gazette,* November 1995, pp. 1–3.

Walrad, Jack. "Prelude to Tarawa." *Marine Corps Gazette,* October 1993, pp. 1–3.